Imre Kertész and Holocaust Literature

Comparative Cultural Studies
Steven Tötösy de Zepetnek, Series Editor

Comparative Cultural Studies is a contextual approach in the study of culture in all of its products and processes. The framework is built on tenets of the discipline of comparative literature and cultural studies and on notions borrowed from a range of thought such as (radical) constructivism, communication theories, systems theories, and literary and culture theory. In comparative cultural studies focus is on theory and method as well as application, and attention is on the how rather than on the what. Colleagues interested in publishing in the series are invited to contact the editor, Steven Totosy, at <clcweb@purdue.edu>.

Volumes in the series are:

Comparative Central European Culture. Ed. Steven Tötösy de Zepetnek. West Lafayette: Purdue UP, 2002. 190 pages, bibliography, index. ISBN 1-55753-240-0 (pbk).

Comparative Literature and Comparative Cultural Studies. Ed. Steven Tötösy de Zepetnek. West Lafayette: Purdue UP, 2003. 356 pages, bibliography, index. ISBN 1-55753-288-5 (ebook), ISBN 1-55753-290-7 (pbk).

Sophia A. McClennen, The Dialectics of Exile: Nation, Time, Language, and Space in Hispanic Literatures. West Lafayette: Purdue UP, 2004. 240 pages, bibliography, index. ISBN 1-55753-315-6 (pbk).

Comparative Cultural Studies and Latin America. Ed. Sophia A. McClennen and Earl E. Fitz. West Lafayette: Purdue UP, 2004. 266 pages, bibliography, index. ISBN 1-55753-358-X (pbk).

Feng, Jin. The New Woman in Early Twentieth-Century Chinese Fiction. West Lafayette: Purdue UP, 2004. 240 pages, bibliography, index. ISBN 1-55753-330-X (pbk).

Comparative Cultural Studies and Michael Ondaatje's Writing. Ed. Steven Tötösy de Zepetnek. West Lafayette: Purdue UP, 2005. 154 pages, bibliography, index. ISBN 1-55753-378-4 (pbk.).

Camilla Fojas, Cosmopolitanism in the Americas. West Lafayette: Purdue UP, 2005. 162 pages, bibliography, index. ISBN 1-55753-382-2 (pbk).

Imre Kertész and Holocaust Literature. Ed. Louise O. Vasvári and Steven Tötösy de Zepetnek. West Lafayette: Purdue UP, 2005. 340 pages, bibliography, index. ISBN 1-55753-396-2 (pbk).

Imre Kertész and Holocaust Literature

Edited by Louise O. Vasvári
and Steven Tötösy de Zepetnek

Purdue University Press
West Lafayette, Indiana

ISBN 978-1-55753-396-8
ISBN 1-55753-396-2

Printed in the United States of America.

Library of Congress Cataloging-in-Publication Data
Imre Kertész and Holocaust literature / edited by Louise O. Vasvári and Steven Tötösy de Zepetnek.
    p. cm. -- (Comparative cultural studies)
  Includes bibliographical references and index.
  ISBN 1-55753-396-2
  1. Kertész, Imre, 1929--Criticism and interpretation. 2. Holocaust, Jewish (1939-1945), in literature. 3. Hungarian literature--20th century--History and criticism. I. Vasvári, Louise O. (Louise Olga), 1943- II. Tötösy de Zepetnek, Steven, 1950- III. Series.
  PH3281.K3815Z72 2005
  894'.511334--dc22
                                                                            2005012735

Contents

Bibliography

Introduction to *Imre Kertész and Holocaust Literature*

Steven Tötösy de Zepetnek and Louise O. Vasvári

Imre Kertész received the Nobel Prize for Literature in 2002, the first Nobel Prize for writing in Hungarian, a rather difficult language of a minor culture in Central Europe. More important is the fact that the Nobel Prize was awarded to an author who writes about the Holocaust—that single event that defines Europe in the twentieth century—and that the author of this writing is a survivor of the Holocaust. As with all prizes, controversy abounds. In the case of Kertész, however, controversy about the Prize erupted in a country where the Holocaust and matters Jewish represent an unresolved and uncomfortable problematic and where the acceptance of the equal standing of another minor culture—even more minor than Hungarian itself—along with the Hungarian is not a given, not self-evident. In Hungary, as in most cultures elsewhere, the belief in and insistence on nation defined as a homogeneous culture, are tantamount to a social, intellectual, political, and cultural standard and force. This essentialist ideology, in turn, allows and promotes the exclusion of the Other and thus the controversy about whether Kertész as a Jewish-Hungarian writer is Hungarian and whether Hungarians—that is, the country's nationalist and conservative sections of society—should or should not endorse the award, and why. This is of course most unfortunate and in our opinion a sign that Hungarian society as one of the newest members of the European Union is in sore need to develop its newly acquired adherence to democratic values further. At the same time, the Kertész controversy will prove unimportant and short lived while the fact remains that Kertész writes in Hungarian, his native language, whose literature he is at home in and loves, and it is for texts written in that language about the Holocaust that he received the Nobel Prize in Literature.

The papers in the volume are about the work of Imre Kertész in the context of Holocaust literature. As seen in the abstracts of the papers below, a number of the papers are about his novels, several papers are historical and cultural, about the Jewry in Hungary in particular and in Central and East Europe in general, while others are about aspects of the controversy in Hungary surrounding Kertész and the Nobel Prize he received. Of importance is that authors of the papers are from a variety of fields—literary studies, cultural studies, history, sociology, cinema studies—and from several countries—Hungary, Canada, Germany, New Zealand, Croatia, the United Kingdom, and the U.S.—thus demonstrating the international appeal of Kertész's work on the landscape of scholarship. The sequence of the papers and of the abstracts in the volume is by alphabetical order of the authors' surnames.

Enikő Molnár Basa explains in her paper "Imre Kertész and Hungarian Literature" that Kertész, although not a popular author in his native country, was recognized by the literary establishment in the decades before his Nobel Prize. It was Kertész's *Sorstalanság* (*Fatelessness*) that captured the imagination of foreign readers, a novel that recounts his alter ego's experiences in and survival of the Nazi concentration camp. At the same time, the theme of Kertész's works is not only the Holocaust but the suppression of human values and the endangerment of human life. The Holocaust, Kertész proposes, is a deadly version of inhumanity, but Communism is no less virulent, as he points out in *Kaddis a meg nem született gyermekért* (*Kaddish for an Unborn Child*), *A kudarc* (The Failure), and *Az angol lobogó* (The English Flag). In his talks and writings after the fall of Communism, Kertész has spoken out about the Holocaust and its relation to Communist rule, pointing out that totalitarianism and dictatorships do not differ in essence. The Holocaust is a unique experience not because its victims were primarily Jews, but because it defined persons on religious and ethnic or national grounds.

Sara D. Cohen, in her paper "Imre Kertész, Jewishness in Hungary, and the Choice of Identity," analyzes how in his writing Kertész grapples with the twinned concepts of Hungarianness and Jewishness. As an Auschwitz survivor, he is haunted by the problem of his own identity and also by the struggle to come to an understanding of his Jewish background that is independent of his wartime experiences. Cohen examines the prevalence of this tension in Kertész's works, with particular attention to the novels *Fatelessness*, *Kaddish for an Unborn Child*, and *Un autre, chronique d'une métamorphose* as well as to some of his shorter essays and speeches. Kertész's struggle is analyzed by Cohen within the framework of theories of Jewish identity: Kertész and his characters reject the legal, religious, racial, cultural, and reactive definitions of Jewishness, finding them restrictive, or otherwise unsatisfying. The only characters who have found some degree of peace with their identification as a Jew are those who make their Jewishness a choice, much the same way Kertész himself appears to have come to terms with the concept. Although Kertész leaves us with more questions than answers, he and his characters offer us one more possibility for a definition of post-war Jewish self-identification.

Robert Eaglestone discusses in his paper, "The Aporia of Imre Kertész," that, in response to his experience of the Holocaust, Kertész develops an aporetic form of agency and that this could be revealed only through the form of the novel. That is, to regard his work simply as eyewitness testimony is to underestimate its genesis and its achievement. Eaglestone contrasts Kertész's work with other testimonies and highlights the differences. Holocaust testimonies have generic "family resemblances" over the generation of identification, the responses of those who have not experienced the Holocaust, the lack of closure, epiphantic moments, and chronology. In *Fatelessness*, Kertész reuses these to make a case about aporia facing him (and us): "Either the consequentiality of fate or the absurdity of fate." In *Kaddish for an Unborn Child* this aporia is developed into a position in which the refusal of agency—to avoid complicity with the "father culture" responsible for Auschwitz—is itself an act of agency. In turn, this reveals a further aporia, namely that even to refuse agency is a form of usurping power, the self's power over the self.

Amos Friedland, in his paper, "Imre Kertész, Hegel, and the Philosophy of Reconciliation," analyzes Hegel's dialectical logic of reconciliation and Hegel's arguments for the necessity of reconciliation, forgiveness, and conversion on the stage of world history. Friedland contrasts this logic with a post-Holocaust response of "resolute resentment"—a stance that refuses this "inescapable" and total Hegelian reconciliation—in the works of Jean Améry, Vladimir Jankélévitch, and Imre Kertész. Friedland explores the "logic" of Kertész's "No!" in his *Kaddish for an Unborn Child* and discusses the question of the possibility of a "sovereign resentment." Can it resist, or remain left over from, the Hegelian reconciliation? By way of an "absurd" persistence, these "resolute resenters"—Améry, Jankélévitch, Kertész—articulate their strategies for refusing the dialectic equation and constitute a remainder to Hegel's total reconciliation.

András Gerő, in his paper, "Identities of the Jew and the Hungarian," explores aspects of Jewish and Hungarian identity in the context Hungarian history, with focus on the twentieth century. Thus, the paper provides a historical background for Imre Kertész's work. Gerő proposes that while anti-Semitism could be lived with in the pre-Holocaust periods of Hungary, ultimately race-based anti-Semitism became final and total and thus in the logic of the events of the Holocaust, identity became worthless. Nonetheless, the Holocaust did not change the historical nature of the disintegrated Jewish identity established during the assimilationist period of Hungarian Jewry. In Gerő's view, the defining force in the birth of Hungarian national consciousness was the inability of a feudal and aristocratic society to satisfy bourgeois needs via the accustomed means of Christian universalism. Bourgeois energies could only be nourished by creation of a new community, one in which as many people as possible had an interest in operating and maintaining it. Privileges had to be spread wider, and in a way that the new form of social organization maximized its own potential. An essentialist national identity here meant that the privileged community was replaced by a linguistic, i.e., a cultural community. While the nation as a linguistic-cultural community is a structural element in the formation of every nation, a quirk of the Hungarian case, with a unique implication for the identity question, is that fear was one of the inspirations for nation-formation, and indeed one of its results. Finally, Gerő argues for a much overdue concept of identity formation beyond the Jew and the Hungarian.

Bettina von Jagow's paper, "Representing the Holocaust: Kertész's *Fatelessness* and Benigni's *La vita è bella*," is a comparison of Kertész's novel and Roberto Benigni's film in order to point out the differences between the so-called first and later generations in what can be called using "truth" in fiction. Kertész's questions about the Holocaust are also about the discourse of truth and the ability to depict, to render into image the Holocaust. Jagow also discusses the specific kinds of memory used by Kertész and Benigni. Their uses of memory display a special aesthetics that could be called "portraying the Holocaust as culture." It becomes clear that wherever memory is no longer able to stretch the limits of what can be described, it recurs to fiction. Fictitious and imaginary structures, such as the ones brought forward by the child as narrator in Kertész's work or the child as the recipient of a narrative in Benigni's film, both point out and close the gap between ratio and imagination and use imagination to describe the indescribable. This process fills "Auschwitz" with anthropologic value and turns it into a "cultural product," as Kertész suggests himself.

Julia Karolle offers in her paper "Imre Kertész's *Fatelessness* as Historical Fiction" an interpretation of Kertész's novel as a work of historical fiction. Karolle's reading provides a framework for understanding the protagonist, George Koves, in the context of Kertész's ambitions of achieving authenticity in the work. Entering into the discussion is how Kertész, as an author of historical fiction, incorporates historical events into a narrative construction that supports reading the work as authentic. Here, the author blends provocatively authenticity with fictionality, distancing himself from the work by dismissing any claims of autobiography in it. Kertész opts instead for a narrative voice that exposes the near impossibility of subjectivity yet also the fatelessness of objectivity. The model of authenticity that emerges in *Fateless* is thus one based on a particular relationship between the narrator and his subject, in which mere fragments of authentic details must suffice.

Imre Kertész's *Galley Boat-Log* (*Gályanapló*): Excerpts" is a translation by Tim Wilkinson from Kertész's *Gályanapló* (1992). Anyone who seeks to analyze the literary works of Kertész would do well to take into account the excerpts from the author's own "journal," which appeared in two installments during the 1990s. *Gályanapló* is more in the nature of a Camus-style notebook or commonplace book—certainly not the catalogue of events of daily life that one normally expects in a diary. Covering the period from when Kertész decided to forgo secure employment at the beginning of the 1960s through to Hungary's re-emergence as an independent state in the early 1990s, it is an irregular but always illuminating record of what the writer was reading and thinking, the concerns that were being thrown up by his creative work and his often hard-pressed circumstances—typically for years on end. The comments are sometimes gnomic but often throw direct light on the literary works, not least on the quotation-world that they draw on. The extracts translated here relate mainly to Kertész's first two full-length novels, *Sorsta-*

lanság (*Fatelessness*) and *A kudarc* (The Failure), although there is also a hint of *Kaddis a meg nem született gyermekért* (*Kaddish for an Unborn Child*).

Adrienne Kertzer's paper "Reading Imre Kertész in English" is about the fact that the work of Kertész is rarely the subject of North American scholarship on the Holocaust or Holocaust literature. Although the canon of Holocaust writers discussed in North America includes many who do not write in English, Kertész is, despite his Nobel Prize, not to be found in this group. His absence, both caused by and reflected in the lack of interest in translating his work, points to the distance between his fiction and popular patterns of Holocaust representation in North America. Acknowledging the limitations of reading Kertész only in English, Kertzer reads his translated text as multiply challenging the overly simplistic representations of Kertész's identity that followed the announcement of the Nobel Prize. Trying to make sense of an award for a writer whom their readers did/do not know, the press coverage often compares him to Elie Wiesel, a Holocaust writer particularly well respected in North America. A more productive way to approach Kertész is to think of his work as radically opposed to Wiesel's. This contrast may also explain why Kertész's work is not better known in North America.

Kornélia Koltai argues in her paper "Imre Kertész's *Fatelessness* and the Myth about Auschwitz in Hungary" that Kertész's existential experience is that of totalitarianism. His first novel, *Fatelessness* is a phenomenological representation of this experience from an existentialist point of view. In the novel, Kertész depicts life in the death camp as a concentrated state of being. He interprets it as the authentic realization of an absurd world that—when portrayed as an all-encompassing universe —becomes the metaphor of human totalitarianism. In the Hungary of the Kádár era the novel could not be published because it did not coincide with the official rules of the representation of the Holocaust. The rejection of *Fatelessness* had great influence on Kertész's later career. It served as proof of how the totalitarian system functioned and at the same time it became a new code of interpretation for the reading of *Fatelessness*. In the terms of Kertész's oeuvre, failing to publish the novel can be seen as the first step toward its evolution into myth. Kertész's search for the writer's role becomes evident in a number of his texts after *Fatelessness*.

András Kovács, in his paper "The Historians' Debate about the Holocaust in Hungary" offers a discussion on the debate about the Holocaust in Hungary by historians, thus providing further aspects of the historical background of Kertész's work. It was in the 1980s when after the long decades of silence a debate broke out about the Holocaust in Hungary. The Hungarian historians' debate was provoked by Randolph L. Braham's *The Politics of Genocide*, with the main question of the debate being whether the Holocaust in Hungary could have been averted. There was general agreement that the majority of Hungary's Jewish population could have survived the war, if the German occupation of Hungary could somehow have been avoided. The question that had to be asked, therefore, was whether the German occupation of the country could have been averted. According to Braham, the

1944 catastrophe suffered by the Hungarian Jews proves the total failure of a process often described as successful assimilation. Braham considers the events of 1944 as part of Jewish history temporarily entangled with Hungarian history. Kovács analyzes the positions of several influential Hungarian historians about the problematics of the Jewish-Hungarian Holocaust.

Magdalena Marsovszky, in her paper "Imre Kertész and Hungary Today," analyzes the reception of Kertész's Nobel Prize in Hungary in the context of anti-Semitic discourse present in the country today. Owing to the politics of "culture wars" in Hungary between "authentic" Hungarians on the political right and the "cosmopolitans" on the political left, in particular since 1989 and the end of communist rule, Hungary has become a country divided along social, political, cultural, and psychological fault lines. And Kertész and his writing have become one of the symbolic figures in the "culture wars" and a focus of anti-Semitic agitation. Marsovszky discusses the reasons of anti-Semitism in contemporary Hungary and concludes that its origins can be found in the fixation on a romantic ideal of the nation, the ethnicization of the notion of people as Hungariannes (*magyarság*), and cultural ethnocentrism. In Marsovszky's opinion, the result of this particular configuration is that anti-Semitism in Hungary has become a cultural attitude.

Sára Molnár, in her paper, "Imre Kertész's Aesthetics of the Holocaust," discusses aspects of Nobel Laureate Imre Kertész's reception in Hungary with focus on the aesthetic features of the author's use of language. Molnár's study illuminates the problem of authorship and questions relating to intersections of fiction and autobiography in Kertész's oeuvre. Molnár's argument is that although the author's personal history is indeed important in his texts, this "author" should not be identified with Kertész himself and that although Kertész's themes and subjects appear to be autobiographical, not even his diaries should or can be interpreted as autobiographical documents. According to Molnár, in discussions about Kertész's texts in Hungarian media and scholarship an autobiographical interpretation represents a simplification and neglect of the fictional characters called into life in the author's narratives. Further, Molnár suggests that Kertész, influenced by other texts in Holocaust literature, such as works by Tadeusz Borowski, Primo Lévi, Jean Améry, or Paul Celan, has found a language and an aesthetic to present Holocaust literature authentically, where his writing is also relevant to issues and problems of our time.

Marie Peguy, in her paper, "The Dichotomy of Perspectives in the Work of Imre Kertész and Jorge Semprún," analyzes how the two authors share the common experience of having been confronted with the destructive force of totalitarianism at its utmost degree, the concentration camps and extermination. Still, their individual paths and patent ways of shaping their narratives testify to the complexity of the impact on their identities during that gruesome episode of the twentieth century. The Jewish-Hungarian concentration camp survivor and the communist Spanish resistance fighter are both bearers of an individual yet collective history and their writing allows us to try to understand how the almost dissolved ego—absent, as it were, to itself—can take in order to survive and to give a meaning to a fate un-chosen. The oeuvre of Kertész and Semprún provides us with testimonies of their idiosyncratic capacities to resist. If Semprún owns up to the subjectivity of experience and translates it into a highly aesthetic literary act, Kertész opposes to that a total unobtrusiveness of the subject, reduced to the part of an irresponsive observer.

Catherine Portuges discusses in her paper, "Imre Kertész and the Filming of *Sorstalanság (Fatelessness)*," the filmic adaptation of the novel in Hungary. Selected for the 2002 Nobel Prize in Literature "for writing that upholds the fragile experience of the individual against the barbaric arbitrariness of history," Kertész, deported as an adolescent in 1944 to Auschwitz and Buchenwald, draws upon his own tragic experience as a Jew under Nazism and Stalinism in his 1975 novel, *Sorstalanság (Fatelessness)*. One result of his recent visibility is a film adaptation of the novel, based on Kertész's own scenario, to be directed by the Hungarian cinematographer and multiple Academy Award nominee, Lajos Koltai, who had attempted unsuccessfully for years to secure funding for *Fatelessness*. Based on production documents, interviews with the writer, director, literary and film historians, and the international press, as well as personal access to the work in progress, Portuges analyzes the history and trajectory of the production of *Fatelessness* and the debates engendered by the Nobel Laureate as a living text that addresses the status of contemporary Jewish identity in post–1989 Hungary.

Rosana Ratkovčić, in her paper, "Danilo Kiš, Imre Kertész, and the Myth of the Holocaust," compares aspects of the work of these two important Central European writers. Following a brief definition of her own notion of "the myth of the Holocaust," Ratkovčić explores Kiš's and Kertész's narratives about the Holocaust by pointing to common points in their approach. Although the two writers are of a similar background, coming from socialist countries with similar attitudes towards the Holocaust and who published their texts in the same period of time—in the 1970s—their writing has of yet not been frequently compared. Ratkovčić explores common points in selected texts by Kertész and Kiš with regard to the genre characteristics of autobiographical fiction, whereby Kiš's work is autobiographical fiction in the second generation dealing with his father who perished in the concentration camp, while Kertész's fiction is that of a Holocaust survivor.

Tamás Scheibner argues in his paper "Imre Kertész's *Jegyzőkönyv (Sworn Statement)* and the Self Deprived of Itself" that the central problematic of Kertész's oeuvre is the exploration of the constructability of personality and its parallel questions regarding the nature and existence of freedom. Scheibner proposes that the answers to these fundamental questions in Kertész's work are inconsistent. Following his postulate, Scheibner investigates Kertész's collection of short stories, *Jegyzőkönyv*. Analyzing the acts of identification of the text and those which react against these, Scheibner exposes precisely that dual consciousness which is apparent in the work of Kertész and which can be described in terms of an oscillation between autonomous personality and a form of internalized external determination, or automatism. From Scheibner's point of view, Kertész's subtle and tension-filled portrayal of a "schizoid" condition is the belletristic construct that locates the short stories in *Jegyzőkönyv* among his most significant texts.

Eluned Summers-Bremner proposes in her paper "Imre Kertész's *Kaddish for a Child Not Born*" that Kertész's short novel marks a particular absence, namely the narrator's sense of the impossibility of bringing a child into a post-Holocaust world. This impossibility is the result of the incorporation of the Jews into pre-Second World War Hungarian life and the incorporation of Hungary into the German mindset that, with the Second World War, would see the Jewish-Hungarian population all but annihilated. Summers-Bremner reads *Kaddish* as an intervention in this history that is faithful to the function of the *kaddish* (mourning prayer), which is incumbent upon Jewish sons to recite daily for the first year of mourning for their fathers. Paradoxically a prayer of praise within Judaism, the function of the ritual *kaddish*—to mark desolation—is at odds with its subject. Yet, it calls on a community to witness or to incorporate actively this repeated act. In reversing the son-father dynamic, Kertész's narrator produces a similar paradox for a community of readers. Instead of the prayer in the synagogue, we have the physical fact of the book, whose writing and reading, although it begins with a "no," call us to witness the active struggle that takes the place of the child not born.

Steven Tötösy de Zepetnek, in his paper, "Imre Kertész's Nobel Prize in Literature in the Print Media," discusses aspects of media coverage in German-, Hungarian-, and English-language newspapers and magazines of the 2002 Nobel Prize in Literature, awarded to Imre Kertész. The perspective of Tötösy's analysis is to gauge the importance and impact of media coverage comparatively in the three cultural and media landscapes. Based on selected examples from newspapers and magazines with an international scope, Tötösy argues that the reception of Kertész's Nobel Prize suggests the convergence of the media (as the message) and the contents of the message within public discourse, resulting in Kertész's role as a public intellectual despite his reluctance to assume this role. Tötösy demonstrates that the media discourse reveals significant differences in the reception of the prize, pointing to different stages in democratic values in the context of the relevance of the Holocaust today. In addition, the media reception reveals how far a particular society accepts (Germany, the U.S., and Canada) or rejects (Hungary) the historical relevance of Kertész's work as unique in the literature of the Holocaust.

Paul Várnai, in his paper, "Holocaust Literature and Imre Kertész," analyzes the work of the 2002 Nobel Laureate in the comparative context of Holocaust literature. Várnai explores the work of Kertész in the context of a number of Hungarian Holocaust texts such as Olga Lengyel's *Five Chimneys*, Miklós Nyiszli's *Auschwitz: A Doctor's Eyewitness Account*, György Gera's *Terelőút*, and György Konrád's *Elindulás és hazatérés*. Várnai's reading of Kertész's work focuses on the

Nobel Laureate's view of the reasons why Communist dictatorships played down the importance of the Holocaust and comes to the conclusion that just as Borowski in his *This Way to the Gas Ladies and Gentlemen*, Kertész, too, challenges the division into persecutors and victims: No one is innocent, including the survivor. According to Kertész, dictatorship deprives a person of his fate and responsibility, even his name, even infantalizing him. Kertész's texts shock their readers when he tells them about their own share of responsibility.

Louise O. Vasvári, in her paper "The Novelness of Imre Kertész's *Sorstalanság (Fatelessness)*" discusses how Kertész perverts deliberately the "serious" values of Holocaust literary culture by overturning every clichéd convention of Holocaust literature by converting it into almost "clinical discourse" and by producing a text that is difficult for a general readership, including in its translated versions. In Vasvári's analysis Kertész is a social realist whose narrative must be sought in its primary debt to existentialism and to the postmodern novel. Further, Vasvári discusses the similarity between *Fatelessness* and Albert Camus's *L'Étranger* as philosophical tracts masquerading as fiction, as well as their startling degree of textual similarity. Thus, the protagonist in Kertész's novel is a younger version of Camus's Meursault, the "indifferent man," who does not have the ability to experience communion with the world and who accepts everything that happens to him with indifference. Vasvári also compares Kertész with authors such as Philip Roth and Benjamin Wilkomirski, who problematize, in turn, authorial and narrative voice, as well as diminish intentionally the barrier between fiction and reality. In this context Kertész's work is best understood as autofiction or as pseudo-autobiographical novel. Vasvári concludes that Kertész's daringly innovative text functions as the ultimate Holocaust novel, which subverts the rhetorical and narrative myths of its predecessors.

Judy Young, in her paper, "The Media and Imre Kertész's Nobel Prize in Literature," reviews the print media responses to the Kertész Nobel Prize in the period from the announcement of the prize on 10 October 2002 to the awarding of the prize on 10 December 2002, and a few weeks following the award ceremony. Young reviews articles, news items, and published interviews primarily from the Hungarian-language press. An analysis of the material gathered from Hungary indicates that the responses to this literary award reflect not so much the literary but the political state of affairs in the country. Reviews and opinions are largely aligned with the political/ideological axes of a polarized society; because of actual and perceived attacks on the writer by conservative and right-wing journalists, the literary establishment in Hungary saw itself forced to defend Kertész and in this way helped to perpetuate an ongoing ideological struggle.

As a brief look at current scholarship about the problematics of the Holocaust, the papers in the volume are followed by Barbara Breisach's book review article, "Jewish Identity and Anti-Semitism in Central European Culture (Books by Lamping, Gilman and Steinecke, Goltschnigg and Steinecke, Suleiman and Forgács, and Wallas)." The volume includes also "A Bibliography of Imre Kertész's Oeuvre and Publications about His Work," compiled by Steven Tötösy de Zepetnek, and a list of bioprofiles of the contributors to the volume.

A note about the English translation of Kertész's *Sorstalanság:* The correct translation of the title is Fatelessness (and not Fateless), as in Imre Kertész, *Fatelessness*, translated by Tim Wilkinson (New York: Vintage, 2004). However, authors in the volume quote from *Fateless*, translated by Christopher C. Wilson and Katharina M. Wilson (Evanston: Northwestern UP, 1992) as the Wilkinson translation was not available at the time of the writing and editing of the papers. In instances where there is no direct quote in the paper from the book, the correct title, *Fatelessness*, is used. Although Kertész has criticized the Wilson & Wilson translation repeatedly, it should be noted in defense of the translators—Christopher C. Wilson and Katharina M. Wilson—that at the time when their translation of *Sorstalanság* appeared, in 1992, outside of Germany and in a few of the Nordic countries, no one has heard of Kertész, certainly not in the English-speaking world, and that the publication of the book was a risky proposition in the context of publishing an unknown author in English in the U.S., to say the least. Thus, the publisher's insistence to release a translation for a readership for whom a "simplified" text would perhaps be more palatable and thus a moderate sale of the books would be possible, made good sense from a publishing point of view. Now, with the Nobel Prize, more accurate translations of Kertész's work are forthcoming.

The papers in the volume speak for themselves and we hope they will be instrumental in creating interest in the work of the Nobel Laureate, both in the context of Holocaust literature and culture and literature per se. Kertész's work represents innovative narration of the Holocaust, as well as, and parallel to the narration of universal values and universal questions concerning humanity. It is thus that scholarship about Kertész's work would be of interest to all, but especially to scholars of literature and culture in the English-speaking world, as well as for all who explore scholarship from the many languages and cultures with English as a tool of scholarship and communication.

Winchester & Halle and New York & Budapest
December 2004

Imre Kertész and Hungarian Literature

Enikő Molnár Basa

When the Swedish Academy announced the winner of the Nobel Prize in Literature for 2002, most people asked, "Who is Imre Kertész?" Of course, it could have been almost any Hungarian author and the reaction would have been the same. Still, Kertész is less well known in the United States than, for example, the novels of Péter Esterházy or Péter Nádas, whose works have received much more attention. It is, however, not unusual for the prize to go to a relatively unknown writer, and, in fact, Kertész had been considered among the contenders for a few years. The Nobel Prize was awarded "for writing that upholds the fragile experience of the individual against the barbaric arbitrariness of history" (see *Nobel Prize in Literature: Laureates* (2002): <http://www.nobel.se/literature/laureates/index.html>). The Academy noted that the topic of his work has been Auschwitz, which "for him . . . is not an exceptional occurrence that like an alien body subsists outside the normal history of Western Europe. It is the ultimate truth about human degradation in modern existence" (see *Nobel Prize in Literature: Laureates* (2002): <http://www. nobel.se/literature/laureates/index.html>). As I point out later, it is also a concept that goes beyond the one camp to embrace all such camps, Nazi or Communist. *Sorstalanság* (1975, translated as *Fateless*, 1992; although *Fatelessness* is the correct translation [see the new translation by Tim Wilkinson] and as Wilkinson's translation is scheduled to appear after the writing of my paper, I am quoting from the Wilson & Wilson translation) was Kertész's first novel and defines his work. *Kaddis a meg nem született gyermekért* (1990, *Kaddish for a Child Not Born* 1997 and *Kaddish for an Unborn Child* 2004), and *A kudarc* (1988, The Failure) elaborate on his examination of what becomes for him the central question of twentieth-century Western thinking. I do not agree with the Academy that for Kertész "the spiritual dimension of man lies in his inability to adapt to life," or that "individual experience seems useless" when "considered in the light of the needs and interests of the human collective" (see *Nobel Prize in Literature: Laureates* (2002): <http:// www.nobel.se/literature/laureates/index.html>). Rather, he has taken from this negative experience and affirmed the humanistic values of Western civilization. As he said in his Nobel speech: "In the Holocaust I have always recognized the human condition, the final end of the great adventure to which European man has arrived after two thousand years of ethical and moral culture. . . . This serious situation was perhaps most precisely identified by the Hungarian Roman Catholic poet János Pilinszky when he called it a 'scandal,' meaning that Auschwitz occurred within Christian culture and so it cannot be lived down. . . . We have to create our own values, from day to day, and with that steadfast, yet invisible ethical activity which will finally bring these values to the surface, and will possibly in time become empowered in a new European culture" ("Heureka!" 3; all translations from the Hungarian are mine unless noted otherwise).

Kertész was born 1929 in Budapest and deported to Auschwitz in 1944. Actually, he spent only a few days in Auschwitz before being transferred to Buchenwald and Zeitz. However, as he points out, Auschwitz has gained a symbolic meaning that goes beyond the one geographical location ("Táborok maradandósága" 11). He returned to Budapest in 1945 and worked for the newspaper *Világosság* from 1948 to 1951, when the consolidation of Communist rule and the Stalinist dictatorship led to his dismissal. For a while he worked in a factory, and later he supported himself, like so many other authors who could not—or would not—publish during those years, as a translator from German. *Sorstalanság* was not published until 1975, in a censored version and in a small press run which seems to have been quietly withdrawn from the bookstores. He had begun writing it in 1960 and completed it in 1973.

In reporting the news of the Nobel Prize, the international press has pointed out that Kertész was a loner on the Hungarian literary scene; that he was not well known even in Hungary. It is true that he did not belong to any of the organized groups, refusing even to join the Hungarian Writers Association because, he said, "I refuse to adapt or integrate myself" (qtd. in Riding, "Nobel Hero" E5; see also Riding, "Nobel"). On the other hand, he had not been unknown. Reviews of *Sorstalanság* appeared in the leading newspapers and several journals upon its publication (on this, see Marsovszky; Tötösy; Young). Most were favorable, yet it was another ten years before his work began to receive the attention it deserved. By then his second novel had been published and the cultural climate had also changed. György Spiró published a study in the literary weekly, *Élet és Irodalom*, in 1983, and included a slightly longer version in his collection of essays, *Magániktató* (Self-Recorder), published in 1985. A review of Kertesz's *Gályanapló* (Galley Boat-Log, 1992) by Péter Dávidházi appeared in *Holmi* in 1993 and again in Dávidházi's book *Per passivam resistanciam* in 1998. Others recognized Kertész as an important representative of postmodernism as well, and literary prizes also came his way—at least twelve in Hungary between 1983 and 1997, including Hungary's highest award, the Kossuth Prize, and several prizes in Germany as well. In April 2002 a conference was held on his works, and *Az értelmezés szükségszerűsége* (The Necessity of Interpretation), based on these presentations and edited by Dávidházi, was already in the works before the Nobel Prize was announced. Kertész has hardly been absent from the Hungarian literary scene, yet he himself commented: "I have been deeply touched by this outpouring of love. But I know my books are not so popular here because the Holocaust is not embedded in Hungarian consciousness" (Kertész qtd. in Kirk <http://core.ujcfedweb.org/content_ display.html?ArticleID=62804>).

The Holocaust is the theme of his novels, but his writing has also been influenced by his living forty years under Communism. "My work is a form of commitment to myself, to memory, and to humanity," he has said in an interview (qtd. in Riding, "Nobel Hero" E5). His novel *Angol lobogó* (The English Flag, 1991) depicts the years of "catastrophe" in the 1950s and the Hungarian Uprising of 1956, and his next one addresses the problems of life under Communism: "This will be my last novel about the Holocaust. It takes place in Budapest at the time of the change of political system and deals with people who did not experience the Holocaust directly, the second generation, who still have to deal with the Holocaust," he pointed out (Kertész qtd. in Kirk <http://core.ujcfedweb.org/content _display.html?ArticleID=62804>). In the interview given to Harace Engdahl on the occasion of the awarding of the Nobel Prize, he refines his to indicate that this is the last of the approaches he will take to the topic. But we must not take the portrayal of the Holocaust literally, for his is basically a symbolic approach. I return to this again in the comments below, as it is impossible to discuss Kertész without discussing the philosophical underpinnings of his work. And, as pessimistic as his appraisal that the Holocaust showed the failure of Western civilization is, Kertész actually draws positive values from it. What he argues is that the values we have accepted as a legacy of Western culture must be created from within us. Only then will they not fail in the face of challenges. As Dániel Lányi points out, "one reason *Sorstalanság* is a great novel lies in its ability to turn around the rationale of the concentration camps, which reduced man to a body, to matter that could be terminated, burned, used up, by circumventing the ethical categories and traditional thinking that had failed in the face of Auschwitz" (671).

Some years before the Nobel Prize, in an interview given to the online version of the magazine *Magyar Narancs*, Kertész noted: "I wished to traumatize the reader. The conception of my work is based on the premise that the fear, the loss of footing, which is cited as lacking in the narrator [of *Sorstalanság*] should be found in the reader" (Kertész Interview, *Magyar Narancs* <http://www.mancs.hu/ index. php?gc.Page=public/hir.phg&id=757>). This imperative to involve the reader accounts for the success of the work. It is a mark of Kertész's mastery of the art of narrative and of his skillful and precise use of language that he is successful. Significantly, his models were Voltaire, Flaubert, Dostoyevsky, Kafka, and Camus. He was not influenced by earlier Hungarian writers in this work, although Gyula Krúdy and Sándor Márai are models in his later works. Indeed, his ironic style is outside the tradition of Hungarian literature, although not outside contemporary concerns.

Spiró notes in his essay that Kertész presents a "philosophy of existence which almost explodes the boundaries of literature" (381). The reader is brought into the experience slowly, almost imperceptibly, while the narrator seems to accept each step as "natural." Thinking he is being taken simply to work, he "mistakes" the concentration camp inmates for real convicts—criminals serving sentences. He finds himself carried along inexorably by the crowd until the realization of where he is *almost* sinks in: "I don't know who took action, nor what happened exactly. I can only remember that some pressure weighed on me, some momentum moved, thrust me, stumbling a little yet in my new shoes, amid a cloud of dust and behind me a sound of strange thumps as if someone's back were possibly being hit, ever forward, towards newer yards, newer barbed wire gates, barbed wire enclosures, expanding and enclosing fences finally swimming together and becoming disturbingly entangled before my eyes" (*Fateless* 112). In time, the hunger, deprivation, work, and dehumanizing conditions do affect him, and he gives up, surviving only by seeing his own body as something separate and foreign: "For my own part, I did not doubt that I lived, if only flickering, as if with the flame turned entirely down, but something still burned within me, the flame of life, as they say, that is, my body was here, I knew everything about it, merely myself, somehow, no longer lived inside it" (*Fateless* 208). It is as an observer that he relates his rescue when he is not dumped on the heap of bodies headed for the crematorium. A voice—his own, barely recognizable to himself—mutters " I . . . ob . . . ject" and he is taken to the hospital ward instead (*Fateless* 136). Inexplicably, here he is treated well. Again the irony becomes apparent as he notes:

> At any rate, after a while, even if only little by little, guardedly, carefully, I had to see, had to accept the proof of facts, namely that—it seems—this is also possible, this is also believable, merely that it is more unusual, and then undoubtedly more pleasant of course, but for all that essentially not in the least stranger, if I think of it, from any other strangeness, which in the final analysis—in a concentration camp—all, all is possible and believable, like this, and also the reverse, truly natural. But on the other hand, precisely this is what perplexed me, disturbed, undermined in a certain way my security: after all, if I looked at it rationally, I could see no reason for it; nothing logical, nothing familiar, nor was I able to find any motive acceptable to my reason that I should be here, as it happens, and not rather somewhere else. (*Fateless* 230–31)

Susanna Nirenstein comments: "Nothing is obvious; in fact, what he lives through and how he lives through this harbors a strange duality: The reader knows the history and dimensions of the concentration camp, the narrator 'I' does not" (4).

Only upon his return home does the narrator begin to understand—to reflect upon—what had happened. Answering laconically the questions of a journalist, he says finally: "'In a concentration camp,' I said, 'they are very natural'" (*Fateless* 180); namely: hatred, horrors, deprivation. It is in this logic—or denial of logic—that the incomprehensibility of Auschwitz is expressed. György Vári sees the pres-

ervation of the "senselessness" of Auschwitz as the goal of the novel at a time
when the memory of Auschwitz is being ritualized (7). I believe, however, that
there is more to the novel than that. Even in the eyes of the narrator his experience
assumes significance because he does not dismiss it merely as something he passively endured. Unlike those who remained at home and lived through their own
horrors, he has changed. That is why he argues with his neighbors Fleischmann
and Steiner. They relate the events as something that happened to them: "The star-
marked house 'came,' October 15 'came', the Arrow Cross 'came', the Ghetto
'came' the Danube bank 'came,' liberation 'came'" (*Fateless* 284). Moreover, it all
seems as if compressed into a moment in time. The narrator, however, points out:
"'But it was not quite so, that it 'came': We also went. Only now does everything
seem complete, finished, unalterable, final, so immensely fast and so terribly
blurred, so that 'it came': Now, only afterwards, when we look at it backwards,
from the reverse side'" (*Fateless* 287). Spiró takes this train of thought to explain
the conclusion drawn by the novel. "The hero changed: Here he can fully expound
the outlook which in the beginning of the novel lurked in the irony of the style. . . .
And this is the question which ties the novel to the already known question, and
whose variations we must face at least in our century" (389). The explanation of
the title of the novel is also found in Kertész's statement: "If there is fate, then
freedom is not possible; if on the other hand . . . there is freedom, then there is no
fate. That is . . . then we ourselves are fate" (*Fateless* 289).

The message emerges slowly in the last pages, and it is well demonstrated in
the essay "Fikcióalkotás és történelemszemlélet" ("The Creation of Fiction and the
Perspective of History') by Gábor Tamás Molnár. Molnár points out that the narrator regains his identity only in the last pages, as a result of his conversations with
the journalist and the two old friends who make him articulate his thoughts (10).
He takes responsibility for his past because, as he says, "they can't take everything
from me, it's not possible that I be neither victor nor victim, that I could not be
right and that I could not be mistaken either, that I be neither the cause nor the consequence, simply . . . I cannot accept that stupid bitterness that I am merely innocent" (*Fateless* 290). I believe this is what leads the narrator to affirm life and yet
to feel a certain nostalgia for the concentration camp: "I am here, and I well know
that I accept all reasons as the price for being able to live" (*Fateless* 291). As Molnár points out, if one "accepts Auschwitz as 'completed' from where the innocent
victims returned, he cannot make it speak and must abdicate from self analysis"
(10). The puzzling and possibly disturbing statement about happiness in the camp
is explained by Imre Szász as part of the instinct for self-preservation, which, the
young Köves asserts, enabled him to survive. When the narrator says, "Why even
there, beside the chimneys there was something in the pauses between torments
which resembled happiness. Everyone only asks about the vicissitudes, the 'horrors' whereas for me maybe this experience remains the most memorable. Yes, this
is what I should talk about to them, the happiness of the concentration camps, next

time, when they ask" (*Fateless* 291), it does not mitigate the horror, but makes it deeper (54).

Sorstalanság/Fatelessness is the most precise and literal evocation of Kertész's basic theme, but his other works serve to broaden the concept. His contention that Auschwitz is symbolic, that in a sense it is a tragedy of the mass culture and mass rule that characterizes twentieth-century dictatorships, is developed in later works and expounded in his statements. Deep in each of his self-reflexive heroes, however, is the will to live and the conviction that by making a choice he asserts his humanity. Tamás Turai argues that the true theme of Kertész's work is survival, which actually can only be understood in terms of avoiding death. Such survival, however, is basically an intellectual act and the survivor becomes a witness (310–11). These ideas are developed in his later works, which I now discuss.

A kudarc (1988, The Failure) is in a sense a continuation of *Sorstalanság*, relating the story—in the novel within the novel—of Köves as a young man making his way through the senselessness that the Communist regime had brought to Hungary. While death and executions are not an everyday occurrence, fear and uncertainty rule the lives of all. The "hero" is almost as clueless and innocent as in the first novel. The frame is provided by the narrator's diffident efforts to write the novel, connecting the narrator of the 1980s with the protagonist of the 1950s. In order to make his naïveté believable and to emphasize the senselessness of the bureaucracy he faces, Kertész has his hero arrive at his destination expecting to visit a friend who had emigrated to the West, only to find himself in what is strangely familiar yet still unfamiliar territory. This Kafkaesque setting thus introduces the Budapest of the late 1940s or early 1950s, although both the locale and the date are left vague. As Miklós Győrffy puts it: "Köves arrived from Budapest to Budapest for in one sense he came back from the today, the eighties, from the present of the Old One; in another, having survived the concentration camp, he arrives home, to another city than that from which he had been dragged away, as a different man from the one who left. A different man to such an extent that it is as if his past did not even exist in the story; we can only infer from it, that the novel whose idea finally emerges in his mind is the same as that which the Old One has already written, that it is about Auschwitz" (986).

In *A kudarc*, grayness, neglect, ruins, broken-down streetcars, trucks full of families being "relocated," soldiers and policemen rule the streets. A group he takes to be customs officers are omnipresent and wield mysterious power: They assign his place of residence and decide where he will work, for example. It is not hard to make the leap from the Hungarian word for the customs officer, *Vámos*, to ÁVÓS, i.e., the state (secret) police (ÁVÓ: Állaravédelmi Hatóság). Everything is decided by "someone," who of course is never named. The decisions are completely arbitrary and invariably harmful. He is dismissed from his job before he even gets to start working there and assigned to a factory. On the first night he shares a park bench with a pianist who does not return home, lest he be dragged away from his bed in the middle of the night. The pianist is nevertheless arrested and spends time tending corn and pigs before being forced to play for his guards under such circumstances that he becomes disgusted and gives up music. The president of his building is also taken away, probably "resettled" in some village or farm, and . . . slowly goes mad with guilt for a mysterious past, probably as an executioner for the regime. And fortunate turns are just as inexplicable. For example, Köves is called into a manager's office and scolded for working in the factory when he should be doing intellectual work, and reflects: "They throw him out of everywhere, they are barely willing to employ him in a steel mill, as a grown man he must become an apprentice locksmith, and then they reproach him, as if it had been his idea to become a fitter?" (*A kudarc* 261). When he protests that he is not suitable for a job in the Press Office of the Ministry, he is told that "a higher design" decided and he must accept (265). His ignorance is only excused because he has just returned from abroad. The corruption of the system and the way everyone is implicated is also made clear. It turns out that he actually got the job through his friend Sziklai and loses it because his boss suspects he saw through an allegorical ballad he was asked to critique. Sziklai, who does seizes the opportunity and leaves in 1956, represents the type of con man who could survive and even prosper in those turbulent years. He manages to ingratiate himself into positions of power and knows exactly how to use connections, bribery and threats to turn the corruption of the system to his advantage.

Az angol lobogó (1991, The English Flag) distills the experience of the same era into a tight monologue. Viktória Radics calls it a *Bildungsroman,* and in the old professor's reminiscences we find traces of his youthful career and a sense of the steps that brought him to the present moment (137). The motto, taken from Mihály Babits, "before us fog, behind us fog, and beneath us a sunken country," captures the essence in a tale where the crux is the "friendly, maybe even sympathetic" wave of a British diplomat as he leaves the streets of Budapest to the Soviet tanks (*A kudarc* 17). The terror, the senselessness of life, the feeling that some power was always threatening, permeates the story: "Anyone, at any time, can be taken away by the black car' (5). Gyula Illyés had distilled the essence of tyranny in 1950 in his famous poem, "A Sentence about Tyranny" ("Egy mondat a zsarnokságról"), and Kertész presents it here from the distance of a philosophically inclined old gentleman, but its message is just as gripping.

Kaddish a meg nem született gyermekért (1990, *Kaddish for a Child Not Born* 1997, *Kaddish for an Unborn Child* 2004) approaches what is Kertész's central motif—the problem of the value of human life in a totalitarian system—through a breathless musical movement that reflects Celan's "Todesfuge," a few lines of which serve as the motto for the book. The recurring "No" forms a refrain-like thread that allows him to express his views on life: Can we chose who we are, or do others chose this for us? What are our choices, and the possibilities of choice? What is the relationship of free will and constrains? The role of goodness?

In one section he reflects how he had become a writer and translator only by subterfuge and cleverly evading the "bull-headed monster" which had not meant him to be this and even so they trampled him, for "they did not tolerate thought in any form, except perhaps in the form of prisoner-thoughts, that is, in no way at all, these circumstances only praised slave labor" (*Kaddish* 111–12). Through the story of the teacher who gives his portion of food to another even in the concentration camp, Kertész asserts that there "exists a pure concept, an idea, not so contaminated by our bodies, our souls, our wild animals which lives in all our minds equally and as the same" (*Kaddish* 112). As Erzsébet Berkes points out, this is "not the novel of the Jewish minority experience, but an accounting of the life that can be chosen" (118).

Kertész himself makes it clear that he is writing not about one particular camp but that he has made Auschwitz the symbol of all such atrocities. At a gathering all the people name the place where they had suffered: Mauthausen, Recsk, Siberia, the villages of the resettlement, the prisons after 1956, etc., but Auschwitz trumps all because it stands for all suffering endured by man at the hands of totalitarian regimes (see *A holokauszt* 56). Here he comes close to the poet János Pilinszky, as Márton Szilágyi points out: "For both, Auschwitz is the axis of the interpretation of the world, but according to Pilinszky, since 'sin showed itself in proportions not seen to this time' in Auschwitz, the ever-present strength of a triumphant redemption also becomes recognizable through it." For Szilágyi, Kertész does not claim something contrary to this; rather, he accepts the full tragic weight of the Heideggerian death experience (72). The wisdom that emerges is a quiet acceptance—expressed poignantly in the "Amen" that concludes the novel, so that Szilágyi is right when he calls the novel "a synthetic summary of all that cultural heritage which we in a word call European" (73).

Gályanapló (1992, Galley Boat-Log) is a diary novel culled from entries ranging from 1961 to 1991. It provides a glimpse into the genesis of Kertész's works, biographical details, and philosophical deliberations. In it, perhaps more clearly than in the novels, he addresses the problem of determination and free will and "seeks the possibilities of the individual in a totalitarian dictatorship"; the entries "ponder the essence of today's culture and arts, its task and its possibilities" (Gács 857). Thus in December 1980 he writes that in the twentieth century the masses rule and this has had disastrous consequences. The intellectuals too often join some mass movement and thus they cease to be the "carriers of that denial" which in today's mob-society, mob-life, mass destruction and destructiveness could be the only thing that is authentic, true, authoritative. The masses and thought were always opposite concepts. But the masses had never before been in *power,* in monopolistic, in total power . . . the masses, more precisely the power which seeks to legitimize itself through the masses, is a position that it can destroy all higher forms of life; and without that there is no value (and I fear no reason) for life. This is a twentieth-century phenomenon" (*Gályanapló* 91). This also sheds light on

Kertész's other statements about the rule of the masses, which of course he does not equate with the rule of the people but that of a mob controlled by a small clique who have seized power without knowing how to use it, or what to use it for. As the arrests and trials of the inner circles of such systems show, they cannot even use it for their own good, while the good of others is automatically excluded from their thinking. Kertész explores the problem of the individual versus power, of freedom versus tyranny, not in isolation but within the context of the twentieth century. In my view, it is this that makes his message so immediate and important. An entry for July 1990 reads: "I saw the dissolution of the Buchenwald concentration camp in '45, the settling in of the red abomination in '48, its dissolution in '56, its reestablishment in '57, etc. . . . It would be foolish to believe that this is merely the failure of the so-called Communist empire, and not that of the whole human world. Of the moral and rational world." For the seventy years of the one (and the twelve years of the other) favored "irrationality, chaos, terror, and the vegetative possibilities of the lowest human form" while camps, killings, general psychopathy, abasement, repression were daily occurrences (*Gályanapló* 214). Still, he escaped, and so did others, and it is this "miracle" that gives hope for a better future, founded on principles of the spirit, of creativity, of life, that a new civilization can rise on the ashes of the old, preserving its values but not its vulnerabilities.

In later statements Kertész makes the universality of this lesson even more explicit. He states that the concept embraced by the word "Auschwitz" actually applies to all totalitarian dictatorships. Thus, the lessons to be learned, the lesson that the narrator of *Sorstalanság*—as indeed the narrators/heroes of his other works—learned does not only concern Jews or a particular historical situation. The Holocaust is a defining concept in the twentieth century because it is open to this universal interpretation. The horrors are not so much the expression of ideology or prejudice as of totalitarianism: "The Jews—it is true—did not die because of their religion, and they were not killed—it is true—in the name of another religion. Totalitarianism killed them, the totalitarian state, the totalitarian party power—this monster, this epidemic, this plague of the century which is more destructive than any destructive religion. . . . Totalitarianism exiles from itself and places outside of law *man* himself" (*A holokauszt* 28).

In one of his other talks on the meaning of the Holocaust Kertész is even more explicit in defining this as a central theme in Western consciousness: Auschwitz has become "a universal example, on which the seal of permanence has been placed; which encompassed in its simple name the whole world of the Nazi concentration camps, the shock of the universal spirit over this, and whose mythical locale has to be maintained so that pilgrims can visit it, as they visit, for example, the hill of Golgotha. . . . In Auschwitz, not for a moment are good and evil blurred" (*A holokauszt* 11); and "There is no benchmark for suffering, there is no thermometer for injustice. The Gulag, the Nazi camp system were created by the same goals, and that they reached their goal, millions of victims are the witness" (*A holokauszt* 18–

19). Whether all of this was clear in the author's mind when he began writing *Sorstalanság* may be debated, but his later works and comments certainly support the realization, which is seminal in his first novel, that the Holocaust was a catastrophe for all of European civilization. In an interview he elaborated on this: "The Holocaust is not history's one-time mistake. It belongs to European history, and with it, the European values of the Enlightenment collapsed" (qtd. in Riding, "Nobel Hero" E1). In view of the kinship Kertész feels with another newly "discovered" Hungarian writer, Sándor Márai, it is interesting to note his comments on how he became a writer and how he preserved his independence under Communist rule. In 1955 he had a vision of people representing "forgetfulness, conformism, resignation. Belonging to this marching group meant losing my identity. I had to step out of line. It was why I decided to become a writer" (qtd. in Riding, "Nobel Hero" E1). But he also chose to remain outside the "establishment, as he noted in a recent interview: "I have always remained an outside observer, sometimes frightened, sometimes shocked, sometimes indifferent, but always an outsider" (qtd. in Riding, "Nobel Hero" E1). But whereas Márai, who was an established writer in 1948 when he decided to leave Hungary, Kertész did not choose to leave. As an outsider, he notes, "Your perspective on life is totally your own and cannot be influenced. . . . You are not thinking about being successful. You expect to make no impact. It's hopeless. And if its hopeless, you might as well stick to the truth. And you have an awful lot of time to think. I had nothing else to do all day. The isolation and hopelessness of the situation gave you freedom" (qtd. in Riding, "Nobel Hero" E1).

In contrast, for Márai, leaving was the only alternative: "I had to leave it not just because the Communists would not let me write freely, but mainly and even much more so because they would not let me be silent freely" (357). This is also why the totalitarian regimes of Central and East Europe did not want to face the Holocaust—that would have meant a self-examination, which leads to cleansing, which in turn is the means of an ascent and of joining a spiritual Europe. The dictatorship, however, wished only disunity and the permanence of disunity, for this served its purpose" (*A holokauszt* 26). Iva Lurincz writes in the *Sydney Morning Herald:* "With the tools of irony and satire, *Fateless* held a mirror that not many could bear to look into. If Hungarian society had understood Auschwitz, the death of the spirit, the conformity with suppression and the loss of the faculty of evaluation, then it would surely have understood the experience of 1956 as well: The inanity of totalitarianism, the people's willingness to keep silent, their eagerness to be appeased by cheap goods, their grotesque and almost perverted gratefulness for not being destroyed" (2). In extending Kertész's thought, I argue that in all fairness it must be admitted that only an exceptional person would take on the task of questioning. A whole population cannot be faulted for not continuing to run into the face of tanks when all hope is lost, nor for trying to salvage what humanity and dignity can be found in passive resistance. And perhaps not even the writers, the intellectual and cultural leaders of that society, can be faulted: There are many ways of resistance, as Dávidházi points out in his *Per passivam resistenciam*.

Paradoxically, Kertész also feels that it was the very denial of the Holocaust in the Communist world which allowed him to work through this dilemma and retain an optimistic outlook on life. Many of his contemporaries, Auschwitz survivors who wrestled with the problem, committed suicide. After Auschwitz the Stalinist society in which he found himself proved that there can be no question of "freedom, liberation, a great catharsis, etc.: All that of which in a more fortunate world intellectuals, thinkers, philosophers not only spoke, but in which they clearly believed; [this society] guaranteed a prison life for him which excluded all possibility of error. . . . Since not only was I a prisoner, but the nation in which I lived was a prisoner also, I had no problems of identity" (*A holokauszt* 42–43). In the interpretation of his works, too, the universality of Kertész's message is connected to humanity's responsibility. As he says in "Táborok maradandósága" ("The Endurance of Camps"), "Since we learned from Nietzsche that god is dead, the question of who is responsible for man . . . has become a real problem . . . before whose sight do we lead our lives, to whom is man responsible for reckoning, in the ethical sense of the word, and yes . . . in its transcendental sense" (*A holokauszt* 9). Poet Zsófia Balla comments with feeling on how Kertész's definition of the Holocaust affects everyone, even one like herself, born four years after the war, but one who spent years in the "hard" dictatorship of Romania: The "shadow of the Holocaust falls over all of civilization, since "anything, that is everything, can happen to a person, because in his defenselessness neither god, nor morals, nor custom protects him. Barbarity not only vanquishes culture and trust; it not only dispossesses it, but also mocks it with degradation in suffering" (3). Unfortunately, the twentieth century was marked by "the methodical, institutionalized degradation and killing that was tolerated by everyone, that was excused, became routine" (3). Only through the artistic expression of memory can human dignity be preserved. It is against the acceptance of this process as merely history, as merely facts, that Kertész writes. All acts of humanity are a rejection of Auschwitz. Kertész suggests this role for his work on the Holocaust when he writes in *A holokauszt mint kultúra* (The Holocaust as Culture) that its "tragic world view" may renew a European consciousness struggling with its own crisis as the Greek spirit, facing the barbarian Persians, created the "eternal example of antique tragedy. If the Holocaust has created a culture for today—as undeniably it has happened and is happening—its literature is from here: It takes its inspiration from Holy Scriptures and the Greek tragedies, the two sources of European culture, so that an unredeemed reality can bring forth redemption, the spirit, the catharsis" (47).

Note: This article is an updated version of Enikő Molnár Basa, "The Victory of the Individual over History: Imre Kertész" in *AHEA: American Hungarian Educators Association* 27.1–2 (2004): <http://hungaria.org/ahea/index.php?halid=11&menuid=239>.

Works Cited

Balla, Zsófia. "Ajándék" ("Gift"). *Élet és Irodalom* 46.43 (25 October 2002): 3.

Berkes, Erzsébet. "Az ésszerű lét nyomorúsága." *Mozgó Világ* 16.11 (November 1990): 118–21.

Dávidházi, Péter. "Révben a gálya" ("The Galley Has Arrived in Port"). *Holmi* 7 (1993): 1017–21.

Dávidházi, Péter. *Per passivam resistenciam. Változatok hatalom és írás témájára* (Per passivam resistenciam: Versions on the Theme of Power and Writing). Budapest: Argumentum, 1998.

Dávidházi, Péter. *Az értelem szükségszerűsége. Tanulmányok Kertész Imréről* (The Necessity of Meaning: Studies on Imre Kertész). Budapest: L'Harmattan, 2002.

Gács, Anna. "Egy különös regény" ("A Curious Novel"). *Jelenkor* 35.10 (1992): 857–60.

Győrffy, Miklós. "A kő és a hegy. Kertész Imre: *A kudarc*" ("The Rock and the Mountain: Imre Kertész's The Failure"). *Jelenkor* 10 (1989): 985–87.

Illyés, Gyula. "A Sentence about Tyranny / Egy mondat a zsarnokságról." 1950. Trans. George Szirtes. *The Hungarian Quarterly* 36 (1995): <http://www. hungarianquarterly.com/no139/p15.html>.

Kertész, Imre. *Sorstalanság*. Budapest: Szépirodalmi, 1975.

Kertész, Imre. *A kudarc* (The Failure). Budapest: Szépirodalmi, 1988.

Kertész, Imre. *Kaddish a meg nem született gyermekért* (*Kaddish for a Child Not Born*). Budapest: Magvető, 1990.

Kertész, Imre. *Fateless.*Trans. Christopher C. Wilson and Katharina M. Wilson. Evanston: Northwestern UP, 1992.

Kertész, Imre. *A holokauszt mint kultúra. Három előadás* (The Holocaust as Culture: Three Lectures). Budapest: Századvég, 1993.

Kertész, Imre. Interview by Tamás Szőnyei. "Nem érzem magam téves helyen, amikor Németországban olvasok fel (Kertész Imre író)" ("I Do Not Feel Out of Place When I Read My Work in Germany [Imre Kertész, Writer]"). *Magyar Narancs (Archive)* (12 December 1996): <http://www.mancs.hu/index.php?gc. Page=public/ hir.phg&id=757>.

Kertész, Imre. *Kaddish for a Cild Not Born.* Trans. Christopher C. Wilson and Katharina M. Wilson. Evanston: Hydra Books, 1997.

Kertész, Imre. *Az angol logogó. Elbeszélések* (The English Flag: Short Stories). Budapest: Magvető, 2001.

Kertész, Imre. "Heureka!" *Élet és Irodalom* 46.49 (8 December 2002): 1–3.

Kertész, Imre. *Fatelessness*. Trans. Tim Wilkinson. New York: Vintage, 2004.

Kertész, Imre. *Kaddish for an Unborn Child*. Trans. Tim Wilkinson. New York: Vintage, 2004.

Kirk, Karl Peter. "Hungary's Nobel Prize Winner Remains Critical Towards Homeland." *ABC News.com* (18 October 2002): <http://core.ujcfedweb.org/ content_display.html?ArticleID=62804>.

Lányi, Dániel. "A *Sorstalanság* kisérletete" ("The Attempts of *Fatelessness*"). *Holmi* 7.5 (May 1995): 665–74.

Lurincz, Iva. "An Ordinary Day at Auschwitz." *Sydney Morning Herald* (23 November 2002): 1–2.

Marsovszky, Magdalena. "Imre Kertész and Hungary Today." Trans. Eszter Pásztor. *Imre Kertész and Holocaust Literature*. Ed. Louise O. Vasvári and Steven Tötösy de Zepetnek. West Lafayette: Purdue UP, 2005. 148–61.

Márai, Sándor. *Memoir of Hungary, 1944–1948*. Trans. Albert Tezla. Budapest: Corvina and Central European UP, 1996.

Márton, Gábor. "A *Sorstalanság* folyamatossága" ("The Continuity of *Fatelessness*"). *Népszabadság* (21 October 1985): 7.

Molnár, Gábor Tamás. "Fikcióalkotás és történelemszemlélet. Kertész Imre: *Sorstalanság*" ("The Creation of Fiction and the Perspective of History: Imre Kertész's *Fatelessness*"). *Alföld* 47.8 (1996): <http://gizi.dote.hu/~hajnal/alf9608/molnar.html>.

Nirenstein, Susanna. "Aki megmenekült Auschwitz poklából" ("One Who Escaped the Hell of Auschwitz"). *Élet és Irodalom* 46.42 (18 October 2002): 4.

Nobel Prize in Literature, The. Laureates (2002): <http://www.nobel.se/literature/laureates/index.html>.

Radics, Viktória. "A rejtőzködő kreatúra" ("The Hidden Creature"). *Holmi* 4.1 (January 1992): 134–37.

Riding, Alan. "Nobel for Hungarian Writer Who Survived Death Camps." *The New York Times* (11 October 2002): A1, A6.

Riding, Alan. "Nobel Hero Insists Hungary Face Its Past." *The New York Times* (4 December 2002): E1; E5.

Spiró, György. *Magániktató* (Self-Recorder). Budapest: Szépirodalmi, 1985.

Spiró, György. "Non habent sua fata. A *Sorstalanság*—ujraolvasva" ("Non habent sua fata: *Fatelessness*—reread"). *Élet és irodalom* 30 (1983): 5.

Szász, Imre. *Háló nélkül* (Without a Net). Budapest: Szépirodalmi, 1978.

Szilágyi, Márton. "Kertész Imre: *Kaddish a meg nem született gyermekért*." *Alföld* 41.12 (December 1990): 72–73.

Tötösy de Zepetnek, Steven. "Imre Kertész's Nobel Prize in Literature and the Print Media." *Imre Kertész and Holocaust Literature*. Ed. Louise O. Vasvári and Steven Tötösy de Zepetnek. West Lafayette: Purdue UP, 2005. 232–46.

Turai, Tamás. "A hiten túl, a pusztulás előtt" ("Beyond Faith, Before Destruction"). *Jelenkor* 34.4 (April 1992): 310–16.

Vári, György. "A *Sorstalanság* történelemszemléletéről" ("About the Historical Perspective of *Fatelessness*"). *Élet és Irodalom* 46.42 (18 October 2002): 7.

Young, Judy. "The Media and Imre Kertész's Nobel Prize in Literature." *Imre Kertész and Holocaust Literature*. Ed. Louise O. Vasvári and Steven Tötösy de Zepetnek. West Lafayette: Purdue UP, 2005. 271–85.

Imre Kertész, Jewishness in Hungary, and the Choice of Identity

Sara D. Cohen

Imre Kertész was awarded the Nobel Prize for Literature in December 2002 for "writing that upholds the fragile experience of the individual against the barbaric arbitrariness of history" (see *Nobel Prize in Literature: Laureates* [2002]: <http://www.nobel.se/literature/laureates/index.html>). This encompasses a body of work that has addressed the experience of concentration camps, the struggle to understand the world that created Auschwitz, and attempts to define the world Kertész returned to after liberation. In the process, Kertész explores the concept of a Jewish identity and the desire to find a way of making one's Jewishness positive and enriching. Péter Nádas has said of Kertész that his "literary work, for the greater part, has always been obscured by his subject, and it will take a goodly lapse of time yet for that not to obscure it" (38). For Nádas, that subject is Auschwitz and the Shoah, and Kertész's work is significant in its attempts to address these topics. For others, the question of Jewish identity in Kertész's work is secondary. György Spiró laments that "he has been obliged . . . to arrive at some kind of response to questions regarding his identity: Whether he is Hungarian or Jewish, or possibly a Hungarian Jew, not to say a Jewish Hungarian, or rather a European who happens to write in Hungarian and is either just a little bit or very Jewish indeed. These are ideological and political issues which serve only to distract him from the cultivation of serious literature" (29). Nevertheless, Kertész returns to the problem of his own identity with a regularity that reveals the extent to which the question is a preoccupation. Even in his Nobel Prize acceptance speech, Kertész opened with a reference to the struggle to "dissolve the duality and fuse the two selves within me" (*Nobel Prize in Literature: Laureates* [2002]: <http://www.nobel.se/literature/laureates/index.html>). Kertész's view of Jewish identity, as revealed in his writings, provides us with a case study of the effects of the Shoah on the self-identification of assimilated Jewry in Hungary. In my paper, I present Kertész's life prior to his deportation to Auschwitz in 1944, as well as his early career, followed by an analysis of the construct of Jewish identity in his works. For this purpose I focus on the novels *Sorstalanság* (1975; translated as *Fateless* 1992; *Fatelessness* 2004*), Kaddis a meg nem született gyerekért* (1990; translated as *Kaddish for a*

24

Child Not Born 1997; *Kaddish for an Unborn Child* 2004), and *Valaki más. A változások krónikája* (*Un autre. Chronique d'une métamorphose* 1999; as there is no English translation available of this text, I am using the French translation), and on some of Kertész's shorter essays.

Kertész was born in Budapest on 9 November 1929 into a family of Jewish descent, whose immediate members were non-practising. Theirs was a standard, middle-class family, who lived comfortably in Budapest and who, in the early years of Kertész's life, were largely unaffected by anti-Semitic prejudices and sanctions. He describes his grandparents as people who "still lit the Sabbath candles every Friday night, but [who] changed their name to a Hungarian one, and it was natural for them to consider Judaism their religion and Hungary their homeland" (*Nobel Prize in Literature: Laureates* [2002]: <http://www.nobel.se/literature/laureates/index.html>). This duality, also evident in the broader history of Hungarian Jewry, combined with Kertész's wartime experiences, has led him to realise that "Being a Jew to me is . . . first and foremost, a moral challenge" (*Nobel Prize in Literature: Laureates* [2002]: <http://www.nobel.se/literature/laureates/index.html>). Kertész's parents divorced when he was five years old; he was sent to boarding school for six years while they fought for custody. Much like George Koves, the protagonist of Kertész's first novel, *Sorstalanság,* Kertész was then sent to live with his father from the time he attended high school. By 1940, Hungary's First and Second Jewish Laws had been enacted; Kertész was enrolled in a separate Jewish class. His father was sent to a forced labour camp, where he died. Kertész himself was deported to Auschwitz in 1944. He arrived at Auschwitz and lied about his age, claiming to have been born in 1927, which would have made him sixteen. This qualified him for labour service, and he thereby escaped being sent straight to the gas chambers. He was subsequently sent to Buchenwald, and then to Zeitz, an affiliated camp. He was then returned to Buchenwald, and was liberated in 1945, whereupon he returned to Hungary.

Kertész went to live with his mother, who had lived out the duration of the war in Budapest, and completed high school. He joined the Communist Party in 1946, became disillusioned after the takeover in 1948, and began working as a journalist in Budapest for the newspaper *Világosság*. He was dismissed in 1950 for his political views, was briefly employed in a factory, and did his obligatory military service from 1951 to 1953. He then turned to writing, producing comedies and radio plays to ensure a steady income while also writing what he considered to be more serious pieces. He taught himself Italian, English, and German, and began translating Western authors into Hungarian (Spiró 34). His translations were primarily of German and Austrian writers, including Hugo von Hofmannsthal, Elias Canetti, Joseph Roth, and Arthur Schnitzler, as well as philosophers such as Friedrich Nietzsche, Sigmund Freud, and Ludwig Wittgenstein. He lived with his wife, Albina—who supported them on a waitress's salary—in a small apartment in Budapest, where he wrote his novels and worked on translations. His first major work appeared in 1975; he had worked on *Sorstalanság* between 1962 and 1972 (Kertész chronicles the struggle to find a publisher in the opening chapter of *A Kudarc* [1988, The Failure]). His subject matter was seen as unpalatable in Socialist Hungary and his depiction of it was perceived of as naïve and vulgar. He was even accused of anti-Semitism by the director of the Magvető publishing house in the early 1970s for suggesting there were moments of "happiness" in the concentration camps (the director himself was Jewish Hungarian; Spiró 36). When *Sorstalanság* was published in 1975, it was to little acclaim. György Spiró recounts that the critics' responses amounted to "one very nice, laudatory review . . . along with two other well-disposed little pats on the back" (29), but nothing further. The novel broke with convention in that it even attempted to address the question of the Shoah and Jewish identity in Socialist Hungary. Kertész is credited with making one of the "first public statements on Jewish themes after the Communist take-over of Hungary in 1948" (Sherwood 21). For Spiró, however, the importance of *Sorstalanság* goes beyond the fact that "someone had written a readable novel about the camps in Hungarian" (34); rather, the power of the novel was rooted in the "seemingly ingenuous yet deeply ironic tone, the strange and unique amalgam of viewpoints of the protagonist as both a fifteen-year-old boy and the later adult that Kertész perfected for himself over ten years of labour, straining for exactly the right inflection for every single sentence—that was something we had encountered in nobody else's works" (Spiró 34).

Critics, then, appreciated both the content and the style of Kertész's contribution. The political situation in Hungary at the time precluded a more obvious show of appreciation. Yet, despite the low profile of responses, *Sorstalanság* began to garner a following among those contemporaries who, like Spiró, considered it to be a masterpiece (Spiró 31). Spiró himself published an essay about the novel in the 1980s, using his own reputation as a successful playwright to promote *Sorstalanság* in the leading intellectual journal, *Élet és Irodalom* (*Life and Literature*). Kertész published steadily through the 1970s and early 1980s, but it was not until the fall of Communism in 1989 that he achieved popularity and respect in Hungary, as well as in Germany. The majority of his works were translated into German in the 1990s and he is the recipient of the Brandenburger Literaturpreis (1995), the Leipziger Buchpreis zur europäischen Verständigung (1997), the Herder-Preis and the WELT-Literaturpreis (2000), the Ehrenpreis der Robert-Bosch-Stiftung (2001), and the Hans-Sahl-Preis (2002). Some of his works have already appeared in French while others continue to be translated, and a number have also been published in Swedish.

Kertész is best known to Western readers in German translation and it is the influence of this market that has been credited with his recent successes. Spiró has observed that "there is not a trace of anti-German sentiment in Kertész's books" (31), which is accurate; Kertész does not blame the Germans for his treatment at Auschwitz, and his protagonist is impressed by German efficiency, cleanliness, and presentability. The author has stated categorically that he has "never tried to see the complex of problems referred to as the Holocaust merely as the insolvable conflict between Germans and Jews" (*Nobel Prize in Literature: Laureates* [2002]: <http://www.nobel.se/literature/laureates/index.html>) because for him the root of Auschwitz lies in the culmination of European modernity, rather than in the interaction between two peoples who are, after all, not entirely distinct from each other. He does, however, take the Germans to task for destroying consciously those Jewish intellectuals in Central and Eastern Europe who wrote in German, and laments the loss of those "once partially German cultural zones . . . from, say, the Crimean peninsula through Bukovina to Galicia in the north [which] no longer enrich German culture, and the only ones responsible for this loss are the Germans themselves" ("The Language of Exile" <http://books. guardian.co.uk/review/story/0,12084,814056,00.html>).

Kertész returned to Budapest after liberation in 1945 and has explained that "for reasons having to do with the language I spoke, I decided, after the suppression of the 1956 revolt, to remain in Hungary" (*Nobel Prize in Literature: Laureates* [2002]: <http://www.nobel.se/literature/laureates/index.html>). As a chronicler of his Auschwitz experiences, he has addressed the impossibility of expressing this experience in any language, save one that is "so terrifying, so lugubrious that it would destroy those who speak it" ("The Language of Exile" <http://books. guardian.co.uk/review/story/0,12084,814056,00.html>). He has also referred to the decision to write in Hungarian as a means of making him "more acutely aware of the impossibility of writing," since it places him within a tradition that cannot encompass the literature of the persecution and identity crises of those who claim to be located within it ("The Language of Exile" <http://books.guardian.co.uk/ review/story/0,12084,814056,00.html>). Nevertheless it is the language he is most comfortable with; hence his happiness at being able to deliver his Nobel speech in Hungarian (*Nobel Prize in Literature: Laureates* [2002]: <http://www.nobel.se/ literature/laureates/index.html>). The decision to remain in Hungary, and the use of the Hungarian language, demonstrate Kertész's identification as a Hungarian: Hungary is his chosen home.

However, this home is not an idyllic one. Spiró has observed that there is nothing anti-Hungarian about Kertész's work (36), which is true as far as his chronicling of the deportations is concerned, although his novels do address the issue of Hungarian culpability. Kertész is unsettled by the alienation he feels from contemporary Hungary, where he "act[s] like a stranger" and with whose countrymen he is ill at ease ("The Language of Exile" <http://books.guardian.co.uk/review/ story/0,12084,814056,00.html>). He has explained that "in the dictatorship called socialism, this was a natural state, and I more or less learned to live with it. Getting accustomed to racism in a democracy takes more time" ("The Language of Exile" <http://books.guardian.co.uk/review/story/0,12084,814056,00.html>). It is the feeling that anti-Semitism persists in Hungary that alienates Kertész from his surroundings, the feeling that "in 1944 they put a yellow star on me, which in a symbolic sense is still there; to this day I have not been able to remove it" ("The Language of Exile" <http://books.guardian.co.uk/review/story/0,12084,814056,00.html>).

How, then, does Kertész approach and define Jewishness? In his *The "Jewish Question" in German Literature*, Ritchie Robertson identifies the evolution of five main criteria for the determination of Jewishness in order to establish what is meant by the term "Jew," also applicable in the Central European context: 1) legal criterion, by which a Jew is simply the child of two Jews, or a non-Jewish father and a Jewish mother, or a convert to Judaism; 2) the religious definition, according to which a Jew is someone who has embraced Judaism, believes in one God who is indivisible, and still awaits the coming of the Messiah; 3) the criterion of race or biology, according to which Jews are believed to have certain physical features which are quantifiable and measurable; 4) cultural criterion, whereby Jewishness is not a matter of a specific relationship to God or of transmitted physical traits but rather a confluence of transitory values that are rooted in changing historical contexts and experiences; and 5) the criterion of reactivity, whereby a Jew is considered to be a Jew, and considers himself to be one, because anti-Semites assign them this label. The definition is then internalised, leading to "Jewish self-hatred." Jewish identity becomes delineated by negative portrayals, and Jews come to resent themselves on the basis of the perceptions of others (Robertson 5–8).

Kertész and his characters grapple with all five of these variations of Jewish identity, discarding each identity eventually as insufficient to meet their needs for satisfactory self-definition. If one rejects all of these criteria, and still feels Jewish, how can this be explained? What conclusions can be drawn about the roots of one's Jewishness in this case? What we are left with is dissimilation, "the affirmation of Jewishness in response to an unwelcoming society" (Robertson 8). Here we find the revaluing of traditional societies, the idea that Jews were Semitic peoples and therefore could not be expected to feel comfortable amongst Europeans, and Zionism, with its goals of transplanting the Jews to a home in the East (Robertson 8).

I would argue that we also find Kertész here, in his decision to make Jewishness a choice that is liberating rather than restrictive. Kertész is an author who decided to remain in a society that expelled him, and then welcomed him back on condition that he forget about his experience in the camps. His characters likewise return to Hungary after liberation, determined to make their experience and their Jewishness valid and positive. They refuse to be punished for their Jewish identity, and they do not lament others' awareness of it. This may not be quite in line with Robertson's identification of an almost spiteful response to a sense of otherness; still, it is a life-affirming reaction through an acceptance of the very thing that was considered to be worthy of the death penalty. But in making it a conscious choice to accept this identity to internalise it, Kertész, and his characters, are able to survive with the fashioning of a new identity that, while it may not yet resonate or be accepted by their non-Jewish neighbours, is still a step toward integrated coexistence, and living at peace with history.

Stephen Poppel explains that "Jewry was defined primarily by its adherence to Jewish law and, in Christian eyes, by its continued non-recognition of Jesus as the Messiah. (Indeed, one clear indication of the essentially religious nature of this definition was the fact that conversion to Christianity was by itself sufficient to secure full acceptance into the dominant group)" (Poppel 4). In other words, premodern Jewish communities have been characterised as autonomous in terms of law, culture, and values. These Jews were isolated from the rest of medieval society, dependent upon charters or privileges granted by the crown or lesser lords for existence, but free to regulate the internal affairs of the community. They were, however, viewed in terms of their confession, and not in terms of any distinctive culture or homogenous ethnic identity that they may have developed in their isolation. Nevertheless, although defined purely in confessional terms, this separation from the broader society allowed Jews to develop a sense of shared history, tradition and heritage. This was a time when, "in the considerable isolation of the ghetto, Jewish existence possessed an all-encompassing and unquestioned character" (Meyer 8).

In modern times, these definitions still resonated, although they were complemented by other views of Jewishness. Kertész himself rejects the religious aspects of Jewish identity yet still claims Jewishness. His Nobel acceptance speech contains a reference to the death of God, followed by the assertion that "since Auschwitz, we are more alone" (*Nobel Prize in Literature: Laureates* [2002]: <http://www.nobel.se/literature/laureates/index.html>). The religious aspects of Jewish identity are also rejected by Kertész's protagonists, all of whom encounter observant Jews whose beliefs they do not understand. In *Fatelessness*, it is clear that George Koves does not have any respect for biblical texts or prescribed modes of worship. When we first meet him he is hurrying home to spend a few hours with his father before Mr Koves leaves for forced labor service. At the family's farewell gathering for George, he is pulled aside by his Uncle Lajos, who explains George's position as a Jew and how this should link him to other Jews: "'Now,' he said, 'you too are part of the common Jewish fate.' . . . This fate meant a 'millennium of continuing persecutions' that Jews had had to accept 'with acquiescence and self-sacrificing patience' because the punishment was doled out by God for the sins of our ancestors" (*Fateless* 15).

George listens to this narration of predestined martyrdom and self-sacrifice uncomprehendingly. He is then told to pray, something that would not have occurred to him without prompting (16). The experience is completely devoid of meaning for him, as he recounts: "at first it went quite well, but soon I got a little tired of this work, and I was a little annoyed that I didn't understand a single word of what we were telling God, because He had to be addressed in Hebrew, and I don't speak that language" (16). The spirituality of Judaism is alien and mystifying for George, and is therefore rendered uninteresting and unappealing. He is distracted and resentful, and cannot establish what meaning, if any, he is supposed to derive from this episode. Koves encounters other observant Jews in the camps, where he again feels alienated by their spiritual Jewishness. By this point, however, he is more uncomfortable with the thought that observant Jews view him as not Jewish enough than he is with their prayers. It is the exclusionary nature of the religious definition of Jews that is problematic; Koves has begun to identify as a Jew even though he does not pray and does not believe in a Jewish God, and he resents the implication that he does not qualify.

At Zeitz, he encounters a group he is told are called "Finns" (orthodox Jews). They are strange creatures, "mumbling their prayers endlessly like a debt that can never be paid off and rocking rhythmically back and forth" (101–02). He tries to avoid them as much as possible, but one day finds himself in their midst. When they realise Koves does not speak Yiddish, they have no interest in further conversation, dismissing him cursorily with an abrupt "You are no Jew" (102). Koves is unsettled and recounts: "That day I also experienced that very same tenseness, that same itchy feeling and clumsiness that came over me when I was with them, that I had occasionally felt at home: as if I weren't entirely okay, as if I didn't entirely conform to the ideal; in other words, somehow as if I were Jewish. That was a rather strange feeling, because, after all, I was among Jews and in a concentration camp" (102). Koves is not Jewish enough for these Jews; he does not know their prayers; he does not speak Yiddish. Yet this is the first time that he feels like what he supposes a Jew to be. Through exclusion and dismissal on arbitrary grounds, he starts to claim his Jewishness. After all, he is in a concentration camp, surrounded by Jews, wearing a yellow Star of David. That is not enough for them, but their dismissal causes Koves to rebel internally against their treatment of him, and he begins to see himself as a Jew. Koves's personal concept of his Jewishness is definitely not spiritual, which is what matters to the orthodox Jews; nevertheless, it has been awakened, and although nebulous, is becoming increasingly important.

For the Old Man in *Kaddish for a Child Not Born,* there is a similar rejection of religious identity followed by a redefinition and reclaiming of Jewish identity. The Old Man recalls visiting relatives in rural Hungary as a child. This was his first encounter with "real genuine Jews" (*Kaddish* 16), who were unlike any type of Jews he had ever encountered. Although he acknowledges that there can be different types of Jews, his categories are based entirely on adherence to religious doctrine. Our protagonist's family were "city Jews, Budapest Jews, that is to say, not Jews at all, but of course not Christians either; we were the kind of non-Jewish Jews who still observe holy days, long fasts, or at least, definitely, until lunch" (16). By contrast, real Jews are those who observed "prayer in the morning, prayer in the evening, prayer before food, prayer with the wine" (16). These rituals are foreign and tiresome due to the alienation they provoke. To the old man these distinctions become less clear; the title of the novel refers to Judaism's prayer for the dead, and it concludes with the invocation "I may drown/Lord God/let me drown/

forever,/Amen" (95). Yet the protagonist does not mention either prayer or Jewish ritual during the course of the exegesis of his life. If the kaddish of the title is taken to mean the novel itself, which is an explanation of a failed marriage and of the decision not to have children, it is a secular, personal prayer.

The shift in legal and religious definitions of Jews occurred as a result of emancipation, brought about by the Enlightenment. The goals of emancipation were to grant the Jews freedom of movement, occupation, and education. Robert Wistrich, among others, credits the Enlightenment with the end of the definition of the Jews as "a people, at least in the ethnic sense" (9), accompanied as it was by a new means of applying the religious definition. Although the premodern Jew was also defined solely according to the religion he practiced, his isolation offered scope to develop a more nuanced identity. The secular aspects of Enlightenment thought encouraged the view that denominational choice was the sole component of Jewish identity, and was one that should be abandoned in favour of integration within the broader social setting.

This was the impetus for the assimilation and acculturation that has been seen to characterise urban Hungarian post-emancipation Jewry, and that characterised urban Jewish communities throughout Central Europe. We have also seen, however, that many still viewed the Jews as separate from the mainstream despite their demonstrated Hungarianness (*magyarság*; on the history of the assimilation and destruction of Jews in Hungary, see, e.g., Ozsváth; Suleiman; Tötösy) and this was the case in other regions as well. Although the assimilated Jews of Central Europe have been heralded as "successfully and almost totally assimilated" (Rozenblit 2), an ambiguity developed in attitudes toward Jewish identity that arose out of living as an assimilated person of Jewish descent in a climate of nationalism and anti-Semitism (Wistrich 2). Assimilation was indeed prevalent, especially among those stunning examples that are often given of Jewish contributions to nineteenth- and twentieth-century culture across Central and Eastern Europe: Walter Benjamin, Sigmund Freud, Franz Kafka, Rosa Luxemburg, Gustav Mahler, Karl Marx, Joseph Roth, Arnold Schoenberg, and Ludwig Wittgenstein, to name only a few. However, Marsha Rozenblit stresses that "one must not judge Jewish assimilation into European society on the basis of these intellectuals alone" (2), especially since the ramifications of Jewish descent were still a concern for many of these figures. Instead, one can see the global situation of the Jews as a pattern of integration instead of complete assimilation, in which Jews and those of Jewish descent were set apart from the larger societies with which they interacted. This tension provoked a crisis of identity; as Michael Meyer insists, with the age of Enlightenment the Jewish identity "becomes segmental and hence problematic" (8). If Jews could supposedly cease to be Jews through conversion or atheism, then why were they still perceived as a separate group? What characteristics of this group go deeper than denominational choice? The answers to these questions were sought in the racial definition of the Jew. Religion had become a means of quantifying rather than qualifying those of Jewish descent. Mitchell Hart observes that "Juda-

ism, as a set of ritual beliefs and practices, was important now more and more in a
sociological sense, insofar as it functioned to bring about or retard particular Jewish
characteristics" (16). Implicit in this statement is that while the Jews could be defined
using religious criteria, there were inherent characteristics these people shared, and
transmitted to future generations. These characteristics then became the objects of
study.

The term "race" came to be generally applied to the Jews by the mid-
nineteenth century. Used imprecisely, the term signified a "sort" or a "kind" (Lindemann 70). This implies an adherence extraneous to the geographic region a
given Jew lived in. If considered a Jew, this meant that one was something other
than, or perhaps additional to, French, English, German, or Magyar (Hungarian).
The term "race" was as nebulously defined as the term "Jew" in this period, although a "consensus was emerging that race entailed an unchangeable, inherent
physical type" (Lindemann 70). For Jews, this meant that one could no longer stop
being a Jew through conversion, for Jewishness was a matter of inheritance
through blood and genealogy. This notion of blood was an important one, for Jews
were often held to be examples of a "pure" "race." Their tendency to marry other
Jews informed notions of cleanliness, purity, and a preservable essence that was
transmitted through bloodlines (Lindemann 75). The use of the term "race" allowed this otherness to be expressed in a way that lent it overtones of objectivity
and quantification. As Robert Lindemann points out, "race was considered to be a
more palpable, measurable term, based on scientific inquiry" (75–76). Yet this notion of objective race science was still tainted with considerations of history and
culture; as John Efron observes, "*fin-de-siècle* notions of race impinged upon questions of history, so that even a purely scientific approach to the Jewish racial question meant the necessary introduction of discussions about the other categories of
the Jewish problem" (4). Even in this age of scientific measurement, Jewishness
could never be objectively quantified and always included reference to cultural and
historical signifiers. The genetic essence of Jewishness was never defined: "the
physique of the Jew seemed infinitely malleable" (Robertson 5). It was not until
twentieth-century Nazi and pro-Nazi legislation began laying out ways of determining who was to be considered a Jew that the questions of culture and history
were laid aside. Considerations of one's ancestry replaced notions of culture, and
Jews came to be defined once again solely in terms of their parentage. However,
the influence of race theory on Nazi policy entailed that once the group was defined in this way steps could be taken to eliminate the entire category, eliminating
genetic Jewish traits in the process.

Kertész views Jews as a distinct group within Hungarian society. We have
already seen that he feels alienated from contemporary Hungary, although he does
not refer to Jews in terms of biological traits. He refers instead to the innateness of
Jewishness, stating simply "I was born a Jew" ("The Language of Exile" <http://
books.guardian.co.uk/review/story/0,12084,814056,00.html>); he treats this as a

fact that must be understood if it is to have any relevance to his self-definition. For his characters, the question of inherited Jewishness is a pressing one. In *Sorstalanság*, Koves and his girlfriend, Anne-Marie, visit two sisters in a neighbouring flat to play cards. The girls are also Jewish, and the eldest has begun to question the wearing of the yellow star. She senses the animosity of those around her, and asks plaintively "shouldn't one know why one is hated?" (*Fateless* 27). The only answer she can provide for herself is that "'we Jews are different from other people, and this difference or otherness is the essence of a rationale about why people detest us" (27). Her means of engaging with the imposed category of "Jew" is to attempt to understand Jews as a cohesive group, joined together in some definable way, and distinct from their non-Jewish neighbours. She has concluded that what sets her apart is something internal and inherited: "we carry this otherness within ourselves" (27), she says. Koves does not agree. Whereas the sister is trying to understand her Jewishness in terms of innate characteristics, George believes that Jewishness is predicated by external forces: in this case the authorities who have mandated the wearing of the yellow stars. George tries to set her mind at rest by explaining that she has only come to these conclusions because she has been told to wear the yellow star, and that, had she been switched at birth with someone permitted to carry the documentation to avoid this, "she would never consider thinking of or even imagining any sort of otherness" (28). This episode takes place before Koves is sent to Auschwitz; at this point Koves considers his Jewishness important only if someone else decides it to be so. Koves first encounters non-Hungarian Jews when he arrives at Auschwitz. He immediately resorts to a racial generalisation of them, noticing that "their faces . . . were not particularly trustworthy: they had widespread ears, protruding noses, and sunken, cunning, tiny little eyes. Indeed, they looked like Jews in every respect" (58). Koves wears a Star of David, he has watched his family pray, and yet he thinks of Jews as something outside himself, and describes them in terms of physical characteristics he does not share. After Koves has come to identify himself as a Jew, he concludes that Jews cannot conform to a certain physical type. This is influenced in large part by the levelling effect of the camps, where "what [people] looked like, their faces, hair color, features . . . usually change entirely" (175).

In *Kaddish for a Child Not Born*, it is the Old Man's wife who articulates this notion of genetically inherited Jewishness, and rejects it, for it does not resonate with her. She is expressing her difficulty in coming to any suitable definition of her Jewish identity and concludes with the exclamation that "nothing, nothing whatsoever, differentiates her from these others around her unless it is some secret ancient message hidden in her genes which she herself can't hear and therefore cannot know" (64). Biological, inherited identity, then, is not satisfactory; if the traits have indeed been passed down, she cannot experience it empirically, cannot find any meaning in this legacy, and can take no comfort from it. A meaningful definition of Jewishness, then, according to Kertész, must be based on other criteria. There is nothing tying Kertész's characters to broader notions of Jewishness and Jewish tradition. While they are alienated from Hungarian society, and have broken with the assimilated identity they brought to Auschwitz, they have not supplanted this with a sense of communal Jewish identity. Their identification is a purely personal one, born of personal experience and necessity.

The first indication we have that Koves has distanced himself from Hungarians is in the Buchenwald infirmary. He is attempting to converse with the boys around him, and is asked where he is from. His answer is greeted with laughter and derogatory comments. This is upsetting for Koves not because he is the object of derision, but because he sees his answer as a mistake, and feels that he should not be considered Hungarian. He has realised that "the Hungarians don't consider me one of them" (144). More to the point, "to a great degree [he] shared the boys' views of them, and [he] found it strange indeed, even unfair, that here [he] was ostracized precisely because of them" (144). In a later conversation, a Czech inmate tells him that he does not like Hungarians. Koves confessed that "he had a point and that generally I found little reason for liking them either" (162). Once again, Koves has his identity, this time a Hungarian one, imposed by others, and once again he rebels against it, finding nothing about the Hungarians or their treatment of him that would make him want to identify as one. The reaction intensifies the longer Koves stays at Buchenwald. After the liberation he returns to Budapest, the only home he knows aside from the camp itself. When asked how he feels upon seeing the city and the people he had left, Koves responds quite simply, "Hatred" (180). The alienation from a community of Jews is made clear in *Kaddish*. The protagonist has written a story about a Christian boy who discovers he is considered a Jew, and is sent to a concentration camp. We are never told why the character is considered to be a Jew; the importance lies in the arbitrariness of the label, and the challenge it provides to his self-definition. The character's background and his new identity make him realise he is simply an individual subject to fate; that "by being excluded from one community one does not automatically become a member of another" (58). For the Old Man's wife, born in a post-Auschwitz environment, the question of Jewish identity is also problematic. Unlike her husband, she has been raised to acknowledge her Jewishness and see herself as a testimony to Jewish survival, having been "made aware of her Jewishness and everything that went along with it at an early age" (61). These reminders make her feel as though "she no longer existed, that she couldn't lay claim to any individual feelings or thoughts, and that she was merely entitled to *Jewish feelings* and *Jewish thoughts*, exclusively for the simple reason that she was born a Jew" (62). This assumption that she is part of a large group of Jews by virtue of neither conscious choice nor affinity provokes her struggle with self-definition, since "neither language nor lifestyle, nothing, nothing whatsoever, differentiates her from these others around her" (64). This is a struggle that must be resolved by a more satisfactory concept of the basis of Jewish identity.

The hopelessness and alienation the Old Man's wife experiences lead us to our final category. According to the theory of reactive Jewish identity, one is only a Jew because anti-Semites say so. Among the diary entries in *Un autre, chronique d'une métamorphose*, Kertész has written, "My Jewishness is much too interesting (or, if you like: significant) for me to consider it as the mere refraction of a madness called anti-Semitism" (83). His characters have the most trouble with this possible reason for their identity. Those who have returned from Auschwitz feel that their Jewishness should come from something other than the threat of persecution and annihilation. Others, like the Old Man's wife, see this negative definition of Jewish identity as restrictive. She describes the constant reminder of her Jewishness as feeling "as if her face were stuck in the mud" (*Kaddish* 60). Her identity has become something she was forced to accept and from which she could never escape. This leads her to the sense that being a Jew was "synonymous with her sense of utter hopelessness: a sense of defeat, despondency, suspicion, hidden fears" (*Kaddish* 61). Here we see the self-hatred Robertson warns of, stemming from Jews' self-defining in response to being defined by others. Kertész has labelled this self-hatred "the purest form of anti-Semitism, that enables us to study its development and operation at the highest level" (*Un autre* 18). The circular relationship between reactive Jewish identity, self-hatred, and anti-Semitism is unfulfilling and therefore unsatisfactory. As we have seen, Kertész and his characters have rejected all five of Robertson's criteria of Jewishness. Self-identification, then, must come from some other source.

Dissimilation affirms the Jewishness that others have criticised, while at the same time maintaining the Jewish otherness and redefining it along positive lines, giving it a place as a segment of society, rather than a fully integrated component. Kertész is not a Zionist, nor does he seek to validate isolated Jews. He sees Hungarian Jews as a separate group of people, but tries to be comfortable in that separateness. In *Un autre*, he declares the impossibility of being both a Hungarian and a Jew, since "in our time (and these times have already lasted for more than seventy years) for a Jew to be accepted as a Hungarian, he must meet certain requirements that, in short, lead to the denial of the self" (101). Instead, Kertész chooses Jewishness over the denial of the self, and makes it an affirmation of existence, rather than just survival. This view is fully developed by the wife in *Kaddish*, in response to her husband's inability to do more than just survive. She is inspired by his writing and feels liberated from the restrictions of legal, religious, racial, communal, and reactive Jewish identity. She has learned that "one can make a decision concerning one's Jewishness" and that this has "taught her to live" (60) as a Jew with a future ahead of her, and the possibility to exist and be happy. The tragedy of the protagonist, who is writing after their divorce, is that he is unable to embrace the internal liberation he describes in his stories. The character does not represent Kertész's experience; rather, his story is a study of the crisis of identity that can ensue if one does not make this choice to be Jewish and be affirmed by it. Kertész has made his choice, and he presents it to his readers as the resolution of over a hundred years of identity crisis. In the words of the Laureate himself, "I have to view my Jewishness . . . as a task to be completed; a decision in favour of total existence or self-denial. If I choose a full life, everything at once turns to my advantage. In the end, the fact that I am a Jew is the result of a decision; having made it, not only will I not be plunged into a so-called identity crisis, but a sharper light will also be cast on my entire existence" ("The Language of Exile" <http://books.guardian.co.uk/review/story/0,12084,814056,00.html>).

Works Cited

Efron, John. *Defenders of the Race*. New Haven: Yale UP, 1994.

Hart, Mitchell. *Social Science and the Politics of Modern Jewish Identity*. Stanford: Stanford UP, 2000.

Kertész, Imre. *Un Autre. Chronique d'une métamorphose*. Trans. Natalia Zaremba and Charles Zaremba. Arles: Actes Sud, 1999.

Kertész, Imre. *Fateless*. Trans. Christopher C. Wilson and Katharina M. Wilson. Evanston: Northwestern UP, 1992.

Kertész, Imre. *Fatelessness*. Trans. Tim Wilkinson. New York: Vintage, 2004.

Kertész, Imre. *Kaddish for a Child Not Born*. Trans. Christopher C. Wilson and Katharina M. Wilson. Evanston: Northwestern UP, 1997.

Kertész, Imre. "The Language of Exile." Trans. Ivan Sanders. *Guardian* (19 October 2002): <http://books.guardian.co.uk/review/story/0,12084,814056,00.html>.

Kertész, Imre. *Kaddish for an Unborn Child*. Trans. Tim Wilkinson. New York: Vintage, 2004.

Kertész, Imre. *Le Refus*. Trans. Natalia Zaremba-Huzsvai and Charles Zaremba. Paris: Actes Sud, 2001.

Lindemann, Robert S. *Esau's Tears: Modern Anti-Semitism and the Rise of the Jews*. Budapest: Central European UP, 1997.

Meyer, Michael. *The Origins of the Modern Jew: Jewish Identity and European Culture in Germany, 1749–1824*. Detroit: Wayne State UP, 1967.

Nádas, Péter. "Imre Kertész's Work and his Subject." *The Hungarian Quarterly* 168 (2002): 38–40.

Nobel Prize in Literature, The. Laureates (2002): <http://www.nobel.se/literature/laureates/index.html>.

Ozsváth, Zsuzsanna. "Radnóti, Celan, and the Aesthetic Shifts in Central European Holocaust Poetry." *Comparative Central European Culture*. Ed. Steven Tötösy de Zepetnek. West Lafayette: Purdue UP, 2002. 51–69.

Poppel, Stephen. *Zionism in Germany 1897–1933: The Shaping of a Jewish Identity*. Philadelphia: Jewish Publication, 1976.

Robertson, Ritchie. *The "Jewish Question" in German Literature 1749–1939*. London: Oxford UP, 1999.

Rozenblit, Marsha. *The Jews of Vienna 1867–1914: Assimilation and Identity*. Albany: State U of New York P, 1983.

Sherwood, Peter. "Survival Techniques." *The Times Literary Supplement* (15 January 1993): 18–21.

Spiró, György. "In Art Only the Radical Exists." *The Hungarian Quarterly* 43 (Winter 2002): 29–37.

Suleiman, Susan Rubin. "Central Europe, Jewish Family History, and *Sunshine*." *Comparative Central European Culture*. Ed. Steven Tötösy de Zepetnek. West Lafayette: Purdue UP, 2002. 169–88.

Tötösy de Zepetnek, Steven. "And the 2002 Nobel Prize for Literature Goes to Imre Kertész, Jew and Hungarian." *CLCWeb: Comparative Literature and Culture* 5.1 (2003): <http://clcwebjournal.lib.purdue.edu/clcweb03–1/totosy03.hml>.

Wistrich, Robert. *Between Redemption and Perdition: Modern Antisemitism and Jewish Identity*. London: Routledge, 1990.

The Aporia of Imre Kertész

Robert Eaglestone

Does Imre Kertész write testimony or fiction? Even his Nobel citation, "for writing that upholds the fragile experience of the individual against the barbaric arbitrariness of history," remains carefully neutral on this (*Nobel Prize in Literature: Laureates* (2002): <http://www.nobel.se/literature/laureates/index.html>). This question goes to the core of his achievement and asks wider comparative questions about Holocaust literature. Despite the proliferation of fictions and films, many agree with Elie Wiesel—a "novel about Treblinka is either not a novel or not about Treblinka" (Wiesel, "The Holocaust" 7)—and feel Adorno's despair at the ways in which the "victims are turned into works of art, tossed out to be gobbled up by the world that did them in" (Adorno, *Notes* 88). Many more agree with Leslie Epstein, who wrote that "I have come finally and reluctantly to the conclusion that almost any honest eyewitness testimony of the Holocaust is more moving and more successful at creating a sense of what it must have been like in the ghettos and the camps than almost any fictional account of the same events. I am not sure why this should be so" (qtd. in Friedländer 99). Yet, while *Fatelessness* is clearly a testimony of sorts—it shares many textual generic and metatextual characteristics of testimony, as I argue below, and has been taken as testimony by critics like Andrea Reiter—I argue that Kertész uses the possibilities offered by the form of novel to think through, aesthetically, issues of fate, agency, and choice in a way that would be impossible in a testimony and would come out very differently had he chosen to write distinctive meditative essays in the mode of Primo Lévi or Jean Améry. That is to say, it is the use of fiction, rather than eyewitness testimony, by Kertész that allows the texts to offer his unique response to the Holocaust (on this, see also Vasvári). This, too, is central to *Kaddish for an Unborn Child*, which, in its form, takes on and develops the central themes of *Fatelessness*. (As a caveat, I would like to point out here that I do not read Hungarian; however I am aware that the translations are, in part, open to question; on this, see Wilkinson. See also the new translation by Wilkinson, *Fatelessness*, where the title of *Sorstalanság* is translated correctly, and *Kaddish for an Unborn Child*, also translated by Wilkinson. As the new translations are not available at the writing of this paper, I quote from the Wilson and Wilson translations, *Fateless* and *Kaddish for a Child Not Born*.) All this is also to argue, following the "New Aestheticism" (see Joughin and Malpas) that

38

art has a role to offer truths which are not reducible to historical accounts or philosophical theses.

These characteristics of Kertész's work are best highlighted in comparison to the huge array of Holocaust testimony and fiction. *Fatelessness* shows how Kertész reuses the often-implicit generic tropes of Holocaust testimony to reach his conclusions, and *Kaddish for an Unborn Child* is a message from a survivor to the next. I take testimony texts to be those written by survivors of the Holocaust which bear witness along the lines Kelly Oliver suggests: "Witnessing is addressed to another and to a community; and witnessing—in both senses, as addressing and responding, testifying and listening—is a commitment to embrace the responsibility of constitution of communities, the responsibility inherent in subjectivity itself" (64–65). While testimony texts maintain what, in the light of the Wilkomirski affair, is called the autobiographical "moral pact" (Mächler 275; on the Wilkomirski affair, see also Vasvári), they all vary to some degree, reflecting what James Young calls the "epistemological climate" (Young 26) from which the authors write. However, as I have argued elsewhere (see Eaglestone), in the range of testimony, there are some generic similarities, "family resemblances" rather than clear-cut taxonomic features, and it is clear that *Fatelessness* shares some of these. However, one of the factors that makes the work exceptional is the way in which it reuses these tropes for its own purposes, and it is in this reuse that its nature as a novel emerges.

One of the most important characteristics of testimony texts is the way in which they deal with the identification, the "embarrassingly ordinary process" (Fuss 1) that often takes place in reading. With Holocaust writing, this can be a profound problem, since fiction encourages (and often relies on) identification, and—in as much as it, like fiction, is a prose narrative—testimonies do, too. However, at the same time testimony aims to prohibit identification on epistemological grounds (a reader really cannot become, or become identified, with the narrator of a testimony: any such identification is a illusion) and on ethical grounds (a reader should not become identified with a narrator of a testimony, as it reduces and "normalizes" or consumes the otherness of the narrator's experience and the illusion that such an identification creates is possibly pernicious). While *Fatelessness* has the form of a realist prose narrative, it manages to resist the easy pressure to identify with the main character in a number of ways. First, and perhaps most significantly, while there are moments of internal description, most of the novel functions in a way which puts a barrier up between the narrator and the reader: rather as if the first-person narrator is describing not his own experiences, but those of another, a third person. Things happen to the narrator, even when he does them himself: his agency—even his internal agency—is limited, and this makes him a hard figure with whom to identify. For example, his father's farewell is almost something that happens to another: the narrator does not describe his feelings, but that his "tears started flowing" (*Fateless* 20), and he is not even sure of the reason (exhaustion? expectation? what was expected of him?). In his Nobel speech, Kertész he says that "I have been feeling the steady, searching gaze of a dispassionate observer on my back" ("Heureka!" 604), and the short story *Az angol lobogó. Elbeszélések* (The English Flag: Short Stories) stresses this by using the pronoun form "he (I)" a number of times. This trope—the internal/external observer—is perhaps key to his work. This stripping of agency is crucial to the argument of *Fatelessness*.

Another, linked factor is that the narrator's responses are simply not what we expect: he does not find the SS troops "the least bit scary" (*Fateless* 61), for example, and wishes to "live a little longer in the beautiful concentration camp!" (138). Finally, everyone "will ask me about the depravations, the 'terrors of the camps', but for me, the happiness there will always be the most memorable experience, perhaps" (191). Andrea Reiter argues that this technique is employed because the protagonist is a child and that the narrator "never departs from the perspective of the child, nor does he explain with hindsight he knows better" (232). However, this seems to me mistaken. Rather, this choice of style is central to the crucial revelation of the novel—the idea of fate and fatelessness and the impossibility of agency. Moreover, these moments are so unlike the received wisdom, and such a reminder of the variability of the interpretation of human experience even in the Holocaust, that they stress the huge void between the knowledge and experience of the post-Holocaust author and the audience and make identification across this gulf much harder.

This gulf is emphasised again by another trope that *Fatelessness* shares with many testimony texts. In Charlotte Delbo's *The Measure of Our Days*, the narrator meets Pierre, the husband of her "camp sister" Marie-Louise. He has a great interest in the experiences of his wife—he has read her notebooks, visited Auschwitz. In fact, he has colonised totally and erroneously his wife's memory of the camps. The first half of Jorge Semprún's *Literature or Life* is made up of accounts of similar moments (on Semprún and Kertész, see Peguy). These are "allegories of failed understanding": the survivors meet characters who think they have comprehended the events, but, because they were not there, cannot. These characters have taken up the reading position of those who did not experience the Holocaust and a warning, in Lawrence Langer's words, against using the "grim details" of the Holocaust "to fortify a prior commitment to an ideal of moral reality, community responsibility, or religious belief that leaves us with space to retain faith in their pristine value in a post-Holocaust world" (1). At the end of the novel, George meets a well-intentioned journalist who wants to know about the camps. George tell him about the passage of time in the camps, and the journalist "covered his face with his hands . . . then said 'No, you can't imagine it.' I for my part, thought to myself: 'That's why they probably say "hell" instead'" (*Fateless* 182). The journalist wants to turn George's story into precisely that, a story, to "mobilise public opinion" (183). George shows by his actions—throwing away the journalist's phone number—that he thinks this is impossible, and that the experience cannot simply be reduced to propaganda (as, of course, it was in Central and Eastern Europe: a character from Arnost Lustig's *Night and Hope* has his hopes raised by "a country so large that he could not imagine her otherwise than as a bear . . . a she-bear determined to protect all her children" [203]). Later, too, George meets survivors and neighbours who counsel him to forget the camps and tell him that "life wasn't easy at home either" (185). Here, the journalist and former neighbours, in different ways, cannot but fail to understand the events, and want to turn them into something different (propaganda, oblivion and a new life). Yet the events have given him a revelation which cannot be taken back.

Testimony texts offer a lack of closure, in two ways. First, textually, the texts finish but do not end. Again, Lévi is an example here. In the last chapter of *If This Is a Man*, he dreams of the "dawn command of Auschwitz . . . get up, 'Wstawàch'" (380), which condemns him to re-awake in the camp, in a sense, forever. Kertész's novel, too, ends not with a triumphant homecoming, but with George, in a penniless state, en route to his mother, failing to find solace. In contrast to the "stereotyped picture" of ending and release, for the "majority of cases, the hour of liberation was neither joyful nor light hearted" (Lévi, *The Drowned* 52). And this lack of closure in the text is echoed by the wider sense of the lack of closure outside the text. While it has been suggested that "great majority of Holocaust memoirists fall silent when they have completed their tales" (Foley 339), I argue that the opposite is true. Their tales, once told, are told again and again. Lack of closure also occurs in—or more accurately, *as*—the oeuvre of a writer; survivors return again and again to write about the Holocaust. As Wiesel writes, "I could spend the rest of my days recounting the weeks, months and eternities I lived in Auschwitz" (*Night* 89). This is true of Kertész, too: "I write about a single subject" (*Fateless* 607). Finally, testimonies are also marked by epiphantic moments, in which the truth of the death camps is revealed. A celebrated example is the guard's response to Lévi's question "warum?": "There is no why here" (Lévi, *If This Is a Man* 35). In Semprún's *The Long Voyage*, too, the death of the Jewish children is the central, structuring moment to which the testimony builds up. For George, this moment of revelation occurs in the final pages: "if there is such a thing as fate, then there is no freedom . . . if on the other hand there is freedom, there is no fate. That is . . . we ourselves are fate. I recognized this all of a sudden and with such clarity that I had never seen before" (189).

It is this realization about fate that lies at the core of his work. Yet this is a complex revelation of an aporia. At first glance, it might look like an existentialist declaration of authenticity ("we ourselves are fate"). However, it is not. It does not rule out "fate," some force (God, history) over which the individual has no control, nor does it rule out the freedom of the individual to make the world, as a stereotype of a Marxist position might. It leaves these two undecided, aporeitic. We can think of ourselves and act or be acted upon as victims of T. S. Eliot's "vast impersonal forces"; we can also think of ourselves as our own fate, active agents. For Kertész, these two possibilities—there is no middle ground between them—are constantly before us. However, crucially, what Kertész in *Az angol lobogó* understands as either the consequentiality of fate or the absurdity of fate is in any event our fate. They still happen, they cannot be avoided, however much, like the narrator in *Kaddish*, one digs and hides. What happens, happens, and if one wills it, one is also an impersonal force acting on oneself ("He [I]"). *Fatelessness* is precisely about the life that leads to this insight and *Kaddish*—in which the act is not to act—is its clear sequel. Yet this realization is affective: It cannot be logically argued for, only shown, or lived through.

The relationship between fate and choice leads Kertész's texts to eschew more straightforward generic markers of testimony. For example, while testimony texts generally follow a linear autobiographical chronology, many intersperse this with historical discourse, and even historical documents or sourced evidence. Rudolph Vrba's testimony has two appendices including a sworn affidavit submitted to the Eichmann trial. Testimony texts often interrupt their chronologies in other ways, too; Lévi is not alone in describing the death camps through various excursions which describe events not in the narrative sequence but instead illustrate his time in Auschwitz more generally. Some use such odd narrative sequences—the narrator and readers know what the narrator earlier did not—for terrible irony; for example, Olga Lengyel asks "one of the guides, and old inmate, about this structure. 'It is a camp bakery she replied'. We absorbed that without the slightest suspicion. Had she revealed the truth we would not have believed her" (33–34). These various recurring formal tropes—mixing genres, playing with the flow of time, narrative devices and frames—occur frequently in testimony texts. Yet *Fatelessness* does not use any of these, but maintains a consistent, linear narrative. The reasons for this emerge in Kertész's Nobel lecture and illuminate the core of the novels. One reason is, of course, his political and social context: "I have to conclude that in the West, in a free society, I probably would not have been able to write the novel known by readers today as *Fateless*" ("Heureka!" 606). Accounts such as Peter Novick's *The Holocaust in American Life* have shown how changing political and historical contexts influenced Holocaust memory. Other accounts, perhaps not so full, exist for other countries and contexts. And it is clear that these political contexts play a role simply in what gets published, well-reviewed, made into films and so on. But for Kertész, the political situation has a deeper significance. In the "free marketplace of books and ideas" he might have wanted "to produce a showier fiction" by, for example, breaking up time and narrating "only the most powerful scenes" ("Heureka!" 606). But—and this seems to be the crucial revelation— "the hero of my novel does not live his own time in the concentration camps, for neither his time nor his language, not even his own person, is really his. He doesn't remember; he exists. So he has to languish, poor boy, in the dreary trap of linearity, and cannot shake off the painful details. Instead of a spectacular series of great and tragic moments, he has to live through everything, which is oppressive and offers little variety, like life itself!" ("Heureka!" 606).

This very linearity is crucial for Kertész: "It did not allow me, say, to skip cavalierly over twenty minutes of time, if only because those twenty minutes were there before me, like a gaping, terrifying black hole, like a mass grave. I am speaking of the twenty minutes spent on the arrival platform of the Birkenau extermination camp—the time it took people clambering down from the train to reach the officer doing the selecting" ("Heureka!" 606). For Kertész, these twenty minutes ("in principle a rather long stretch of time"; *Fateless* 187) constitute the central point of being stripped of agency: "were we gassed right now, or were we given a momentary reprieve?" (*Fateless* 187). This moment gives him the two interlinked insights I discussed above. These are not given, *pace* Reiter, from a child's perspective, but underlie, perhaps, all of Kertész's work. The first is about the relationship between fate and choice, between individual agency and the impersonal forces over which the individual has no control. The second is the insight that what happens, happens anyway, and agency, wresting one's subjectivity from the impersonal, however authentically, is no guard against atrocity; worse, it in fact re-inscribes the same gesture. Kertész's memory, his reading of the work of writers like Borowski and of the photographs in what is called the *Auschwitz Album* (a photographic series of Hungarian Jews arriving at Auschwitz-Birkenau; see Gutman and Guterman) all suggest that these twenty minutes are recalled and passed over too quickly: "I saw lovely, smiling women and bright-eyed young men, all of them well-intentioned, eager to cooperate. Now I understood how and why those humiliating twenty minutes of idleness and helplessness faded from their memories. And when I thought how all this was repeated the same way for days, weeks, months and years on end, I gained an insight into the mechanism of horror; I learned how it became possible to turn human nature against one's own life" ("Heureka!" 607). The very moments of agency are turned against life; as he stated in his Nobel speech, "I understood that hope is an instrument of evil, and the Kantian categorical imperative—ethics in general—is but the pliable handmaiden of self-preservation" ("Heureka!" 606).

Fatelessness is a novel, not for the facile reason that the narrator and author have different names. It is the insights about the nature of fate and the ways in which these are enacted though the novel, in its style, in its narrative, in its linear form, that mark it as a novel. Only in the novel can these be carried through at the level of form and style. Testimonies are, in many ways, formed chronicles: here, the central motif of the text is foregrounded in that very formation, to a point at which it must be called a novel. Paralleling Kertész, Emmanuel Levinas argues that if "I am reduced to my role in history I remain unrecognised" (252). History, he writes, "recounts enslavement, forgetting the life that struggles against slavery" and historians "interpret, that is, utilize the works of the dead" (228). Thus, the "virile judgement of history . . . is cruel" (243). Kertész in *Fatelessness* uses the novel form to stand for history itself; George is trapped in the linear, novel form. The finish of the novel (not an ending) occurs when George in a sense recognizes this trap. The novel itself, an allegory in Paul de Man's sense, enacts the fate/fatelessness that is revealed to its protagonist. It is the trap of this novel, and the novel in general, that turns "all that remained of the whole experience . . . a few muddled impressions, a few anecdotes" ("Heureka!" 606) for Kertész into a full, linear account. Indeed, as he writes, it is precisely the linearity, the not choosing specific anecdotes—"true captivity is really a row of grey, everyday days" (*Fateless* 99)—that reveals the truth the camps tell. In the camps, George has only the fate assigned him. And wrestling with and with the idea that to make fate is to impose it, an internal or external "Moloch" (*Fateless* 604) marks out the advance made in *Kaddish.*

Some testimonies—although fewer than one might think—refer to the relationship between the survivor and the world afterwards. Kitty Hart's second account, *Return to Auschwitz*, describes how postwar Britain has no interest in her experiences in Auschwitz: Her uncle, almost as soon as he meets her, says, "there's one thing I must make quite clear. On no account are you to talk about any of the things that have happened to you. Not in my house, I don't want my girls upset. And I don't want to know" (14). She goes on to describe the psychological and social aftermath of the Holocaust and how everyone "I have met since the war slots in my mind into an Auschwitz setting" (Hart 214). However, this is not as excoriating as Kertész's *Kaddish*, a prose poem for child he has decided not to have. While this message to the next generation is exceptional, the genre of writing to which it compares interestingly is, following Marianne Hirsch, who designates this as Holocaust "post-memory." These are all texts by the children of survivors and represent the ways in which the Holocaust is taken up, reworked by these children as an active force in their lives. Such texts include Spiegelman's *Maus*, George Perec's *W*, Sarah Kofman's *Rue Ordener Rue Labat*, Anca Vlasopolos's *No Return Address,* Alain Finkielkraut's *The Imaginary Jew*, Anne Karpf's *The War After* and Leon Wieseltier's *Kaddish* (on second-generation memoirs of the Holocaust, see also Tötösy de Zepetnek). Like testimonies, they are a disparate group of texts, about which any generalisation is provisional, but some overall lines might be drawn that in turn illuminate Kertész's message to the next generation, not least because it seems so at odds with them.

Central to these texts is the idea of mourning. Indeed, Leon Wieseltier's *Kaddish* is based around mourning his father and, in turn, opening up to a wider mourning for the murdered Jews of Europe. But this mourning for the Holocaust's victims is understood as being in process, developing, from which a different and stronger self develops. With this is a coming to terms with the communal, usually though their sense of Judaism. Alain Finkielkraut in *The Imaginary Jew* develops a leftist "ethical," if not religious, Judaism. The lack he feels—from the destruction of European Jewry and a feeling of exile—is precisely what turns him back to Judaism, not to fill this lack but as an awareness of transcendence, of the fragility of his own identity under the "gaze of the other" (Finkielkraut 15). In contrast, Wieseltier turns to a more conservative Judaism and feels himself part of "a cable running through time" (410). In New York, when he takes his father's seat at *shul,* he has "a physical sensation of inheritance" (218). These texts help focus what is at the core of *Kaddish*, a text with which these "post-memory" texts seem almost to be in dialogue. *Kaddish* brings to the fore a strand of ideas that other survivors have rarely expressed. What makes it such a powerful work is the ways in which these ideas are bound together, and this "binding together" is, again, what makes the text a novel and not simply an account; the "binding" is part of its literary style. The book is about refusal in the light of fate. That is, unlike *Fatelessness*, which is about being the victim of fate, *Kaddish* is about both being the victim of this fate, about claiming what agency is possible in that dark light and the ineluctable perils of that claim. This is its "narrative" development from *Fatelessness*. In it, three strands are interwoven.

The first strand is the narrator's relationship to Judaism. For the narrator the recurring image of Jewishness comes from accidentally seeing his aunt without her wig: "the horror of seeing a bald woman sitting in front of a mirror" (*Fateless* 17). Judaism is not, as it is for survivors like Wiesel or Levinas and for children of survivors like Wieseltier and Finkielkraut, something to be cherished or inhabited, but rather something that has to be endured. His rejection of Judaism, of community, summed up in his refusal to have a child, is the core of the book. This rejection has some parallels with others: Améry writes of "the Necessity and Impossibility of Being a Jew" (82). From an assimilated family, like the narrator—"city Jews, Budapest Jews, that is to say, not Jews at all, but of course not Christian either" (*Kaddish* 16), Améry writes that if "being a Jew implies having a cultural heritage or religious ties, then I was not one and can never become one" but that if "to myself and to the world . . . I say: I am a Jew, then I mean by that those realities and possibilities that are summed up in the Auschwitz number" (94). Yet, in the final pages, as his marriage breaks up, the narrator writes that "it doesn't matter a hill of beans whether I am a Jew or a non-Jew, although being a Jew does have a large advantage here and in this respect . . . labeled a Jew, I was allowed to be in Auschwitz and that on account of my Jewishness I experienced something and survived something and faced something and now I know something once and for all, and irrevocably, something that I won't let go of, will never let go of" (*Kaddish* 93). This statement, taking something from Auschwitz, is clearly at odds with what one might expect a survivor to say. But similar sorts of things emerge in some testimonies: Kitty Hart, too, writes: "While being interviewed . . . I said something which sounded strange to my own ears. I declared that I thought the experience had been worthwhile. This was not at all what I meant. No such horror and such slaughter of innocents could ever in any sense have been worthwhile. What I was trying to convey, and what I say now, is that if such a terrible thing had to happen, or was allowed to by human negligence and human wickedness to happen, then personally I would sooner have gone through it than not gone through it. But I would not wish that anyone in the world should ever have to suffer such agonies again" (223). These remarks seem to suggest that in Auschwitz something was gained or revealed. For Hugo Gryn, it was an ethical mission (258); for Wiesel, the night that "murdered my God and my Soul and turned my dreams to dust" (*Night* 45); for Hart, facing the extreme. What the narrator takes is a bleakness, but a creative bleakness.

This is the second strand of *Kaddish*, which puts this text again at odds with the accounts by the children of survivors in the West. They often find the Holocaust—if not anti-Semitism—to be an aberration, and they attempt to salvage culture; they often find themselves consciously taking on roles—as parents, as children, taking up responsibility. In contrast, for Kertész, Auschwitz reveals that the world has always been like that, is beyond the possibility of salvage. It is, for the narrator, not Auschwitz but "precisely the absence of Auschwitz" in previous history "that could not be explained. Consequently Auschwitz must have been hanging in the air for a long, long time, centuries, perhaps like a dark fruit slowly ripening in the sparkling rays of innumerable ignominious deeds, waiting to finally drop on one head (*Kaddish* 28). In his usual laconic style, Raul Hilberg writes that in August 1944 the capacity of the Birkenau death camp was "approaching the point of being unlimited"; this "took years to work out in the constant application of administrative techniques. It took millennia in the development of Western culture" (251). It is this insight—that what underlies Auschwitz underlies everything—which leads the narrator to reject fatherhood, indeed "all Führers, Chancellors and other sundry titled usurpers" (*Kaddish* 29). The narrator's schooling reflects this; the Director who pulled open the door "like the Gestapo" (83) from whom "orders descended" (82); "in fact" these orders "often . . . weren't even expressed wishes but wishes attributed to him or, one could say, anticipated of him" (82) (this is an even more accurate image of Hitler, as is shown by recent historical studies, such as Peter Longerich's *The Unwritten Order*); afternoon *rapports* on Saturdays "like the appel at Auschwitz" (85); laws which "while I feared them, I never respected" (86). All "this is the earlier culture, this father culture, this universal father complex" (80). The narrator's father, whose rule was a "warm-hearted tyranny" (86), and despite the narrator's boyhood pity for him, was preparing the narrator for "the same thing, the same 'culture'" (87). Auschwitz was "an elaboration of those virtues in which I have been indoctrinated since childhood" (88) and "appears to me in the image of a father . . . the two terms, Auschwitz and father, resonate the same echoes in me" (88). "And," the narrator continues, "if the observation is that God is an exalted father, then God too, is revealed to me in the image of Auschwitz" (88). It is this that the narrator has seen in Auschwitz. The whole world is, and has been, a death camp, that the structures of power are the same throughout; "the absurd order of chance, which reigns over our lives with the whim of a death squad, exposing us to inhuman powers, monstrous tyrannies" ("Heureka!" 609).

For Kertész, then, the Holocaust is not, as some popular views have it, the insolvable conflict between Germans and Jews, nor a one-time aberration, nor the "longest hatred" of anti-Semitism, "the "latest chapter in the history of Jewish suffering, which followed logically from their earlier trials and tribulations" ("Heureka!" 607). "What I discovered in Auschwitz is the human condition, the end point of a great adventure, where the European traveller arrived after his two-thousand-year-old moral and cultural history" ("Heureka!" 607). This is the reason that the narrator refuses to have a child. It is not only that he fears bringing a Jewish child into the world: "I would have to walk with lowered head before the child . . . because I couldn't give the child . . . anything no explanation, no faith, no ammunition" (*Kaddish* 69). It is because he will not take on the role of the father culture, of which Auschwitz is part: "I could never be another person's father, fate, god" (71). The narrator refuses any complicity with Auschwitz, and the "murder" of his unborn child and his refusal of fatherhood is the cost. One might speculate that this sense that the whole culture is like a death camp stems in part from Kertész's experience of the totalitarian oppression in Hungary: "a spiders web seemed to cover everything" (Márai 305), forcing and persuading people into complicity. However, it is clear that it is the barbarism of all of European culture that the narrator is addressing: "In the West, at least, one is allowed to say so" (Adorno, *Negative Dialectics* 367). This refusal, which is so negative and so final, is, in fact, his ethical response to Auschwitz. This is the third strand of the book, the narrator's taking up of his fate. His repeated denial—in an English tradition, it might be described as a Miltonic Satanic denial—viewed in a Blakean light is, in fact, a taking up of a burden. His denial of a community is the making of a point. This is why the text is called a *kaddish:* it is both a mourning, and, as such, an affirmation of the community. His Jewishness exists in a negative sense, and his affirmation of the community is its denial. He is taking on his own fate himself and so declaring himself not fateless. He has chosen—a choice that leads to mourning rather than to happiness—and eschewed victimhood for agency. The only agency available to him, the only way to avoid complicity with Auschwitz, is this negative space, a choice which leads, purposefully, nowhere.

Yet, once again, the author is trapped; the logical conclusion of his refusal to be "father, fate, god" (*Kaddish* 71) is his refusal to be his own father, fate, god. The narrator refuses any complicity, even his own self-authorship. The narrator's refusal of agency and community includes even his own agency—thus, an aporietic form of agency, "the spiritual form of the survival instinct that no longer can survive, doesn't want to survive, and probably is no longer capable of survival, but one that still and because of it all demands its . . . own formation . . . so that it could continue to exist" (94). Thus, "let me drown" (95), the command to make commanding impossible, the choice for the impossibility of choice. He has made peace with "the absurd order of chance, which reigns over our lives with the whim of a death squad" ("Heureka!" 609) by surrendering himself even to himself, to maintain himself.

Kertész's novels *Fatelessness* and *Kaddish*, then, make up two moments of an arc of argument that can only be made in an artwork. The idea of fate, of the power of history, is not—is no longer—an idea open to philosophers or to most historians. Yet it is precisely the sort of orienting concept that shapes and forms our lives, described, perhaps, in other ways. Alastair MacIntyre, for example, writes that "Man is in his actions and practice, as well as in his fictions, essentially a storytelling animal. He is not essentially, but becomes through his history, a teller of stories that aspire to truth . . . I can only answer the question 'What am I to do?' if I can answer the prior question 'Of what story or stories do I find myself a part?'" (216). Kertész's novels respond to this precisely by locating George as the agentless victim of the "story," and then the narrator of *Kaddish* as a man who, in response, takes up what little agency is left him. The two novels, with the sense of a linearity of time, bear this out. This arc—and the intellectual and aesthetic achievement it represents—is most clearly seen in contrast with other texts of Holocaust literature. The work of a Nobel laureate and the work of any Holocaust survivor is exceptional. Yet, in stressing the nature of the failure of choice and agency as aporia rather than either tragedy or redemption, Kertész's work, in my opinion, is an exception in a literature of exceptions.

Works Cited

Adorno, Theodor. *Negative Dialectics*. Trans. E. B. Ashton. London: Routledge, 1973.

Adorno, Theodor. *Notes to Literature*. Ed. Rolf Tiedemann. Trans. Shierry Weber Nicholson. New York: Columbia UP, 1993.

Améry, Jean. *At the Mind's Limits*. Trans. Sidney Rosenfeld and Stella P. Rosenfeld. London: Granta, 1999.

Delbo, Charlotte. *Mesure de nos jours*. Paris: Éditions de Minuit, 1971.

Eaglestone, Robert. "Identification and the Genre of Testimony." *Immigrants and Minorities* 21 (2003): 117–40.

Finkielkraut, Alain. *The Imaginary Jew*. Trans. Kevin O'Neill and David B. Suchoff. Lincoln: U of Nebraska P, 1994.

Foley, Barbara. "Fact, Fiction, Fascism: Testimony and Mimesis in Holocaust Narratives." *Comparative Literature* 34 (1982): 330–60.

Friedländer, Saul. *Reflections on Nazism: An Essay on Kitsch and Death*. Trans. Thomas Weyr. Bloomington: Indiana UP, 1993.

Fuss, Diana. *Identification Papers*. London: Routledge, 1995.

Gryn, Hugo, with Naomi Gryn. *Chasing Shadows*. London: Penguin, 2001.

Gutman, Israel, and Belah Guterman, eds. *The Auschwitz Album: The Story of a Transport*. Jerusalem and Oświęcim: Yad Vashem and Auschwitz-Birkenau State Museum, 2002.

Hart, Kitty. *Return to Auschwitz*. London: Panther, 1983.

Hilberg, Raul. *The Destruction of the European Jews*. London: Holmes and Meier, 1985.

Joughin, John J., and Simon Malpas, eds. *The New Aestheticism*. Manchester: Manchester UP, 2003.

Kertész, Imre. *Az angol lobogó. Elbeszélések* (The English Flag: Short Stories). Budapest: Magvető, 2001.

Kertész, Imre. *Fateless*. Trans. Christopher C. Wilson and Katharina M. Wilson. Evanston: Northwestern UP, 1992.

Kertész, Imre. *Fatelessness*. Trans. Tim Wilkinson. New York: Vintage, 2004.

Kertész, Imre. "Heureka!" *PMLA: Publications of the Modern Language Association of America* 118:3 (2003): 604–14.

Kertész, Imre. *Kaddish for a Child Not Born*. Trans. Christopher C. Wilson and Katharina M. Wilson. Evanston: Hydra Books, 1997.

Kertész, Imre. *Kaddish for an Unborn Child*. Trans. Tim Wilkinson. New York: Vintage, 2004.

Langer, Lawrence. *Pre-empting the Holocaust*. New Haven: Yale UP, 1998.

Lévi, Primo. *The Drowned and the Saved*. Trans. Raymond Rosenthal. London: Abacus, 1988.

Lévi, Primo. *If This Is a Man and the Truce*. Trans. Stuart Woolf. London: Abacus, 1979.

Levinas, Emmanuel. *Totality and Infinity*. Trans. Alphonso Lingis. London: Kluwer, 1991.

Longerich, Peter. *The Unwritten Order: Hitler's Role in the Final Solution*. Stroud: Tempus, 2001.

Lustig, Arnost. *Night and Hope*. Trans. George Theiner. Washington: Inscape P, 1976.

MacIntyre, Alastair. *After Virtue*. London: Duckworth, 1985.

Márai, Sándor. *Memoir of Hungary, 1944–1948*. Trans. Albert Tezla. Budapest: Corvina, 1996.

Mächler, Stefan. *The Wilkomirski Affair*. Trans. John Woods. London: Picador, 2001.

Marchitello, Howard, ed. *What Happens to History: The Renewal of Ethics in Contemporary Thought*. London: Routledge, 2001.

Nobel Prize in Literature, The. Laureates (2002): <http://www.nobel.se/literature/laureates/index.html>.

Novick, Peter. *The Holocaust and Collective Memory*. London: Bloomsbury, 2000.

Novick, Peter. *The Holocaust in American Life*. Boston : Houghton Mifflin, 1999.

Oliver, Kelly. "Witnessing Otherness in History." *The Renewal of Ethics in Contemporary Thought*. Ed. Howard Marchitello. London: Routledge, 2001. 41–66.

Peguy, Marie. "The Dichotomy of Perspectives in the Work of Imre Kertész and Jorge Semprún." *Imre Kertész and Holocaust Literature*. Ed. Louise O. Vasvári and Steven Tötösy de Zepetnek. West Lafayette: Purdue UP, 2005. 171–81.

Reiter, Andrea. *Narrating the Holocaust*. Trans. Patrick Camiler. London: Continuum, 2000.

Semprún, Jorge. *Literature or Life*. New York: Viking, 1997.

Semprún, Jorge. *The Long Voyage*. Trans. Richard Seaver. London: Penguin, 1997.

Vrba, Rudolf, and Alan Bestic. *I Cannot Forgive*. London: Didgwick and Jackson and Anthony Gibbs and Phillips, 1963.

Tötösy de Zepetnek, Steven. "Comparative Cultural Studies and the Study of Central European Culture." *Comparative Central European Culture*. Ed. Steven Tötösy de Zepetnek. West Lafayette: Purdue UP, 2002. 1–32.

Vasvári, Louise O. "The Novelness of Imre Kertész's *Fatelessness*." *Imre Kertész and Holocaust Literature*. Ed. Louise O. Vasvári and Steven Tötösy de Zepetnek. West Lafayette: Purdue UP, 2005. 258–270.

Wiesel, Elie. "The Holocaust as Literary Inspiration." *Dimensions of the Holocaust*. Ed. Elie Wiesel, Lucy Dawidowicz, Dorothy Rabinowitz, and Robert McAfee Brown. Evanston: Northwestern UP, 1990. 3–23.

Wiesel, Elie. *Night*. Trans Stella Rodway. London: Penguin, 1981.

Wieseltier, Leon. *Kaddish*. London: Picador, 2000.

Wilkinson, Tim. "Kaddish for a Stillborn Child?" *The Hungarian Quarterly* 43 (2002): 168–70.

Young, James. *Writing and Rewriting the Holocaust: Narrative and the Consequences of Interpretation*. Bloomington: Indiana UP, 1990.

Imre Kertész, Hegel,
and the Philosophy of Reconciliation

Amos Friedland

Within the scope of the dominant philosophical and theological tradition of "the West," the themes of forgiveness and reconciliation occupy a privileged place. The apotheosis of these themes occurs in the work of G.W.F. Hegel, for whom reconciliation is the process by which every sundering is repaired and overcome, every rupture healed and raised to a higher level, until even the gulf that would separate humanity from God is transcended. Hegel held it to be his great insight that this process is necessary and inescapable, precisely because that which would resist, evade, or attempt to escape it ends up being the fertilizer for its soil. The attempt to think through resentment from its own side is, post-Hegel, something of a paradox. For in this context resentment is at once the enemy of forgiveness and reconciliation, yet also the necessary "moment" to be superseded by a reconciling forgiveness. In its enmity to reconciliation, resentment is also essential to this movement of forgiveness: Resentment, in effect, propels, enables, or makes possible the very movement of forgiveness and reconciliation that it aims to resist and fight against. Any resistance turns out to be in vain, for the fruit of resentment's labors is precisely what it resisted: A forgiveness that, in its movement of reconciliation, defeats and contains it, renders it but a moment within its all-encompassing totality. Is there a resentment that does not inevitably find itself playing out the divine comedy of forgiveness and reconciliation, which resists forgiveness without enabling or necessitating it; or one that remains in spite of reconciliation's unfolding? What is this "remaining," these "remains"? How can they be spoken of?

Under this rubric of "sovereign resentment" I attempt here to situate the post-Holocaust thought of Jean Améry and Vladimir Jankélévitch, and above all, the literary work of Imre Kertész (on this, see also Friedland, *Forgiveness*). Rejecting the drive to forgiveness, Améry, Jankélévitch, and Kertész (each in his own way) articulate stances of resentment aligned with the eternal, resisting, to the point of absurdity, all compulsion towards reconciliation. Their resentment resists and persists even and especially as reconciliation inevitably proceeds in spite of it, in the work of time and history. Resentment absents itself from this "path of spirit," and its resistance is not solely that of a dialectical order, even of a fragmentary sort (as the fragmentary "work of mending" still is for Emil Fackenheim, under his idea of "resistance," which still takes place in the "broken Hegelian middle," in which "dialectical . . . fragments remain, [which] seek each other and flee each other, flee each other and seek each other" (see Fackenheim, "Retrospective" 222, *To Mend*). Resentment is, for those we will consider here, a remainder or remains left over from this process and progress, situated on the hither side of life, love, and happiness—and on the hither side of time. These "resolute resenters" follow another moral imperative, and the remains of resentment turn out to be the "remains of time." Although I am especially concerned to open up a space for thinking of resentment in a way that does not inevitably lead to forgiveness, or to reconciliation, my analysis nevertheless demonstrates the impossible difficulty of articulating this sovereign resentment, one not eventually subsumed by reconciliation. Thus the sections on Améry, Jankélévitch, and Kertész which follow Hegel replay the Hegelian symphony—its Divine Comedy—but in a minor key, as variations on a resentful theme, such that we may hear otherwise the dialectics of reconciliation. The absurd combination of the necessity and the impossibility of this resentment "after Auschwitz" yields the concept of an eternal resentment "left over," as a remainder or remains to the Hegelian *Aufhebung*. Reconciliation may have always already made of resentment a moment in its own unfolding, yet in this *Aufhebung* something is left over of resentment, a remainder or a remains outside of the "equation" of reconciliation: "The disaster is . . . a remainder which would bar with invisibility and illegibility all that shows and is said—a remainder which is neither a result (as in subtraction), nor a quantity left over (as in division). . . . The *Aufhebung* turns inoperable, ceases" (Blanchot 40).

In her famous speech, addressed to Shylock from beneath a disguise, Portia anticipates, in an almost uncanny way, the young Hegel's thoughts on forgiveness, Judaism, and Christianity: "The quality of mercy is not strained; / It droppeth as the gentle [there is a constant punning between 'gentle' and 'gentile' throughout the play] rain from heaven / Upon the place beneath. It is twice blest; / It blesseth him that gives and him that takes. / 'Tis mightiest in the mightiest; it becomes / The thronèd monarch better than his crown. / . . . / But mercy is above this scept'red sway; / It is enthroned in the heart of kings, / It is an attribute of God himself, / And earthly power doth then show likest God's / When mercy seasons justice. Therefore, Jew, / Though justice be thy plea, consider this: / That in the course of justice, none of us / Should see salvation. We do pray for mercy" (*The Merchant of Venice*, IV. i. 183–99).

The same mythical tropes of the Jew and the Christian that Shakespeare uses in *The Merchant of Venice* are marshaled by Hegel in his early theological writings in order to explicate the spiritual journey from, on one hand, the "hard heart" of justice, resentment, and law (the "spirit of Judaism"); to, on the other hand, the "open heart" of love, forgiveness, and universal reconciliation (the "spirit of Christianity"). In both Portia and the early Hegel Christianity-as-forgiveness-and-

reconciliation and Judaism-as-justice-and-resentment are not opposed as alien
stances. Rather, forgiveness is understood as the very essence of justice: It is justice
raised above justice, to its height and its truth—that is, forgiveness is more just than
justice. Forgiveness is the *Aufhebung*, the dialectical conclusion of the internal contradictions immanent within the stance of justice, law, and resentment. Forgiveness
is the logical "must" of justice and resentment, and we can compare Portia's earlier
injunction "Then must the Jew be merciful" (IV. i., 182) with Hegel's conclusion,
in the *Phenomenology of Spirit*, that "the breaking of the hard heart," and the
"wounds of spirit heal[ing], and leav[ing] no scars behind," is "necessitated and already contained" within resentment's stance itself (*Phenomenology* 407).

    In addition to the "necessity" of forgiveness, there is an equally necessary
"logic of conversion" implicit in Shakespeare and in Hegel: Shylock will be
granted forgiveness on condition of his double conversion (that is, conversion of
his daughter through marriage to a Christian, as well as his personal conversion to
Christianity); and the Jew, for Hegel, is fated to escape his Jewish fate, only insofar
as he accepts his higher, Christian fate, realized through love and reconciliation, in
the conversion to Christianity (it is, Hegel says, the "consequences and elabora-
tions of their original fate" that "they will be continually maltreated until they ap-
pease it by the spirit of beauty and so annul it in reconciliation" [Hegel, "Spirit of
Christianity" 200]). Thus the pre-dialectical Hegel is already here proto-dialectical;
this will be made explicit not only in the *Phenomenology of Spirit*, where what is at
question in the "breaking of the hard heart" is a "logical forgiveness" (Harris 2
503); an also in the late *Lectures on the Philosophy of Religion*.

    In these latter lectures, Hegel is concerned to explicate nothing less than how
the Absolute becomes cognized, and therefore actual, in the course of the history of
the unfolding of religion. The story culminates, of course, with the "consummate
religion," Christianity. Christianity stands logically at the end of history, for Hegel,
because only within its sphere is reconciliation taken to its final point, wherein the
distinction between the finite and the supposedly inaccessible infinite is transcended—and transcended from both sides, from God's and Man's. Judaism is the
last stage just prior to this final (and necessary) reconciliation: In *Phenomenology*,
Hegel says of the Jews that "it is precisely because they stand before the portal of
salvation that they are, and have been, most reprobate and rejected" (206). This distance must be overcome, and this happens in the dual movement of Christ dying on
the cross and being resurrected, on the one hand ("The resurrection is something
that belongs just as essentially to faith [as the crucifixion]. . . . The death of Christ
is the death of this death itself, the negation of negation" [Hegel, *Lectures* 3 324]);
and the communal doctrine of confession and forgiveness within the Protestant
church: "It is not a matter of overcoming evil because evil has been overcome in
and for itself. The child, inasmuch as it is born into the church, has been born in
freedom and to freedom. For one who has been so born, there is no longer an absolute otherness; this otherness is posited as something overcome, as already con-

quered. . . . Spirit has the power to undo evil" (*Lectures* 3 336). Bluntly put: in the doctrine of the crucifixion *and* resurrection of the Christ, Easter always comes after Good Friday.

The transition (conversion or assimilation) from Judaism to Christianity, accomplished in and through reconciliation and forgiveness (through love), was already Hegel's strong intuition in his early theological writings on the "Spirit of Christianity." Yet it is in the *Religion* that this intuition is actually given its full determination, since only at this later point in Hegel's thought is the *necessity* of the transition—its inescapable logic—given determination in a dialectical way. The section on "Evil and Forgiveness" in the *Phenomenology* anticipates this and makes this necessity explicit. But it is given its strongest undergirding in the analysis of the finite and infinite (the "bad infinite" and the "true infinite") in the dense section on "Force and Understanding" earlier on in the *Phenomenology*: "It is itself and its opposite in one unity. Only thus is it difference as inner difference, or difference in its own self, or difference as an infinity" (*Phenomenology* 99), and in the sections on the "limit," the "finite infinite," and the "true infinite" in *The Science of Logic*. Because any un-reconciled distance between the finite and the infinite is, for Hegel, an extreme contradiction; and because, moreover, the very idea of limit already conceives the transcending of any limit ("Something has a limitation in so far as it has negation in its determination, and the determination is also the accomplished sublation of the limitation. . . . [Thus,] it is the very nature of the finite to transcend itself, to negate its negation, and to become infinite" [*Science* 132–33]); the transition in the Religion is therefore necessitated between the stage in religion (Judaism) that would stubbornly hold onto and reify just this limit and distance, and another (Christianity) which would, in its ultimate form, reconcile every distance between God and Man, between the infinite and the finite, in the dual movement of God becoming man and man becoming God. (The obvious additional conclusion here is that Christianity becomes indiscernible from secularism; and that therefore the inner truth of secularism is itself a Christian one.)

It is thus as an inevitable and inescapable conclusion that Hegel posits the completeness of forgiveness and reconciliation, understood as the immanently necessitated conversion of spirit into its Absolute self. Out of the "No" of dialectical negation there emerges the universal "Yea," wherein the hard and resentful heart breaks and opens to its other, and thereby transcends itself in a movement in which it becomes itself. The truth of this Yea, held by Hegel to be inescapable, is the truth of conversion—and the true fate of the Jew (as opposed to his "miserable Jewish fate") is thus just this Yes—the Yes that forgives all and reconciles. It is counter to Hegel's Yes that we turn now to our counterpuntal "resentful variations": first Améry's *At the Mind's Limits*; then Jankélévitch's "Should We Pardon Them?"; and finally Kertész's novels, *Fatelessness*, *Kaddish for an Unborn Child*, and *Liquidation*. Since my main aim is to situate Kertész, I turn freely to his novels throughout these sections. I move from Hegel's resonant Yes of reconciliation to

Kertész's explicit "No!" of resentment. In doing so, I explore what I have else-where called Kertész's "logic of survival" (Friedland, "Review"); but also show how that logic implies a particular logic of persistence, and also a logic of the re-mainder.

Améry concludes the 1976 preface to his book *At the Mind's Limits* with this declaration: "Nothing is resolved, no conflict is settled, no remembering has be-come mere memory. What happened, happened. But *that* it happened cannot be so easily accepted. I rebel: against my past, against history, and against a present that places the incomprehensible in the cold storage of history and thus falsifies it in a revolting way. Nothing has healed" (xxi). These are also the concerns of Améry's essay "Resentments": The need to rebel, to take a resolute stance against a process that nevertheless proceeds and accomplishes itself. "Clarification," the resolving of the case, that sense of "having done with this"—resentment rebels and rejects this movement of history, this process, this work of time. Against the world in which reconciliation, forgiveness, and the personal and collective "work of mourning" de-fine the processes of time, of history, of life, Améry juxtaposes a "stubbornness," a "totally obstinate, morally condemnable hate" (69). This resentment, Améry ac-knowledges, is both "psychologically disordered" and "logically inconsistent": "Resentment is not only an unnatural but also a logically inconsistent condition. . . . Absurdly, it demands that the irreversible be turned around, that the event be un-done. Resentment blocks the exit to the genuine human dimension, the future. . . . The time sense of the person trapped in resentment is twisted around, dis-ordered" (*Mind's Limits* 68). The rupture of time and of history is one of the motifs I want to highlight here, and one that I discern in other authors as well, for example in Cyn-thia Ozick's novel, *The Shawl*, where Rosa says, "Before is a dream. After is a joke. Only during stays. And to call it life is a lie" (58). Freud, of course, speaks of the "work of mourning"—and also the process of "working-through"—as a "work of time": this work may take a long time, but it is that which allows time to proceed (one's own personal lived time, and also collective world-historical time). This work of mourning bequeaths the ability to work and to love—to live (see Freud, "Mourning," "Remembering").

The contrast with Améry's "absurd" "disordered time sense" of resentment shows up certain basic tenets shared by both Freud and Hegel, namely: that resis-tance alone enables the work to proceed, and that, therefore, the significance of re-sistance as such lies ultimately in relation to the work; that the process aims at a reconciliation that opens on to the future, or the possibility of the future; that the time and the suffering inherent in the work process are essential; and that the truth is not achieved through any immediate insight, but must be endured and "tarried with" if progress is to occur. In short, in both Freud and Hegel, time is the time of work (just as work is the work of time), the time of suffering, and ultimately—although in a very different way for each thinker—the time of redemption, where the suffering and resistance that propelled the process are "fulfilled" in a kind of reconciliation that allows for a future. It is this "time that heals all wounds" that Améry (and, indeed our other "resolute resenters") rejects ("Nothing is healed"). But what is the logical status of this "rejection"? What does it mean to "reject" time? Is there any sense that can be given to this "rejection"? It cannot claim that time works or "moves" in a different way, for the movement of time is (Améry insists) the movement of healing. Time does move, life does "go on," forgetting (even and especially forgetting by way of remembering, commemorating, clarifying—the "mereness of memory" of which Améry speaks in his preface) does do its work: the work of time and mourning. So it must be in the name of something higher that one absurdly, unnaturally, illogically—indeed, vainly—situates oneself on the hither side of time, history, healing, working, loving, living. Améry calls this "other side" a "higher moral order," a moral "uniqueness," a "shining light of morals and morality" (Améry 68, 70, 71).

By doing so, one achieves nothing, for achievement occurs precisely within work, achieving is the movement of time and of history. We can begin here to understand the positioning of Kertész's narrator B. in *Kaddish* and *Liquidation*. Thus, for example, "failure, failure alone is left as the sole fulfillable experience" (*Kaddish* 45); thus the rejection of the "more ambitious literary work" that would trace survivor's "path of a striving from darkness to light, a struggle to attain joy, engagement in this struggle as an obligation, *happiness viewed as a duty*" (*Kaddish* 82)—rejected, no doubt, as a "false note" (10); thus B.'s conclusion that his pen is his "spade," and that he must reject (as likewise a false note) "the seductive ulterior motive of *achievement, literature*, or maybe *success*" (84; in *Liquidation*, this imaginary novel that B. will not write is the story of his improbable survival as an infant born in Auschwitz, which "happened, yet [is] still not true," since it cannot be written except as "kitsch" [*Liquidation* 32–33]). Améry's insight—that any "achievement" cannot but confirm what he struggles against—is in fact one of the deep structuring motifs of Kertész's work.

Setting oneself resolutely on the side of resentment is absurd, unnatural, illogical. Resentment persists, resists, and insists, but does not live, heal, work, or love. As Ozick's Rosa says: The "during" stays, and one then stays with the "during." One endures the during that knows no future: Améry speaks of the "exit to the future," "exit" as opposed to "entrance," implies departure, leaving, even escape or fleeing. The future, any future, would be the escape or flight from the enduring of the during. This staying or enduring that does not, cannot, and will not move on, is not life or living—on the hither side of time, it is also on the hither side of life. Thus Ozick's Rosa, "to call it life is a lie." Kertész's narrator in *Kaddish*, B., declares this as well : "I lived . . . in a way that was not quite living and indisputably not quite a life, rather it was just being alive, yes, *surviving* to be more precise" (58). And later, in *Liquidation*, B.'s suicide letter will speak of the "strangeness that separates me from life," and state "I was already dead while I was living" (76; This theme of the blurring of boundaries—between life and death, between the

human and the non-human—is one of the deepest in Holocaust testimony, literature, and philosophy. It is a structuring theme of Giorgio Agamben's work and
plays a dominant role throughout Emil Fackenheim's post-Holocaust philosophy
and theology as well; a constant referent for both is the *Muselmann*, starkly described by Primo Lévi: "One hesitates to call them living; one hesitates to call their
death death" [Lévi 82; *Muselmann* was the term used by inmates to describe those
who had been so broken psychically and physically by their concentration camp
existence that they became automaton-like]). Kertész, in *Fatelessness*, too, writes
about the *Muselmann*; indeed, George comes precariously close to becoming a
Muselmann himself.

Resentment cannot be a moment within the working out of history, for then
it would indeed "rise up," as Hegel would say, to reconciliation. A witnessing that
constitutes itself as a resolute resentment is futile, Améry acknowledges, but must
be endured. This "must" of resentment, too, has significance, but of another order
than the "must of forgiveness" to which Shakespeare's Portia and, later, Hegel
speak. Against the logical or dialectical must of reconciliation and the movement
of time and history, Améry and others posit the moral must. This must allays itself
with the eternal, the "never" and the "forever." Resentment is "what remains," the
(absurd) remainder left over after or while history and time nevertheless proceed.
This proceeding (which is of the order of the "logical" and the "natural," Améry
concedes) cannot but prove Hegel right, in advance, for natural death—the universality of mere being—will break the particularity of the hard heart if forgiveness—
the universality of spirit—will not (*Phenomenology* 406–07). Améry holds no illusions at this level, and he concludes his essay on resentment with the "immensity
and monstrosity of the natural time-sense": "The world, which forgives and forgets, has sentenced me, not those who murdered or allowed the murder to occur. I
and others like me are the Shylocks, not only morally condemnable in the eyes of
the nations, but already cheated of our pound of flesh too. Time did its work, very
quietly. . . . We victims must finish with our retroactive rancor, in the sense that the
KZ argot once gave to the word 'finish'; it meant as much as 'to kill.' Soon we
must and will be finished. Until that time has come, we request of those whose
peace is disturbed by our grudge that they be patient" (Améry, *Mind's Limits* 75,
81).

In "Should We Pardon Them?" Jankélévitch raises the question of the "imprescriptable." The imprescriptable defines the limits, or rather the limitlessness, of
"crimes against humanity." Jankélévitch distinguishes between those crimes that
are of the order of humanity, and that take place in time and in history (a history
that heals and reconciles, forgets and moves on); and those crimes that are of another order, that rupture or create a breach within time and history itself, and that
remain irrecuperable, inexpiable, irreparable, utterly unforgivable. He concludes
that, in Auschwitz, forgiveness—a presumably a-historical command—itself dies
(and thus, paradoxically, enters history—in a way that it never had before—in or-

der to die and to rupture this very history): "Pardoning died in the death camps. Our horror over that which properly speaking reason cannot conceive would smother pity at its birth" (Jankélévitch 567). Thus the death camps also kill time, they kill the power of time that is the power of healing and the power of forgiveness; and they kill time for all time. The crimes that rupture history are imprescriptable, crimes that can never be sufficiently punished, but which can and must be prosecuted "until the end of time" (This is not unlike Arendt's conception, in *The Human Condition*, of "radical evil" that can be neither punished nor forgiven, where one "can indeed only repeat with Jesus: 'It were better for him that a millstone were hanged about his neck, and he cast into the sea'" [Arendt 241; see also Friedland "Evil"]). One "must take a stand," and this stand can no longer find its place in the movement of time. The resentful stance invoked here must take itself up on the other side of time, outside time, in the irreparable breach of time. It must stand on the side of the eternal, even and especially if time yet proceeds in its healing work. It takes its stand and declares, from the eternal standpoint it assumes, that time is null and void: "The time that dulls all things, the time that uses up sorrow as it erodes mountains, the time that favors pardon and forgetfulness, the time that consoles, settling and healing time, does not diminish in the least the colossal slaughter; on the contrary, it never ceases to revive the horror. . . . Crimes against humanity are *imprescriptable*, that is, the penalties against them *cannot* lapse; time has no hold on them. . . . It is in general incomprehensible that time, a natural process without normative value, could have a diminishing effect on the unbearable horror of Auschwitz" (Jankélévitch 556–57). One who takes a stance of resentment must, instead of entering into a movement of time, dwell, endure, or vigilantly stand by the "never" and the "forever." Time, Jankélévitch states, does its own work, so it cannot be with or in time that this work of "serious hatred" takes place: "Forgetfulness had already done its work before . . . Such is the case with the past in general; the past needs us to help it, to recall it to the forgetful, the frivolous, and the indifferent. . . . The past needs our memory. No, the struggle between the irresistible tide of forgetfulness that eventually overwhelms everything and the desperate, intermittent protestations of memory is not a fair fight; in advising forgetfulness, the proponents of pardoning thus recommend something that does not need to be recommended. The forgetful will take care of that themselves" (Jankélévitch 566, 571).

The stance of resentment counters time itself; like Améry, Jankélévitch allays himself—perhaps absurdly—against the movement of time, understood as an inevitable movement of forgetting and reconciliation. Thus he takes his stand, not in time, but "at the end of time"—and on the side of the "never" and the "forever": "We dwell indefinitely on the litanies of bitterness. . . . This is our resentment [*ressentiment*]. For *ressentiment* can also be the renewed and intensely lived feeling of the inexpiable thing; it protects against a moral amnesty that is nothing but shameful amnesia; it maintains the sacred flame of disquiet and faith in invisible things. . . . Because this agony will last until the end of the world" (Jankélévitch 569, 572).

These same themes—of an eternal and irrevocable resentment situated on the other side of life, love, happiness, work, time, and history—also resound in Kertész's work. Already at the end of *Fatelessness* the narrator, George, anticipates the "accumulating readiness to continue my uncontinuable life," and then speaks with curious words of happiness "keeping a watch on me on my journey, like some inescapable trap" (262). In words that anticipate B.'s declaration in *Liquidation*, "*it would be possible for me to destroy the whole world with my resentment*" (75), George replies to the naïve reporter (after this reporter suggests that "the main thing is that it's over, in the past") that his return home elicits "hatred" for "everyone" (247). He replies even more strongly to Fleischmann and Steiner, who, speaking of the "future," tell him that "you must put the horrors behind you." Yes, he acknowledges, without doing this, he will not "be able to live," to "live freely," or "start a new life" (256). But, he replies, "we can never start a new life, only ever carry on the old one" (259). Hannah Arendt, too, speaks of the "new beginning," under the category of "natality," the birth that allows the new into the world. And she links this category to the power of forgiveness, which alone frees one from the past, and therefore opens up to the possibility of the new, the future. Although she limits the scope of forgiveness, stating that certain acts of evil cannot be comprehended, punished, or forgiven, she nonetheless concludes the chapter on forgiveness in *The Human Condition* with an invocation of the Gospels, the "New Beginning," "the miracle that saves the world," and the "glad tidings" that "a child has been born unto us" (Arendt 247). There is a not dissimilar principle of natality in Nietzsche's work—in *Zarathustra* the philosopher must become the child—though Nietzsche places it not under the heading of forgiveness, which he suspects is always contaminated with a Christian *ressentiment*, but rather forgetting: The "active forgetting" necessary for life, for vitality, for happiness. B., in *Kaddish*, situates himself explicitly against this Nietzschean forgetting—which has captivated his wife—and the happiness and vitality that is bequeathed by it (78).

Obviously, it is in response to this idea of the "new beginning," in all of its guises, that Kertész writes *Kaddish*, whose structuring motif is the refusal to give birth or have a child—and the No! to everything that this refusal involves. Whereas the chapter on "Evil and Forgiveness" in Hegel's *Phenomenology* ends with the reconciling and universalizing Yes of Spirit realizing itself through forgiveness, Kertész's novel begins with, and takes up as a refrain, a screaming No! This "No!" is the lament or death prayer for a non-born or still-born child, the child the narrator could never say "Yes" to. The No to the child is at once the No to life, to love, to happiness, to reconciliation. The rejection of any "new beginning" is given a new variant in the "experiment" Kertész enacts in *Liquidation:* what happens if you do obliterate any concrete memories of the camps, if you subtract the duration of George's life from B.'s age in *Kaddish?* That would place the "new beginning" in the ashes of Auschwitz itself. In obliterating the possibility of any concrete memories of the camp, Kertész tries out his family's neighbors', Fleischmann's and Steiner's, suggestion; he does "give orders to [his] memory," he does make himself "reborn," he reverses, to a certain degree "that what had happened had happened" (*Fatelessness* 256). Yet this experiment, this perverse subtraction—already spoken of in *Fatelessness* as an "affliction" or "disease of the mind"—changes nothing; B.'s task here as well is that of "self-liquidation." Auschwitz is the irrevocable, and B.'s farewell letter to his ex-wife, in *Liquidation*, wherein he instructs her to burn his novel (is it *Kaddish?*) and declares that *"for you, and for you alone, I revoke Auschwitz"* (*Liquidation* 121), is eclipsed by the new husband's revocation of the revocation: "No one can revoke Auschwitz, Judit. No one, and by virtue of no authority. Auschwitz is irrevocable" (*Liquidation* 123), above all because these words are anticipated in advance by B., they are the words he places in their mouths in his play "Liquidation," which play structures and directs (or at least anticipates) the actions and words of all of its "real life" characters in the aftermath of his self-liquidation. B. writes the declaration of revocation, but he also himself writes the revocation of this revocation (I will not say the "negation of the negation" here). He revokes Judit's happiness, her marriage, her "new" life, and her love as well, as if reiterating his claim from *Kaddish*, "there is no cure for Auschwitz, nobody will ever recover from the disease of Auschwitz" (77).

This "disease of Auschwitz" is the irrevocable because Auschwitz is not a discrete event; it is not that it "did" exist, but rather it *"does"* exist. Auschwitz does not rupture history for Kertész—it is the inevitable and necessary outcome, the logical conclusion, of this history, one that "has been hanging around in the air since long ago . . . perhaps for centuries," and "it is necessary because it is" (*Kaddish* 36). (Its logic can also be traced through his personal life, his own pre-Auschwitz childhood: "Auschwitz . . . seemed to me to be just an exaggeration of the very same virtues to which I had been educated since early childhood. Yes, childhood and education were the start of the inexcusable process of breaking me, the survival that I never survived" (*Kaddish* 112). Here Kertész invokes Hegel explicitly and acknowledges that he "was moreover absolutely right about this," that "the history of the world presents us with a rational process" and that "to him who looks upon the world rationally the *world* in turn presents a rational aspect" (*Kaddish* 36, 37). Yet the question remains open: "*what kind* of rational process [is it] . . . that world history presents to us[?]" (*Kaddish* 37).

The logic of history is inescapable, and we cannot avoid, evade, or revoke Auschwitz. *Liquidation* makes this point all the more clearly by eclipsing the distinct event named Auschwitz, to show up that the aftermath—our contemporary situation, which can itself, Kertész says, also be named "Auschwitz"—remains the same even minus the experience of the camp. B. is still a survivor, half-alive, living "the Auschwitz mode of existence: He felt that he had been born illegally, had remained alive for no reason, and nothing could justify this existence unless he were to 'decipher the code named Auschwitz'": "He sought to apprehend Auschwitz in his own life, his own daily life, in the way he lived. He wished to register on himself . . . the destructive forces, the survival urge, the mechanism of accommodation, in the same way as physicians of the past used to inject themselves with a poison in order to experience its effects for themselves" (*Liquidation* 110, 111). Although this logic cannot be escaped, one can still resist it—not in any way that can change the outcome of this logic (per Fackenheim's idea of resistance, for example), but solely as a persistence, a refusal to go away: "To rebel is / TO STAY ALIVE / The great insubordination is / for us to live our lives to the end" (*Liquidation* 57), a recusant stance that will not assimilate to this process, this "principle of life, which is actually just the principle of accommodation," this "*total assimilation* to the extant, the extant circumstances and existing conditions": "It is *our . . . decision*, our decision to carry out total assimilation, or not to carry out total assimilation. . . . Already in early childhood I could see clearly that I was incapable of it, incapable of assimilating to the extant, the existing, *to life*, and despite that . . . I am nevertheless extant, I exist and I live" (*Kaddish* 118).

B. harangues his wife about his recusant stance to life just as she has announced that she is leaving him in order to "move on," to live and to love—and that there is another man, who is "not a Jew." B.'s scandalous, virtually blasphemous reply (a reply that echoes and extends his nostalgic invocation of the "beautiful concentration camp" and, later, the "happiness of the concentration camps" in *Fatelessness* (189, 262) is the penultimate moment of the novel, his scream of refusal: "*From this* unique *perspective alone* am I willing to be Jewish, exclusively from this unique perspective do I regard it as a fortunate, even especially fortunate, indeed a blessing, to be a Jew, because I don't care a hoot . . . what I am, but to have had the opportunity to be in Auschwitz as a branded Jew and yet, through my Jewishness, to have lived through something and confronted something; and I know, once and for all, and I know irrevocably something that I will not relinquish, will never relinquish" (*Kaddish* 118–19). It is not a matter of learning how to live on, or if one can live on or resume life. Kertész—but also Améry and Jankélévitch—refuse this "getting on with life," in a decision (perhaps a decision that is no decision [*Kaddish* 30–31]) to stand absurdly on the side of the never and the forever, against time that goes on regardless and does its work: the work of healing, work of mourning, work of reconciliation. This irreconcilable No! links up with the "forever" and the "never" ("I know irrevocably something that I will not relinquish, will never relinquish" [*Kaddish* 120] and "let me submerge / for ever and ever"), with the "until the end of the world" (Jankélévitch 572). Life goes on, but this life does not live, or only half lives; it survives and lives on, but this living on is not quite living. It is the persistence and resistance within life and time against life and time: "During these years I became aware of my life, on the one hand, as fact, on the other, as a *cerebral mode of existence*, to be more precise, a certain mode of existence that would no longer survive, did not wish to survive, indeed was probably not even capable of surviving survival, a life which nevertheless has its own demand, namely, that it be *formed*, like a rounded, rock-hard object, in order that it should *persist*, after all, no matter why, no matter for whom—*for everybody and nobody*, for whoever it is or isn't, it's all the same" (*Kaddish* 119).

We recall that for Hegel forgiveness and reconciliation were not merely juxtaposed to resentment, as if Christian and Jew stood in an unbridgeable opposition to each other, separated by some sort of gulf. Rather—and this is both the strength and the insidiousness of the dialectic—forgiveness emerged out of the internal contradiction and inner diremption immanent within resentment itself. Reconciliation—the Yes of forgiveness—was the dialectical necessity and logical "must" of resentment, and the "conversion" to Christianity the logical must inherent within the Jewish fate itself. We do not refute Hegel here—to attempt to do so would be to contest him, thereby entering into the dialectic ourselves, wherein our attempted "anti-Hegelianism," as Foucault notes perceptively, could itself be "one of his tricks directed against us, at the end of which he stands, motionless, waiting for us" (235). Rather we must, as the above authors implicitly or explicitly have, acknowledge the absolute truth of reconciliation and the healing Yes of time, such that the No of resentment might remain, leave its remains, or constitute a remainder in the total system that is, ipso facto (that is, qua "total"), without remainder. Blanchot, in *The Writing of Disaster,* strategizes his battle against Hegel in a similar way:

> The correct criticism of the System does not consist (as is often, complacently, supposed) in finding fault with it, or in interpreting it insufficiently . . . but rather in rendering it invincible, invulnerable to criticism or, as they say, inevitable. Then, since nothing escapes it because of its omnipresent unity and the perfect cohesion of everything, there remains no place for fragmentary writing unless it comes into focus as the impossible necessary: as that which is written in the time outside time, in the sheer suspense which without restraint breaks the seal of unity by, precisely, not breaking it, but by leaving it aside without this abandon's ever being able to be known. . . . Something rings false in the dialectic, but only the dialectical process, in its inexhaustible demand, in its ever-maintained completion, allows us to think what is excluded from it—not on account of weakness or because it is unacceptable, but in the course of the process's functioning and in order that this functioning be interminably pursued all the way to its term. All the way, that is, to the end of history . . . For first it must be ascertained what authorizes doubt that the dialectic can ever be, I wouldn't say refuted (the possibility of refutation is part of its development), but simply refused. . . . Or does something of the refusal remain, perhaps, in the dialectical process? Would it not persist, all the while modifying itself, until it gives place to something one might call a non-dialectical imperative? Or better, could what rings false in the dialectic and yet makes it function ever separate itself off from the dialectic? . . . . But yet again, let us consider whether it is not by attending to the refusal that accompanies it and alters and consolidates it—let us wonder if it is not

by obstinately playing its own game—that we might come to outplay the dialectic or to defeat it in its very inability to fail. (Blanchot 61, 72, 74)

Just as it was demonstrated that reconciliation emerged out of resentment as its dialectical and inevitable truth, so resentment must be shown as the remainder to, or the remains of, the dialectical process of time and history, in which reconciliation was, with its Yes, shown to overcome and preserve without remainder, what it had necessarily emerged from. This remainder, or these remains, of resentment return, come back, haunt. They are the left-over, the "still-there" within and apart from the life-process, the Spirit-progress, the time of love and forgiveness, healing and mourning. They are the No! yet there within the Yea of reconciliation, the latter said to have emerged from and sublimated this No!: "Sometimes I still scurry through the city like a bedraggled weasel that has managed to make it through a big extermination drive. I start at each sound or sight, as if the scent of faltering memories were assailing my calloused, sluggish senses from the other world" (*Kaddish* 120).

Note: This paper is dedicated to Ágnes Heller.

Works Cited

Améry, Jean. *At the Mind's Limits*. Trans. Sidney and Stella Rosenfeld. New York: Schocken, 1990.

Arendt, Hannah. *The Human Condition*. Chicago: U of Chicago P, 1958.

Blanchot, Maurice. *The Writing of the Disaster*. Trans. Ann Smock. Lincoln: U of Nebraska P, 1986.

Fackenheim, Emil L. *To Mend the World: Foundations of Post Holocaust Jewish Thought*. New York: Schocken, 1989.

Fackenheim, Emil L. "A Retrospective of My Thought." *Jewish Philosophers and Jewish Philosophy*. Ed. Michael L. Morgan. Bloomington: Indiana UP, 1996. 215–26.

Foucault, Michel. "The Discourse on Language." *The Archaeology of Knowledge and the Discourse on Language*. Trans. A. M. Sheridan Smith. New York: Pantheon, 1972. 215–37.

Freud, Sigmund. "Mourning and Melancholia." *The Standard Edition of the Complete Psychological Works of Sigmund Freud*. Ed. James Strachey. London: Hogarth P, 1954– . 14: 243–58.

Freud, Sigmund. "Remembering, Repeating, and Working-Through." *The Standard Edition of the Complete Psychological Works of Sigmund Freud*. Ed. James Strachey. London: Hogarth Press, 1954– . 12: 147–56.

Friedland, Amos. *Forgiveness, Reconciliation, and the Remains of Resentment*. Ph.D. Dissertation. New York: New School U, 2002.

Friedland, Amos. "Evil and Forgiveness: Transitions." *Perspectives on Evil and Human Wickedness* 1.4 (2004): 24–47 <http://www.wickedness.net/ejv1n4/friedland_amos.pdf>.

Friedland, Amos. Review of Imre Kertész *Liquidation*. *Globe & Mail Book Review* (27 November 2004): D43.

Harris, H. S. *The Odyssey of Spirit: Hegel's Ladder*. Indianapolis: Hackett, 1997. 2 vols.

Hegel, G. W. F. *Lectures on the Philosophy of Religion*. Ed. Peter C. Hodgson. Berkeley: U of California P, 1985. 3 vols.

Hegel, G. W. F. *Phenomenology of Spirit*. Trans. A. V. Miller. Oxford: Oxford UP, 1977.

Hegel, G. W. F. *Science of Logic*. Trans. A.V. Miller. Atlantic Highlands: Humanities P, 1989.

Hegel, G. W. G. "The Spirit of Christianity and Its Fate." *Early Theological Writings*. Trans. T. M. Knox. Philadelphia: U of Pennsylvania P, 1971. 282–301.

Jankélévitch, Vladimir. "Should We Pardon Them?" Trans. Ann Hobart. *Critical Inquiry* 22.3 (1996): 552–72.

Kertész, Imre. *Fatelessness*. Trans. Tim Wilkinson. New York: Vintage, 2004.

Kertész, Imre. *Kaddish for an Unborn Child*. Trans. Tim Wilkinson. New York: Vintage, 2004.

Kertész, Imre. *Liquidation*. Trans. Tim Wilkinson. New York: Knopf, 2004.

Lévi, Primo. *Survival in Auschwitz*. Trans. Stuart Woolf. New York: Orion P, 1959.

Ozick, Cynthia. *The Shawl*. New York: Vintage, 1990.

Shakespeare, William. *The Merchant of Venice*. New York: Signet Classics, 1965.

Identities of the Jew and the Hungarian

András Gerő

Our concepts often present themselves as ready interpretations. Their casual use saves us much effort by making something appear "self-evident" that would otherwise demand an explanation. The word "Jew" is used as a more or less self-evident category of identity, even though the content it conveys has been just as much transformed by secularization, modernization, assimilation, and acculturation as any other category of identity. Whatever meaning we ascribe to it, the word "Jew" denotes a minority throughout the diaspora, and as with every minority, what is decisive is the content of the category expressing the majority, and how that content changes. Majority and minority—under any interpretation—contextualize each other and take their meanings with reference to each other. The question of what is what, and how we define things, is a matter of decoding or, more precisely, the means of decoding. For this, of course, we also need the words and concepts by which we attempt to say anything at all. The means of decoding is history itself. History can be interpreted as the story of society, the course of politics, and as many other things such as awareness, identity, self-identity, and classifications of ourselves made or expressed by others. This is true for Jews, Hungarians, Communists, etc. Seemingly straightforward identities could be ambiguous, and sometimes mutually entangled, or even deliberately confused. Interpretation is more and more difficult, if for no other reason than we also have to interpret the interpreter.

In the Europe before secularization and the modern idea of the nation—up to the nineteenth century in Hungary—a Jew was a person whose religion was Jewish. The Jewish religious enlightenment in German-speaking Europe reinterpreted much of religion and religious rules, and thus created major differences among believers of the same religion (there is a substantial amount of scholarship on this subject, see, e.g., Katz; Katzburg). Followers of the diverging movements may have criticized, indeed vilified, each other, but this did nothing to change the fact that Jewishness meant Judaism, even if there were wider and wider differences as to what was regarded as Judaism. Jews argued and wrangled with each other, but everyone else regarded them as Jews on the grounds of their religion. In consequence, prejudices against Jews was known as anti-Judaism, since it was expressed in the name of Christianity, against Jews as followers of Judaism. However, the internal cracks caused the Judaism-based concept of Jewishness in Hungary to fall apart within a couple of decades. By the late nineteenth and early twentieth centuries, religious identity and self-identity had broken into three distinct groups: The neology, the orthodoxy, and the *status quo ante* movements (see McCagg; Venetiáner). Depending on the movement they adhered to, Jews went to different synagogues, dressed differently, and led different lives. As Judaism's cracks deepened, Jews in Hungary became divided. Their uniform image in the eyes of non-Jews could, of course, have remained intact, but other changes were taking their effect on the concept of the Jew.

In the nineteenth century Jews in Hungary experienced the results of a combination of existing social prejudices, the tradition of anti-Judaism, and the beginnings of equal rights. They also experienced the Hungarian national uprising against Austrian rule, with the promise of equality, followed by riots involving anti-Judaist rhetoric and a tendency towards and early emergence of modern anti-Semitism. And of course they experienced the—somewhat belated—acceptance to equal rank by the modern Hungarian national consciousness when an Act of Parliament was passed on the issue in 1849. Beset with pitfalls and setbacks as it was, the process nonetheless gained further reinforcement immediately after the Compromise with Austria in 1867, when equal rights and emancipation for Jews was enshrined in law (on the history of Jews in Hungary in the nineteenth-century and in the Austro-Hungarian Monarchy, see Bernstein; Bányai; Gerő; Gerő, Patterson, and Koncz; Miskolczy). The possibility and challenge of national identity became an increasingly broader reality under the liberal political disposition in the years that followed. The rising current of assimilation—a term that covers a highly complex set of phenomena—swelled to become the mainstream of Jewish affairs. Examining the appeal that assimilation held for Jews explains much in social terms of what was behind religious fragmentation. The power of neologism grew from national—and thus secular—identification. Jews, at least in the minds of many, became Hungarian, or, more precisely, Hungarians of the Mosaic faith. The power and depth of assimilation may seem less convincing in retrospect, but the fact remains that more and more Jews saw themselves as Hungarians, and were increasingly looked on first of all as Hungarians, and only secondarily as Jews, just like others for whom national identity was primary, with other considerations—such as being Catholic or Protestant—coming only in second place. It was this momentum of change that created the political conditions for the divorce of church and state (on Jewish secularization and modernization in Hungary, see, e.g., Karády).

At the turn of the nineteenth to the twentieth century, however, the picture changed again. It was a two-way change, stemming both from intra-Jewish affairs and from a discourse that reflected various processes and led to a new framework of attitudes. Many Jews, as traditional Judaism gradually waned and identification with worldly affairs spread, began to regard religious Jewishness as a burden that could be shed. It was a burden in the first place because, even after reforms, it prescribed many regulations obstructing everyday secular life. It was simply uncomfortable. But abandoning religious constraints also made it easier to escape from prejudices against Jews. And on the spiritual side, the personal need for Jewish religion diminished because it was replaced in many respects by membership in a community (on the history of the turn of the century in this context, see, in particular, Beller; Boyer; Hanák; Schorske; Vermes). Responses varied depending on individuals' positions: The Hungarianization of foreign surnames (*magyarosítás*) became common, and not a few people, after rising in society, converted to Christianity in the hope of securing their rise social status and making themselves Hungarian more firmly. And then there came the opportunity to identify with something universal and very secular, going well beyond national essentialism, namely socialism. In many ways, socialism's promise and its rituals made it the universal religion of international and worldly redemption, sweeping aside every religious, national, and other inherited cultural dimensions. The result was the hitherto unthinkable phenomenon of the Jew who was no longer a Jew. None of this ran to a final consummation, of course, and it was the divergences along the way that lent the traditional view of the process, the fragmentation and disintegration of the Jewry, its characteristic features. It was a double incompleteness. Firstly, no single approach proved to have sufficient merits to eliminate completely, liquidate, or prevent the progress of the other approaches. By the early twentieth century, there were living in the same country the traditionally recognizable figures of religious orthodoxy, the muscular communities of reformed Jews, ambitious converted "Jews" who made it right up to ministerial ranks, socialist intellectual agitators, and more-Magyar-than-the-Magyars writers, poets, and patriotic poetasters (see Venetiáner). Then there was incompleteness of the individual kind. It was possible to take up diverging processes simultaneously, or to vary the tempo, and a single person or family often declined to follow one route or another to its conclusion. Socialist-minded young intellectuals pursued their studies with the financial support of families who maintained and cultivated Jewish traditions; the relations of converted Jews remained Jewish; and intellectuals declaring identification with Hungarian culture looked, actually, towards German culture. There was wide scope for variation and innumerable "inconsistencies," all signs that the concept of "the" Jew, established previously, had been shattered. The external world not only tolerated this but encouraged it and often granted confirmation of it. Encouragement, toleration, and confirmation ensured the authenticity of a wide diversity and choice of identities, however aesthetically jarring some or all of them might be. But while Jewishness was disintegrating, a reaction was developing against Jews that identified as its enemy the "total Jew" (see, among others, Tamási). Aspirations to integration crumbled, and the question from then on was: If Jewish identity has fragmented, but the imaginary creature of the total Jew was being identified as the enemy, what will happen next? This question could only be answered by the majority, which we will refer to collectively as Hungarians.

Hungarian national consciousness and Hungarian nationalism followed without many deviations the same standard structural course of birth and formation as for other nations. What is important here, however, is the kind of national consciousness into which Jews assimilated and how the internal content of that national consciousness changed in the twentieth century. The defining force in the birth of Hungarian national consciousness was the inability of a feudal and aristocratic society to satisfy bourgeois needs via the accustomed means of Christian universalism. Bourgeois energies could only be nourished by creation of a new community, one in which as many people as possible had an interest in operating and maintaining it. Privileges had to be spread wider, and in a way that the new form of social organization maximized its own potential. National identity here meant that the privileged community was replaced by a linguistic, i.e., a cultural community. The nation as a linguistic-cultural community is a structural element in the formation of every nation. A quirk of the Hungarian case, with a unique implication for the identity question, is that fear was one of the inspirations for nation-formation, and indeed one of its results. The "inspirational" fear was that if the Hungarians did not become a European nation, then they would be left out of the current of European civilization and be cast into poverty.

There was only one solution offering real prospects, and the culture-based national consciousness found the appropriate response almost immediately: This response asserted the insufficiency of thinking in terms of a cultural community alone. There was also a need to form a consciousness of a political community. The content of political community could be none other than civil liberty. Civil liberty was the only course that could ensure the leading social role of the existing elite while offering the peasantry—which made up the mass of the country's inhabitants—some real prospects, and something they could identify with. The political concept of the nation remained alongside the cultural even after the Compromise of 1867 between Austria and Hungary, since the same liberty applied to everyone regardless of national affiliation in the cultural sense. There was no national distinction in terms of rights, and the universal value of freedom took expression in the Hungarian political nation (from the large amount of scholarship on Hungarian national consciousness perhaps the most comprehensive is the multivolume *Hungarian Liberals* I edited). Hungarian national identity had its own visions and versions of the enemy. By the turn of the nineteenth to the twentieth century, Hungarians—not least because of Jewish assimilation to the liberal Hungarian identity—had become the ethnic majority in Hungary. This fact, coupled with the problems created by a sclerotic system unable to make social reforms, strengthened the national consciousness seeking in an internal enemy just as much as the appearance of social-political radicalism in various forms. The latter put the main emphasis on social and political, rather than national identity, and by this means sought to distinguish between good and evil. The former, the narrowing national consciousness, partly in reaction to socio-political radicalism, found more and more criteria for not admitting, indeed for excluding people from the nation. The original, "traditional" national consciousness sounded increasingly empty, since it was least able to supply what there was the greatest demand for at the turn of the century: an internal enemy.

For a brief moment, the First World War gave new strength to the traditional national consciousness, since the population had above all to be mobilized against an external enemy. At the end of the war, the avoidance of the consequences of defeat preferred the socially radical "Magyar" concept or—when this seemed to be insufficient—class-based internationalism going beyond Hungary. But the consequences of defeat in war proved unavoidable. It was this, and not the revolutions, that dictated the content of Hungarian national consciousness. In the remnant country, Hungarians became an overwhelming majority, but Hungarian nationalism suffered a catastrophic defeat, losing two-thirds of its historic state territory, and a third of people declaring themselves Hungarian found themselves subject to another state (on this complex issue, see Romsics). With the concept of "Hungarian" having branched in many directions, the ideology of the inter-war period under Admiral Horthy followed the path of constriction and exclusion. This ideology prescribed that Hungarianness (*magyarság*) was incompatible with the concepts of equality under the law and the indivisibility of civil liberty. A program of legislation instituted discrimination on religious grounds by targeting, primarily, Jewish Hungarians. However, at least until the late 1930s, the system did not yield to pressure for a national concept based on race, and the guiding state principle remained that of cultural restrictions. However, by the 1930s, the culturally-restricting national consciousness was gradually losing its official endorsement, giving way to a proposition of identity aimed at defining Hungarianness in terms of race. This demanded more than just Christianity, since according to this twisted thinking racial origin derived from pagan Magyar roots, to which Christianity was just a mongrel addition (this resulted in comical situations: the prime minister Gyula Gömbös, a prominent apostle of the racial idea, had German forebears, and the Arrow Cross nazi and racial fanatic, Ferenc Szálasi, was of Armenian parentage; see Gergely). State power essentially adopted variations of the national consciousness that sought restrictions of rights. The choice of exactly which variation, and when, was guided by domestic and international affairs.

Thus, from the late 1930s laws were passed depriving people of rights on racial grounds with the aim of excluding gradually in particular one group of Hungarian citizens, the Jews, from the nation (extensive documentation of racially-based legislation is in Vértes; on the thinking on the background to the legislation, see Csizmadia). Since this arose as a racial and not a religious issue, the widely divergent complex of Jewish identities, and identities of people who had renounced their Jewishness, was reduced to a single category. It then became irrelevant whether somebody was orthodox, neologist, converted, atheist, or any of the many other possibilities. In turn, those who had assimilated, had assimilated into another

Hungarian national consciousness. They cited their patriotic figures, their contribution to the elevation of the Hungarian nation, their propagation of culture, and many other things. But they were addressing a national consciousness that no longer existed, at least not in the realms of power. The new, racially-motivated national consciousness, relegating legal equality in the name of protection of the race, was simply deaf to the voice of the old Hungarian national consciousness, as was in its interests, an integral part of its self-definition. In my view, the 1944 endgame cannot be blamed solely on the Nazi invasion. The essential mental and state preparations had already been made, and the racially-based, liberty-depriving Hungarian national consciousness was already in place. Years before the Holocaust of Hungarian Jewry, officialdom had spelled out what and how much could be taken away from the Jews, and had made it acceptable to take someone's rightful property and give it to someone else. The Jews, clinging to the coordinates of traditional Hungarian national consciousness, retreated by intensifying their loyalty, their respect for the law, and thereby their own defenselessness, since anything that could have made them eligible for being regarded as the enemy was completely absent from their own identity (see Hofmann; Schmidt; Sándor). This racial and disenfranchising Hungarian national consciousness resulted in unbroken victory. The scope of life for Jews narrowed, they were deprived of everything that had been theirs, including, for many, life itself (on the Holocaust of Hungarian Jews, see Braham; Karsai). It counted for little whether one was an Olympic champion, an eminent scholar of Hungarian literature, a great poet, or a law-abiding citizen.

The Holocaust brought unparalleled destruction. Some forms of Jewish identity lost much of their pre-genocide sociological weight within the Jewish-Hungarian community through sheer physical elimination. Such was orthodoxy, which had been strong in some parts of the country outside Budapest. Since the vast majority of non-Budapest Jews were liquidated, it effectively vanished (unfortunately, the subject of the Hungarian Jews and Jewish identity in all its forms in the post-Second World War period has been neglected; however, on religious life and the intellectual life surrounding religion, see Csorba; Ungvári). At the same time, the Holocaust created a unifying experience for very diverse identities and a common history. This common history brought together those who had long been far apart from each other. It could also be said that whereas anti-Semitism could be lived with, got round, or got over, the Holocaust did not permit this behavior and attitude of avoidance. The words of racially-based anti-Semitism became final and total acts, and the acts could not be ignored. In the logic of the events of the Holocaust, identity became worthless, giving way to an inexorable common history and shared suffering. Nonetheless, the Holocaust did not change the historical nature of the disintegrated Jewish identity. At most, it altered the internal proportions. The anti-Semitic logic of the "total Jew," even though it took the lives of hundreds of thousands in Hungary, did not come out victorious in the history of identity. Some Jews who survived, having in many cases lost their families, left the country and—

out of conviction, need, or for emotional reasons—chose the Zionist solution, becoming Israelis. Some left the country for countries other than the newly-forming Israel. They could no longer live in Hungary, but that did not mean they broke from their Hungarian identities. The neologist consciousness also remained, but its adherents were much reduced in number and dwindled even further under the later pressure of state secularization. Many also chose Christianity. And there also remained that other established routes out of Jewishness and class-based identity. The latter also became strongly articulated, since the formation of the Communist system reduced or eliminated the opportunity for expressing other identities. The suppression and obscuration of alternative forms of consciousness was a special feature of the Communist system—one of the reasons it is referred to as a dictatorship—and was not restricted to Jewish self-expression. This all meant that old self-definitions of Jewish identity as Hungarianness, in the forms of minor property owner, petit bourgeois or grand bourgeois, could not appear publicly, but they still existed and lived on in the ritual of private lives.

However, for those seeking a way to cast off their Jewishness, the communist-socialist identity meant more than just another familiar option, even if it had already existed before the war. To abandon Jewishness was now an act supported and promoted by the authorities. It should be re-emphasized here that a commitment to class-based and universal self-identification, if pursued consistently, meant abandoning any form of Jewish identity. Taking such a step was influenced by both repulsion and attraction: repulsion from retaining any aspect of Jewishness and attraction to class-based Communist identity with its negligible national content. The repulsive forces fed on the weakness of existing bonds, the lack of comfort offered by Jewish spirituality for the radical stigmatization and disadvantage experienced during the Holocaust, the failure of any Hungarian form of Jewish identity to provide a relevant response, and the reduction of Jewishness in direct memory to no more than shared suffering. The attraction was that Communism at least promised to overcome anti-Semitism, so that no one would be suppressed (at the same time, not to be neglected are the instances of Jewish persecution even after the war, see Pelle).

The attraction of Communism was not confined to Jews of assorted backgrounds. But the motivation for post-Holocaust Jews to identify with Communism stemmed from more than the promise that the Communist order would overcome anti-Semitism. What was on offer was a world-view in which anti-Semites themselves, and the perpetrators of the Holocaust themselves, were held up as the principal enemies. Nazis and fascists were fixed as the antithesis of Communist identity. Of course there were internal dissonances. The dissonances did not in the main derive from an identification of the strong similarities between Nazi and Communist methods and ways of thinking. The ideal of "class war" and the savagery of the war had obscured these, or at least made them subject to argument. The strength of emotional and political legitimization of the struggle against the "evil class enemy" and the Nazi brute proved powerful enough to keep the doubts at bay. A much bigger problem was that in the model country of socialism, the Soviet Union, anti-Semitism had been incorporated into official policy. However, anti-Semitism was a much lesser part of socialist politics in Hungary than in the Soviet Union, and identity did not become so detached from experience, which is perhaps why the socio-psychological phenomenon of cognitive dissonance did not occur so strongly here. The conception that Communist identity held up anti-Semitism as the image of the enemy could thus be more or less sustained. But there was one factor that made the choice of Communist identity easier for those who had a national identity, in this case a Hungarian national identity. Communism in Hungary—despite stereotypes to the contrary—set out to assert its power by means of vigorous national propaganda, although the emphasis and strength of the national rhetoric changed its nature somewhat during the socialist period (I have dealt with this problem in my *Az államosított forradalom* [The Nationalized Revolution]). It is undoubtedly true that the "national" world-view was highly selective, containing only what proved useful currently for socialist ideology. In general, two elements were highlighted: one was the "progressive" aspect of national history and the other was the aspect of independence. It might be summed up by saying that the more authoritarian the system became, the more it promoted insurgents as its precursors, the less independent the country, the more it touted the historical personalities of independence. But the desire for identification was little moved by such paradoxes: after all, every religious world-view had always carried with it irresolvable contradictions. So now those Jews who had survived assimilation, had a Hungarian consciousness, and treated anti-Semitism as the enemy, became the potential and actual subjects of Communist identity.

People whose Jewishness retained a religious meaning or to whom middle-class lifestyle and personal property were important, naturally enough, regarded Communism not so much an attraction as a development to keep their distance from. The reaction of each individual was thus a combination of the above described repulsions and attractions. Some became party members to avoid trouble, more as a "tribute" paid to the dictatorship than identification with it. With racially-based deportation out of the way, some nonetheless found themselves sitting on a train again, this time the victims of their class situation. But there were some who adopted a Communist identity with faith and identification, and it was a matter of chance, or the strength of character, whether they became propagandists of the new faith, or its inquisitors. So it was not to avenge the Jews that they took this step but to escape from any kind of Jewishness, and find relief in a new identity. Vengeance for the Jews was out of the question in any case, because those retaining Jewish or Jewish-middle-class status were oppressed by the system just like everyone else. Either because they were religious or because they dared to show themselves as secular Jewish citizens (the formation of secular Jewish consciousness merits study of its own, since both the secular socialist world and the resolutely anti-Israeli

Communist propaganda were both involved in its creation. This form of Jewish identity became especially visible following the political transition, although its precedents had already appeared in the discourse, in urban folklore, and in dedicated samizdat publications). The anti-Semitic and disenfranchising Hungarian national consciousness said: "it doesn't matter what you are—if I say you are a Jew, you are a Jew." Communism said: "it doesn't matter what you are, if you are not a Communist, you cannot be anything else." Communism—in its aims and for a while in practice—wanted to expunge and suppress any identities differing from it, thus forcing people into disguise or self-deception. It was to be feared, and fear is something that can be escaped into. A large section of Jews in Hungary, whatever kind of Jewish identity they adhered to, took the option of disguise: "do not talk about it, forget it, cover it up." It was something like an administratively enforced assimilation (on these issues, see Erős; M. Kovács; A. Kovács, Erős; Sanders). But this applied equally to dissenting articulations of Hungarian national consciousness. As if national identity, at least formally, had dozed into some kind of "socialist patriotism." And all the time, every identity that had entered the twentieth century was still there, sleeping, taking cover, being articulated only in the barest outlines, if at all. Life seemed to take its course along curious paths, with strange mythologies and counter-mythologies, from novice rabbi to Communist, from Communist to security policeman, from security policeman to a critical pressure-release valve within the system. Starting as a Jew, they found that everything that was Jewish had disappeared by the time grown up. And the process sometimes went into reverse: From Jew to Communist and back to Jew again. And of course there were those who lived here, beheld the specter of Communism, and just wanted to survive (in this sense, István Szabó's film *The Taste of Sunshine* is pure history of identity and one of the strengths of the film is the demonstration that what gave rise to Communism does not exonerate the horrors of Communism; e.g., see Suleiman).

As Jews and Hungarians today, in the clear air of freedom, we discover the existence of things we had never seen, and found many things whose existence we had assumed to be mere illusions. What seemed to have disappeared was here all the time and what was here may no longer exist. What is with us is the past and the need to interpret it. And interpret we must, because we have to come to terms with everything that happened. Or if not come to terms, at least to understand, to get the past in proportion, and put it in its place. We need all this to interpret individual lives; to interpret our utterances; to understand ourselves; because we ourselves are the full history of identity.

Works Cited

Bányai, Viktória. *Zsidó oktatásügy Magyarországon 1780–1850* (Jewish Education in Hungary 1780–1850). Doctoral Dissertation. Budapest: Eötvös Loránt University, 2001.

Beller, Steven. *Vienna and the Jews 1867–1938: A Cultural History*. Cambridge: Cambridge UP, 1989.

Bernstein, Béla. *A negyvennyolcas magyar szabadságharc és a zsidók* (The 1848 Hungarian War of Independence and the Jews). 1898. Budapest: Múlt és Jövő, 1998.

Boyer, John W. *Political Radicalism in Late Imperial Vienna: Origins of the Christian Social Movement 1848–1897*. Chicago: Chicago UP, 1981.

Boyer, John W. *Culture and Political Crisis in Vienna: Christian Socialism in Power 1897–1918*. Chicago: Chicago UP, 1995.

Braham, Randolph L. *The Politics of Genocide: The Holocaust in Hungary*. New York: Columbia UP, 1981. 2 vols.

Braham, Randolph L. *A magyar holokauszt* (The Hungarian Holocaust). Trans. Mária Schmidt. Budapest: Gondolat, 1988. 2 vols.

Csizmadia, Ervin. *Makkai János*. Budapest: Új Mandátum, 2001.

Csorba, László. "Izraelita felekezeti élet Magyarországon a vészkorszaktól a nyolcvanas évekig" ("Israelite Sects in Hungary from the Age of Peril to the Eighties"). *Hét évtized a hazai zsidóság életében* (Seven Decades in the Lives of Hungarian Jews). Ed. Ferenc L. Lendvai L., Anikó Sohár, and Pál Horváth. Budapest: Hungarian Academy of Sciences, 1990. Vol. 2., 61–190.

Gergely, Jenő. *Gömbös Gyula: Egy politikai karrier* (Gyula Gömbös: A Political Career). Budapest: Vince, 2001.

Gerő, András. *Az államosított forradalom. 1848 centenáriuma* (The Nationalized Revolution: The Centenary of 1848). Budapest: Új Mandátum, 1998.

Gerő, András, ed. *Hungarian Liberals: Portraits*. Budapest: Új Mandátum, 1998. 14 vols.

Gerő, András, James Patterson, and Enikő Koncz, eds. *Modern Hungarian Society in the Making: The Unfinished Experience*. Budapest: Central European UP, 1995.

Hanák, Péter. *A kert és a műhely* (The Garden and the Workshop). Budapest: Gondolat, 1988.

Karády, Viktor. *Zsidóság és társadalmi egyenlőtlenségek, 1867–1945* (Jews and Social Inequalities, 1867–1945). Budapest: Replika, 2000.

Karsai, László. *Holokauszt*. Budapest: Pannonica, 2001.

Katz, Jacob. *Kifelé a gettóból. A zsidó emancipáció évszázada 1770–1870* (Out of the Ghetto: The Century of Jewish Emancipation 1770–1870). Budapest: Hungarian Academy of Sciences, 1995.

Katz, Jacob. *Végzetes szakadás. Az ortodoxia kiválása a zsidó hitközségekből Magyarországon és Németországban* (Final Break: How Orthodoxy Split from the Jewish Religious Community in Hungary and Germany). Budapest: Múlt és Jövő, 1999.

Katzburg, Nathaniel. *Fejezetek az újkori zsidó történelemből Magyarországon* (Chapters from Modern Jewish History in Hungary). Budapest: Hungarian Academy of Sciences, 1999.

Kovács, András, ed. *Modern Antiszemitizmus*. Budapest: Új Mandátum, 2000.

Kovács, M. Mária, Yitzhak M. Kashtia, and Ferenc Erős, eds. *Zsidóság, identitás, történelem* (Jewishness, Identity, History). Budapest: T-Twins, 1992.

McCagg, William O., Jr. *A History of Habsburg Jews, 1670–1918.* Bloomington: Indiana UP, 1989.

Miskolczy, Ambrus. *A zsidó emancipáció Magyarországon 1849-ben* (Jewish Emancipation in Hungary in 1849). Budapest: Múlt és Jövő, 1999.

Pelle, János. *Az utolsó vérvádak. Az etnikai gyűlölet és a politikai manipuláció keleteurópai történetéről* (The Last Blood Libel: The History of Ethnic Hatred and Political Manipulation in Eastern Europe). Budapest: Pelikán, 1995.

Romsics, Ignác. *Hungary in the 20th Century.* Trans. Timothy Wilkinson. Budapest: Corvina, 1999.

Sanders, Iván. "Metakommunikáció haladóknak. Nádas Péter *Emlékiratok* könyvének zsidó olvasata. A határ és a határolt" ("Advanced Metacommunication: The Jewish Reading of Péter Nádas's *A Book of Memories*"). *A határ és a határolt. Töprengések a magyar-zsidó irodalom létformáiról* (The Boundary and the Restricted: Thoughts on Forms of Hungarian-Jewish Literature). Ed. Petra Török. Budapest: Országos Rabbi Képző Intézet, 1997. 373–87.

Sándor, Tibor. *Őrségváltás után. A zsidókérdés és a filmpolitika, 1938–1944* (After the Change of the Guard: The Jewish Question and Film Policy, 1938–1944). Budapest: Magyar Filmintézet, 1997.

Schmidt, Mária. *Kollaboráció vagy kooperáció. A Budapesti Zsidó Tanács* (Collaboration or Cooperation? The Budapest Jewish Council). Budapest: Minerva, 1990.

Schorske, Carl E. *Fin-de-Siècle Vienna: Politics and Culture.* New York: Vintage, 1981.

Suleiman, Susan Rubin. "Central Europe, Jewish Family History, and *Sunshine.*" *Comparative Central European Culture.* Ed. Steven Tötösy de Zepetnek. West Lafayette: Purdue UP, 2002. 169–88.

Tamási, Györgyi. "Zsidó szellemi élet Magyarországon 1945 után" ("Jewish Intellectual Life in Hungary after 1945"). *Hét évtized a hazai zsidóság életében* (Seven Decades in the Lives of Hungarian Jews). Ed. Ferenc L. Lendvai, Anikó Sohár, and Pál Horváth. Budapest: Hungarian Academy of Sciences, 1990. Vol. 2, 61–300.

Ungvári, Tamás. *Ahasvérus és Shylock: A "zsidókérdés" Magyarországon* (Ahasverus and Shylock: The Jewish Question in Hungary). Budapest: Akadémiai, 1999.

Venetiáner, Lajos. *A magyar zsidóság története a honfoglalástól a világháború kitöréséig, különös tekintettel a gazdasági és művelődési fejlődésre* (History of the Hungarian Jews from the Conquest to the Outbreak of the Great War, with Particular Attention to Economic and Cultural Development). Budapest: Fővárosi, 1922.

Vermes, Gábor. *Tisza István.* Budapest: Századvég, 1994.

Vértes, Róbert, ed. *Magyarországi zsidótörvények és rendeletek, 1938–1849* (Laws and Decrees against Jews in Hungary, 1938–1945). Budapest: Polgár, 1997.

Representing the Holocaust, Kertész's *Fatelessness* and Benigni's *La vita è bella*

Bettina von Jagow

Translated from the German by Sabine Prechter

Imre Kertész—Hungarian Jew, concentration camp survivor, and Nobel Laureate for his work on the spiritual and existential consequences of the Holocaust—has managed to depict the Holocaust in his novel *Fatelessness* in a way that can almost be called scandalous. From the protagonist's own perspective, it tells the story of fourteen-year-old George, beginning with the boy's bidding farewell to his father who leaves home because he has to go to a so-called "work camp," then going on to recount George's own deportation, first to Auschwitz-Birkenau, then to Buchenwald-Zeitz, and ending with the liberation of the camp by the Americans, which leaves George free to go home to his native Budapest. This description can be called "almost scandalous" because it includes every single of the all too well known details of this symbolic era and at the same time manages to do without interpretations or evaluations. George always tries to understand, to find explanations for the general hatred of Jews he encounters, for his life as a prisoner and for the actions and reactions of those Germans that work in the concentration camps. He never doubts his own fate, but rather takes it as a given and accepts his situation in all rationality. Yet, in spite of all the sobriety with which the story is told, the reader cannot but marvel in disbelief at what happens in this narrative (although I am quoting in this paper from the Wilson & Wilson translation of Kertész's *Sorstalanság, Fateless,* I am aware that the correct translation from the Hungarian is *Fatelessness;* see the 2004 translation by Wilkinson).

A completely different trigger for this kind of disbelief and amazement is Roberto Benigni's movie *La vita è bella*. This, too, is an attempt at depicting the Holocaust: Guido, the main character, finds his true love Dora through many turbulences—yet Dora is already promised to another, a rich and renowned man in their hometown. By pulling out all the stops and using his sense of humor and his chaotic warm-heartedness in an often almost Chaplinesque manner, Guido manages to win Dora over. After a cut and a love scene hinted at rather than shown, Guido appears as a family man with Dora and his son Giosuè. This cut is also the symbolic cut between the superficially jolly world outside and the tragic world inside the concentration camp. Benigni's presentation of daily life inside the camp is just as consequent as Kertész's, but much more humorous, in that Guido continues with his slapstick routines and keeps playing the funny "Bappo" for his son, to whom he pretends that "Auschwitz" is a game that they both play together; a game that starts on Giosuè's birthday, the day of their deportation, and the goal of which it is to score a total of 1000 points in order to win a real tank—for Giosuè the gift of his dreams. This way of presenting the Holocaust, in a humorous manner, has stirred many a discussion—in ways that also show the difference in how the first and the second or third generation handle this topic. The main question is always that of authenticity, of entitlement and ownership of "an Auschwitz discourse." Imre Kertész explains this as follows: "Ours is not the time of anti-Semitism, but of Auschwitz. And today's anti-Semites do not wish to distance themselves from Jews, they want Auschwitz" ("Unsere Zeit ist nicht die Zeit des Antisemitismus, sondern die von Auschwitz. Und der Antisemit unserer Zeit will nicht mehr von den Juden abrücken, er will Auschwitz") ("Der Holocaust als Kultur" 63; all subsequent translation is by Sabine Prechter unless noted otherwise).

The need for remembering the Holocaust is seen as a given—but there is still the question as to the how. It is obvious that the larger the chronological distance, the harsher the tone in the acts of memory—in a time that sees specific types of memory, such as the learning memory, the educational memory, and also the experiential memory of Holocaust survivors coming close to extinction. Aleida Assmann (14–15) points out that in order to keep the survivors' memory alive, we need to translate their experiential memory into cultural memory. These translations, on their part, however, often trigger strong criticism that refers to the chosen discourse—an excellent example (among many) of this is W. Michael Blumenthal's 1999 article "Streit um die Erinnerung." Given these facts, it almost seems scandalous that Kertész—in his essay "Der Holocaust als Kultur"—uses Jean Améry's ideas as his starting point for a clear provocation: "On the other hand we cannot help but realize that all these reflexions and their manifestations eventually are a manifestation or even more, namely a product of culture" ("Andererseits kann unserer Aufmerksamkeit nicht entgehen, daß diese Überlegungen und ihre Erscheinungsformen letzten Endes eine Manifestation von Kultur, mehr noch: ein Kulturprodukt darstellen") (59). He also asks whether the Holocaust can be a value-creating instance—his own answer draws on a positive anthropology that marks his dealing with the Holocaust in general: "To be able to survive, a society has to keep alive and constantly renew its knowledge, its awareness of itself, and its own conditions. And if a society decides to maintain the dark obsequies for the Holocaust as an indispensable element of this awareness, this decision is not based on some kind of commiseration or regret but on a vital value judgment. The Holocaust is a value in itself because it has led—over un-measurable tragedy—to unfathomable knowledge and thus holds unmeasurable moral resources" ("Eine lebensfähige Gesellschaft muß ihr Wissen, ihr Bewußtsein von sich selbst und von den eigenen Bedingungen wachhalten und ständig erneuern. Und wenn ihre Entscheidung lautet, daß die schwere, schwarze Trauerfeier für den Holocaust ein unverzichtbarer Bestandteil dieses Bewußtseins ist, dann gründet diese Entscheidung nicht auf irgendwelchem Beileid oder Bedauern, sondern auf einem vitalen Werturteil. Der Holocaust ist ein Wert, weil er über unermeßliches Leid zu unermeßlichem Wissen geführt hat und damit eine unermeßliche moralische Reserve birgt") ("Der Holocaust als Kultur" 68).

In this paper, I compare the "producers"/"manufacturers" of these two works in order to point out the differences between the so-called first and later generations in what can be called using truth in fiction. Kertész's question about the values of the Holocaust is also the question about the discourse of truth and the depictability of the Holocaust. I also focus on the specific kinds of memory as used by Kertész and Benigni—neither uses consequently the productive and ironic way of describing the Holocaust; rather, they employ these elements according to what could be called an apory of memory (on this, see also Eaglestone). These instances display a very special aesthetics that could be called "portraying the Holocaust as culture," an assumption I illustrate with an exemplary analysis of the two works. It becomes clear that wherever memory is no longer able to stretch the limits of what can be described, it recurs to fiction (on second- and third-generation "memoirs" of the Holocaust, see Tötösy de Zepetnek). Fictitious and imaginary structures, such as the ones brought forward by the child as narrator in Kertész's work or the child as the recipient of a narrative in Benigni's film, both point out and close the gap between ratio and imagination and use imagination to describe the indescribable. This process fills "Auschwitz" with anthropologic values and turns it into a "cultural product."

Kertész and Benigni cover the Holocaust in its entirety and both see the presentation of one clipping in the history of anti-Semitism and of the attempt at annihilating this people as their central focus. Both use an abrupt start for their works: in *Sorstalanság* George, the protagonist, tells that "today" he only went to school for a brief while, the introductory sequence of *La vita è bella* makes the viewer believe he is attending a romantic comedy. Both plots lead relatively directly to the clearly connotated world inside the concentration camp, both stories address similar topics such as forced labor or the shortage of food. And a child plays the central role in both stories: in *Sorstalanság* fourteen-year-old George tells his own story, in *La vita è bella* it is Giosuè, the little son that makes Guido tell the story the way it is told, resulting in a structural idiosyncrasy that creates a certain alienating effect. However, in spite of these similarities, the two narratives are very different, the main one being the different perceptional angle on the recipient's part, which Jan Strümpel explains as follows: "Holocaust literature is not accessible only through its texts. Both text and author form an inseparable unit; without the author's reliable integrity, authenticated through his biography, no reliable statements can be made about his work" ("Literatur zum Holocaust erschließt sich nicht allein von ihren Texten her. Text und Autor bilden eine unhintergehbare Einheit; ohne Verlaß auf die biographisch verbürgte Integrität des Autors scheint nichts Verläßliches über dessen Schreiben sagbar") (16–17).

Kertész has himself lived through what he tells in *Sorstalanság;* Benigni, on the other hand, belongs to a generation that needs to rely on texts, images, and narratives for their view of the Holocaust. This difference might bring about certain differences in both perception and depiction and also the question as to which way of depicting the Holocaust may be seen as adequate (see Köppen and Scherpe 1–12). These questions center around the notion of a so-called "ethics of memory" and is answered for Kertész by taking the notion of authenticity into account and for Benigni by recurring to Kertész. In his article "Wem gehört Auschwitz?" ("Who Owns Auschwitz?"), written on the occasion of Benigni's film, Kertész deals with this thematic field, and I discuss this article, together with other texts by Kertész, to illustrate his specific concept of remembering the Holocaust. Peter Szondi's variation on Adorno's claim that no poetry is possible after Auschwitz might serve as a starting point for a definition of Kertész's concept of memory in *Sorstalanság*. Szondi adds that no poetry is possible unless it is *because* of Auschwitz. Kertész's novel shows that there is language after and even a language specifically for Auschwitz and he stresses the indispensability of the actual use of this language (102). In his *Gályanapló* (*Galeerentagebuch*/Galley Boat-Log) Kertész claims that "The concentration camp can only be pictured as a literary oeuvre, not as anything real. (Not even—and even less so—by someone experiencing it.)" / Das Konzentrationslager ist ausschließlich als Literatur vorstellbar, als Realität nicht. (Auch nicht—und sogar am wenigsten—wenn wir es erleben.)" (253). Kertész stresses the need for memory by saying that time has taught him that remembering is the only way to liberation. As a writer, he stages memory in the realm of fiction and for that he needs imagination—just like Benigni in his work as a director. Kertész (*Dank des Preisträgers* 36) used his speech of acceptance in Leipzig to illustrate his views of the function of imagination:

> It is imagination that causes the problem . . . and talking about literature and the Holocaust means talking about imagination. Since it is here that lies the big paradox, the *contradictio in adiecto*, because only through aesthetic imagination is it that we are able to create an image of the Holocaust, this unseizable and inscrutable reality. Yet thinking the Holocaust is such an immense project by itself, an almost physical effort, that it usually means asking too much of those who try to do so. The fact that all this has truly happened makes it difficult to even think about it. And how can horror be the object of aesthetization since it is true horror and holds nothing original? Instead of a paradigmatic kind of death, these facts have only heaps of corpses to offer.

> Ja, der Phantasie; das ist hier das Problem . . . und wenn von Literatur und Holocaust gesprochen wird, dann muß von ihr gesprochen werden. Hier nämlich liegt das große Paradoxon, die *contradictio in adjecto* verborgen;

> denn vom Holocaust, dieser unfaßlichen und undurchschaubaren Wirklich-
> keit, ist es uns einzig mit Hilfe der ästhetischen Vorstellungskraft möglich,
> uns eine wirkliche Vorstellung zu machen. Indes ist den Holocaust zu
> denken an sich schon ein so ungeheures Unterfangen, eine Schultern zer-
> malmende Anstrengung, daß sie zumeist über die Belastbarkeit derjenigen
> geht, die sich darum bemühen. Daß es wirklich geschehen ist, macht schon
> die einfache Vorstellung daran schwer. Und wie kann das Entsetzen Gegen-
> stand des Ästhetischen sein, da es ein Wirkliches ist und nichts Originelles
> enthält? Die Tatsachen können anstelle eines paradigmatischen Todes nur
> Berge von Leichen bieten. (*Dank des Preisträgers* 36)

Thus, Kertész sees real and fictitious discourse on Auschwitz as basically equivalent; for him, authenticity is not a matter of reconstructing events exactly but of
representing the aura of the experience. This is why for him there is no difference
between historiography and poetry on Auschwitz. This point of view situates
Kertész in the tradition of Hayden White's train of thought: White claims that historical description differs from fictitious events in exactly the way Aristotle describes this difference. The question as to whether facticity and narrativity may be
seen as equal in depictions of the Holocaust has stirred up many a discussion (see,
e.g., Diner). Yet, for *Fatelessness* it is relatively safe to claim this equivalence,
judging from several autopoetic statements by Kertész, who, however, stresses the
need for a clear "ethics of memory" for each depiction ("Wem gehört Auschwitz?"
56), an ethics for which he claims the following criteria: he wants to see the far-
reaching ethical consequences of Auschwitz implicated in the work—a characteristic which he defines as "the HUMAN BEING written in capital letters at its heart"
("der mit Großbuchstabe geschriebene MENSCH—und mit ihm das Ideal des
Humanen") ("Wem gehört Auschwitz?" 150). He also wants to see a clear statement about "the organic interrelation between our deformed way of life both in
public and private and the possibility for another Holocaust" ("[den] organische[n]
Zusammenhang zwischen unserer in der Zivilisation wie im Privaten deformierten
Lebensweise und der Möglichkeit des Holocaust") ("Wem gehört Auschwitz?"
150) which means that he does not want to see Auschwitz as a historical exception
but to integrate it into the humanly as much as this is possible. He also postulates
that Auschwitz has to be seen as a global experience and not just an "issue between
Jews and Germans" as two separate collectives ("Wem gehört Auschwitz?" 151).
This is why Kertész sees any imaginable depiction of Auschwitz as adequate as long
as it exemplifies the values of civilization, humanity, and freedom against the in-
credible breach of civilization that started even earlier than 1933 and saw its apo-
gee in the Second World War.

For those who see the Holocaust as a breach of civilization, there is no way
for its representations to follow any conventional aesthetics. Kertész sees the continuous transition of places and ideas of memory as his way of remembering
Auschwitz, even if he chooses a very specific angle for his depiction, the sober per-

spective of a fourteen-year-old protagonist. Benigni, on the other hand, who is not a survivor himself, can only make a claim to authenticity in that his depiction supports an original experience. His is a re-production of Auschwitz and an example of how "writing" in the realm of fiction approaches somehow the metaphorical "reading" of historical facts. Thus the historical knowledge about the Holocaust is necessarily of a literary nature (see Young; Hillis Miller). It is this literary aspect that Benigni stresses in his humorous contributions in *La vita è bella* (see Steinlein 97–106)—contributions such as Guido's amorous escapades, for instance with a beautiful young woman falling into his arms directly from the hayloft on one of his trips to the countryside, or his own strategies such as running around an entire block just to meet his beloved Dora "by accident" in the city, but also contributions such as Guido's clownish routines in the camp that make the reader choke on the disparity of the serious topic and the way the "hero" treats it. Comedy is staged on both the *histoire* and the discourse levels. Comparing the depiction of the protagonists to an omniscient auctorial narrator's perspective, one has to state that the more is told, the more the discourse level undermines the *histoire* level by turning the comic value away from the what to the how in Guido's experience—and that is where a relieving kind of laughter becomes inhibited.

The starting point for this might be the scene with Guido imitating the school inspector from Rome, explaining to the children the "race manifesto" by referring to impeccable earlobes, good shanks, and a well-shaped belly button. Although Guido's attempt at impressing Dora is obvious, there is more than just a hint of bitterness in this scene—just as in Guido's last comic scene, in which he passes Giosuè on his way to his execution. Giosuè does not know that this is the last time he will ever see his father and Guido does his Chaplinesque routine in order for Giosuè to remember him forever as his funny "Bappo." It is this abrupt transition from an uninhibited to an inhibited laughter that illustrates Benigni's intention not just to make a comic movie—it is actually and in particular the function of the comic elements that shows his seriousness: after Guido's and Giosuè's deportation, it is their function to give Giosuè a chance to survive what is happening; whenever Giosuè might feel terrified, Guido invents stories or evokes the "rules of the game" he has invented. Those phenomena that make clear that the sober way of telling the story in *Fatelessness* is no longer possible in being treated in a comic way in Benigni's movie—one might suspect that these are the exact phenomena that make it necessary for the imaginary to be told. Both presentations, as different as they may be, make the spectator marvel at the stories they tell, and both seemingly incarnate a strong testimonial power—a characteristic Kertész, too, appears to see as indispensable: "and if we see the need to keep the memory of what has happened alive, this will not be through official speeches but through witnesses" (*Fateless* 55). This is why Kertész sees more truth in Benigni's movie than in Spielberg's *Schindler's List*—and this "truth" is not about authenticity, but it is, in Kertész's words, "the soul" of a depiction of the Holocaust ("Wem gehört Auschwitz?" 152). This truth explains the credibility of Benigni's work—the invented game is part of experienced reality, which can only become credible in the discourse of fiction.

Unlike Benigni's film, Kertész's novel is not situated entirely in the realm of the unreal; rather, it suggests to the reader that he/she finds himself in the middle of an at least partially autobiographic report on the experiences of a young boy in Budapest and later in Auschwitz-Birkenau and Buchenwald. The tone of the narrative, however, is intriguing: the reader appears always to be ahead of the boy, already imagining the horror scenarios that are to follow George's reading the name of Auschwitz-Birkenau out to the other deportees on the train. Yet George's own description makes everything seem like a first-time experience while we as readers know that it is just a fictitious reliving of factual history. However, there are passages in *Fatelessness* that do not correspond to this style or structure, and I employ two of these key passages to illustrate the function of "Auschwitz" as a "cultural product." The first example is George's attempt at "conveying the idea of being a Jew" (*Fateless* 43) to a girl his age who lives in the same house. We know that George is a regular boy from Budapest, just like the other kids who live in his apartment building and he does not speak Yiddish, nor does he understand the prayers his Uncle Lajos tries to recite with him before his father's departure. Given a situation in which he thinks he has to explain what is different about Jews, what makes them appear as despicable as they seem to most inhabitants of the city, he starts in his very individual manner, using the example of the baker who always cuts thinner pieces of bread for Jews than for non-Jews:

> He didn't respond to my greeting. It was common knowledge in the neighborhood that he couldn't stand Jews. That's why he tossed me a piece of bread a few grams short of the allotment. But I heard some talk that this was how he also kept some of the bread. And somehow, from his angry glance and his clever movements, I understood at that moment why he had no choice but to dislike Jews. For if he liked them, he'd be left with the unpleasant feeling that he was cheating them. This way he acted according to his convictions, his acts being governed by an ideal, and that made everything entirely different, of course. (*Fateless* 9–10)

The girl does not understand this argument, and thus George tries to illustrate "the idea of being Jewish" with the simpler symbol of the yellow star. Again, the girl objects, saying that there have to be internal and not only external differences, and although George does not agree, he still tries to explain. His last straw is the story of the prince and the pauper: two children, interchanged shortly after birth, and just as the pauper, who should be the prince, has to live a pauper's life, the girl has to live her life as a Jew. And this seems to be the convincing explanation—the girl does not ask any further questions and seems to have understood (*Fateless* 44–45). This pattern displays the poetological core of Kertész's depiction of the Holocaust: Once George finds himself at a loss of words to explain a situation rationally, he starts telling a story, using his imagination to answer the girl's question. The hatred of Jews, which cannot be explained or understood rationally, is made explicit with the help of imagination, and what is even more astonishing is the finishing sentence of George's narration, describing his feelings after the girl's understanding has made her break out in tears: "But still, somehow, I felt uncomfortable. Who knows why, but now for the first time I felt something like shame" (*Fateless* 29). This is one of the rare moments in *Fatelessness* where feelings are involved, the other one being a scene where, after his descriptions of his itinerary via Auschwitz-Birkenau and Buchenwald, his camp experiences in Zeitz and his way back to Buchenwald, his thoughts about what is going on around him display a positive anthropological dimension in a depiction of what is un-representable.

This thinking about the outside and the inside, the visible and the invisible is a central notion in this novel. It appears already in George's focus on the visible symbol of the yellow star and it is also a visual impression, that of beautiful and clean uniforms, that leaves a mark on him upon his arrival in Auschwitz-Birkenau: "He too, like the prisoner in the baths, wore tailored clothes, and he had hair that seemed unusual to me, with a dark-blue cap covering it, known at home as a Basque cap. On his feet were some good-looking yellow shoes, and on his arm a red ribbon immediately announced his authority. I at once saw that I'd have to revise, it seemed, a concept that they had taught me at home, according to which clothes don't make the man" (76). Yet, once the crimes committed in Auschwitz are no longer disguised, this way of thinking changes completely. George withdraws from his—failing—body into some spiritual existence: "Yet as far as my living was concerned, I doubtless existed, even if I was only sputtering along with the flame turned entirely down. But still something within me burned—the flame of life, as they used to say—in other words my body was still there. I was thoroughly familiar with it, only somehow I myself no longer lived inside it" (134–35)—his only chance to survive. He creates a room of his own, and again this is a deeply emotional scene: "the bodies pressing against mine no longer disturbed me. Somehow I was even glad that they were there with me, that their bodies and mine were so connected and so similar, and now for the first time I felt a strange, unusual, somewhat shy, almost clumsy feeling toward them. Perhaps it was love, I think" (135).

Had he relied on rationality, George might not have survived the concentration camp. The language of rationality would not have covered much of what he has gone through. George's strategy is a deeply human one—feelings like shame and love grow and lead to a rationalization of the situation in which they appear, and the fear that is present in the situation described above would not have been bearable without the love that is evoked in the very same situation. Benigni does the same, albeit in a very different way. His is also a work of translation; he, too, tries to engrave facts from the extinction of the Jews between into some kind of cultural memory. Also his work is based on a positive anthropology. It is this "translatory" aspect that becomes most strikingly important in the scene in which an SS officer wants to explain the camp rules to the newly arrived. Guido volunteers as an interpreter—and what follows is a discourse split paradoxically, two sequences of utterances meant to be semantically equivalent, but in reality entirely different. Under the commando voice of the SS officer, who is explaining the cruel rules, Guido uses simultaneous translation to explain the rules of the game he has invented, one of these rules being that no inmate is to demand a jelly sandwich unless he wants to lose points—Guido's way of controlling all the fears he has with regard to Giosuè's behaviors that might prove fatal in the camp context:

German SS man to prisoners:	Guido to Giosuè:
— Listen, I won't repeat what I am telling you now.	— The game begins—only those present are allowed to take part.
— There is only one reason you have been deported to this camp...	— In order to win, you need to score 1,000 points. The first prize is a real tank.
— . . . you're here to work.	— Lucky blighter!
— Any attempt at sabotage will be punished by the death penalty. The execution will be carried out with shots in the back and will take place in the main yard.	— The current ranking will be announced over loudspeaker every day. The last one in the ranking will be labeled as "donkey," with a sign being put on his back.
— It is a great honor for you to be able to work for our great country and to contribute to the building of the Greater German Reich.	— We belong to the screaming bad guys. The scared ones will lose points.
— There are three basic rules that you should never forget: 1) Do not try to escape. 2) Follow every order, do not ask any questions. 3) Any attempt at mutiny will be punished by death through hanging. Have I made myself clear?	— There are three cases in which a player uses all of his points. 1) If he cries. 2) If he wants to go home to his mommy. 3) If he asks for food. There is none!
— You should be happy to work here. If you follow the rules no harm will be done to you.	— Hungry players easily lose points. I lost 40 points myself just for wanting a jelly sandwich.
— Obedience is everything.	— With apricot preserve.
— Another thing:	— With him, it was strawberry preserve.
— If you here this whistle, just hurry outside into the yard. And be quick.	— Don't ask for lollipops, you won't get any since we eat them ourselves.
— Form up in rows by two!	— I had twenty myself yesterday.
— Silence!	— Did my tummy ache!
-- Every morning ...	— But they were great.
— . . . there is a roll call.	— But let's not talk about that.
— One more thing I'd like to show you: you are going to work in that area back there. You will soon grasp the dimensions of the camp.	— Please excuse my leaving in such a hurry—but I am playing hide-and-seek and do not want to get caught.

On the other hand, Guido's translation also shows the impossibility of translating the officer's words rationally. Other instances of plays on words and language are the riddles that Dr. Lessing and Guido come up with for each other—easy ones like "From the dwarves to Snow White—solve the riddle in the time the answer allows you." The ritual language use between these two men turns into something imaginary and acquires the status of a "cultural product" as soon as the topic treated is a meaningful one. One of the most striking scenes in this context takes place in the camp commander's house, where Dr Lessing has helped Guido obtain the position of a servant, originally to make it easier for Guido to escape from the camp. Giosuè is also present when Guido tells Dr Lessing that his wife is also an inmate—a piece of information that destroys Lessing's plans for helping Guido. He tells this with the help of an unambiguous riddle and stresses his own helplessness by saying "Help me, Guido. Please help me." His narrative rationalizes his concern, and it is the concrete context of fear that give meaning to his words that help naming the unnamable, his guilty conscience that leads him to say things like "I can't sleep any more."

During the hours in this hostile situation something happens that endangers Giosuè—Guido starts the scene by telling his son that this last round of the game is called the "silent round." Giosuè has to be silent so that the German children and servants around cannot find out that he is an Italian Jew. Giosuè is usually a very good and meticulous player and follows his father's rules—with minor exceptions. One of these exceptions happens in a scene together with the German children, when one of the servants hands him a piece of cake and Giosuè answers with a clear and loud *grazie*. He realizes his blunder immediately when the servant stops and stares at him and rushes out of the room to fetch the elderly nanny, a paragon of Nazi ideology. Guido, too, has witnessed his son's grave mistake and he, too, stands paralyzed in the middle of the room. Then he finds a way out of the terror, with the help of another game: He adopts the role of a teacher and teaches the children how to say *grazie*. All children practice eagerly, and the nanny stands in the doorway, consterned. Thus Guido saves his son and himself, probably also Dr Lessing. His spontaneous idea to pretend in front of the nanny that he had been practicing saying *grazie* with the children for a while—a situation in which the simple word *grazie* acquires a special meaning. The audience never cease to wonder—how can it be possible to find this language of imagination whenever it is needed?

One possible explanation for the astonishing narrative style is the fascination exercized by imagination, the central survival strategy in both works. Amazement is the origin of all reflexion. Aristotle says that *thaumazein* because of not yet explicable phenomena and the search for reasons stem from the desire for higher knowledge (see Höffe 46). In *La vita è bella* the spectator comes closer to Giosuè's final sentence "Yes, it is true," and his exclamation "Mommy, we have won!" represented by a symbol whose usual associative field evokes the opposite of relief and happiness: the tank. The tank makes its first appearance in the first scene with Giosuè—when he should get ready to accompany his mother to work, he cannot find his toy tank. This toy tank is also the symbol of Dora's despair upon seeing the destroyed birthday table and realizing that both her husband and her son have been deported. And in the end it is the real tank as the symbol of the liberation of the camp by the Americans whose rattling chains tell the little boy that his father has told the truth, that he has won the game and that his story of "Auschwitz" is a true one. This means of associative reversal is one that reoccurs throughout the film, a method that sometimes attracts special attention, for instance, when Guido tries to make Giosuè believe that sentences such as "They make buttons and soap out of our bones" or "They will burn us all in one big oven" are not true. But what would have happened if Guido has told his son the truth? He used his own means to save his wife and son, his little ideas and quirks gave them all the strength to survive, and it was especially the idea to invent the "game" that made Giosuè and Dora happy, and not only for a single moment. This interpretation also fills the title of the film with meaning—life as a challenge to man, a challenge that can be mastered by means of values such as humanity and freedom even in the most terrifying situations.

Against this background the final sentences in Kertész's novel—George's view on happiness upon returning to a devastated and deserted Budapest—no longer appear to express the protagonist's concern for the presence: "Even back there, in the shadow of the chimneys, in the breaks between pain, there was something resembling happiness. Everybody will ask me about the deprivations, the 'terrors of the camps,' but for me, the happiness there will always be the most memorable experience, perhaps. Yes, that's what I'll tell them the next time they ask me: about the happiness in those camps. If they ever do ask. And if I don't forget" (191). George has told his story—once read, his words cannot be forgotten. The individual strength of Kertész's work lies not only in the meticulous and uninhibitedly unemotional story-telling, but also and especially in the enormous intellectuality—even if it does not always succeed. But these are the situations that make George rise above the daily essential inferno, just like Guido, Giosuè, and Dora, and these are also the situations that characterize "Auschwitz" as a "cultural product" in these texts and images. They are characteristic of Kertész's and Benigni's specific ways of treating the Holocaust and of remembering the truth in their special ways. Thus the Holocaust is a value-creating phenomenon—in Kertész's words: "If we see it as a given—and it is—that the Holocaust has produced a culture that is present today, its literature may draw on the Bible and the Greek tragedy, these two sources of Occidental culture, for inspiration to find a way to make compensation sprout from a reality that cannot be amended—or spirit, or catharsis" ("Der Holocaust als Kultur" 69).

Works Cited

Assmann, Aleida. *Erinnerungsräume. Formen und Wandlungen des kulturellen Gedächtnisses.* München: Beck, 1999.

Blumenthal, W. Michael. "Streit um die Erinnerung. Über den schwierigen Weg zu einer Ethik des Gedenkens: Der Holocaust und die Öffentlichkeit." *Frankfurter Allgemeine Zeitung* (9 October 1999): Bilder und Zeiten, n.p.

Diner, Dan. "Gestaute Zeit. Massenvernichtung und jüdische Erzählstruktur." *Fünfzig Jahre danach. Zur Nachgeschichte des Nationalsozialismus.* Ed. Sigrid Weigel and Birgit R. Erdle. Zürich: vdf, 1996. 3–16.

Eaglestone, Robert. "The Aporia of Imre Kertész." *Imre Kertész and Holocaust Literature.* Ed. Louise O. Vasvári and Steven Tötösy de Zepetnek. West Lafayette: Purdue UP, 2005. 38–50.

Hillis Miller, J. "Narrative and History." *English Literary History* 41 (1974): 455–73.

Höffe, Otfried. *Aristoteles.* München: Beck, 1996.

Kertész, Imre. *Gályanapló* (Galley Boat-Log). Budapest: Holnap, 1992.

Kertész, Imre. "Wem gehört Auschwitz?" *Eine Gedankenlänge Stille, während das Erschießungskommando neu lädt.* By Imre Kertész. Trans. György Buda. Reinbek bei Hamburg: Rowohlt 1999. 145–54.

Kertész, Imre. "Der Holocaust als Kultur." *Eine Gedankenlänge Stille, während das Erschießungskommando neu lädt.* By Imre Kertész. Trans. György Buda. Reinbek bei Hamburg: Rowohlt, 1999. 54–69.

Kertész, Imre. *Dank des Preisträgers. Leipziger Buchpreis zur Europäischen Verständigung 1997.* Frankfurt: Suhrkamp, 1997.

Kertész, Imre. *Galeerentagebuch.* Trans. Kristin Schwamm. Reinbek bei Hamburg: Rowohlt, 1993.

Kertész, Imre. *Fateless.* Trans. Christopher C. Wilson and Katharina M. Wilson. Evanston: Northwestern UP, 1992.

Kertész, Imre. *Fatelessness.* Trans. Tim Wilkinson. New York: Vintage, 2004.

Köppen, Manuel, and Klaus R. Scherpe. "Vorwort. Zur Einführung. Der Streit um die Darstellbarkeit des Holocaust." *Bilder des Holocaust: Literatur—Film—Bildende Kunst.* Ed. Manuel Köppen and Klaus R. Scherpe. Wien: Böhlau, 1997. 1–12.

Steinlein, Rüdiger. "Das Furchtbarste lächerlich? Komik und Lachen in Texten der deutschen Holocaust-Literatur." *Kunst und Literatur nach Auschwitz.* Ed. Manuel Köppen. Berlin: Erich Schmidt, 1993. 97–106.

Strümpel, Jan. "Im Sog der Erinnerungskultur. Holocaust und Literatur—'Normalität' und ihre Grenzen." *Text und Kritik* 144 (1999): 9–17.

Szondi, Peter. *Celan-Studien.* Frankfurt: Suhrkamp, 1972.

Tötösy de Zepetnek, Steven. "Comparative Cultural Studies and the Study of Central European Culture." *Comparative Central European Culture.* Ed. Steven Tötösy de Zepetnek. West Lafayette: Purdue UP, 2002. 1–32.

White, Hayden. *Auch Klio dichtet oder die Fiktion des Faktischen. Studien zur Tropologie des historischen Diskurses*. Trans. Brigitte Brinkmann-Siepmann and Thomas Siepmann. Stuttgart: Klett-Cotta, 1991.

Young, James E. *Beschreiben des Holocaust*. Trans. Christa Schuenke. Frankfurt: Suhrkamp, 1992.

Imre Kertész's *Fatelessness* as Historical Fiction

Julia Karolle

Although Imre Kertész's novel *Sorstalanság* (*Fatelessness*) first appeared in 1975 and has been available in English—translated as *Fateless* in 1992 and as *Fatelessness* in 2004—it took the Nobel Prize to acquaint many English-speaking readers and scholars with Kertész's contribution to Holocaust literature. In Germany, too—although comparably speaking Kertész's work found more interest there than in the United States—there was limited response to Kertész's first novel until the late 1990s, when its second translation into German (*Roman eines Schicksallosen*, trans. Christina Viragh, 1996) met with critical acclaim. In 1997, when Kertész was awarded the "Jeanette Schocken-Preis" of the city of Bremerhaven, jury member Wolfgang Emmerich explained the long silence surrounding Kertész's work with its departure from the traditions of Holocaust literature (79). I agree that Kertész breaks ranks with the tradition of Holocaust literature, but for different reasons than those mentioned by Emmerich. While Emmerich read *Roman eines Schicksallosen* as a behavioral study and an ethnography, I understand the novel as historical fiction, which involves considering the components usually associated with this genre, including the incorporation of history and a particular narrative presence in the work. Characteristic of the historical-fiction genre is, moreover, a certain provocative blending of authenticity and fictionality in both of these components (see Maxwell 543, 544). I argue that Kertész optimizes this provocative potential in *Fatelessness*, indeed, it can be understood as Kertész's quest for a type of truth, one that takes Holocaust literature's fictionality seriously in its construction of authenticity. (It should be noted that Kertész did not endorse the 1992 translation by Wilson and Wilson of *Sorstalanság* as *Fateless*, rather preferring the later translation by Tim Wilkinson as *Fatelessness*. Because the Wilkinson translation was not available at the time of writing my paper, I refer to the work as *Fatelessness* but quote from the Wilson and Wilson translation.)

While Holocaust literature is more often categorized as its own genre, or as factual historical narrative, many features of Holocaust literature are akin to those of historical fiction, among them fictional form and historical foundation. However, perhaps because the historical-fiction genre more often evokes accounts of

Napoleon's childhood than engagement with issues such as genocide, Holocaust literature does not often appear to be categorized expressly as belonging to this genre. Nevertheless, the scholarly discourse surrounding Holocaust literature reveals implicit association with historical fiction. In establishing curriculum selection standards, for example, educator Margaret Drew classifies explicitly Holocaust literature as historical literature: "First, any historical literature needs to be evaluated both as history and as literature. A book cannot be fully recommended unless it is good history as well as good literature" (11). In an essay from the same collection, Samuel Totten expands upon what "good history" may entail with regard to Holocaust literature: "On a simple, but important level, one needs to ascertain the following: Are the dates of actual events correct? Are the names of actual people correct? Is the chronology of actual events correct? On a more complex level, one must ask: Does the literary work delineate the incidents and events in their varied complexity versus providing a simplistic portrayal that is bereft of the intricacies involved?" (30). Totten's criteria are certainly in line with historical fiction's traditional claim to historical reference, focusing on accurate reportage of dates, names, and chronology. In a similar vein, Kertész describes Holocaust survivors as the most critical readers of historical detail: "Furtive glances cling to every line of every book on the Holocaust, to every foot of every film where the Holocaust is mentioned. Is the representation plausible, the history exact? Did we really say that, feel that way? Is that really where the latrine stood, in precisely that corner of the barracks?" ("Who Owns Auschwitz?" 267).

While Kertész recognizes these criteria as legitimate, his reviews of Steven Spielberg's *Schindler's List* and Roberto Benigni's *Life Is Beautiful* suggest that he employs a different set of criteria to evaluate the films: "Authenticity lies, admittedly, in details, but not necessarily in material details . . . the point here lies in something totally different: the spirit, the soul of *Life Is Beautiful* is authentic, and it moves us with the power of the oldest kind of magic, the magic of fairy tales" ("Who Owns Auschwitz?" 271). *Schindler's List*, based on the actions of a historical figure, Kertész dismisses as kitsch, whereas *Life Is Beautiful*, not a true story, Kertész deems more authentic. Here, as in *Fatelessness*, Kertész questions the very notion of authenticity. In his judgment of *Life Is Beautiful*, authenticity rests not in material detail, but rather a fictionality that is spiritually truer than historical fact (on this, see also Jagow). In *Fatelessness*, Kertész explores similarly the relationship between fiction and history in constructions of authenticity. As a work of historical fiction, "by definition referential, gesturing toward a world commonly understood to have existed" (Nünning 548), *Fatelessness* includes many of the signposts of historical authenticity. Yet, also as a work of historical fiction, *Fatelessness* "lay[s] claim to neither verifiability nor truth" (Nünning 548).

At the narrative core of historical fiction, and certainly Holocaust literature, is the calendar. Reference to calendrical time in Holocaust literature in particular allows the reader to do more than merely establish associations with historical reality. Even if the reader's knowledge of the Holocaust amounts to little more than the delimiting dates, this knowledge steers expectations of possible narrative outcomes. For example, a narrative explicitly taking place in 1941 will raise greater expectations of heroism than survival; one taking place in 1945, on the other hand, leads the reader to expect a story of liberation. Historical anchoring in *Fatelessness* includes mention of the introduction of stricter laws governing Hungarian Jews (21), the landing of the Allied forces (22), and ultimately the aggressive rounding up and deportation of Jews after German forces occupied Hungary in 1944, all of which allow the reader to fix the novel's plot to the last year of the war. Toward the end of the novel, when a physician mentions to the protagonist George Köves that he has been interned for twelve years (155), the reader may conclude that the year is now 1945.

Kertész does not avoid historical contextualization in *Fatelessness*, yet it is striking that nowhere in the work is a specific year mentioned, and only once a specific month, April (172). By contrast, the long-time paradigm of Holocaust narrative, Anne Frank's *Diary of a Young Girl*, prominently displays calendar time in correlation with Anne's life in hiding, and in Hans-Peter Richter's *Damals war es Friedrich*, a year follows each chapter heading in the table of contents. By contrast, Kertész makes it more difficult for his reader to match events to the calendar and thus to order *Fatelessness* among Holocaust stories as either one of heroism or one of survival. Like George, who cannot glean hope from knowing his position in history, the uninitiated reader will be denied this promise. The reader of *Fatelessness* must therefore either read George's story outside of history (i.e., as events unfolding without the benefit of retrospect) or activate her own knowledge of history to validate the work's historical authenticity.

The chronological ordering of events is a crucial component in both Holocaust literature and historical fiction, indeed, it is the premise upon which all narratives are founded. In his Nobel lecture, Kertész explicitly commented on the construction of chronology in *Fatelessness:* "The hero of my novel does not live his own time in the concentration camps, for neither his time nor his language, not even his own person, is really his. He doesn't remember, he exists. So he must languish, poor boy, in the dreary trap of linearity, unable to shake off the painful details" ("Heureka!" 606). Although Kertész states that Köves only narrates in the present tense and that the narrative progression is strictly linear, this observation is perhaps truer in its intention than its practice. George does remember home (115–16), and even hints that he has spent many more days in prison beyond the first few he had just narrated (75). For Kertész, the "dreary trap of linearity"—a narrative feat, incidentally, that Gérard Genette claims is "virtually *impossible* for any narrator to sustain" (758)—is an expression of George's powerlessness. Yet elsewhere in his lecture, the author suggests, more importantly, that George's powerlessness precludes any significant rational engagement with his environment: "If the world is an objective reality that exists independently of us, then humans themselves, even in their own eyes, are nothing more than objects, and their life stories merely a series of disconnected historical accidents, which they may wonder at but which they themselves have nothing to do with" ("Heureka!" 604–05). By comparison, while Primo Lévi's narrator in Auschwitz is driven by a "need to understand, categorize, and analyze" (qtd. in Yudkin 25), Kertész places George in this world but leaves him to merely wonder at his own life story.

Readers have resisted understanding *Fatelessness* as a narrative of "disconnected accidents," that is, as a story that possesses only chronology and not causality between events. Several early reviews of the novel in German translation speak of logic, be it George's encounter with the "logic of annihilation" (Emmerich 80; all subsequent translations are mine unless noted otherwise), or George's "ready identification with the logic of others" in the absence of his own (Breitenstein 4). Indeed, H. Porter Abbott suggests that the will to perceive logic, reason, and ultimately causality is part of human nature: "We are made in such a way that we continually look for the causes of things. The inevitable linearity of story makes narrative a powerful means of gratifying this need (whether accurately or not is another issue)" (37). Abbott continues by observing that we may be so intent on finding causation that we will perceive it in events connected to each other by nothing more than consecution (39). Indeed, if there *is* a logic governing life at a concentration camp, it is only partially accessible to George and thus the coherence it lends his narrative is imperfect; for the balance, correlation stands in for causation.

Kertész's (putatively) linear narration in *Fatelessness* and his audience's search for logic in it reveal the abuses that reason must endure in order to create *any* story or history about the Holocaust. Like Lévi's character, readers use narrative to "understand, categorize, and analyze." But as Kertész seems to suggest, if he is to remain true to historical events, he cannot narrate them using the conventions we rely upon. Ultimately, Kertész challenges the reader not to make up for the lack of logic in *Fatelessness*, but rather to consider the nature of its absence. In his choice of narrative stance, Kertész further challenges distinctions between historical narrative—in this case, autobiography—and historical fiction. As Genette has observed, the first-person novel has long been fraught with ambiguity; Käte Hamburger argued in the 1950s that it fell into the category of the make-believe, not entirely fiction and not entirely historical, for it "proceeds mainly by borrowing or simulating the narrative behavior of authentic autobiographical narrative" (qtd. in Genette 771). Holocaust literature told in first-person has not been exempted from this confusion; while Hans-Peter Richter has confirmed the autobiographical nature of his fictional works, "I am reporting how I lived through that time and what I saw—no more" (*I Was There* n.p.), Elie Wiesel has found it necessary to assert that *Night* is not a novel (271). For his part, Kertész has indicated cryptically that there is nothing in *Fatelessness* that is autobiographical (qtd. in Földényi 202). Despite the fact that both author and narrator experienced concentration camps in the last years of the war, Kertész distances himself explicitly from one of the most compelling assertions of authenticity possible: that the story told here is *his* story. By denying that author and narrator are one, Kertész refuses to align his work with historical narrative. What remains is a fictional narrative which, to speak with Genette, is "a type of narrative for the veracity of which the author does not seriously vouch" (764). If the reader is to discern authenticity in *Fatelessness*, it will not come from the conventional equation of author with narrator. Instead, the reader will have to glean authenticity from the relationship between the narrator and his subject matter.

Although Kertész distances himself from his narrator and thus reinforces the fictionality of George's narrative presence, the narrator's voice nevertheless emulates the style of autobiography. The first two chapters open with sentences such as "Today I skipped school" (3), and "It has been two months now since we said good-bye to my father" (21) which evoke intercalated narration, as if each chapter were an diary entry that the narrator composes following each new episode. While some direct speech appears in the work, few conversations are reproduced in full, yielding to reporter-style quoting of single phrases embedded in indirect speech: "[Vili's] opinion is respected in the family because before he opened a betting office, he was in the newspaper business. Now, too, he wanted to inform us about some interested news that he had from 'reliable sources' that he called 'absolutely trustworthy'" (13). Hamburger has suggested that extended dialogue is a signature of fictional narrative, and while Genette admits that historical narrative is not barred from including dialogue, quoting conversations at length "somewhat transgresses historical narrative's verisimilitude ('How do you know that?')" (761). In the context of *Fatelessness*, George's reporting style suggests that the narrator is only sharing what he has been able to reconstruct reliably. Indeed, when more complete utterances are included, they may be accompanied by assertions of veracity: "This was her phrasing" (*Fateless* 4), "Those were his words" (77) and "to quote him in full: 'Well, by the time we shit them full, we'll be free'" (98). This strategy reinforces George's authority—be it historical or fictional—over the text; as he draws on outside sources to verify his narrative, he never turns over control to other speakers for more than one or two sentences. While Kertész pointed out that George was trapped in a time and language not his own, George's maintenance of narrative authority may be seen as a means of asserting power elsewhere compromised. Instead of imbuing George with the claim of autobiographical authenticity, Kertész leaves his narrator to make a more modest claim. Given the limits of human reason, memory, and emotion, George's narrative reveals that there is precious little that can be asserted with absolute certainty of truth and honesty. His judgments are embarrassing, his emotions impenetrable, and his reconstruction of landscapes and people fragmentary, and yet the implication is that this narration is more authentic than one claiming autobiographical foundations.

Despite George's attempt to provide an authoritative narrative, he often conveys his own opinions in *Fatelessness* as they take shape, evident in turns of phrase such as "I totally agreed with him" (*Fateless* 68), "I didn't find any difficulty accepting his useful suggestion" (68), and "I thought he was correct" (69). At other times, he admits that his interpretations may be imperfect and possibly erroneous, "Unless I'm mistaken" (8), "if I understood correctly" (64), and "Of course, I was probably mistaken" (74). All of these phrases intone a self-conscious subjectivity which—even in autobiographical (i.e., factual) historical narrative—Yudkin deems inevitable: "as events do not exist only in themselves but in a symbiotic relationship with the observer, this testimony is multilayered. The witness sees only part, and what is seen is shaded by subjectivity" (16). First-person narratives—fictional or factual—admit a limited scope of representation. Despite Yudkin's ready acceptance of subjectivity in the context of Holocaust literature, in particular, the *degree* of subjectivity perceived appropriate is contentious. Margaret Drew, for one, argues that Frank's *Diary of a Young Girl* is too subjective to stand alone as an exemplar of Holocaust literature: "This failure to confront the full horror of the Holocaust or to examine the historical facts of the period occurs in Anne's diary because it is primarily about her personal life. That is, Anne is writing about what she knows, which is the impact of events on her own life; not the events themselves" (12). For his part, George may admit error and misinterpretation, but his ultimate goal is to interpret his situation with "cold, rational pondering" (150), which is perhaps why the narrator's subjectivity is rarely invoked. Instead, George has been interpreted as maintaining the eye of an outsider (Breitenstein); he wants to keep perspective on everything, to which his foreignness, distance and otherness must all contribute (Rudtke 50–51).

In an interview Kertész indicated that he has to offend his readers because this is the only manner in which one can speak about Auschwitz, and Zsuzsanna Gahse has concluded that it is precisely the surprising and unusual perspective in *Fatelessness* that causes this offense (69). While Wiesel's narrator in *Night* presents "himself both as the adolescent in the camp and as the adult who knows what is to transpire" (Yudkin 24), Kertész maintains the narrative perspective of a fifteen-year-old throughout the text (see Graf). Yet it is not so much George's youth, rather his inability—or refusal—to comprehend and judge his situation that confounds many readers. The interpretations vary; some call George's descriptions consistently naive (Weinzierl), others suggest that George's lack of identity is overcompensated with an excess of it at the end (Breitenstein). Dismissing unreflective ingenuousness, Gahse has suggested that an ironic adult voice speaks behind the young one (70; see also Spiró 34), while Rudtke interprets George as a naive yet picaresque scoundrel akin to Becker's Jakob (51). In any case, if George's intention is to be objective, his very attempt to do so disqualifies him as a reliable narrator. The reader either responds with doubt, rejection, and confusion (Rudtke 57), presumes she knows more than George (Weinzierl; see also Basse 560), or, in the most extreme case, questions whether George is human (Földényi 194). While the appropriate degree of subjectivity has been seen as crucial in Holocaust literature, Kertész counters that subjective narration is impossible. Yet it is precisely George's putatively objective stance that threatens to render him fateless. In order to regain his subjectivity, George has "to step out of the mesmerizing crowd, out of History, which renders you faceless and fateless" ("Heureka!" 606). At the close of the book, George comes closer to (re-)claiming this personal fate, by refusing to participate in the factual historical narrative of Auschwitz (183), to forget what he knows (186), and to be unequivocally categorized as a victim of history (189; see also Basse 561).

I have argued here for exploring Kertész's *Sorstalanság* as historical fiction in order to consider how the author incorporates provocatively standard conventions of that genre into his work. Although the manner in which Kertész structures *Fatelessness* might detract from its historical authenticity, my position here is that the author seeks to achieve a new type of authenticity, one based on spiritual and moral truth over historical truth. Reading *Fatelessness* as historical fiction is certainly validated by Kertész's reference to historical context and his provocative engagement with the devices of the genre, but it falls to the reader to assess whether Kertész's offense—of refusing his narrator subjectivity—still conveys sensitivity toward the subject matter and thus acknowledges *Fatelessness* as Holocaust literature as well. Perhaps Kertész's relative obscurity outside of Hungary is an indication that readers have not yet determined what to make of this offense.

Works Cited

Abbott, H. Porter. *The Cambridge Introduction to Narrative.* Cambridge: Harvard UP, 2002.

Basse, Michael. "Auschwitz als Welterfahrung. Der ungarische Schriftsteller Imre Kertész." *Merkur: Deutsche Zeitschrift für Europäisches Denken* 53.6 (1999): 559–64.

Breitenstein, Andreas. "Schöne Tage in Buchenwald. Imre Kertész' *Roman eines Schicksallosen.*" *Neue Zürcher Zeitung* (27 April 1996): 67.

Drew, Margaret A. "Teaching Holocaust Literature: Issues, Caveats, and Suggestions." *Teaching Holocaust Literature.* Ed. Samuel Totten. Boston: Allyn and Bacon, 2001: 11–23.

Emmerich, Wolfgang. "Keine 'Sinngebung des Sinnlosen.' Kertész lesen." *Die Horen: Zeitschrift für Literatur, Kunst und Kritik* 42.2 (1997): 78–80.

Földényi, László. "'Große Wahrhaftigkeit': *Roman eines Schicksallosen* von Imre Kertész." Trans. Hans Skirecki. *Ein Foto aus Berlin: Essays 1991–94.* By László Földényi. München: Matthes and Seitz, 1996. 193–208.

Frank, Anne. *The Diary of a Young Girl: The Definitive Edition.* Ed. Otto Frank and Miriam Pressler. Trans. Susan Massotty. New York: Bantam, 1997.

Gahse, Zsuzsanna. "Das Unerwartete und Imre Kertész. Eine Laudatio." *Die Horen: Zeitschrift für Literatur, Kunst und Kritik* 42.2 (1997): 67–73.

Genette, Gérard. "Fictional Narrative, Factual Narrative." *Poetics Today* 11.4 (Winter 1990): 755–74.

Graf, Hansjörg. "'Ein durchaus erträglicher Ort': Imre Kertész's *Roman eines Schicksallosen.*" *Süddeutsche Zeitung* (6 April 1996): 27.

Jagow, Bettina von. "Representing the Holocaust, Kertész's *Fatelessness*, and Benigni's *La vita è bella*." Trans. Sabine Prechter. *Imre Kertész and Holocaust Literature.* Ed. Louise O. Vasvári and Steven Tötösy de Zepetnek. West Lafayette: Purdue UP, 2005. 76–88.

Kertész, Imre. *Fateless.* Trans. Christopher C. Wilson and Katharina M. Wilson. Evanston: Northwestern UP, 1992.

Kertész, Imre. "Heureka!" Trans. Ivan Sanders. *PMLA: Publications of the Modern Language Association of America* 118.3 (2003): 604–14.

Kertész, Imre. "Who Owns Auschwitz?" Trans. John MacKay. *Yale Journal of Criticism* 14.1 (2001): 267–72.

Kertész, Imre. *Fatelessness.* Trans. Tim Wilkinson. New York: Vintage, 2004.

Maxwell, Richard. "Historical Novel." *Encyclopedia of the Novel.* Ed. Paul Schellinger. Chicago: Fitzroy Dearborn, 1998. 543–48.

Nünning, Ansgar. "Historical Writing and the Novel." *Encyclopedia of the Novel.* Ed. Paul Schellinger. Chicago: Fitzroy Dearborn, 1998. 548–53.

Richter, Hans Peter. *Friedrich.* Trans. Edite Kroll. New York: Penguin, 1970.

Richter, Hans Peter. *I Was There.* New York: Holt, Rinehart & Winston, 1972.

Rudtke, Tanja. "'Eine kuriose Geschichte.' Die Pikaro-Perspektive im Holocaustroman am Beispiel von Imre Kertész' *Roman eines Schicksallosen.*" *Arcadia: Zeitschrift für Vergleichende Literaturwissenschaft* 18 (1983): 43–57.

Spiró, György. "In Art Only the Radical Exists." *The Hungarian Quarterly* 43 (Winter 2002): 29–37.

Totten, Samuel. "Incorporating Fiction and Poetry into a Study of the Holocaust." *Teaching Holocaust Literature.* Ed. Samuel Totten. Boston: Allyn and Bacon, 2001. 24–62.

Weinzierl, Ulrich. "Verstörendes Glück. Imre Kertész in der Schule des Grauens." *Frankfurter Allgemeine Zeitung* (30 March 1996): B5.

Wiesel, Elie. *All Rivers Run to the Sea: Memoirs.* New York: Schocken, 1995.

Yudkin, Leon I. "Narrative Perspectives in Holocaust Literature." *Hebrew Literature in the Wake of the Holocaust.* Ed. Leon I. Yudkin. Rutherford: Farleigh Dickinson UP, 1993: 13–32.

Galley Boat-Log (*Gályanapló*): Excerpts

Imre Kertész

Translated from the Hungarian by Tim Wilkinson

I. Outward Bound (on the High Seas)

1961

I started work on the novel a year ago. It all has to be thrown away.

* * *

1964

* * *

July: Two weeks in Germany. I visited Buchenwald and the factory at Zeitz. I recognized the sandy path. A young lad in worker's overalls was cycling along it; he carefully mustered me. I must have struck him as foreign. It was narrower than I had remembered (the path, I mean). The factory sounded a greeting as well: the big cooling towers wheezed. I had quite forgotten that sound but recognized it immediately, and what memories it evoked! I believe (am almost certain) I also found the site of the Zeitz camp. A state farm and a huge cattle barn are now standing on the spot. I did not experience great moments of recall. Time, good old time, and as its master, Proust, says: "The reality that I had known no longer existed." And: ". . . houses, roads, avenues are as fleeting, alas, as the years."

* * *

Conformity: When a person does not seek concordance with reality but with the facts. What is reality? In a word, ourselves. What are the facts? In a word, absurdities. The link between the two, put briefly: a moral life, fate. Alternatively, there is no link, which means an acceptance of facts, a series of chance events and adjustment to those events. Thus the conformist himself becomes a fact, an absurdity. He loses his freedom, explodes his core and becomes dispersed in the void of facts. He will never be able to reassemble his alien life from the unknown, perilously sundered fragments. The person turns into his opposite: a machine, a schizophrenic, a monster. He becomes executioner and victim.

* * *

1965

* * *

May 1st: "Novel of Fatelessness" as a possible title, a subtitle at any rate. What do I call a fate? Certainly the possibility of tragedy. The external determinacy, the stigma which constrains our life into a situation, an absurdity, in the given totalitarianism, thwarts this; thus, when we live out the determinacy that is doled out to us as a reality, instead of the necessity that stems from our own (relative) freedom—that is what I would call fatelessness.

What is essential is that our determinacy should always be in conflict with our natural views and inclinations; that is how fatelessness manifests in the chemically pure state.

The two possible modes of protection: we transform into our determinacy (Kafka's centipede), voluntarily so to say, and in that way attempt to assimilate our determinacy to our own fate; or else we rebel against it, and so fall victim to our determinacy. Neither of these is therefore a true solution, for in both cases we are obliged to perceive our determinacy (a totally external arbitrariness that we must accept as, so to say, a natural condition, knowing full well that although it is theoretically subject to our human control, it does not lie within our power to do anything to change it) as *reality*, whilst the determining force, that absurd power, in a way triumphs over us: it gives us a name that is not our name and turns us into an object, even though we were born for other things.

The dilemma of my *"Muslim"*: How can he construct a fate out of his own determinacy. After all, that determinacy can have no continuation; historically it loses its validity and is denied on all sides. Thus nothing remains of it beyond the memory of physical suffering. Oh, and the prospect of fresh determinacies ahead of him.

June: Gide introduced the idea of the *acte gratuite,* the "gratuitous act." I am discovering its opposite—"gratuitous toleration."

For four years I have been working on the novel—or perhaps rather on myself? In order to see? And then be able to speak once I have seen?

It may be that it is not any talent which makes someone a writer but the fact that he does not accept the language and ready-made concepts. At the outset, I think, one is simply stupid, more stupid than all the others, who instantly understand everything. Then one starts to write like someone trying to convalesce from a severe ailment, to master his mental illness—at least as long as he keeps on writing.

The unbelievable blindness of human consciousness can still profoundly shock me. People talk about lunch and midday naps and don't even notice that the couch on which they stretch out is their coffin.

I could never be another person's father.

* * *

1966: A writer cannot create a more irrational world than God.

1) Proportions: The problem of measure and material. Kafka and Faulkner (especially *Light in August*). An abundance and surplus of the pullulating stuff of life mark the latter out as a dark master of life. Yet Kafka still knows more about life, is more familiar with its darker secrets. Why, then, is he the more sublime, the more cheerful and comforting, for all that?—He who knows the law reduces the carver of images to silence.

2) The personality trap, psychology, passion. How much do we really have to do with our passions; exactly how big is our part in them? — Swann's story. Meursault's revolver shot.

Looked at more closely: show the individual psychological motives of deeds in the torture chambers of the totalitarian state. Futile, by the way, because here only the role is significant, the fact that people are capable of being executioner or victim, and how the cogwheels function in the machinery of death, taking no account at all of the individual case. Here individuality, if it finds expression in anyone at all, can at most only lament its past. In this respect, therefore, there is no multifaceted humanity, no complicated and many-layered characters, no extraordinary personalities because the essence of totality is precisely uniformity.

3) Hero of the novel. How can there be one, if man is nothing more than his situation, a situation in the given "actuality"? — Yet perhaps there is something to be salvaged all the same, a tiny foolishness, something ultimately comic and frail that may be a sign of the will to live and still awakens sympathy.

The further question is the impossibility of portraying functional man. If one undertakes to portray him none the less, one is still left with the question of from what viewpoint to portray him.

If one regards his situation as tragic, then one is undoubtedly mourning something non-existent, a false consciousness of the culture that prevailed before Auschwitz (and led to Auschwitz), a humanism that never existed. Isn't that something absurdly anachronistic? Isn't that absurdly innocuous? In other words, isn't it a lie?

The next question, the biggest of all, is therefore: How can one make a portrait from the viewpoint of the totality but without adopting the totalitarian viewpoint as one's own?

Not Jews but a person who happens to be Jewish: The "Jew" as a situation in totalitarianism.

Schopenhauer: "Plan and totality are to be found not in world history . . . but in the life of the individual." And "individuals are what is real." And especially: "Neither our action nor our course of life is our work, but rather our essence and existence, which no one regards as our work."

The thought that anyone at all might understand my secret occupation and the way of life it entails is so strange to me that I am quite capable, even unprompted, of joking about myself to anyone without feeling the least bit ridiculous in doing so.

Shall I be capable of conjuring up the concentration camp in the necessary manner? Is it possible that this constitutes the deeper sense of my peculiar way of life, my voluntary incarceration? And is it possible that my own separate liberation will be effectuated on completion of the novel?

* * *

1968

* * *

G.M. Gilbert's *Nuremberg Diary*, with particular regard to my own work. For example, the words of Keitel, according to whom Hitler attempted to present as "manifest destiny" what was anything but that, which could have happened quite differently, indeed need not even have happened at all. On another level, that is the experience of *fatelessness*. In totalitarianism everything takes place in the name of destiny and fate. The whole purpose of these designations is to disguise the nothingness, the absolute Nothingness, which nevertheless produces mountains of corpses, devastation and atrocities.

About Rudolf Höss, the commandant of Auschwitz, Gilbert writes: "One gets the general impression of a man who is intellectually normal but with the schizoid apathy, insensitivity and lack of empathy that could hardly be more extreme in a frank psychotic." An astute diagnosis, not just for Höss but also for the disease with which totalitarian systems infect mankind. Precisely for that reason, I find G.'s subsequent attempt to impute specific motives to Höss (parents, upbringing, marriage, sexual life, etc.) of no interest. After all, every person has a history, but the said schizoid apathy is not an individual product: it can be attested equally well in Höss's superiors and subordinates and in the inmates at Auschwitz as in Höss himself, even though their individual motivations were totally different.

They were humiliated in order that it could said that they had humiliated themselves.

Dig down to the very depths of the character and the ideas—via the devices of the surface. Communicate only what is communicable and trust that a completed work comprising only what is communicable will, in its completeness and its muteness, say more about the incommunicable than if I were to seek to capture that directly. The story of a depersonalization which unfolds just as slowly and inexorably as if it were that of a personality. Employ the old language of morality in order to show its absurdity. One should think not of Nietzsche ('the first of the immoralists'), no, but of a world in which neither belief nor denial exists, and deeds are manifested in their particularity, their uniqueness, without any binding system of values, in the singular conflict of the exigency of the transformation and in the general conflict of the exigency of the system of those transformations, in accordance with this profound, tormenting secret.—That is why, incidentally, the experience of state totalitarianism is so all-important for the European form of existence and personality type—one which has, so to speak, traumatically undergone a certain ethical culture and tradition; it has completely demolished not only the myth but almost the very concept of personality.

* * *

1969 October: In the next chapter I shall reach Auschwitz.

* * *

1970 December 26th: Christmas. Excitement and indecision. I have a need for clarification and theoretical underpinning for my novel-writing activity. This is what is preoccupying me: through reading Adorno, I again see quite clearly that the technique of my novel emulates the twelve-tone or serial method of integrated composition. It abolishes free characters and the possibility of a free form of narration. Here the characters are thematic motifs making their appearance within the structure of a totality which exercises its control over the novel from outside. The Structure levels all such themes, abolishes all impression of depth in the individual, and those themes "develop" and vary solely in relation to the compositional leitmotif of *fatelessness*. The same applies to the narrative. The Structure determines the narrative plot from the outset, so that twists such as subterfuges, anecdotal partial solutions, reassuring or fantastic elements and "exceptions" cannot come into consideration. Psychological characterization likewise falls by the wayside; the totality of the Structure dictates the narrative, and illumination consists in examining the degree to which we play a part in bringing the Structure into existence. The process, the development of themes, is linear—there are no "reprises," nothing is allowed to reverse or repeat itself—and the composition finishes when the work-up comes to its end, when every possible variant within the sole existing possibility has been exhausted, and yet this ending still leaves everything open.—This would be tantamount to saying that the work, instead of "portraying," *becomes* what it portrays: the external structure becomes an aesthetic structure and the social laws become the laws of the novel's technique. The text itself is not a description but a happening, not an explanation but time and presence—at all times and throughout an essential function, never "external" or "writerly," and therefore never hollow. The starting-point is not the character, metaphysics or psychology of an individual but that exclusive domain of his life, his existence, which was linked—positively or negatively—with the Structure, whether bestowed on or expropriated from it. A structural novel views the other component parts of the individual as negligible, simply because they are indeed negligible.—The novel will be characterized by a certain deficiency as a result, a lack of the "rounded life" that aesthetes demand, a deficiency that incidentally tallies completely with the mutilating times.—This technique will only succeed, by the way, if it is no more "audible" than it is in a piece of dodecaphonic music. On the other hand, if the one-offness, the fantastic (the fantastic of precision), the temporality and fatelessness give the impression of a living experience, that will be a product of the technique.

1971 April: I must come to terms with working with a controlled and controllable material. The obligatory elements of this material are not only not to be avoided but must be adhered to very strictly: the loading up of the railway wagons, the journey, the arrival at Auschwitz, the selection, the bath, the issuing of clothes— everything as an obligatory succession of moments, exactly like the Stations of the Cross in a medieval passion play. The only big question is how to resolve the seemingly unbridgeable gulf between material and organizing principle, how to avoid the drama which at all times winks out craftily from behind the stylization and, in this setting, is simply inauthentic, insistently intruded by hindsight — "history," that artificial construct which retrospectively pins down events that origi- nally ran a very different course.

* * *

I spend an entire morning reconciling maps. Gradually I work it out: from my per- spective, everything that was on my left is shown as being on the right of the ramp and for the selection officer actually was to his right. With a magnifying glass, I scrutinized photos of new arrivals (maybe those from Tyachev, the village near the northern Transylvanian town of Sighetu Marmatiu, who featured in the Eichmann trial?). Smiles, optimism, trust. Yes, indeed, assuming man clings on to life even under conditions of totalitarianism, he is in essence contributing to the sustenance of totalitarianism: that is the simple trick of organization. The sense of alienation with which a person nevertheless relates to totalitarianism can only be halted by re- alizing this. This realization and its acceptance betoken an act of liberation; yet this act of liberation, this illumination—and with it the acceptance of complicity— always comes up against the censure of the survivors. This is how the "fateless" fate comes into being, how people pass from one alienation to the next; this is how nothing ever has an end: the dead themselves are threatened with resurrection.

Anyone who in a literary sense emerges "triumphantly" or "successfully" from concentration camp material is dead certain to be a liar and cheat: write your novel accordingly.

* * *

1972: The fantastic and the anecdotal: That can only be justified when it is obvious that it too is only a part, indeed a truly regular element, of the Structure. The act of being saved is just as much an absurdity, structurally speaking, as the acts of arrest and delivery to the camp and as such, in musical terms, nothing more than a retrogression of the *Reihe*, the tone row, but (or rather, therefore) of essentially the same material.

June: I believe my novel's character is like no other in the sense that he is constituted entirely of determinacies, reflections and tropisms: at all times and in all places it is solely the torment he suffers at the hands of the world that makes him speak up, otherwise he would be unable to speak at all; it is never he who induces the world to speak. (In the way that even Meursault still does, for example: "The sky was green, and I felt happy," or "I left my window open and it was good to feel the summer night flowing over our brown bodies," and so forth.)

* * *

1973

* * *

I am bringing up "this subject" too late, so I am told; it is no longer timely. "This subject" should have been dealt with much earlier, at least ten years ago, etc. For my part, however, I have recently again been surprised that the Auschwitz myth is the only thing that truly interests me. In contemplating a new novel, I can only think about Auschwitz again. Whatever I think about, I always think about Auschwitz. Even if I may seem to be talking about something quite different, I am still talking about Auschwitz. I am a medium for the spirit of Auschwitz; Auschwitz speaks through me. Everything else strikes me as inane by comparison. And not just for personal reasons either, that is for sure, absolutely sure. Auschwitz and everything bound up with it (but then what does not have something to do with it?) is the greatest trauma for the people of Europe since the Crucifixion, even if it may take decades or centuries until it dawns on them. If it doesn't, then it makes no difference anyway. But then why write at all? And for whom?

* * *

1974

* * *

Leafing through my *Galley Boat-Log:* Where are my everydays? Where is my life? Is it so non-existent, or so shameful? Could that be why I am stylizing myself? And with what diminishing conviction! . . . What is to be done about it anyway? I believe less and less in "literature," in fiction. Man does not just consume, he is consumed as well; the bit of him that was reserved for art (the tastiest morsel) seems gradually to be spent. What is left? Perhaps example (existence): both more and also less than art. The compulsion *to bear witness* grows ever stronger within me, all the same, as if I were the last one still alive and able to speak, and I were directing my words, so to say, at those who will survive the flood, acid rain or the Ice Age—biblical times, immense and grave cataclysms, a time of silence. The species steps into man's place; the creation is swept aside by the collective as by a fleeing herd of panic-stricken wild elephants.

* * *

Sorstalanság—Fatelessness—twelve letters. A coincidence maybe, but an indicative one.

* * *

1975 April: *Fatelessness* has been published. I have taken an honest look at myself: I am free and empty. I want nothing at all, feel nothing at all. At most a bit of the ignominy of the process.—The trumpets have fallen silent. "Victory is ours," sighed the army commander and expired.

George Simmel: "That we follow the laws of our own nature—and yet that is what freedom is—will only become graphic and convincing for us and for others too when these manifestations of our nature diverge from those of others; the only proof that our form of existence is not coerced on us by others is our irreplaceability by others."

The masters of thought and ideologies have ruined my thought processes. Turn away from history and towards what can be formulated definitively.

* * *

II. Drifting (amidst Reefs and Shoals)

* * *

1980 May 20th: On a scholarship, East Berlin; two days ago Dresden. Berlin— that monstrous symbol of absurdities, of our disorderly, walled-in life, which has not ceased being the past, which came to a standstill somewhere and whose sole occupation is to swallow up the future: the present is the apathetic poverty of survival. Yet the *direction* of this survival is completely unsure; it may be advancing in time yet it is still not steering *towards* anything—at least not perceptibly. People fill in the cracks between the stones materially as it were, like some sort of stifling, squishy mass: they queue up in shops, at cafés and restaurants. The morality of this human mass, or so it seems to me, is sheer decorum; all that is keeping a tight rein on it is the well-known limit of their possibilities. It is incomprehensible how every night does not bring massacres, arson attacks, blood baths and pillaging, then in the morning everyone would go to work. *Danke sehr, bitte sehr.*

In Dresden all I can see is faces like those in the pictures of the German masters in the Zwinger. What are they doing here if they have already been painted? People have no idea of their own superfluousness.

After two hours of queuing up for a couple of bread rolls, some cold-cut meat, etc., I discover printed on the crude paper bag the words *Freude am Einkauf* — "Shopping is Fun."

The Hotel Neva, Dresden: I read through what I have so far out of *The Failure*. It fits in well with the visible ruins here.—In the morning, swimming trunks, towel, soap, then off by tram to the swimming baths. After asking around, I locate it. The old man at the entrance desk points to a placard hanging resplendent on the wall: "Private individuals—Tuesdays only 20:30–21:15." I slink away. What was it Goethe said? "I was born a private individual." These days it has become an extremely arduous status.

* * *

The green wallpaper of the hotel room in the Dresden dusk. Outside heavy rainfall. Cut off from everything, separated from everything. In one hand Klaus Mann's *The Turning Point*, in the other Camus's *Notebooks* (as counterpoise).

The next day. Cold wind. Acquisitional foray into the city. Booty: 3 cakes, 7 postcards. One could not get into the butcher's shop. —Actually, I rather like the view of Dresden from my window on the fourteenth floor: the railway terminal building, the trains running on the overhead tracks, the roofs beyond that, here and there a curious chimney, dome or weather-cock, the university clock tower, the green hillside further away, its houses tucked amongst the trees. From the very first sight of the railway station a sense of *déjà-vu*. From time to time, it prompts me to step over to the window and just stare, fixedly and brooding, at the broad vista. Today I finally realized that this was the station from which I set off homewards when I got out of Buchenwald in 1945. It was a scorching-hot summer and we had to wait for hours on end for a totally uncertain departure time. If I rightly remember, I spent the entire journey on the steel plate between two coaches. Or was it on the roof? No, because it was from the roof that a Russian soldier with machine gun suddenly let himself down and, to my stupefaction, proceeded to rob me. So there it is, that's the station. I search myself as to whether it means anything. In all honesty, I can only answer: Nothing, nothing at all.

That evening the hotel repair man. He notices straight away from my German accent that I am a Hungarian. He has a Hungarian wife. They have just had a daughter; his wife went to Budapest for the delivery so that the child could be a Hungarian citizen. When she grows up, says the repair man, she will be able to travel, unlike him. "I feel like a criminal," he says. Indeed, I can see that on all sides. A punished people. But then can a people be punished? And even if it can be—since the means to do this are at hand—should it be?

* * *

Inez, my assigned *Betreuerin*, or "minder," my interpreter (and no doubt my informer too, which latter task she may, perhaps, discharge with a congenial partiality towards me), says "We are a front-line state," and shrugs her shoulders.

Seen from here, the peculiar art of living or, one might say, lifestyle of the former Austro-Hungarian Monarchy is suddenly thrown into relief. Already on the journey here the Czech waiter in the dining car of the Prague express radiated an air that is hard to pin down but is recognizably Central and East European. Perhaps it has to do with the skill in survival that has by now degenerated almost into geniality—beyond Good and Evil, beyond everything.

Monstrous, stifling Berlin again. Today I solved the mystery of the clattering noise that never-endingly accompanies one when walking around the city streets: the flags fluttering in the wind make the iron flagpoles rattle about in their pavement mountings. The place is never-endingly decked out with flags, never-ending celebrations; the whole city clatters and rattles. Never-ending boredom, never-ending humiliation of self and by self in turn. A smile, a gesture of politeness, however natural, elicits bafflement and aggression from other people. They simply do not believe that humanity can exist between one person and another.

* * *

May 30th: At the Brandenburg Gate. Behind the Wall, West Berlin tourist buses being shown the local sights over here. I weigh up whether to stay, whether I can stand it. With work I could stand it. Only I am not working.

June 21st: Humiliation of an entire country—no, "country"—and in no small measure by themselves. No solidarity. Concession for the Germans evidently means completely identifying with their situation. And to top it all, a startling, cheapjack provincial patriotism, DDR patriotism. Paralyzing. A twilight stroll to the famed Checkpoint Charley. The car traps, the continual rising and falling of the barriers, the toing and froing of privileged cars. I am repelled.

* * *

Weimar-Eisenach-Naumberg. Goethe's house in Weimar, twice. The second time on my own, as soon as it opened in the morning; an ample tip in order to obtain a lead of at least two rooms over the horde of tourists pressing right behind me. It disquieted me. Only *here* and *then* had *he* been possible. Turning one's back productively on an unproductive present, that is what is called German Classicism. He recognized the timely arena for his untimely genius. At the same time, what frailty, what vulnerability. One has only to reflect that Germany had no place for the more modern Heine, Büchner died, Kleist killed himself—and within the blink of an eye there was the hypermodern Nietzsche.—Then on to the Cranach collection in the castle. In the end, the scramble, the tramping around towns in the company of the tireless Inez, who would stop at every baker's shop in order to buy some disgusting *Kuchen* or other, so exhausted me that I knocked my knee while boarding the train and re-aggravated a knee swelling, which is keeping me tied for the moment to my hotel room in Berlin.—Berlin, Hotel Stadt Berlin: An icy wind outside, 15 degrees Celsius in my room. I limp down to the front desk because I don't trust the phone. Quite a sympathetic young man. I tell him it is cold. If that would be all right with me, he says, he might be able to have a heater sent up. That would be very much all right with me, I answer happily. No heater arrives. One and a half hours later, I call down to say I am still waiting for the heater. They don't know about any heater is the response. I limp downstairs again: in place of the young man is an unprepossessing young woman. "What heater?" she asks. "The one the young man promised earlier," I say. "What young man?" she asks. "The one who was sitting here earlier, in your place," I reply. "No one else has been sitting here," she says, she has been sitting there the whole morning. I start to feel unsure. After all, anything is possible. I tell her that I am freezing. Nothing she can do about that, the woman says. I point out that, when all is said and done, this is supposed to be a first-class hotel; she should have a heater sent up to me. The woman: "We have no heaters." I: "But if I'm freezing?" I then checked twice if I had correctly understood her response. I had: "*Decken Sie sich zu*—Wrap up more warmly!" I take the lift back to my room and switch on the tiny electric plate that I originally brought with me for making coffee and which has a plug that my friend K. has modified to fit any wall-socket in the world. A few minutes later a pleasant stream of warmth is wafting around my neck from the shelf where I placed the cooker plate. I stow my poorly leg on a chair and draw up the other leg so that I can lay my notebook on my knee. It took this painful leg, these two sterile months, and this final indignity to bring me to pick up from where I left off roughly eight weeks ago in Budapest:

'I take a book down from the shelf. The volume exudes a musty smell—the sole trace that a finished work and a completed life can leave behind in the air: the smell of books. *It was on the 28th of August, 1749, at the stroke of twelve noon, that I came into the world in Frankfurt on the Main,* I read. *The constellation was auspicious: the Sun was in Virgo and at its culmination for the day. Jupiter and Venus looked amicably upon it and Mercury was not hostile. Saturn and Mars maintained indifference. Only the Moon. . . .* Yes indeed, that is the way to be born, as a man of the moment—of a moment when who knows how many others were likewise born on this globe. Only the others did not leave a smell of books behind and so they don't count. The cosmic constellation arranged the lucky moment for a single birth. That is how a genius, a great creative figure, sets foot on earth—like a mythical hero. An unfilled place longs yearningly for him, his advent so long overdue that the ground is practically moaning out for it. Now all that has to be done is to await the most favorable constellation, which will assist him just as much through the difficulties of birth as through the uncertain beginnings, the years of hesitancy, until that shining moment when he enters the realm of recognition. Looking back from the pinnacle of his career, there will no longer be room in his life for any contingency, since his very life will have assumed the form of necessity. His every deed and every thought is important as a carrier of the motives of Providence, his every declaration pregnant with the symbolic marks of an exemplary development. 'A poet,' he pronounces later, 'should have a provenance; he must know where he springs from.'

I suppose he is right: that truly is the most important thing.

Well then, at the time I came into the world the Sun was standing in the greatest economic crisis the world had ever known; from the Empire State Building to the Turul-hawk statues on the former Franz Josef Bridge in Budapest, people were diving headlong from every prominence on the face of the earth into water, chasm, onto paving stone—wherever they could; a party leader by the name of Adolf Hitler looked exceedingly inimically upon me from amidst the pages of his book *Mein Kampf;* the first of Hungary's Jewish laws, the so-called *Numerus clausus* stood at its culmination before its place was taken by the remainder. Every earthly sign (I have no idea about the heavenly ones) attested to the superfluousness—indeed, the irrationality—of my birth. On top of which, I arrived as a nuisance for my parents: they were on the point of divorcing. I am the material product of the lovemaking of a couple who did not even love one another, perhaps the fruit of one night's indulgence. Hey presto, suddenly there I was, through Nature's bounty, before any of us had had a chance to think it through properly. I was a healthy child, my milk teeth broke through, I started to burble, my intellect burgeoned; I began to grow into my rapidly proliferating materiality. I was the little son in common of a daddy and mommy who no longer had anything in common with one another; a pupil at a private institution into whose custody they entrusted me whilst they proceeded with their divorce case; a student for the school, a tiny citizen for the state. "I believe in one God, I believe in one homeland, I believe in the resurrection of Hungary," I prayed at the beginning of the school day. "Rump Hungary is no land, reunified Hungary the heavenly land" I read from the caption on a wall map outlined with bloody color. *Navigare necesse est, vivere non est necesse,* I parroted in Latin class. *Sh'ma Yisroel, adonai elohenu, adonai ehod* I learned in religious instruction. I was fenced in on all sides, my consciousness taken into possession: they brought me up. With a loving word here and stern warnings there, they gradually ripened me for slaughter. I never protested, I strove to do what was asked of me; I languished with torpid goodwill into my well-bred neurosis. I was a modestly diligent, if not always impeccably proficient accomplice to the unspoken conspiracy against my life. . . ."

November: Szigliget. Worryingly offhand attitude to the novel. Reading through what has been completed so far: cool affirmation, but nothing stirs me. In the meantime I recall the visit to Buchenwald during my trip to Germany a few months ago: I did not so much as mention it in the diary that I kept there. The mediocrity and shamefulness of it all. Inez's question: Did I want to see Goethe's house first, or rather Buchenwald? Buchenwald, I answered. The bus stop was in quite a different place from the last time (a good fifteen years ago). The road, the landscape even less familiar than then. Heavy rain clouds gathered overhead. Inez and I went through the gate. A fair number of visitors; in front of us a group of youngsters accompanied by a. . . . What should I call him? . . . a death-camp tourist guide. The rain suddenly began to bucket down. We looked for cover in the nearest building; it happened to be the crematorium. The youngsters too crowded in with us. I was pushed up against the originally white- but now yellow-tiled dissection table. The rubber hose that served for washing it down was still there at the table head. Even inside here, the tourist guide, a middle-aged man with brown hair and a rather unsympathetic face, did not interrupt his impassively intoned explanations of how people were shot in the head, bodies incinerated, etc. He pointed out the tiny loophole above the weighing scales on which the inmates were placed for the shot in the back of the neck. Evidently none of this was of interest to the youngsters; a couple of them, at the back, carried on necking unperturbed. Inez quickly remarked that they must be West Germans. However inane the remark may have been, it did at least show her embarrassment and attentiveness towards me. Yet I was not in the least "offended." If anything upset me, it was solely the fact that my "history" obliges me to adopt a certain comportment with which I could not identify in the slightest at that moment. At that moment the only thing I could think about was how even the fact that Buchenwald meant nothing meant nothing. . . . That I had already written a novel about Buchenwald, and then this peculiar and melancholy fact that Buchenwald meant nothing . . . And how I wished so much not to be me, and they not to be who they are, that nothing had happened, that there was no history, and that all of us who happened to be gathered there were fateless like the Gods, as Rilke has it . . . The rain stopped, and we went outside. Inez wanted to know where the Little Camp had been. I couldn't point it out to her. The sun broke through the scudding clouds. On the bare hillside, some sort of plaques in the ground marked out the site of something or other—I could not make out the inscriptions; I found nothing by which to orient myself. I did not dare show Inez that I would have preferred moving on to a more hospitable place. We then strolled towards the gigantic monument along a path, at last unmarked, amidst high-standing weeds, thistles and meadow flowers on which raindrops were still glistening. From the crescent-shaped terracing cut into the hillside, a broad vista over the entire landscape. A group of statues, which was perhaps not too bad "in itself," completely lost its impact in the gentle temperate-zone sunlight, in this spacious setting that just invited one to stroll. We entered the grisly site of grace, an implausible shelter comprising a cross between Inca altars and modern cooling towers. Along the dizzying height of the weather-beaten wall, my eye was caught by an overall, a pail and a couple of empty beer bottles placed on the planks of a masons' scaffolding; the sight of these human artifacts was almost reassuring. Then down the hill by bus, and at lunch we were already back into the mundane swing of things (we were not allowed to sit where we pleased; they would not let us onto the terrace in the Hotel "Elephant," etc.), and I thought no more about Buchenwald. But I had understood where the boundaries of historical receptiveness lie. They do not admit generosity, although without a measure of generosity no people can understand another—nor itself, for that matter. I felt almost apologetic that I—one of millions—am part of that frame of reference in which the noses of this people, eking out an existence in this spiritual poverty, are rubbed, while the reasons for their oppression, their "punishment," are quite different from those by which they are justified. So, to exaggerate somewhat, it will again be me whom they hate for that. In the same absurd manner as when I was transported to Auschwitz back then because Manfred Weiss, so to say, had exploited the Hungarian people, and meanwhile the same Manfred Weiss and his family were granted travel visas for Portugal. That is how historical false-consciousness operates and is manipulated: falsification, sickness, neurosis, an imposed guilty conscience, the end-result of which is angry aggression—against others as long as that is possible, and when not, then against oneself. That is the inevitable consequence when people are not permitted materially, spiritually or intellectually to rise above their situation, to progress at all. . . .

If I could just discover some time who and what I am. . . .

A Sartre monograph. I am forced to recognize anew that I stem from their world. My roots reach back into the soil of this post-War existentialism. Is fresh nourishment still to be drawn from this soil? I suppose I am an untimely figure. That is not to say that I do not understand this world, but at all events that the world does not understand me (and has no desire to).

December: I have made my peace with my novel. The prologue is completely ready; I deleted bits here and there. It has lost blood as a result but has at least gained a consistency that, even in its slimness, it can carry with pride, like a gaunt aristocrat who keeps up his bearing even in decrepitude. And what is not decrepit? Beckett is, so too is Camus, painting is decrepit, music, everything. An exuberant art does not flourish on bare, burned-out fields. Something has been lost; but maybe precisely out of this loss something will be saved.

It must surely be rough to be dead, but in time one probably gets used to it (as to everything).

* * *

Note: The above text is a translation by Tim Wilkinson from Imre Kertész's *Gályanapló* (Galley Boat-Log). Copyright © 1992 by Imre Kertész. This translation is published by permission of Rowohlt Verlag GmbH, Berlin (2004).

Reading Imre Kertész in English

Adrienne Kertzer

The work of Imre Kertész is rarely the subject of North American scholarship on the Holocaust. Although the canon of Holocaust literature discussed in North America includes many authors who do not write in English—writers such as Elie Wiesel, Primo Lévi, Aharon Appelfeld, Tadeusz Borowski, Ida Fink, and Charlotte Delbo—Kertész is, despite his Nobel Prize, not to be found in this group. His absence, both caused by and reflected in the lack of interest in translating his work, points to the distance between his fiction and popular patterns of Holocaust representation in North America. My Hungarian-born relatives have told me that I cannot pronounce Kertész's name correctly; this paper begins by acknowledging that failure, for its subject is precisely that limitation, the understanding of Kertész that results when one reads him, as I do, only in English.

Other than a few essays and interviews, only two of his eleven works are available for such readers (the three new English translations of 2004 by Tim Wilkinson were not available to me at the time of the writing of this paper; for these, see the Works Cited, below; in the paper, I quote from the Wilson & Wilson translation, *Fateless*): *Sorstalanság* (his first novel, published in 1975, translated in English as *Fateless* in 1992 and as *Fatelessness* in 2004) and *Kaddis a meg nem született gyermekért* (published in 1990, translated as *Kaddish for a Child Not Born* by Cristopher C. Wilson and Katharina M. Wilson and published in 1997, and translated as *Kaddish for an Unborn Child* by Tim Wilkinson and published in 2004). *Fatelessness* and *Kaddish for a Child Not Born* are often described as the first and last part of a trilogy, the second part being the un-translated *A kudarc* (The Failure). Numerous reviewers assume that there is a single narrator in the trilogy and regard him as a veiled portrait of Kertész at different stages of his life, but I regard the narrators as invented characters who are neither identical to Kertész, nor to each other. Here, too, translation affects my reading in that according to the English translation, the narrator of *Fatelessness* is called George Koves whereas the narrator of *Kaddish for a Child Not Born* refers to himself only as B. Although I have read that Kertész is "unhappy with the translations and is eager to have the books retranslated" (Riding E5), I have read such statements only in articles that cite Kertész indirectly, not in interviews in which he actually expresses his unhappiness. István Deák says that the English translation of *Sorstalanság*, *Fateless*, "misses the zest of the Hungarian original" (66), but others regard Wilson & Wilson as "the best-ever translators of Hungarian into English" ("Translators" C7; on the translation of *Kaddish*, see Wilkinson).

Certainly, Kertész shares the problem of language with other Holocaust writers. That language is limited in its ability to represent the Holocaust is an idea often expressed by writers who stress that the everyday language we use—for example, the words for hunger and thirst—cannot describe what hunger and thirst mean in the camps. Kertész observes in his essay "The Exiled Tongue" that we are fortunate that the Holocaust does not have its "own exclusive language," in that such a language "would destroy those who speak it" (qtd. in "The Freedom" 41). His fiction draws attention to the inadequacy of language, for example, in the way that his protagonist George Koves in *Fateless* observes that "'Terrible' . . . is not exactly the term that [he] would use to characterize Auschwitz" (86). In contrast to other writers, however, Kertész does not claim that no words can adequately characterize Auschwitz. He finds the words that he needs in our daily lives. To look for them elsewhere is to fall into the trap of what he calls Holocaust kitsch: "any representation . . . that is incapable of understanding or unwilling to understand the organic connection between our own deformed mode of life . . . and the very possibility of the Holocaust" ("Who Owns Auschwitz?" 270). When George returns to Budapest after liberation, a journalist wants him to write about "the hell of the camps" (181). George rejects the metaphor, and when the journalist falls back upon the predictable response—that the camps are unimaginable—George thinks, "That's probably why they say 'hell' instead" (182).

The fact that the Holocaust does not lie beyond language makes its articulation all the more problematic. Believing that "the Holocaust does not and cannot have its own language" (qtd. in Kertész, "The Freedom" 40), Kertész elected to remain in Hungary after the suppression of the 1956 revolution, not because of any fondness for Communism, but because Hungarian was the language that he wrote in. Despite this decision, he insists that the survivor always writes in a "borrowed language" (qtd. in "The Freedom" 40). Adapting Franz Kafka's reflection upon the multiple impossibilities that face the Jewish writer, Kertész proposes that for the Holocaust survivor/writer, "it is impossible not to write about the Holocaust, impossible to write about it in German, and equally impossible to write about it any other way" (qtd. in "The Freedom" 40). Writing in Hungarian provides the painful pleasure of constantly reminding him of his "exile from his true home, which never existed" (qtd. in "The Freedom" 41). For if he had a true home, he would not have been deported. Thus, for Kertész, there is no way around the problem of language; the language of exile, the language of the country where he was born, is the only language that he can use. Unlike the choice he made in becoming a writer, there was no choice about the religion and language that he was born into. Hungarian is and is not his native tongue: "For a writer, for whom one language, the one he writes in, is always privileged, it is difficult to admit that . . . one language is like another, and none of them are really his" ("The Freedom" 42). To write about the Holocaust is to write from a position of exile.

To write from a position of exile complicates Kertész's relationship with his national literature; it is not surprising that when the Swedish Academy announced on 10 October 2002 that Kertész would receive the Nobel Prize in Literature, most Hungarians were unfamiliar with his work. There are reports that initially news of the prize was reported solely as news from abroad, but very quickly the books that Hungarians had ignored for years were in high demand. Kertész was in Berlin when he learned about the prize; by the time that he returned to Hungary, he found himself "greeted like a hero" (Riding E5). In short order, the Hungarian government revoked the tax on his prize and ensured that his books were available in libraries (Riding E5). In only a few weeks, 70,000 copies of *Fateless* were sold (Riding E5).

Despite the greater familiarity with his work in Germany, France, and Sweden, in most of the world, news that Kertész had won the Nobel Prize was greeted with a great deal of bewilderment and snide comments about how once again the Swedish Academy had chosen a writer whom no one had heard of. In *Fateless*, Kertész demonstrates how eager people are to jump to false conclusions precisely at the moments when they have little evidence to guide them but are desperate for explanations. A similar pattern is evident in the newspaper coverage reporting the prize, for it is obsessed with providing instant analysis of the motivations behind the Swedish Academy's choice. Reporters are far more interested in explaining the symbolism of the prize than in discussing Kertész's writing. Their articles always begin by dutifully quoting from the Academy's 10 October 2002 press release—a necessary step when reporters have to file stories about writers of whom they have never heard—but the articles quickly shift to what the reporters regard as the real reasons behind the prize. In contrast, the Swedish Academy's press release emphasizes that it is the exemplary quality of Kertész's writing that has merited the prize. The press release praises the universality of what he derives from "the decisive event in his life: the period spent in Auschwitz." This phrasing is in itself both revealing and misleading. The emphasis on Auschwitz reflects how the name has become the ultimate symbol of the Holocaust. In *Kaddish for a Child Not Born*, the narrator describes ironically a party game where everyone tells "where he was" (25) during the war—Auschwitz is the place that the party host calls "unbeatable" (26). The academy's reference to Auschwitz also overlooks what is equally significant for Kertész, both the decisive events in Hungary prior to Auschwitz—where in fact he spent only a few days—and the events post Auschwitz—not just his months in Buchenwald, but also his years in Communist Hungary. In his Nobel lecture, "Heureka!" Kertész describes a key moment in an office building in Communist Hungary that compelled his decision to write. He classifies the experience as "an existential self-discovery" (606) in which he realized that writing under a totalitarian regime gave him inner freedom but one that required a "highly allusive [linguistic] medium" (606) in which he could address both of the dictatorships he had experienced.

The complexities of Kertész's life experience prompt the newspaper articles to attribute to him numerous and often conflicting identities. Journalists inform their readers that Kertész received the Nobel Prize because he is 1) a Holocaust survivor, 2) a Jew, 3) a Hungarian, or 4) a European. There are also combinations of these identities, for example, in articles that identify him as a Jewish-Hungarian Holocaust survivor worth celebrating because he also survived Communist Hungary, or as a Jewish-Hungarian Holocaust survivor worth celebrating because he writes as a European, not as a Jew. To draw a distinction between writing as a European and writing as a Jew is troubling, not just because it challenges those who regard Kertész's Nobel Prize as a gesture by the Swedish Academy to signal its disapproval of the recent disturbing increase of anti-Semitic incidents in Europe. It is also evident that the distinction between writing as a European and writing as a Jew affects the way the Academy's press release characterizes Kertész's work: "For him Auschwitz is not an exceptional occurrence that like an alien body subsists outside the normal history of Western Europe" ("Press Release" <http://www.nobel.se/literature/laureates/2002/press.html>). That is, the Academy applauds Kertész for treating the Holocaust as neither unique nor exceptional, but as part of European history, and gives him the prize because in his writing, he finds "the ultimate truth about human degradation in modern existence." The Academy's citation praises Kertész specifically for "uphold[ing] the fragile experience of the individual against the barbaric arbitrariness of history" ("Press Release" <http://www.nobel.se/literature/laureates/2002/press.html>).

In contrast, many newspaper articles concentrate on the challenge of identifying Kertész, both symbolically and specifically. They cannot take for granted that their readers will know the complex history that makes his life so ambiguous, and occasionally betray their own ignorance of that complexity. In a representative article in *The Vancouver Sun*, on 11 October 2002, Kim Gamel reported that Kertész was 72 years old, "a Jew born in Budapest . . . deported in 1944 to the Auschwitz concentration camp in Nazi-occupied Poland, then to the Buchenwald camp in Germany, where he was liberated in 1945" (A11). This biographical information encourages us to place Kertész in the company of Wiesel, who was also liberated from Buchenwald and won the Nobel Prize for Peace in 1986. However, it would be inadvisable to take for granted a commonality between these two survivor/writers, for in his work, Kertész often writes in direct opposition to the religious discourse associated with Wiesel. Gamel does not explore this contrast; instead, she cites, as do many of the newspaper articles, a statement by Wiesel in which he expresses his enthusiasm for the Swedish Academy's decision. Gamel also provides her readers with two factual statements: "Some six million Jews were killed in the Holocaust" and "Kertész is the first Hungarian to win the award" (A11). Again, whatever connection we might make between these two statements runs up against the very history that Kertész depicts. How many of Gamel's Canadian readers know that close to 10% of the Jews who were killed during the Holocaust were Hungarian Jews deported in the Spring and Summer of 1944 or know that many of the Budapest Jews who escaped deportation died at the hands of Hungarian anti-Semites? The history of Hungarian anti-Semitism is one that Kertész says Hungary has not addressed (on the history of anti-Semitism in Hungary, see Gerő; Kovács; Ozsváth; Suleiman; on contemporary anti-Semitism in Hungary, see Marsovszky; Tötösy, "And the 2002 Nobel Prize"; Young). Although Gamel quotes Kertész saying that Hungarians have not "faced up to the Holocaust," she does not explain what such a confrontation would involve.

The novel ends with George Koves very much alienated from his Hungarian background. Granted "the prize of being allowed to live" (*Fateless* 190), he is already aware that people do not want to understand what has happened, and especially not their own complicity. In contrast, many articles, like Gamel's, suggest that giving the prize to Kertész might be regarded in some sense as recognizing both the millions of Holocaust deaths and the literature of Hungary. Gamel may be right that this longing underlies the Academy's decision, but it is hard to recognize both. According to Alan Riding in the *New York Times*, "some extreme rightist Hungarians said they hoped that next time a *real* Hungarian would win the prize, while others sent e-mail messages to the Swedish Academy saying it had fallen victim to an international Jewish conspiracy to destroy Hungarian culture" (E5). The prize was announced just one day after the European Union confirmed the admission of Hungary into the European Union in 2004; whatever the Academy's intention in awarding a Hungarian citizen the Nobel Prize, not all Hungarians were ready to regard Kertész as Hungarian. Neither were they the only ones to challenge the prize. The web site for David Irving's *Action Report* questioned the authenticity of Kertész's story, and on 17 October 2002 posted an entry "Imre Kertész" that continued to question his identity as a Holocaust survivor (*Action Report* <http://www.fpp.co.uk/Auschwitz/stories/Kertesz_Biog.html>).

In yet another group of newspaper profiles, the prize is explained by identifying Kertész as a representative Holocaust survivor (on media reception of Kertész's Nobel Prize, see Marsovszky; Tötösy, "Imre Kertész's Nobel Prize"; Young). The limitation of this category lies in the way it indiscriminately conflates Kertész's Holocaust experience and writing with that of all other Holocaust survivor writers. These articles stress that Kertész is the first Holocaust survivor to win the Nobel Prize for Literature—Wiesel won the prize for Peace—and that therefore the prize in effect recognizes all Holocaust writing. Thus, in the *New York Times*, Thane Rosenbaum, noting how many Holocaust survivors who became writers later committed suicide, proposed that Kertész's prize be viewed as a collective achievement, for all the writers, alive and dead, who had written on the Holocaust. In essence, he was suggesting "A Nobel Prize for literature of the Holocaust" (Rosenbaum A21). In making his argument, Rosenbaum groups Kertész with Elie

Wiesel and Aharon Appelfeld as Holocaust survivor writers who are still alive and who should be honoured not just for surviving, but for surviving their post-Holocaust lives as well. I want to challenge this grouping and to suggest that a more accurate way to understand Imre Kertész is to think of his work as radically opposed to Wiesel's. Despite Wiesel's praise for Kertész and the way that their first novels are often read as autobiographical accounts of their time in Auschwitz and Buchenwald, their writing has little in common. This contrast may also explain why Kertész's work is not better known in North America.

A good place to illustrate the difference between Kertész and Wiesel is in an early section of *Kaddish for a Child Not Born*. The narrator of this novella is a writer and translator who has refused to bring a child into this world. He does so not just because of his experiences during the Holocaust; by the novella's ending, we learn that traumatic events in his childhood prior to the war have also left him determined to say, "No!"—the word that begins nearly every one of the novella's lengthy paragraphs. The narrator's refusal drives his wife to leave him, and as he contemplates his life, he recalls the evening when he first met her. It was at a party when he became enraged by the discussion of a popular Holocaust book. His outburst was unusual, for describing himself as a "private survivor" (12), he positioned himself at some distance from the conventional way of talking about the Holocaust: "I was not willing to give in, like an idiot, to the mass survival hysteria and the breast-pounding oratory" (21). The narrator also calls himself a "Budapest survivor" (21). Such words are provocative—what does it mean to be a survivor of Budapest? Like Kertész, the narrator did not survive the war in Budapest and the term alludes to the non-religious character of many of the assimilated Budapest Jews who were deported. The narrator says that Budapest Jews are "not Jews at all, but of course not Christians either . . . the kind of non-Jewish Jews who still observe holy days, long fasts, or at least, definitely, until lunch" (16). In comparison, Wiesel grew up in a Hasidic background in Sighet, a small village in Romania's Transylvanian region. Wiesel's devoutly religious background is foreign to the narrator of *Kaddish* as it is to Kertész. It enters into the narrator's story only as part of a traumatic memory of his childhood when he first met "real genuine Jews" "in a dusty, stuffy Hungarian village where [he] was sent for a summer vacation" (16). The trauma occurred the morning he opened a bedroom door and saw "a bald woman in a red gown in front of a mirror" (16). Not recognizing that this woman was his orthodox aunt, the narrator confesses that when he later learned that the condition of Judaism "carries the death penalty" (17), he came to identify with the image he saw that morning and to regard it as the emblem of his Jewishness: grotesque, repellent, and shameful. Only by seeing himself as a bald woman in a red gown in front of a mirror could he make sense of the way the world looked at him. The act of misrecognition characterizes the narrator's ignorance regarding Judaism—he had not known that orthodox Jewish women shaved their heads and wore wigs. It also characterizes the anti-Semite who according to Kertész misrecognizes complex humans similarly by labeling them with unambiguous racial identities. Once the trauma of misrecognition occurs, it is hard to escape its power. In "The Freedom of Self-Definition," Kertész admits, "In 1944, they put a yellow star on me, which in a symbolic sense is still there; to this day, I have not been able to remove it" (37).

The narrator says he is "one who makes no fuss over his survival, who does not feel compelled to testify to his survival, to give meaning to it-yes-to turn his survival into a triumph" (21–22). However, he is compelled to make a fuss when the party conversation turns to the "subject of a then-fashionable book" (26). At this point the alienation of the narrator from conventional patterns of representing the Holocaust shifts into a pointed critique of writing such as Wiesel's. Someone at the party quotes a sentence from the fashionable book, "Auschwitz cannot be explained" (26)—exactly the kind of sentence we find in Wiesel—and the narrator is astonished. He is driven to protest at length. How can clever people believe "this idiotically simplistic sentence" (26)? For several pages, he attacks its philosophical flaws. Auschwitz happened; of course, it can be explained. We may not like the explanation, but whatever has happened, can be explained: "Anything that *is* has an explanation" (28). The narrator simply cannot leave the topic alone: "By way of that wretched sentence 'Auschwitz cannot be explained' is the wretched author explaining that we should be silent concerning Auschwitz, that Auschwitz doesn't exist, or, rather, that it didn't, for the only facts that cannot be explained are those that don't or didn't exist. However . . . Auschwitz did exist, or rather, *does* exist, and can, therefore, be explained; what could not be explained is that no Auschwitz ever existed, that is to say, one can't find an explanation for the possibility that Auschwitz didn't exist . . . yes, indeed, it is precisely the absence of Auschwitz that could not be explained" (28). That Auschwitz *does* exist is italicized; it is characteristic of Kertész that his narrators' past tense recollections always conclude in the present tense, as though to write about the Holocaust in the past tense is impossible. We might read this impossibility as demonstrating the ongoing trauma of the Holocaust survivor. However, in his Nobel lecture, Kertész clarifies that he means more than this when he says, "Auschwitz . . . is still not over" ("Heureka!" 607). Believing that "nothing that has happened since Auschwitz . . . could reverse or refute Auschwitz," he explains, "In my writings the Holocaust could never be present in the past tense" ("Heureka!" 607).

The narrator of *Kaddish for a Child Not Born* argues that the explanation for Auschwitz lies in "individual lives and exclusively in individual lives" (29). He dismisses those who would tell him that his "explanation is a tautology, explaining facts with facts" (29). To understand history, he insists, we must pay attention to all of the individual steps that were taken. Auschwitz did not just happen by accident: "Consequently, Auschwitz must have been hanging in the air for a long, long time, centuries, perhaps like a dark fruit slowly ripening in the sparkling rays of innumerable ignominious deeds, waiting to finally drop on one's head" (28). The fruit, like the sword of Damocles that it evokes, does not just happen. The problem of the leap from individual lives to the historical theories that account for centuries is not addressed; the narrator's concerns lie elsewhere. The narrator is scathing about the reluctance to recognize the contribution of individual acts in explaining the Holocaust: "the totality of individual lives and the technique of administering the whole thing, that's the explanation, no more, nothing else" (29). He is contemptuous of theories that rationalize the human willingness to accept the leadership of common criminals by proposing that Hitler was demonic. To offer grand theories about "the social situation . . . the international political situation . . . philosophy and music and other artistic hocus-pocus" (30) is similarly beside the point. It is far easier to explain evil, the narrator insists, than to explain good. It is the good that happened to him during the Holocaust that he cannot explain; the evil makes sense enough.

This is a point that Kertész explores over and over. The problem of Holocaust representation lies neither in the limitations of language nor in the inexplicability of evil. The problem is that we do not want to accept that evil is explicable. In his Presentation Speech for Kertész's Nobel Prize, Torgny Lindgren, a member of the Swedish Academy, says, "The realities that are the subject of Imre Kertész's literary production and form its background cannot be understood or described by any of us who have not experienced them" (Lindgren <http://www.nobel. se/literature/laureates/2002/presentation-speech.html>. But according to Kertész they can be understood if we are willing to listen. It is precisely the problem of finding people who will be willing to listen that concludes George Koves's story in *Fatelessness*. George imagines what he will tell people the next time that they ask him about the camps, but the novel ends with the possibility that they will never ask and that therefore George will not remember the reality of his experience. Similarly, in *Kaddish for a Child Not Born*, the narrator's wife leaves him because she can no longer listen to his "awful childhood and [his] monstrous stories" (91). While it would be a mistake to identify Kertész with his fictional narrators, it would be a greater mistake to set aside his attention to explanation just because we prefer to believe that the Holocaust is unimaginable and inexplicable. For Kertész, it was imagined, and it can be explained. Even if we conclude that his narrators—particularly George Koves—fail to explain the Holocaust adequately, and we believe that a theory of history requires more than a linear account of individual lives, this does not mean that the Holocaust cannot be explained. That such explanation must never lose sight of the small steps taken by each individual accounts for the narrative technique of *Fatelessness*. Consider the opening sentences of each chapter in this novel. Despite the opening sentence of chapter 10—"I have to admit that there is a lot I could never explain . . . not if I tried to base my explanations on reason"—what characterizes these explanatory sentences is their precise and mundane descriptiveness. Explanation resides within the details: the water that the narrator missed on the train; the shrinking food portions. Except for the references to

Buchenwald, in sentence 7, and Zeitz, in sentence 8, nothing marks immediately these sentences as about the Holocaust. Buchenwald is described as it might be in a geography book.

George Koves, who like Kertész was fourteen years old when he was deported, tells his story with a mixture of surprise and acceptance. He never protests; he tries to get along. When he sees other Jews escape by stepping out of line, he is bemused but does not act. He has no particular motive for stepping out of line and his "sense of honor" (42) outweighs the desire to run off. But it is precisely his not stepping out that leads him to the train. It is obvious that George lacks the information that would motivate stepping out, and clearly given the historical circumstances, he might still have ended up in Auschwitz. But the question of when we can step out—when it is too late, and when there is still time for our actions to make a difference—is a constant preoccupation of Kertész. Compare George's language of not stepping out to Kertész's decision to become a writer: "The need to step out of the mesmerizing crowd, out of History, which renders you faceless and fateless" ("Heureka!" 606). In 1950s Hungary, Kertész can and does step out; in 1944, George Koves does not. At the end of his first day in Auschwitz, George is sure that the whole thing has been planned "in the same way that a practical joke is planned" (82). He imagines a group of well-dressed gentlemen—"in respectable suits, with cigars, and with medals on their breasts" (82)—competing with each other to imagine the humiliating and atrocious details. He has no problem imagining this process: "One of them had dreamed up the gas, another the baths, still another the soap. A fourth added the flowers, and so on it went" (82). Confined to George's limited understanding—the reality of how he experiences what happens—the novel relentlessly probes the language of explanation, only to undercut it by pointing to the numerous times that George does not understand. What George comes to understand is the power of incremental steps. He also comes to understand that his ability to "become used to every new step gradually [prevents him having] the detachment [he] needed to actually notice what was happening" (114). Paying attention to what is happening to others, he does not notice what is happening to his own body.

The difficulty with Kertész's narrative technique is characteristic of ironic texts. *Fatelessness* requires a reader who is more perceptive and informed than the narrator; only such a reader can recognize the inappropriateness of many of George's explanations. When George skips school, the explanation—"personal reasons" (3)—that his father provides for the teacher is both correct and incomplete. He skips school because his father has been conscripted into the labour service; George does not mention the racial laws that underlie this. His Judaism has never concerned him; it is merely an accident of birth. When he later is told by orthodox Jews in Buchenwald that his inability to speak Yiddish means that he is not a real Jew, his resulting sense of inadequacy makes him feel that he really is Jewish. The first chapter foregrounds George's lack of understanding, his desire to please his father on this special day, and his boredom—in many ways serving as models of what he will experience in Auschwitz and Buchenwald. His Uncle Lajos tells him that the day's events mark the end of his childhood; George is surprised and admits that he hadn't thought of this. For Kertész, the end of childhood is also a progression of small steps. George takes for granted that what is happening is "natural" (14)—the novel's language is peppered with the words, "naturally" and "of course." Tense with having to behave well, he is relieved when at the end of the day he starts to cry at the separation from his father. How fortunate, he thinks, to send his father "off to labor camp with the memory of a beautiful day" (20). George's ability to call beautiful what we regard as horrible will also affect his later description of Buchenwald. When he returns to Buchenwald from the camp hospital, he admits that he feels like he is returning home and expresses his longing to "live a little longer in this beautiful concentration camp" (138). Such language raises two interpretive problems: how does the reader recognize irony and whose irony is it? In foregrounding problematic aspects of George's language, Kertész never reveals his own position. The adults that George observes are equally confused by what is happening and hungry for grand explanations. One neighbor reports that the present severe actions against Budapest Jews are the result of secret discussions to protect them; another neighbor of the family tells George that he is "part of the common Jewish fate" (15), one which he must accept. Forced to pray, George admits to being "tired" and "annoyed" (16); he does not understand Hebrew and has no interest in understanding it. In contrast to the narrator of Wiesel's *Night* who loses his faith because of what he sees in the camps, George has no faith to lose. There is a famous scene in *Night* where the narrator witnesses a young boy hang, and concludes that God is hanging on the gallows. George watches a similar hanging, but Kertész focuses on George's distance from Judaism, not from God. As he overhears the murmurs of the *kaddish*, the Jewish prayer for the dead, George thinks how absurd and "useless" (119) praying is.

When George is rounded up—the "strange" happening that opens chapter 3—and is deported to Auschwitz, this happens because he is Jewish. However, it also happens because of bad luck, the result of following their neighbor Steiner's advice to take the bus, rather than the streetcar when he goes to work (Steiner is a neighbor of the family in the apartment building they live and not an "uncle" as in the Wilson & Wilson translation: The Hungarian *bácsi* is, in English indeed "uncle"; however, in Hungarian this does not mean "uncle" as in a relative but is a term used to address and refer to an older male by a younger person). Because of the "absurd order of chance" ("Heureka!" 608), George goes to Auschwitz and Steiner survives the war in Budapest. As always, George misunderstands the significance of the roundup; forced to get off the bus, he concludes that the police just want to check his papers; the adults who are deported either blame their "bad luck" or seek for explanations that the novel discredits. In Buchenwald George hears a joke that the "U" of *Ungar* does not mean Hungarian (Ungar is Hungarian in German); it means *unschuldig* (innocent). Whether adult or child, they are all innocent, surprised to discover what is happening. Nevertheless, with time one can get used to anything; on the second day in Auschwitz George eats the disgusting soup, and on the third day he looks forward to it. In one of his most shocking statements, George notes that one can "be bored even in Auschwitz" (87). In fact, this is why George eventually rejects the journalist's metaphor of hell; the difference between hell and Auschwitz is that George imagines hell as a place where one can never be bored. To survive Auschwitz requires boredom, the strange experience of waiting "for nothing to happen" (87). But the only thing that happens in Auschwitz is death; once again, the novel demands a reader who recognizes the irony and who knows that the alternative to boredom is death.

In his Nobel lecture about the burden of surviving the Holocaust—a survival he attributes to "the absurd order of chance" ("Heureka!" 608)—and his mid-life decision to write about it, Kertész admits, "It is not so easy to be an exception" ("Heureka!" 608). In many ways his writing is itself exceptional, in contradiction to the conventions of Holocaust discourse that dominate North America. It is not just that his prose is difficult—the Swedish Academy offers ambivalent praise when it compliments his style for his "refusal to compromise," evident in its resemblance to a "thickset hawthorn hedge, dense and thorny for unsuspecting visitors." Taking on Adorno's prohibition—No Poetry after Auschwitz—Kertész says that fiction is more capable than non-fiction in describing the concentration camps: "The concentration camp is imaginable only and exclusively as literature, never as reality" (from *Gályanapló* [Galley Boat-Log] qtd. in "Who Owns Auschwitz?" 268). Kertész's work is often discussed as autobiography, but he categorizes it as fiction. Fiction can come closer to truth than autobiography: "The drive to survive makes us accustomed to lying as long as possible about the murderous reality in which we are forced to hold our own, while the drive to remember seduces us into sneaking a certain complacent satisfaction into our reminiscences; the balsam of self-pity, the martyr's self-glorification" (from *Gályanapló* qtd. in "Who Owns Auschwitz?" 268). In contrast, Wiesel writes, "A novel about Auschwitz is not a novel, or else it is not about Auschwitz" (qtd. in Horowitz 15).

The need to find the right language of explanation drives George Koves to the language of fairy tales. It has been fashionable recently to belittle Roberto Benigni's *Life Is Beautiful* but Kertész prefers its fairy-tale discourse to the "saurian kitsch" ("Who Owns Auschwitz?" 269) of Steven Spielberg's *Schindler's List*. As George sees his body magically transform into that of an old man in Buchenwald, he comprehends fairy-tale truths about transformation (*Fateless* 121). After months of imprisonment, what he sees still surprises him, but he is certain that if only he can discover the right set of rules for explaining what he sees, the system will make sense. The question of understanding drives him: "What were you to make of all this . . .?" (148). What are the rules that explain why camp hospital doctors want to save his life whereas outside the hospital, this is not the case? Explanations based on conventional logic do not help, and George considers whether the "make-believe world of fantasy" (148) offers more insight. Initially he concludes that maybe he is the subject of a perverse experiment in which he is nursed only to be starved; he recalls rumors that in Auschwitz "they feasted their patients on milk and honey until piece by piece they removed all their organs" (148). Anything is possible, and such rumors are not far from the truth of Nazi medical experiments. Finally George is driven to accept the absurd reality of the hospital: "This place was also possible . . . no stranger than all the other strange possibilities . . . in a concentration camp" (151). As in a fairy tale, inexplicable luck matters more than anything; a series of random acts save his life. Like Primo Lévi, he survives because of the bad luck/good luck of being ill at the end of the war.

Because George emphasizes the accidental, because he comes back from the camps saying he hates everyone "Naturally" (180), because he insists that he experienced no "horrors," he is unwelcome when he returns to Budapest. What makes him particularly unwelcome is his insistence that "we did it step by step" (187). He outrages his neighbours Steiner and Fleischmann: "What? Are we now the guilty ones—we, the victims?" (189). George clings to this belief in personal freedom because he needs to believe that what happened to him was not simply fate, that he did not nearly die because of an accident of birth. He is convinced that Steiner and Fleischmann do not understand and do not want to understand. How much George himself understands is left ambiguous; if according to Kertész survivors deceive themselves, then George's insistence—"The point is in the steps. Everyone stepped forward as long as he could: I, too, took my steps" (188)—may be part of that deception. Deák, calling George a "modern Candide," says that *Sorstalanság* is a devastating satire (65). But as with *Candide*, we might ask what is being satirized, and is the ending part of the satire? Equivalent to Kertész's "Heureka!"—the moment that makes him decide to be a writer—is George's epiphany: "'We ourselves are fate.' I recognized this all of a sudden and with such clarity that I had never seen before" (189). But Kertész provides ample counter-evidence regarding the role of luck and accident, and qualifies George's rhetoric by revealing his desperate desire to see his life as meaningful: "Do you want all this horror and all my previous steps to lose their meaning entirely?" (189).

In writing about the Holocaust, Kertész describes himself as no different from other writers: "Which writer today is not a writer of the Holocaust?" ("Heureka!" 607). In his Nobel lecture, he is more optimistic than his narrators. He is also more willing to use the language of a larger historical perspective. The Holocaust is not a "conflict between Germans and Jews" ("Heureka!" 607) as the historian, Daniel Goldhagen, with his thesis of eliminationist anti-Semitism, has argued. It is not "the latest chapter in the history of Jewish suffering. . . . a one-time aberration, a large-scale pogrom, a precondition for the creation of Israel" ("Heureka!" 607). It is something that happened in Europe and to Europe. In contrast to those who say that the Holocaust cannot be understood, Kertész insists that "what was revealed in the Final Solution . . . cannot be misunderstood" ("Heureka!" 608). Having observed twice "how an entire nation could be made to deny its ideals, and watched the early, cautious moves toward accommodation" ("Heureka!" 606), he knows that "the real problem with Auschwitz is that it happened" ("Heureka!" 608). In his Nobel lecture, he urges us to acknowledge this, and to reflect upon its implications. While the narrator of *Kaddish for a Child Not Born* insists, "one can never recover from Auschwitz" (60), the Nobel Laureate is both more tentative and more hopeful: "the only way survival is possible . . . is if we recognize the zero point that is Auschwitz" ("Heureka!" 608).

Works Cited

Action Report Online: Real History and Fake Auschwitz Survivors. "Imre Kertész." (17 October 2002): <http://www.fpp.co.uk/Auschwitz/stories/Kertesz_Biog.html>.

Deák, István. "Stranger in Hell." Review of *Fateless*, by Imre Kertész. *New York Review of Books* (25 September 2003): 65–68.

Gamel, Kim. "Auschwitz Survivor Awarded Nobel Prize for Literature: Swedish Academy Singles out Imre Kertesz's 1975 Debut Novel *Fateless*." *The Vancouver Sun* (11 October 2002): A11.

Gerő, András. "Identities of the Jew and the Hungarian." *Imre Kertész and Holocaust Literature.* Ed. Louise O. Vasvári and Steven Tötösy de Zepetnek. West Lafayette: Purdue UP, 2005. 65–75.

Horowitz, Sara R. *Voicing the Void: Muteness and Memory in Holocaust Fiction.* Albany: State U of New York P, 1997.

Kertész, Imre. *Gályanapló* (Galley Diary). Budapest: Holnap, 1992.

Kertész, Imre. *Fateless.* Trans. Christopher C. Wilson and Katharina M. Wilson. Evanston: Northwestern UP, 1992.

Kertész, Imre. *Kaddish for a Child Not Born.* Trans. Christopher C. Wilson and Katharina M. Wilson. Evanston: Northwestern UP, 1997.

Kertész, Imre. "Who Owns Auschwitz?" Trans. John MacKay. *Yale Journal of Criticism* 14.1 (2001): 267–72.

Kertész, Imre. "The Freedom of Self-Definition." Trans. Ivan Sanders. *Witness Literature: Proceedings of the Nobel Centennial Symposium.* Ed. Horace Engdahl. New Jersey: World Scientific, 2002. 33–43.

Kertész, Imre. "Heureka!" *PMLA: Publications of the Modern Language Association of America* 118 (2003): 604–14.

Kertész, Imre. *Liquidation.* Trans. Tim Wilkinson. New York: Knopf, 2004.

Kertész, Imre. *Kaddish for an Unborn Child.* Trans. Tim Wilkinson. New York: Vintage, 2004.

Kertész, Imre. *Fatelessness.* Trans. Tim Wilkinson. New York: Vintage, 2004.

Kovács, András. "The Historians' Debate about the Holocaust in Hungary." *Imre Kertész and Holocaust Literature.* Ed. Louise O. Vasvári and Steven Tötösy de Zepetnek. West Lafayette: Purdue UP, 2005. 138–47.

Lindgren, Torgny. "Presentation Speech." *The Nobel Prize in Literature. Laureates* (2002): <http://www.nobel.se/literature/laureates/2002/presentation-speech.html>.

Marsovszky, Magdalena. "Imre Kertész and Hungary Today." Trans. Eszter Pásztor. *Imre Kertész and Holocaust Literature*. Ed. Louise O. Vasvári and Steven Tötösy de Zepetnek. West Lafayette: Purdue UP, 2005. 148–61.

Nobel Prize in Literature, The. Laureates (2002): <http://www.nobel.se/literature/laureates/index.html>.

Ozsváth, Zsuzsanna. "Radnóti, Celan, and the Aesthetic Shifts in Central European Holocaust Poetry." *Comparative Central European Culture*. Ed. Steven Tötösy de Zepetnek. West Lafayette: Purdue UP, 2002. 51–69.

"Press Release 10 October 2002." *The Nobel Prize in Literature. Laureates* (2002): <http://www.nobel.se/literature/laureates/2002/press.html>.

Riding, Alan. "A Holocaust Survivor at Home in Berlin." *New York Times* (4 December 2002): E1+.

Rosenbaum, Thane. "The Survivor Who Survived." *New York Times* (12 October 2002): A21.

Suleiman, Susan Rubin. "Central Europe, Jewish Family History, and *Sunshine.*" *Comparative Central European Culture*. Ed. Steven Tötösy de Zepetnek. West Lafayette: Purdue UP, 2002. 169–88.

Tötösy de Zepetnek, Steven. "And the 2002 Nobel Prize for Literature Goes to Imre Kertész, Jew and Hungarian." *CLCWeb: Comparative Literature and Culture* 5.1 (2003): <http://clcwebjournal.lib.purdue.edu/clcweb03–1/totosy03.html>.

Tötösy de Zepetnek, Steven. "Imre Kertész's Nobel Prize in Literature and the Print Media." *Imre Kertész and Holocaust Literature*. Ed. Louise O. Vasvári and Steven Tötösy de Zepetnek. West Lafayette: Purdue UP, 2005. 232–46.

"Translators to Discuss Prize Winner." *Edmonton Journal* (9 December 2002): C7.

Wiesel, Elie. *Night*. Trans. Stella Rodway. 1960. New York: Discus-Avon, 1969.

Wilkinson, Tim. "Kaddish for a Stillborn Child?" *The Hungarian Quarterly* 43 (2002): 41–43.

Young, Judy. "The Media and Imre Kertész's Nobel Prize in Literature." *Imre Kertész and Holocaust Literature*. Ed. Louise O. Vasvári and Steven Tötösy de Zepetnek. West Lafayette: Purdue UP, 2005. 271–85.

Imre Kertész's *Fatelessness* and the Myth about Auschwitz in Hungary

Kornélia Koltai

Translated from the Hungarian by Katalin Erdődi

The totalitarian system not only called for a certain grade of clarity and simplicity that bordered on one-sidedness; the very structures of its existence were characterized by simplification. Thus, one should not wonder that it was incapable of dealing with a book that, instead offering readily a "single" interpretation, had several. And it was by no means a coincidence that in 1973 when Imre Kertész sent the manuscript of *Sorstalanság* (*Fatelessness*) to the publishing house Magvető, the then "official" literary critics rejected it. When it came to publishing books in the era of János Kádár, it was of utmost importance that the author's political standpoint on the events of the Second World War—when portraying Nazism and the Holocaust—be clearly definable. If the theme of Holocaust was approached from a political perspective in the context of political loyalty, it served to legitimize the very existence of the regime and therefore to reinforce its acceptation by society. The Kádár regime not only strived to control the political factor, it also regulated the scope of artistic expression in the representation of the Holocaust. Since the aim was to convey an indirect political message to large segments of society, emotionalism and the manipulation of emotions became a core element in the portrayal of the Holocaust and in this sense was formulated as a criterion dictated by the politics of literature. Thus it happened that in 1959 Imre Keszi's novel *Elysium* was deemed worthy of publishing because it fulfilled both then required criteria of political stand and literary style. When describing the fate of the protagonist—a boy fallen victim to Nazi sadism—Keszi's book excises strong emotional reaction from the reader and the demise of the main character gives the impression of a genuine tragedy. The reader feels intense empathy and identifies on emotional grounds with the personal views of the author. As a result, the conclusion can be seen as artistically well grounded: the arrival of the Soviet soldier as liberator is undeniably the point of catharsis in the narrative. Looking at *Elysium* and its plot from a historical-political perspective, one recognizes that Keszi's book could appear in print because it convinces the reader that the liberating Soviet army was the only possible solution in the course of events

Hajtű-kanyar (1974, Hairpin Bend), the fictional autobiography of Mária Ember also passed the test, presumably owing to the narrative technique used. Ember blends the narration of events inspired by real-life facts with historical documents. Such interplay of fiction and reality—enhancing the authenticity of a "fictional" story by supporting it with documents—suits perfectly the aims of making an impact of producing the identification of the reader on emotional grounds. At the same time, the technique embedding historical facts in a fictional narrative makes the text and its events easier to remember. Ember's text could also be published because it is in perfect harmony with the totalitarian regime's literary politics, namely the program of "educating" the masses. Pál Bárdos's novel, *Az első évtized* (1975, First Decade) approaches the dominant ideology from a different perspective. His writing underpins the goals of communist totalitarianism's social and language policy, according to which ethnical, religious, and cultural variety could not exist, not even in verbalized form. As a consequence, after the Holocaust the only possible choice of the Jewish-Hungarian population was assimilation and integration into the internationalist system. Bárdos's novel could be published because it called for communism and also declared that Jews should forsake their identity. Naturally, aside from the above-mentioned novels, several others that dealt with the theme of the Holocaust appeared in print in Hungary. Nevertheless, these selected writings can be regarded as representative in illustrating the orientation of the Holocaust literature of the time. In 1973, in line with the then official politics of literature, *Sorstalanság* did not fit into any of the categories defined for Holocaust portrayals and Kertész's work was found unsuitable in the context of the Holocaust representation adopted by the communist regime.

The rejection of *Sorstalanság* by the publishing house and the novel's "failure" at first can be seen as a decisive turning point in Kertész's career. With the passing of time the failure experienced evolves into a source of inspiration and was transformed into a driving force that enriches Kertész's work. In his collection of essays *Gályanapló* (1992, Galley Boat-Log) that contain his writings and entries between 1961 and 1991, and also in his novel *A kudarc* (1988, The Failure), the fact that the manuscript was rejected is verbalized explicitly by Kertész. At one point he includes the letter of the publisher—word for word—in his own text: "Concerning 'this theme,' I am too late, or so I have heard. It is out-of-date. 'This theme' would have been of interest earlier, at least ten years ago" (*Gályanapló* 26): "It was a regular, ordinary business letter, with date (27 August 1973), with administrator (not named), with subject (not specified), with registration number (483/73), without address: 'Your manuscript was read by the publishing house's readers . . . who all shared the opinion that you failed to demonstrate the necessary artistic skills in wording your personal experience'" and "my novel was rejected" (*A kudarc* 75). After coming to terms with the rejection, Kertész himself acknowledges that such an act of rejection can be seen as characteristic of the mechanisms of the world he portrays. Therefore, the refusal to publish his writing serves as proof of how the totalitarian regime works and at the same time becomes a new code of interpretation for Kertész. How the decision to publish his work came about is also very typical of the era: It was made possible not out of an appreciation or consideration of its artistic and aesthetical merit but by the rivalry of the two publishing houses that monopolized by official decree the Hungarian book market. Two years after its rejection, in 1975 *Sorstalanság* appeared in a censored version by the publishing house Szépirodalmi. In his diary entries, Kertész writes about the "successful" publication of *Sorstalanság*: "April 1975, *Sorstalanság* is published" (*Gályanapló* 34). Naturally, its reception was negligible, as befitted the regime. It was just as natural that the slow, but nonetheless steady ideological change that began in the 1980s initiated a search for classified files, archives until then concealed and forgotten, and with that revealed new horizons for the re-interpretation, criticism, and rethinking of past events. This was the time when Kertész was discovered and *Sorstalanság* reread and new editions of the novel appeared in 1983 and 1985. People found that the key to understanding his writing and the only possible way to "read" his books was to recognize the primacy of the formal approach.

The entries referring to the publication of *Sorstalanság* show that Kertész likes to document the workings of his mind, as well as the events of the surrounding world. He ponders and reflects on these thoughts, many times not only in a descriptive sense, but showing inclination to a normative interpretive approach. He also makes note of coming up with the idea to write *Sorstalanság*: He not only records accurately this event in documentary fashion but interprets the moment retrospectively. His "afterthoughts" in the *Gályanapló* date from 1964 and the reference in *A kudarc* recounts how the idea took form from even greater distance in time: "In life there comes a time when all of a sudden, you realize who you are and are overcome by a sense of power. From this moment on, we can take ourselves into account; this is when we are actually born" (*Gályanapló* 13). When recalling in *A kudarc* the moment of inspiration to write *Sorstalanság*, Kertész points to 1956, the year of the Hungarian Uprising against communism and Soviet rule. With hopes of liberation and great change running high, the author found himself compelled to reckon with the events of his past. This reckoning did not happen voluntarily: it was an answer to the demand of the outer world and external powers, conveyed to the writer in the form of dreams, visions, and an inner process of revelation. Fulfilling this demand was beyond his power and causes him suffering. In fact, as Kertész records his mental state during the course of writing the novel and after its publication, it is clear that his was an all-consuming sacrifice: "I am free and empty. I desire nothing, I feel nothing. . . . Victory!—sighed the general and died" (*Gályanapló* 34) and "Oh, what emptiness, what a fall!" (*Gályanapló* 27).

In his later works, Kertész regards the writing of *Sorstalanság* as getting a quasi obligatory job done and sacrificing himself while completing the task. I read this in the context of a familiar phenomenon in the world of mythology and mystics where the hero sacrifices himself for the sake of humankind and dies while performing his good deed. By conceiving the process of being emptied and applying the metaphor of death to the act of writing, Kertész places the novel itself on a mythological pedestal. Therefore, the retrospective interpretation in Kertész's case can be proposed as a kind of mythicized re-defining of his work. The mythical hero is stigmatized: He is God's anointed; he is stigmatized because he is one of God's people. The "border-line situation" (the notion is taken from Jaspers and used in its existentialist sense) of 1956 makes Kertész realize that the theme of the book he must write can be no other than Auschwitz: "As a result of his revelation, he appointed himself to his task" (*A kudarc* 139). His all-encompassing existential prose is the concentrated life story of the mythical hero himself.

Sorstalanság begins *in medias res:* "Today I skipped school" (3; while I quote from the Wilson & Wilson translation, *Fateless*, in the paper I use otherwise the correct translation of *Sorstalanság* as in Tim Wilkinson's translation of the novel, *Fatelessness*, at the time of the writing of this paper not yet available). The tone Kertész strikes in the beginning goes a long way in determining the style and quality characteristic of the whole novel. All through his work, simplicity of expression and often in the strictest grammatical sense, assertive sentences prevail. Kertész's narrative abides by the "obligatory" contents of a book on Holocaust, on surviving Auschwitz. By drawing a parallel between this conventional pattern and the guiding principles of passion plays, Kertész makes the genre sacral and defines the following stations of suffering: Living in the ghetto, traveling in the cattle cars, arriving at Auschwitz, becoming a prisoner, the alternative, the coincidence, the survival of survival. The plot begins with leaving home and ends with arriving home. Thus, Kertész creates a framed structure but also sustains the causal and linear (chronological) structure characteristic of classical narration. The time span of the story told is one year, which can also symbolize a certain integrity and completeness. Since the narrator of the story is the protagonist and it is through the eyes of this teenage boy that we are made familiar with the events, it is possible to approach and understand the narrative technique used as an expression of his mentality. The detached, matter-of-fact narrative technique can be seen as a manifestation of his attitudes and views, given that the teenaged boy regards the events as something self evident. For example, "All of this . . . we all agreed sounded feasible. Besides, we had to obey him" (*Fateless* 33). At the same time, such detachedness supposes that the boy considers himself an outsider, a mere spectator: "Without any doubt, I thought he was correct, although the question didn't really concern me" (*Fateless* 69). The technique of alienation is especially evident when he uses formulas reminiscent of official or scientific-documentary style of language, such as "at this particular time her stomach was unable to keep down any kind of food" (11) and "Buchenwald lies in a mountainous region at the crest of a hill. Its air is clean. In the camp one's eyes were delighted by various views: forests were all around, and the red roofs of village houses lay in the valley below" (91). The combination and constant interaction of being a naïve onlooker and becoming a victim, along with the fact that the narrator knows less about the situation on the whole than the reader, results in producing a peculiar tension.

It is highly unusual that anyone should portray "the greatest trauma since the crucifixion" (*Fateless* 27; *A holokauszt* 11) from the perspective of an indifferently naïve teenager: The narrative technique, tone and style of the novel make it possible to draw an analogy between its protagonist and narrator, Gyuri Köves and Meursault, the protagonist of Camus's novel *L'Étranger*, and as a consequence, to call to mind the views of the existentialists. The course of the events appears natural, but in fact, it is absurd. Only when taking the absurdity of existence as a starting point, can such events seem "normal." Only from a functional point of view, when "bracketing existence" (drawing on Husserl's phenomenological category) can all this be considered necessary and with no alternative. By evoking the existentialists' philosophy in *Fatelessness*, Kertész makes Auschwitz the metaphor and myth of universal totalitarianism. The narrative technique used in the novel not only implies a linear structure, it also entails making advance with some kind of aim. Such purposeful linearity is well illustrated by the change in the quality of the novel's non-characterizing character-study.

In the beginning (at home), the family's portrayal is extended to each member. Aside from becoming familiar with their outer appearance, one also gains brief insights into their lives through anecdotes, such as "before he opened a betting office, he was in the newspaper business" (*Fateless* 13). The representation of the micro society at the customs house (in the ghetto) is detailed and implicit, inclined to be concentrated in character: "The other man then lapsed back into lamenting his bad fortune" (*Fateless* 38). Later in the death camp even the non-characterization becomes simpler. The narrator describes Bandi Citrom with no more than a few bits of information relevant to the actual situation: "He had ended up here, I learned, from a labor camp. . . . He had qualified for labor service because of his age, blood, and state of health . . . That's all I could pull out of him" (*Fateless* 96, 97). And the stripping, the denudation of the character study escalates further: in the hospital, Pjetyka's character is outlined exclusively in view of his obligatory tasks: "Take Pjetyka, for example. . . . The impeccable ordering of the room, the wiping of its floor . . . all this was the work of his hands" (*Fateless* 152). The way the character study is stripped bare can be seen as a telling side effect, a consequence of the destruction of personality: the different stations of suffering are at the same time the individual's Stations of the Calvary. The naïve outsider, the unknowing boy in a peculiar guest-prisoner position—"At first I felt myself, so to speak, like a guest in the world of convicts" (75)—acquires knowledge gradually: "The first day didn't come to a close without getting a clear view of everything, by and large" (80) and adopts eventually to, grows into the life of a prisoner. Thus, the death camp can be regarded as an existence, a state of being, in which personality is destroyed but at the same time it can lead to a certain knowledge.

In the "borderline situation" of the death camp the teenage boy grasps the finality and also the absurdity of existence, that is, hidden within this revelation, he acquires knowledge needed to encompass Being, to comprehend Existence: "I felt that some irreparable damage had been done to me; from that point on I was convinced that every morning would be the last morning . . . that every move would be my last" (125). The subjective, concentrated, and intensely lived time spent in the death camp—"seven days are seven years" (21)—makes him realize how relative existence is: "Certain things . . . that I had previously considered tremendously, almost incomprehensibly important now lost all value in my eyes" (125). The absurdity of the concentration camp restores the real meaning of words: "He asked me if I was willing, and I was amazed because he looked at me like someone who was indeed waiting for my answer, even my agreement" (129). And with death drawing very near, the absolute is manifested: "the bodies pressing against mine no longer disturbed me. Somehow I was even glad that they were there with me, that their bodies and mine were so connected and so similar, and now for the first time I felt a strange, unusual, somewhat shy, almost clumsy feeling toward them. Perhaps it was love, I think" (135). In Kertész's novel, the concentrated existence of the death camp can be seen as *the* genuine articulation of absurd existence. Our hero is merely playing a role which casts him as being in a state of "fatelessness," he can only escape the Jewish fate imposed upon him if he is able to face death. Only in the shadow of death is he able to fulfill his own destiny, that is, to reflect on existence. The intense existence experienced in the death camp is no other than the very essence of Being, here and now, *the* authentic existence. In *Fatelessness* Auschwitz represents the ultimate absurdity of Jewish existence, it appears as the exclusive and indispensable prerequisite of authentic revelation.

After the death camp, "outside Auschwitz," the grown-up boy is again confronted with "bracketing existence," but this time in the grasp of the "truth" revealed to him. The existence of "fatelessness" can only be combated—surviving survival can only be accomplished—by passing on the revealed and empirically experienced truth "in the shadow of chimneys, in the breaks between pain, there was something resembling happiness" and "Yes, that's what I'll tell them the next time they ask me: about the happiness in those camps" (191). This is how Auschwitz becomes the prerequisite of surviving survival. Resolution is found in establishing life about Auschwitz as the subject of literature. So it is that after Auschwitz—in a reversal and subversion of Adorno—one cannot write anything other than poetry, and "after Auschwitz one cannot write poetry about anything other than Auschwitz" (*A holokauszt* 22). However, as I introduced above, totalitarianism, the "bracketed existence" of the Kádár regime "silences the muse": Kertész's myth of Auschwitz, his account of "happiness in the concentration camps" could by no means reach the public in 1973 and was received with a total lack of understanding and interest in

1975 while at the same time the rejection of the novel led to the creation of a myth by the novel itself.

In *A nyomkereső* (1977, The Pathfinder), Kertész documents his returning after thirty years to Buchenwald and Zeitz. In *Gályanapló* Kertész tells us of the autobiographical connection: "Meanwhile, I recalled my visit to Buchenwald during my trip to Germany a few months ago" (85). The protagonist of the novelette is a man in his forties: the "delegate." One day, this man goes to examine former crime scenes. During his extraordinary expedition he gets caught up in adventures and affairs that are all examples illustrative of the historical trauma's still painful memory. Alas, on the surface the wound afflicted by history, by events of the past, seems healed but face to face with the scene it causes disappointment. When looking back at the years of writing *A nyomkereső* in the *Gályanapló*, Kertész uses the metaphor of wandering in the desert: "Wandering on and on through the desert, plodding along in the sand, staggering along the desolate plain, for forty biblical years now (plus six), still manna does not fall, no fresh water spring can be found, there is no way out, no flower blooms" (48). These images also appear—almost word for word—in *A nyomkereső*, such as "this barren landscape . . . this place exposed to the murderous heat of the noon sun" (53). The delegate's pilgrimage to the land of long ago can be seen as a version of wandering in the desert, an exploration, a groping-around for the adequate form of expression in order to return and reclaim the knowledge lost.

The search for form calls to mind the visions of Dante: "Its sulfur-spouting cauldrons, burbling circles" (*A nyomkereső* 102) and is riddled with apocalyptic images such as "are the dies irae trumpets being blown?" (86). The wandering is the consequence of the fruitless search for a way out, but "it has failed" (103), "To flee from here! . . . These objects . . . remain here forever, solid and unredeemable" (104-05). Kertész's decision is symbolized by the suicide of the veiled woman in mourning, who after coming face to face with the "scene," when she realizes that her loved ones are forever lost and past events cannot be reversed: "Her veil of mourning was wound around her neck like a rope" (*A nyomkereső* 111). This is the only way the wanderer is able to carry on his mission, changing course, but not ceasing to "weave through reefs and ledges," as the title of the second part of *Gályanapló* suggests.

The second novelette of the volume entitled *A nyomkereső* is *Detektívtörténet* (Detective Story). When assessing Kertész's work, the two long short stories can also be regarded as parts of a whole. While *A nyomkereső* contributed to maturing the idea from which *A kudarc* was to stem, *Detektívtörténet* makes headway in context of the form. *Detektívtörténet* depicts a structure—an allegory of Auschwitz—with crime story clichés. The fictional state is set in South America. The events are narrated by Martens, a detective-turned hangman. *Detektívtörténet* is his confession, the portrayal of a malicious state body striving, illegally, for control of the state. The events are recounted as diary entries, in confessional form. This technique results in escalating tension and by showing the workings of the mind, by looking inwards creates an increasingly authentic effect. The method of "displacing the scene"—that is, setting the plot in Latin America—makes possible a constant vibrating between references and allows for identification with Hungary in the 1950s. The tension mounts if one takes into account the actual time of writing the novel: the dictatorial system of the 1970s does not yet tolerate such in-depth and analytical uncovering of the 1950s. The network of references has three dimensions: Latin America, the setting and the time of the story; Hungary in the 1950s, the time and place with which the reader identifies the story; and Hungary in 1970s, the actual time, the dictatorial setting of the story's conception. The triadic structure is also characteristic of the formal structure: the manuscript of the diary complemented by the commentaries of the lawyer. Martens's manuscript saw light only after he was convicted and executed with the help of his officially appointed lawyer. This diary, however, contains part of another diary, the diary of a young man (Enrique) whose thinking and sensitivity sets him apart from the "assimilated" masses of society and this in turn costs him his life. Enrique's non-existentialist philosophical fragment evokes the ideological backdrop of *Fatelessness*, while the dramaturgy of the triadic role play already paves the way for the Old man Köves-Berg's alterego in *A kudarc*. Thus, *A nyomkereső* and *Detektívtörténet* are essential parts of Kertész's oeuvre, as in them the myths of totality and Auschwitz take shape. At the same time, the two novelettes are also imprints of the crises of Kertész's search for forms of artistic expression, as of his search for his place in the world. Only the transition, the change of system, puts an end to the crisis caused by the hardships of dealing with the myth of Auschwitz. Kertész had to wait until totalitarianism's next "borderline situation" to recognize and develop the adequate approach to his prose.

The pertinent passage of *Gályanapló* and that also reflects on writing *A kudarc* informs us of close ties with *Sorstalanság*, in terms of the novel's motives and the author's motivations. In the case of *A kudarc*, a novel of Camus can again be pointed out as a source of inspiration, and in general, the intellectual impact of existentialism can also be felt: "In a mood for confession. Something from that sphere, like 'The Fall' ('A bukás')" (51) and "A Sartre monograph. Again I am forced to recognize, I am of their world. I stem from the existentialism that evolved following the war" (87). Furthermore, both novels are marked by atonality as the underlying principle of his narrative technique. In *Sorstalanság* atonality is designed to separate the autobiographical dimension from illustrated historicism while in *A kudarc* the role of atonality is further elaborated as it appears directly as a constituent of the plot: "The narration of the events appears to follow a linear structure, but in the end, it turns out that it has made a full circle. It is an epic estimation of the setting, without its domination" (61). At the same time, "no process can be compensated or substituted by analysis" (64). The use of the first person narration is an additional link connecting the two pieces of writing. In both, self-expression dominates, as does understanding the world as determined by the ego, as well as the all-encompassing character of totalitarianism as creative environment and illustrated milieu. *A kudarc* is a novel that relates a writer's career by supplying two different versions: in the introduction the author-protagonist recalls with documentary accuracy the stages of his career, from writing his first novel until the present. Subsequently, the novel within the novel, that is, the actual novel portrays an earlier stage: it relates how the writer presented in the introduction became one. The form applied in the introduction of *A kudarc* reflects how Kertész's theoretical approach grows more and more profound. He still makes use of the phenome-nologically-grounded descriptive technique applied in *Sorstalanság*, but here it forms part of a continuous interpretation and re-interpretation.

The mechanism of totalitarianism is "beyond comprehension" (*Gályanapló* 87). This incomprehensibility is increased further by the absurdity of language. Al-though objectively put, the language is incapable of grasping the essence of exis-tence, Kertész attempts to overcome at least the obstacles that impede comprehen-sion and do not make sense (at this point his views can be linked to the theses of Wittgenstein). The relativity of concepts entails striving for precision and makes an increasingly accurate description necessary. The re-interpretation, as well as the application of different linguistic techniques thereby serves the clearer transmission of concepts. The frequent use of brackets and hyphens can be seen as an example of techniques applied to the ends of increased accuracy: "he was not old (nor was he young) (that is precisely why they call him 'old man')" (*A kudarc* 12). Further examples are the increasingly complex syntactic structures which at the same time make a growing flow of information possible and the *terminus technicus* of distinct linguistic strata. For example, "In terms of the Decree (No. 1/1970.III. 20. MM) is-sued in agreement with the President of the National Price Office and the National Council of Syndicates" (*A kudarc* 16). The repetitions, the topics (constant ele-ments) and the intra-textuality all serve a more precise depiction of the writer-protagonist's world (in its totality), since absurd existence itself is cyclical, repeti-tive and constant. A further form of representing totality is pushing the concept to its extremes, using a form of composition based on the paradox. For example, "al-though he was registered only as temporary resident, it was his permanent home" (*A kudarc* 9). The paradox, especially characteristic of the technique used in his later works, not only conveys the relativity of existence, but also demonstrates the combination of contradictory qualities of tone. Aside from suggesting the absurdity of the world and language itself through the novel's formal solutions, Kertész also defies the conventional treatment of time. In the introduction of *A kudarc*, he breaks with the linear, chronological structure and instead continuously alternates between the portrayal of present and past events, trying simultaneously to maintain his grasp of both dimensions. Thus, the evolving plot also includes the alternating use of various types of text, since past events are recalled in the form of diary en-tries and embedded texts.

By exploring the scope of linguistic possibilities to its extremes, portraying the totality of the temporal dimension, and using simultaneously different bodies of text and, at the same time, striking a grotesque tone, *A kudarc* is Kertész's wording of his views on absurd existence in its most theoretical and theoretizing form. This attempt to systematize and re-interpret coincides with the end of the 1980s, the time of transition, when people expected a summary, an explanation of past events, and the creation and realization of myths. This is the atmosphere, introduced previously, that was responsible for renewed interest in *Sorstalanság*, when the novel began to be reread and new editions were published. This is the time when it becomes clear to Kertész that the myth of Auschwitz should form part of the cultural heritage of human kind. It is in this self documentation and reflective-creative period that he decides that the novel *Fateless* should be elevated to the mythical heights of his lifework.

As I have shown earlier, the reading of *Sorstalanság* can be pre-determined by retrospective re-interpretation. In the introduction of *A kudarc*, the "old man" not only relates how the task of writing a novel was appointed to him ("Many years afterwards. . . . I came to know that I had a novel to write" [29]), he also words the mythical process of fulfilling the task: "I never believed . . . in my existence. While writing the novel this handicap of mine became my work tool, it disintegrated in my daily routine. After getting tired of pouring it into words, it bothered me no more" (34). Kertész's views on being a failure are incorporated in his writing: "there is no greater acknowledgement, no lesser glory for a writer than the blindness of his contemporaries with regard to his work. The crowning of this glory is when the blindness is paired with his silencing. . . . I felt apprehension at the alarming glory heralded by my failure" (*A kudarc* 75). Further, he expounds his theory on the novel, on the reason for *Sorstalanság*'s separate existence and in connection with this, on the existence of the creative process. "All of a sudden, I came into the possession of a material that finally offered a concrete reality instead of my excited, but constantly disintegrating visions... I was possessed by a peculiar feeling of ecstasy. Mine was a dual life: there was my present which I lived half-heartedly, and my past in the concentration camp, lived as the harsh reality of the present" (*A kudarc* 81). Finally, he offers an evaluation of his identity as author: "My intention was also no other than communication, indeed if it had not been so, I wouldn't have written a novel. To communicate . . . the material within my possibilities, my material, myself . . . Alas, there is one thing . . . I didn't take into consideration: we can never communicate ourselves to ourselves. 'I' was taken by a real train, not an imaginary one, to Auschwitz" (82). In the novel-within-the-novel of *A kudarc*, the reader encounters the literary interpretation of the myths of Auschwitz. Following the search for form in *A nyomkereső* and *Detektívtörténet*, the actual novel of *A kudarc* can be regarded as a stage of utmost importance in Kertész's artistic work because it embodies the best possible approach to Auschwitz.

The novel-within-the-novel is the work of the protagonist of the introduction. The writer elaborates the theme of embedded texts found in the introduction, this time in the form of fiction. After traveling for a long time, Köves arrives to an unknown place. In spite of finding himself in an absurd world, he behaves as if he were living his former life. In fact, this absurd world bears haunting resemblance to Budapest, the scene of his former life. By such interplay of two worlds Kertész calls to mind the novelistic form used by Kafka. The "scheme," the pattern of Köves's absurd life, can be illustrated by the stages of Kertész's life story: working as a journalist after the arrival/homecoming, followed by writing comedies, work in the factory and at the press department, and finally the revelation, the moment of discovering the purpose of life. The totalitarianism of the novel is the dictatorship of the 1950s: Kertész portrays the absurdity of the power structure with psychological accuracy. During the course of his life, the protagonist becomes acquainted with several people but most of the time these relationships only serve to make him aware and to reinforce his feeling of being alone, a metaphysical solitude. Berg, the insane "hangman" imprisoned in his room, is the only person with whom his relationship is worth mentioning. Berg is the one who can offer the writer the most help and prompting in finding his individual task. Berg is the only one who can overcome the absurdity of existence by facing it, by putting it into words, by writing a crude and unfinished fragment of a novel. The catharsis of *A kudarc*'s novel-within-the novel is the scene when Berg reads the part he has already finished to Köves. In this dramatic scene the existential philosophy of Kertész is assessed: the idea of totalitarianism, of an inner force compelling him to write, the illusory character of existence ("bracketed existence"), where all is incidental: redemption, moral and values, and finally "man is a mere redundancy . . . on what perilous grounds does his moral equilibrium stand" (333) and "What a victory it is to love! What tyranny! And what slavery!" (342).

With the gradual dissolution of Berg's mental state Kertész illustrates the dissolution of social values by drawing on the formal criteria of tragedy. Berg's character can therefore be regarded as an example of fate's alternative in a world of fatelessness. As Kertész expounds in *Gályanapló*, in contrast with the functionality of life, only fate is capable of bearing the "possibility of tragedy" (10, 15). The work portrayed in *A kudarc* is Sisyphean: Köves is destined to roll the stone of the myth elaborated by the author. Over and over again, he has to interpret the same subject—totalitarianism as the absurdity of existence, symbolized by Auschwitz, and the story of being in the state of fatelessness in a state order labeled totalitarianism—only to fall back into the abyss at the point of catharsis (the Berg scene in the novel), making the completion of the task constant and superfluous. At the same time, aimlessness is only one of the aspects of the Sisyphean stone rolling, there is another factor that makes the work meaningful. The Sisyphean fulfillment of the task (writing) also includes, paradoxically, the joy of never ceasing to interpret the epic material, thereby making the completion of the individual task constantly possible. Accordingly, the Sisyphean work entails the incessant creation and re-creation of the authentic existential experience: Fate is fulfilled continually and this is what makes the writer-protagonist happy.

Is it possible to write happily about Auschwitz? Is it possible to write about the "intervals of suffering" and the "happiness of Auschwitz"? Is it possible to write happily about Auschwitz in a way that the absurdity of the death camps also portrays the greatest and most painful catastrophe of humankind? Kertész succeeds in accomplishing this task. He writes about the truth revealed to him in Auschwitz: about the happiness of Auschwitz and at the same time, about the ever-painful memory of the trauma. He writes about the paradox that Auschwitz represents: For Kertész, the task of surviving survival is the task of a lifetime and the continuous writing about the Holocaust where, in turn, writing is his existence.

Works Cited

Bán, Zoltán András. "Körkörös monológ" ("A Roundabout Monologue"). *Magyar Napló* 24 (1990): 13.

Bárdos, Pál. *Első évtized* (First Decade). Budapest: Szépirodalmi, 1975.

Csáki, Judit. "Sors és sorstalanság. Beszélgetés Kertész Imrével" ("Fate and Fatelessness: An Interview with Imre Kertész"). *Kritika* 3 (1992): 24–26.

Ember, Mária. *Hajtű-kanyar* (Hairpin Bend). Budapest: Szépirodalmi, 1974.

Győrffy, Miklós. "A kő és a hegy. Kertész Imre: *A kudarc*" ("The Rock and the Mountain: Imre Kertész's The Failure"). *Jelenkor* 10 (1989): 985–87.

György, Péter. "Egy mondat értelmezéséhez" ("On the Interpretation of a Sentence"). *Orpheus* 7 (1991): 39–40.

Hima, Gabriella. Review. "Kertész Imre: *A kudarc.*" *Alföld* 6 (1989): 86–88.

Kertész, Imre. *Sorstalanság* (*Fatelessness*). Budapest: Szépirodalmi, 1975.

Kertész, Imre. *A nyomkereső* (The Pathfinder). Budapest: Szépirodalmi, 1977

Kertész, Imre. *A kudarc* (The Failure). Budapest: Szépirodalmi, 1988.

Kertész, Imre. *Kaddis egy meg nem született gyermekért* (*Kaddish for an Unborn Child*). Budapest: Magvető, 1990

Kertész, Imre. *Gályanapló* (Galley Boat-Log). Budapest: Holnap, 1992.

Kertész, Imre. *Fateless*. Trans. Christopher C. Wilson and Katharina M. Wilson. Evanston: Northwestern UP, 1992.

Kertész, Imre. *A holokauszt mint kultúra* (The Holocaust as Culture). Budapest: Századvég, 1993.

Kertész, Imre. *Fatelessness*. Trans. Tim Wilkinson. New York: Vintage, 2004.

Keszi, Imre. *Elysium*. Budapest: Szépirodalmi, 1958.

Marno, János. "Sziszifusz, az öreg—Köves és Berg" ("Sisyphus the Old: Köves and Berg"). *Kortárs* 3 (1989): 155–61.

Spiró, György. "Non habent sua fata. A *Sorstalanság*—ujraolvasva" ("Non habent sua fata: *Fatelessness*—Reread"). *Élet és Irodalom* 30 (1983): 5.

Székely, János. "Találkozások a terrorral" ("Meetings with Terror"). *Élet és Irodalom* 22 (1977): 10.

Wirth, Imre. Review. "Kertész Imre: *Kaddis a meg nem született gyermekért.*" *Vigília* 11 (1990): 876–77.

The Historians' Debate about the
Holocaust in Hungary

András Kovács

At the time of the first publication of Imre Kertész's *Sorstalanság* (*Fatelessness*), the memory of the Holocaust in Hungary belonged mainly to the realm of private/personal memory. After the Communist take-over in 1947–1949, the animated public discussions of the first post-war years on the uneasy questions of involvement, responsibility, moral and material re-compensation, etc., were adjourned forcefully and the ruling official narrative on the persecution of Jews excluded all serious exchange on the historical explanation and the historical and moral consequences of the Hungarian Holocaust. The subject, if at all, appeared only in few literary works, mostly surrounded by silence, as the book of Kertész itself. However, in the first half of the 1980s after the long decades of silence a vivid debate broke out on the Holocaust in Hungary. Characteristically, the debate was not provoked by a Hungarian publication, but of the monumental work of Randolph L. Braham's *The Politics of Genocide*, which became a standard work on the Holocaust. In Hungary, the book was published finally seven year after its American publication, and the reception of it has shown immediately the uneasiness of Hungarian historians of the period (see Braham 1981, 1988).

György Ránki, a prominent historian of the time and director of the Institute of History of the Hungarian Academy of Sciences and who contributed to the discussion on Braham's book with several articles (see below), signalized already certain reservations in a review, written on the American publication of Braham's book and incorporated into the introduction of Iván T. Berend to the Hungarian edition of the two-volume work. Ránki expressed the opinion that the thoroughness of the research and description was the strongest feature of Braham's book, but, as he put it in his "Introduction," "The eminent author does a better job in describing when and how these things happened than in analysing why the catastrophe took place" (Ránki, "A Magyar Holocaust" 7; Berend, Introduction 12; all subsequent translations from the Hungarian are mine unless noted otherwise). What is lacking from Braham's book, according to Ránki, is "the uniquely Hungarian aspect of the tragedy of Hungarian Jewry" (Ránki, "A Magyar Holocaust" 7–8). By this Ránki means that while the assimilated Jewry of West and Central Europe shared in the fate of their countries and while the Jewish population of East Europe—unaffected by assimilation—experienced the events as the inevitable workings of the eternal Jewish fate, the Jews of Hungary, who had considered themselves to be Hungarians, perished "without a fate" (7). Their national identity—which had seemed so uncomplicated up till then—was devastated by the brutality of the deportations and by the indifference with which the Hungarian authorities and a significant part of the public watched the process (on this, see, e.g., also Gerő; Ozsváth; Suleiman). This was, indeed, a distinctly Hungarian aspect of the tragedy, although in my opinion it was not as unique as Ránki assumes. As the persistently recurring French debates on collaboration in the deportations in France suggest, a similar feeling of "being deprived of a fate" might also be shared by the Jews of France. Nevertheless, I do not believe that the answer to why the catastrophe actually took place lies in the uniqueness of the tragedy of Hungary's Jewish population—as Ránki's criticism suggests. Braham does, actually, inquire into the origins of the catastrophe, but he approaches this from a different perspective. What he wants to know is whether the destruction of hundreds of thousands of Hungarian Jews was inevitable or whether the Hungarian Holocaust could have been averted. On this point the author takes a firm stand—it is therefore not surprising that the book stirred up heated controversy as soon as it was published.

Could the Hungarian Holocaust have been averted? Those participating in the debate prompted by Braham's book listed the factors which had affected—i.e., improved or reduced—the chances of the survival of the Jews in the European countries under Germany's influence (the debate was prompted by István Deák's review of Braham's book, see Deák; Benton et al.). It is difficult to draw a general conclusion. The geographical position of the given country most certainly played a part; so did the character of the state (democratic or authoritarian); the historically-developed relationship between the Jewish and the non-Jewish population; the reaction of the Churches; and—most importantly—the goals of German foreign policy with regard to that particular country. The various factors weighed differently, but perhaps the last factor on the list carried the greatest weight. Everyone who participated in the debate agreed that the majority of Hungary's Jewish population could have survived the war if the German occupation of Hungary could somehow have been avoided. The question that has to be asked, therefore, is whether the German occupation of the country could have been averted.

This question is difficult to answer, for the simple reason that historians have to this day been unable to agree on the real motive behind Germany's decision to occupy Hungary in March 1944. If we were to accept that one of the ultimate goals of Hitler's wars was the eradication of the "enemy race" and it was really a "war against the Jews," as Lucy Dawidowicz, an author often quoted in the Braham debate, firmly believes, then Hungary's chances of escaping German occupation were indeed small, considering that up until the country's occupation the Hungarian authorities had resisted the German demands to deport Jews. Of all the participants of the debate, William O. McCagg Jr. seems most inclined to share this view. He believes that in the case of countries with a small Jewish population, it might perhaps be worth examining whether Hitler subordinated his primary goal—the eradication of the "enemy race"—to rational considerations, either strategic or political. However, in Hungary, which even as late as March 1944, had a Jewish population of 900,000, the ultimate motive for the occupation must have been the enforcement of the "final solution" and in this sense the occupation of Hungary was unavoidable.

Braham, together with Helen Fein and István Deák, is of a different opinion. According to Braham, "the Germans' decision to occupy Hungary resulted from a series of complex political/military factors: the unsolved 'Jewish question,' though important, was not the determining one" (Braham, *The Politics of Genocide* 1 362). He believes that the Germans followed primarily strategic goals: in the worsening military situation they wanted to secure the unconditional loyalty and obedience of their allies. They were extremely worried about the political developments in Hungary, most notably about the attempts of the Kállay government to reduce the war effort and to make contact with the Allied Powers. Braham believes that Miklós Kállay, who wished to avoid occupation both by Germany and by the Soviet Union, was an incompetent politician. Kállay's illusions about the possibility of arranging for a separate armistice with the Allied Powers proved completely unfounded; he failed to make the necessary military arrangements; he failed to rid the political and military leadership of pro-Nazi elements; and his "secret" Western connections were monitored throughout by German intelligence. Braham concludes: "His failure to take any precautionary military measures at home facilitated first the German and then the Soviet occupation" (362). It is probable that even if Kállay had avoided all shortcomings, he could not have prevented the inevitable Soviet occupation; at best he could possibly have dissuaded the Germans from wasting their desperately needed forces on the occupation of a loyal country—but this, of course, would have made the crucial difference for the Hungarian Jewish community" (Braham, *The Politics of Genocide* 1 248.). Braham states explicitly: "Ironically, it appears in retrospect that had Hungary continued to remain a militarily passive but politically vocal ally of the Third Reich instead of provocatively engaging in diplomatic manoeuvres that were essentially fruitless, if not merely aimed at establishing an alibi, the Jews of Hungary might possibly have survived the war relatively unscathed" (Braham, *The Politics of Genocide* 1 225–26.)

It appears Deák, the eminent Columbia University historian, shares Braham's opinion. In his review essay, Deák sums up the conclusion of Braham's book with provocative sharpness: "The frightening conclusion we must draw is that for the Jews in a given country to have had a chance of survival, that country had to be loyal to the Germans" (164). Therefore, Deák, too, holds the opinion that greater political shrewdness on the part of the Hungarian government (that is, a better show of collaboration) could have saved the country from occupation and the Jews from deportation. Deák refers to the theory advanced by Lucjan Dobroszycki, who believes that in any given country the fate of the Jews depended largely on the status of that country among the European countries that were either under German occupation or under German influence at the time. According to Dobroszycki, in countries under German influence the measures against the Jews took three different forms. In certain countries, primarily in Poland and the Soviet Union, there were special SS units to carry out the mass murders directly. Elsewhere the German authorities arranged for the setting up of Jewish councils, which was an indirect way to effect the introduction of discriminatory measures and deportations. Finally, there were regions where the Germans tried to achieve the same results by putting pressure on the national governments. It was only in this last case that sabotage of the organized and full-scale deportations could be attempted. According to Deák, the third scenario applied to Hungary up until April 1944, when it was replaced by the second scenario, that was to prove so fatal to Hungary's Jewish population; this continued to apply until July 1944. When the deportations were suspended in July 1944, the Hungarian government once again regained some measure of control over events. Then, following Horthy's radio announcement on 15 October of a cease-fire between Hungary and the Allied Powers, the situation grew once again to resemble the second scenario. Deák infers from all this that there was a direct connection between the Hungarian government's attempt to break away from the German alliance and the worsening of the Hungarian Jews' chances of survival.

What makes Deák's final conclusion so frightening—in McCagg's opinion—is that it challenges the established, anti-Fascist view. Deák's conclusion suggests that when attempting to determine the moral responsibility of the collaborating regimes, instead of treating them with sweeping condemnation, these governments should be judged on an individual basis, always bearing in mind the concrete form of their collaboration, as well as its consequences. Although McCagg agrees with this in principle, he believes that in the Hungarian example Deák was unable to follow his own guidelines since he failed to take into account important historical circumstances and his declaration on the question of the links between collaboration and the Jews' chances of survival was far too general. According to McCagg, it was not the defiance of the Regent, Miklós Horthy, that delayed the start of deportations; the simple truth was that Hitler did not think the time was right for their execution efficiently. Until 6 June 1944, when the Allied Powers landed in Normandy, the chances of survival for the Jews were indeed better in those countries where the government collaborated with the Germans in one way or another. Nevertheless, in countries with a large Jewish presence this collaboration could only postpone the deportations. After D-Day, however, the national governments found themselves in a position to be able to save Jewish lives. By that time Hitler was unable to commit troops to fighting governments which defied his orders. When Horthy suspended the deportation of Jews on 7 July 1944, the Germans could do nothing about it. This particular fact, by the way, has some relevance for determining the responsibility of Hungary's political leadership: for a whole month, this leadership continued passively to watch the full-scale deportation of Jews, taking no advantage of the new strategic situation at a time when they were already informed about the atrocities of Auschwitz: it has been established by Braham as well as others that Horthy had been aware of these atrocities latest since June 1944. But the newly found and analyzed reports of the Hungarian ambassadors in the neighboring countries, sent to the Ministry of Foreign Affairs, suggest, that the Hungarian authorities must have known what had happened to the Jews of Croatia, Slovakia, etc., as early as 1942 (see Karsai; on the history of Jews in Europe, see Kovács).

Braham, Deák, and McCagg, therefore, agree basically that collaboration with the Germans—at least under certain circumstances—could have helped the persecuted Jews and historians should accordingly be prepared to face the unpleasant truth of Deák's conclusion: the interests of the Allies, whose aim was to end the war quickly, did not always coincide with the interests of the Jews who were trying to survive it. Now, more than twenty years after the discussion on Braham's provocative thesis, we know much more about the circumstances of the German occupation of Hungary, about the motives and intentions of the Nazi leadership. The conclusion seems to be less frightening, as twenty years ago. It is most probable, that "satisfactory collaboration" in the eyes of the German authorities could not have meant less than the physical persecution of the Jews. However, historians seem to agree that the direct motivation of the invasion was of pragmatic nature. On the one hand, the German political and military leaders were afraid that Hungary could quit the German alliance, and, on the other, they wanted eagerly to mobilize the partly still untouched Hungarian economic and military resources for their purposes (see Gerlach and Aly 91–113). But they put these pragmatic considerations into the ideological context of the anti-Semitic policy. They explained the reluctance of the Hungarian authorities to participate more intensively in the German war efforts by the presence of a large Jewish population in the country and by the influence of the Jewish elite on the Hungarian political decision makers. On the other hand, by forcing the Hungarian authorities to carry out the deportation of the Hungarian Jews, they wanted to clog the way of the Hungarian government to negotiations with the allies by making them accomplices in the most serious war crimes (this factor is stressed by Longerich 565–70). Thus, the direct motives of the German invasion were pragmatic, while the annihilation of the Hungarian Jews was a logical part of these pragmatic considerations in the eyes of the German authorities.

The new historical debates are concentrating more on the problem of the Hungarian collaboration and responsibility. The most debated issue is whether the Eichmann *Kommando* had arrived with a ready-made blueprint of the deportation of all Jews from Hungary or whether they decided on the total annihilation of the

Hungarian Jews only when they had seen the readiness of the Hungarian authorities to collaborate. Christian Gerlach and Götz Aly and the Hungarian historian László Varga share the view that the Germans did not know exactly how strong the Hungarians—the authorities as well as the population—would resist the deportation of the Hungarian Jews from the country, and that in the case of strong passive resistance, they would have given up the idea of a total deportation and would have agreed with achieving more limited aim, such as the total expropriation of property, long-term ghettoization inside of the country, compulsory forced labor, etc. What all this means is that Hungarian collaboration is the key issue in the explanation of events following the German invasion of Hungary.

Exactly these question of collaboration and responsibility were those which motivated Ránki, the most renowned expert of the period, to enter the discussion at the beginning of the 1980s (for Ránki, see the Works Cited). The conclusion about the eventual contradiction of Jewish and antifascist interests, drawn by Deák and others, was unacceptable to the leading Hungarian historian of the epoch. Ránki disagreed to such an extent that in his review, written in 1982 and included in the Hungarian edition's introduction, he went as far as to declare that the suggestion that Horthy's attempt to arrange for a separate armistice actually led to the destruction of Hungary's Jewish population could only be based on superficial evidence: "The Hungarian government's success in preventing the deportation of the Jews in 1942–43 was not due to its loyalty toward Hitler but to its not being altogether loyal," he wrote (Ránki, "A Magyar Holocaust" 8; Berend, Introduction 14). One of the causes of the eventual Jewish catastrophe, according to Ránki, was precisely that the Kállay government did not go far enough and did not seek new legitimating for its policies. In other words, he blamed the Kállay government for agreeing in principle with the Germans on the Jewish question as well as on the question of the war and when rejecting the German demands, referring only to practical problems, instead of also renouncing their earlier policies on principle.

The problem of collaboration and responsibility continued to interest Ránki and he returned to it in a number of his later writings (see, e.g., "A németek szerepe"). In a lecture given in the United States in the Spring of 1984 which was subsequently published both in English and in Hungarian, he went to some lengths to explain his views (see "The Germans"). On the one hand, he appears convinced that the majority of Hungary's Jews could not have survived the war because with the worsening of their military situation, the Germans would in any case have occupied the country sooner or later. His other critical comment is more direct. According to Ránki, the Kállay government was already preparing for the post-war situation. The protection given to the Jews was meant to show the Kállay government's loyalty to the Allied Powers, and to establish, as it were, an alibi for Hungary's foreign policy in the war. Neither can Hungary's half-hearted efforts to withdraw from the war be condemned outright, as Braham's conclusions would suggest, for having such fatal consequences for the Jews. Ránki writes that from the viewpoint of the Hungarian nation it was not at all an inconsequential matter which side Hungary was on when the war finished. These two arguments can be found in both the English and the Hungarian version of Ránki's essay, although the latter did not contain a line of argument which the author felt necessary to add when addressing the American audience: If the Jews were part of the Hungarian nation, they could not have been indifferent to the future of the nation; if however, they were merely a special-interest group, their interests had to be adapted to the overall interests of the nation (see Ránki, "The Germans" 49).

Ránki argues that Braham's theory is an abstract speculation, and as such, a-historical. It is true that by discussing a historical hypothesis—an alternative course never actually realized in history—a historian can easily loose his footing. Never-theless, in itself the idea of putting forward such hypotheses can hardly be consid-ered inadmissible. Of course, in order to be of any use in scholarship, the hypothe-sized course of action should not be a priori less likely than the one realized in history; it should also conflict neither with the existing conditions nor with the opinion of those involved in the course of events. Braham never makes such mis-takes, since the question he asks is not whether the Kállay government did every-thing possible to prevent the deportation of Jews, but whether its actions were ap-propriate to achieve the goal it had set itself: The circumvention of the German occupation of Hungary, in turn, led directly to the deportation of Hungarian Jews. With reference to the problem as defined by Braham, Ránki could perhaps argue that in the given historical situation Miklós Kállay, along with István Bethlen and his pro-British circle, regarded Hungary's rejection of the German request to trans-port Jews and the Hungarian negotiations for drawing up a separate armistice with the Allied Powers as two phases of the same policy, and that the Jews, too, seem to have felt that the negotiations increased, rather than reduced, their chances of sur-vival. In this sense, it might indeed be somewhat ahistorical to separate the two sides of the Kállay government's policy. But instead of making this point, Ránki puts forward a rather contradictory view. On the one hand, he claims that between 1942 and 1944 it was not the government's collaboration that saved the Jews from deportation but its resistance to German requests. He even implies that firmer resis-tance could perhaps have improved the Hungarian Jews' chances, since in that case Döme Sztójay would not have been able to take over the government so easily in 1944 and the systematic deportations could perhaps have been avoided. On the other hand, Ránki also claims that the deportations would have eventually taken place anyway, and, therefore, collaboration was contrary to national interests. However, he overlooks the argument that a more resolute opposition by Hungary to Nazi foreign policy would, in all probability, have hastened the German occupa-tion of the country. This would have further reduced the Hungarian Jews' chances of survival, considering that an organized resistance movement did not exist in Hungary and that anti-Semitism was running high in the country.

Ránki was, of course, far too good a historian to get entangled in such contradictions without any apparent reason. There is nothing surprising in this, nor in the passion of Ránki's rejection of Braham's (and Deák's) arguments. Both can be explained by noting that beneath the two interpretations lies a fundamental conceptual difference. According to Braham, the 1944 catastrophe suffered by the Hungarian Jews was in part the ultimate consequence of a process often described as successful assimilation. He thinks that what Ránki regarded as the distinctly Hungarian aspect in the history of Hungary's Jewry proved a fatal mistake that was corrected in the end by the tragic conclusion, the Holocaust, which, in the words of Jacob Katz, united the Jews "in the fate of a people singular in its suffering and unique in the mystery of its existence" (qtd. in Braham, *The Uniqueness* 190). By contrast, Ránki suggests that there was no historical alternative to assimilation, and Braham's theory is therefore, nothing but "being wise after the event" (Ránki, "A német megszálláshoz" 229). Braham considers the events of 1944 as part of Jewish history temporarily entangled with Hungarian history; Ránki regards these same events entirely as matter of Hungarian history. This explains why the latter feels that in tracing the causes of the Holocaust in Hungary, the point of departure should be this distinctly Hungarian aspect which led to the perishing of Hungarian Jews "without a fate." Braham raises the same question from the viewpoint of the Jews who became disillusioned with assimilation after the trauma of 1944. In the final analysis, this is what lies at the heart of their disagreement. It is possible to argue—as Ránki does—about whether Braham's views regarding the assimilation of Jews was "being wise after the event" (see above). For the people deported to Auschwitz it was completely irrelevant whether the Kállay government shaped its policies with a view to the post-war situation and from this perspective it makes very little sense to talk about the need to reconcile national and group interests.

In discussing the alternatives of collaboration or resistance, or in tackling the questions of moral responsibility, Ránki's arguments reveal an uneasiness and contain contradictions which can be traced back to his failure to specify his own point of reference. In this we can clearly see evidence of Ránki's approach to his work: he felt that as a historian he also had a duty. When discussing sensitive issues that could divide public opinion, he always took into account the composition of his audience. He could, however, never be accused of opportunism. "The unique aspect of the tragedy lay not so much in the brutality of the deportations, but in the fact that the plans for it were prepared by Hungarian administrators," he wrote in the journal *Kortárs* in 1984, addressing a Hungarian audience (Ránki, "A német megszálláshoz" 176). In the spring of the same year, in front of a mainly Jewish-American and Jewish-Hungarian-American audience in New York, he said something completely different: "Even the master plan for the deportation of the Budapest Jews was elaborated by the Germans" (Ránki, "The Germans" 84.)

In common with many others, Ránki felt that diverging opinions in the allocation of responsibility for the Holocaust created great pressure on the relation between Hungary's Jewish and non-Jewish population. At the one end of the spectrum was the rejection of all responsibility; at the other was the view that the Hungarian political leadership as a whole was solely responsible for the tragedy of Hungarian Jews. In his capacity as a historian, Ránki tried to advance the cause of reconciliation. It was for this reason that, facing a Hungarian audience—at variance with Braham—he stressed the responsibility of the collaborationist Hungarian government, both for its indecisiveness, as shown in the attempted breakaway and for the deportations. Addressing an American audience, however, he stressed Germany's responsibility for the destruction of the Hungarian Jews and also maintained that the national interests that justified Hungary's attempted breakaway could not be regarded as extraneous to the Jews. It was Ránki's intention to achieve reconciliation and this took him outside the bounds of historiography—a familiar phenomenon in political systems where historians have to work under strong ideological pressure and feel obliged to undertake tasks quite outside their competence, and often at the risk of damaging their professional reputation, as in the case of in Hungary during the last decades of Communist rule. One lesson of the debate of the historians is that the role of the public intellectual and the historian have to be separated. A debate of historians is absolutely necessary on moot points of national histories, but these debates must follow different rules than public controversies on clearly moral issues. In both areas there remains much more to be done in Hungary.

Works Cited

Benton, Albert B., Helen Fein, and William O. McCagg. "Genocide in Hungary: An Exchange. With the Response by István Deák." *New York Review of Books* 29.9 (1982): 54–56.

Braham, Randolph L. "The Uniqueness of the Holocaust in Hungary." *The Hungarian Holocaust Forty Years Later*. Ed. Randolph L. Braham and Béla Vágó. New York: Columbia UP, 1985). 177–90.

Braham, Randolph L. *A magyar holokauszt* (The Holocaust in Hungary). Budapest and Wilmington: Gondolat and Blackburn International Corp., 1988.

Braham, Randolph L. *The Politics of Genocide: The Holocaust in Hungary*. New York: Columbia UP, 1981. 2 vols.

Berend, Iván T. "Előszó" ("Introduction"). *A magyar holokauszt* (The Holocaust in Hungary). By Randolph L. Braham. Budapest and Wilmington: Gondolat and Blackburn International Corp., 1988. 11–15.

Dawidowicz, Lucy S. *The War against the Jews, 1933–1945*. New York: Bantam, 1976.

Deák, István. "Could the Hungarian Jews Have Survived?" *New York Review of Books* 29.1 (1982): 15–17.

Gerlach, Christian, and Götz Aly. *Das letzte Kapitel. Der Mord an den ungarischen Juden 1944/1945*. Stuttgart: Deutsche Verlag-Anstalt, 2002.

Gerő, András. "Identities of the Jew and the Hungarian." *Imre Kertész and Holocaust Literature*. Ed. Louise O. Vasvári and Steven Tötösy de Zepetnek. West Lafayette: Purdue UP, 2005. 65–75.

Karsai, László. "The Fateful Year: 1942 in the Reports of the Hungarian Diplomats." Lecture at the conference *The Holocaust in Hungary: Sixty Years Later*. Washington: United States Holocaust Memorial Museum, 16–18 March 2004.

Kertész, Imre. *Sorstalanság (Fatelessness)*. Budapest: Szépirodalmi, 1975.

Kertész, Imre. *Fatelessness*. Trans. Tim Wilkinson. New York: Vintage, 2004.

Kovács, András. "The Lost Contract: Europe and Its Jews (Or vice versa)." *Szombat: Jewish Political and Cultural Review* (May 2004): 10–13.

Longerich, Peter. *Politik der Vernichtung. Eine Gesamtdarstellung der nationalsozialistischen Judenverfolgung*. München: Piper, 1998.

McCagg, William O., Jr. *A History of Habsburg Jews, 1670–1918*. Bloomington: Indiana UP, 1989.

Ozsváth, Zsuzsanna. "Radnóti, Celan, and the Aesthetic Shifts in Central European Holocaust Poetry." *Comparative Central European Culture*. Ed. Steven Tötösy de Zepetnek. West Lafayette: Purdue UP, 2002. 51–69.

Ránki, György. "A Magyar Holocaust" ("The Hungarian Holocaust"). *Élet és Irodalom* 25 (1982): 7–8.

Ránki, György. "A német megszálláshoz vezető út" ("The Road Leading to the German Occupation"). *Kortárs* 11 (1984): 1752–759.

Ránki, György. "A németek szerepe a magyar zsidók elpusztításában" ("The Germans and the Destruction of the Hungarian Jewry"). *História* 4 (1984): 18–22.

Ránki, György. "The Germans and the Destruction of the Hungarian Jewry." *The Hungarian Holocaust: Forty Years Later*. Ed. Randolph L. Braham and Béla Vágó. New York: Columbia UP, 1985. 77–91.

Ránki, György. *A Harmadik Birodalom árnyékában* (In the Shadow of the Third Reich). Budapest: Magvető, 1988.

Suleiman, Susan Rubin. "Central Europe, Jewish Family History, and *Sunshine*." *Comparative Central European Culture*. Ed. Steven Tötösy de Zepetnek. West Lafayette: Purdue UP, 2002. 169–88.

Varga, László. "The Logistics of the Holocaust." Lecture at the conference *The Holocaust in Hungary Sixty Years Later: A European Perspective*. Budapest: Hungarian Academy of Sciences, 16–18 April 2004.

Imre Kertész and Hungary Today

Magdalena Marsovszky

Translated from the German by Eszter Pásztor

On the day when news agencies announced that the 2002 Nobel Prize in Literature is awarded this year to a Hungarian writer called Imre Kertész, joy and pride were virtually palpable in Budapest. Yet, the first moments of euphoria were followed by the sobering question: Who is Imre Kertész? The critic and scholar Mária Vásárhelyi points to the fact not a single monograph has ever been published about the work of the Laureate until the Nobel Prize and that the future Nobel Prize winner is not even mentioned in the first history of Hungarian literature published after the fall of the communist regime in 1989, by Ernő Kulcsár Szabó in 1995. Kertész's novel, *Sorstalanság*—first published, in a censored version, in 1975; translated into English as *Fateless* 1992 and, correctly, in 2004 as *Fatelessness*— was known to few readers and during communism scholars and intellectuals would not refer to the work even if it were known to them. Although this silence was broken by the writer and critic György Spiró in 1983, there was little further reaction, and it was only in the early 1990s that discussions of Kertész's work began. By this period, however, signs of a certain "Kertész-cult" became noticeable in a small circle of critics (see Spiró, "Interview"). Surely, by the end of 2002, the time has come for a more general appreciation and a few monographs have already been in the pipeline when the news of the decision by the Swedish Academy was announced. Yet, the real breakthrough took place only after and due to the Nobel Prize (see Heller; Kőbányai; Scheibner and Szücs; Szirák; Vári). In the meantime, Kertész commanded much greater attention in many other countries, first and foremost in Germany, where his works were published. Dávid Kaposi traces the fact that the world of literature in Hungary had little interest in an intensive confrontation with Kertész's works owing to the fact that both during the communist era and after the Holocaust little to no attention. Following Lawrence L. Langer and Craig R. Barclay, Kaposi argues that owing to the social environment, conditions of communication were inadequate and, in contrast, for instance, to Germany, this led to a "conspiracy of silence" about the Holocaust (see in Erős 116–20). The reception of Kertész's Nobel Prize and the strong reactions to it suggest that these conditions still apply in many ways to contemporary Hungary (on this, see also Tötösy de Zepetnek; Young).

Shortly after the announcement of Nobel Prize, a significant number of articles appeared in the liberal press of the country, with headings such as "A Hungarian Nobel Prize Winner" (Sándor 5; translations from the German to English are by Eszter Pásztor and translation from the Hungarian to German are mine, unless noted otherwise), "Great Day of Hungarian Literature" ("A magyar irodalom ünnepe" in *Magyar Hírlap*), "Let Us Rejoice!" (Spiró 26). Yet, an analysis of the right-wing and the national conservative reactions to the news reveals the belief that the Nobel Prize for a Hungarian Jew is assumed to represent an aspect of the "syndrome" (Sándor 5) of the oppression of Hungarian society. The national/conservative media were rather restrained in their statements commenting only on the fact that the Nobel Prize was awarded to Kertész (see, e.g., Haklik "Kertész Imre"). At first, leading politicians of the right-wing and national conservative opposition did welcome the news, but did not congratulate Kertész. Later, this criticism took shape with quotations often taken out of context (see, in particular, Lovas) and with increasingly direct complaints that Kertész was ungrateful to his motherland (see Haklik "Doronggá alázott"; Solymosi). A further example is this: "These days the constellation and the light in which we [Hungarians] appear are favorable and that is why this gesture was made to us" (qtd. by Borcza 6). This extremely guarded statement—made by the president of the Hungarian Writers' Association, Márton Kalász—became provocative when it was repeated in the daily *Magyar Nemzet*, known for its regular right-of-center and right-wing radical publications. One did not have to wait long for a clear-cut formulation. A few days later, in a right-wing radical cultural program on public television, the participants spoke openly about the fact that "the decision-making competencies for this literary prize, as in general, for most literary prizes in the world, lie in the hands of a small circle" (Szentmihályi-Szabó qtd. in Marsovszky "Aus der Rezeption"). In this sense, this "certain gentleman" (i.e., Kertész, whereby they avoided mentioning his name) would be "part of a terror of a minority," which works "so intensively" (Szentmihályi-Szabó qtd. in Marsovszky "Aus der Rezeption") that the "selection of the unfittest" arising as its consequence blocks the channels "through which more valuable intellectual products could be reached" (Szentmihályi-Szabó qtd. in Marsovszky "Aus der Rezeption"). "In the meantime it has gone so far that a political compensation seemed to be in progress," that is to say, "always those political directions and nations received the prize that provided some kind of a service to this cosmopolitan and international society" (Szentmihályi-Szabó qtd. in Marsovszky "Aus der Rezeption"). Through this suggestion of an "international Jewry with an excellent network" and its "favorite" Kertész, the Hungarian "clash of cultures" has been refueled (nota bene: I am quoting terminology used in right-wing and nationalist discourse). Through infighting among scholars, critics, politicians, and the general public raging between the "authentic" Hungarians on the political right and the "cosmopolitans" and "internationals," Jewish Hungarians, Judeophiles, and "design Jews" (Hungarians who are perceived and consequently categorized as Jews by anti-Semites and nationalists since 1989, see below), Hungary has become a country divided along social and psychological fault lines. And Kertész has become one of the symbolic figures of the so-called "non- or un-Hungarians," thus a focus of anti-Semitic agitation. Signs of this division, a "clash of cultures," could be detected already during the period of real socialism and even earlier and can be traced further back to the struggle between the urbanists and the populists between the two world wars (see, e.g., Enzensberger). On the one side there were the urbanists (Central European cosmopolitans, liberal middle-class intellectuals, artists, and writers) and on the other side there were the populists, *völkisch* nationalists and "authentic" Hungarians (see, e.g., Széchenyi; *völkisch* nationalists in Hungary are akin to the German *völkisch* movement between the two World Wars; on the current situation of populism in Hungary, see, e.g., Chiantera-Stutte and Petö <http://clcwebjournal.lib.purdue.edu/clcweb03–4/chiantera&peto03.html>). Since the urban-liberal world of ideas and the traditions of individualism were regarded under the communist period negatively as "bourgeois" while *völkisch* nationalists were perceived to carry a greater overlap with the ideals of socialism (see Eörsi, "Der Schock" 69), the latter were supported by the regime. In consequence, by the second half of the 1970s and in the course of the 1980s two different and oppositional ideological and intellectual camps developed. One group is represented by those intellectuals and dissenters who insisted on the realization of human rights and the freedom of the individual: this group was driven underground and produced a large amount of samizdat literature. In contrast, the second group developed an ideology similar to the ruling ideology, both supporting the myth of a nation of a homogeneous culture inscribed with only positive attributes.

This situation was in fact a consensus between the rulers and the majority of writers and intellectuals, also supported by the majority of the population for the reason that many did not want to lose the privileges the Kádár regime allowed in the decades after the 1956 Uprising, which, in turn, made Hungary into the "happiest barracks of the East." Even West Europe acquiesced to this "collective amnesia" (see Eörsi, "Erinnerung" 25). Former dissidents complained that neither German politicians who, as a result of Willy Brandt's *Ostpolitik* visited Hungary repeatedly, nor were most of the Western journalists were able to distinguish among the cultural, ideological, and political groupings in the country. The consequence of such an odd political leadership was that János Kádár, emerging from the 1956 Uprising, followed by Soviet military intervention and colonialism, was regarded not only in Hungary but also in the West as a more or less legitimate, even beloved father of the land, and hence the contradictions between the "tolerated" and the "genuine" opposition by writers and intellectuals could never really be addressed. The West also contributed to the conservation of the status quo in

Hungary and through it also to the fixation of a romantic ideal of the nation and the ethnicization of the notion of a people.

After the fall of the Soviet empire, the new post-communist right—from which the first democratically elected government was recruited—attempted from the very beginning to construct a new national identity to go with the political independence achieved through the change in regimes. Yet, the basis of this national identity continued to be a notion of people which did not mean *demos*, that is, a "society of free and equal people," but *ethnos*, that is, an "imaginary society based on descent and affiliation" (on this, see Balibar; Francis; Nowotny; Radnóti). This then gave rise to an ethnic understanding of culture whose point of departure was an organic character immanently specific to Hungariannes (*magyarság*) out of which Hungarian national cultural ideas of values should/would grow (see Marsovszky, "The Ethnic Conception," "Die Gefahr"). This would be the standard against which international culture could be measured, with everything to be rejected that is alien to the national culture. Such a view goes hand in hand with a desire for cultural homogeneity, one that represents regression because it perceives foreignness as a disturbance and as a threat. In order to be able to manage this feeling of threat, Hungarianness emphases its own greatness and turns its own people, understood in an ethnic sense, into (wronged) heroes. Here the points of departure are partly clichés or myths, and apocryphal history through which the allegedly thousand-year-old homogeneity in the culture of one's own people can be grounded and its greatness and superiority to other peoples can be stressed. This heroization also attains support, often, from the Roman Catholic Church, with an additional divine legitimization. In consequence, these romanticizing notions are now incorporated in the *völkisch* concept of the Hungarian nation and culture.

The crystallization of cultural ethnocentrism led first and necessarily to the creation of "in-groups" and "out-groups" (see Wehler 54), to "members" and "outsiders" (see Gellner 114) that is, to the creation of images of the "enemy" in relation to the allegedly culturally and ethnically homogeneous society. As Hungarians living beyond the boundaries of the country (Slovakia, Romania, the Ukraine, Serbia and Croatia, etc.) also belong to the "in-groups" who need to be integrated culturally, Hungarian ethnocentrism led automatically to the irredentist notion of Greater Hungary (the claim to the geography of pre-First World War Hungary), while at the same time it created "out-groups" within Hungary proper. Furthermore, cultural ethnocentrism leads, in this case, to anti-Semitism. Consequently, in the discourse of Hungarian *völkisch* nationalism the images of the "enemy" growing out of cultural ethnocentrism are directed generally and most frequently against Jews, rather than against any other group (see Kovács 21; Wehler 51). The specific nature of this type of anti-Semitism is that it is not satisfied with negation and hatred against the Jewish-Hungarian population or against "design Jews" (see Bibó 826); rather, it becomes a problem of identity contra anti-identity, that is, it goes into a *Weltanschauung* (see Holz), and a cultural code (see Volkov), with the consequence that it becomes directed against any type of person or group that does not agree with or does not represent Hungarianness. This constellation determines who is Jewish: Jewish is determined by who is perceived as Jewish, that is, who assumes to represent Hungarianness "undeservedly."

Kertész conforms to this type of individual on two accounts. He does not define himself either as Jewish, nor as Hungarian, nor as Jewish-Hungarian and this "in-between-ness" creates discomfort in a country that defines itself as a culturally homogeneous nation. Indeed, in Hungary it is perceived as a provocation that he does not describe his land of birth as his country of choice. Kertész writes that "The language—that is the only thing that ties me to it. Unique. This foreign language, my mother tongue, which helps me to understand my murderers. . . . I clearly mark myself off from my environment. I seem to withdraw into myself and albeit I strongly cling to it, I do not sink into the depth of depression with it as hitherto and already that will be regarded as provocation, even as a shortage of solidarity, as treachery" (Kertész, *Ich—ein anderer* 29). And he argues further that

> I also belong to this minority that is described eventually as Jews or Jewry, this, however, has nothing to do with my Jewish existence, with my own personal consciousness realised in the context of Jewry—it is my personal consciousness that is tied to it or which breaks me away from it; and, finally, this has nothing to do with genuine Jewry, if there is such a thing. If, on the other hand, we regard the development of the last ten years since Hungary has been free and a so-called democratic state, I have been imprisoned in this cage of "Jewry" (together with my works) even deeper. In the light of this, I cannot develop any kind of national solidarity with the so-called "Hungariannes," which means that I do not have a Hungarian identity and that I do not feel and I do not think together with this desperate Hungarian ideology. And that is sad, because in this way the preconception of the anti-Semites will be confirmed, namely, that the so-called Jew is not interested in the so-called Hungary. . . . One lives in very few countries because of a conviction. We say that many of the Israelis live in Israel because of conviction. But in Hungary? One is born here by chance and then either survives or not. One cannot talk about conviction. (Kertész, "A végső kocsma" 3)

For Hungarian anti-Semitism as a cultural attitude it probably does not matter whether Kertész has a Jewish identity or not. Terminological codes meaning Jewish are used generally to slander the entire intelligentsia that sympathizes with the spectrum of parties on the left, although they are known not to be Jewish, such as, for instance, the former president of the Republic and writer Árpád Göncz (see Bartus 67; Csurka). Also, in Hungary there has traditionally been and survives to this day an associative proximity between notions such as "liberal intelligence" on the one hand and "accomplished" or "educated" and "Jewish" on the other (see Ungvári 46). In the 1920s and 1930s and again even today the term "liberal" is the most important code and synonym for "Jewish" (see Ránki 94). The increasing emphasis on the "national" and the "Christian" triggers and furthers anti-Semitism, as these notions mean traditionally the negation of "Jewish" in conservative Hungarian ideology (see Lukács, "Interview"). In this way, everything and anything that is perceived as non-"authentic"-Hungarian is discarded on the political right as evil, as cosmopolitan, internationalist, and, finally, as Jewish.

The notion of the so-called "reversed assimilation," meaning that Hungarians have in the meantime become a minority in their own motherland because "Jewish liberals" attempt to align the Hungarian nation with their own style and way of thinking has been widely successful propaganda and is today an essential moment and locus in Hungarian anti-Semitism. The first to write about the tenets of reversed assimilation after 1989 was the poet and writer Sándor Csoóri. In 1990 he writes: "These days the tendencies of a reversed assimilation are becoming increasingly and clearly perceptible in the country. The Hungarian Jewry representing liberal principles desires to assimilate Hungarian values to themselves in style and spirit" (Csoóri 6). Csoóri's article marked a watershed in the country's understanding of culture and of the bitter silence between the right and left wings of the Hungarian intelligentsia. Today, there are two parallel societies in the country fighting against one another in vigorous and at times even violent conflicts. When Kertész's exclusion after 1989 began with Csoóri's tenet, Kertész called upon the Writers' Association in a public letter to take a stand. The Association refused to do so and since then Kertész has severed all contact with the Association (see Dalos 15). In the last twelve years, the hatred of the national conservatives pursued him as far as Germany. This is how in his 1999 book, *Ich—ein anderer*, he depicts an incident related to a conference of the Evangelical Academy Tutzing "Central European Dialogue: Hungarians and Germans" in November 1993. At the conference, "a lady very much upset received me with rather strange news. Apparently, the Hungarian side [of the conference participants] expressed the opinion that the list of the Hungarian invitees was one-sided. With regard to myself, they objected to the fact that I wrote only about a single theme (namely, Auschwitz) and therefore I was not representative of the country (namely, Hungary)" (63; see also *Magyar Ház*). Kertész explains that soon after 1989, he no longer felt himself accepted as a Hungarian writer in Hungary:

> Why this almost provocative statement: "Hungarian writer" . . . [in Hungary]? Obviously, because I am not one of them. . . . What should this statement mean? Something like this: One would like to acknowledge and accept me as a "Hungarian writer," although I'm not one. . . . For certain reasons, I do not belong here (I cannot belong here), largely, I do not write for those whose language I speak (I cannot) . . . it is just that the "world" that surrounds me is Hungary, and the real name of my "foreignness" is Jewry; in order, however, for a Jew to be accepted as Hungarian these days (and these days have now lasted for a good seven decades) he has to meet certain conditions which, to be brief and to the point—leads essentially to disowning

one's self. Life is either demonstration or collaboration. (*Ich—ein anderer* 84)

While most comfortable culturally and linguistically in Hungarian, Kertész regards himself as belonging more to the German cultural context and he also expresses his affinity with writers of a similar affinity in Central and East Europe such as Joseph Roth and Franz Kafka (see Radnóti, "Interview"). It is also questionable whether he would ever want to be described as a "Hungarian" writer because in his mind his identity is determined by writing alone: "You don't demand that I have an identity, I let you into the secret: my only identity is that of writing, an identity writing itself" (*Ich—ein anderer* 56). During the year of preparation for the 1999 Frankfurt Book Fair whose theme in that year was Hungary, the waves of anti-Semitic agitation shot particularly high. After the victory of the national-conservative and right-wing Orbán government in 1998, the preparations carried out by the previous socialist-liberal coalition for the book fair were revised and the "one-sided selection" of the authors who should represent Hungary and Hungarian literature in Frankfurt was supplemented (see Pröhle, "Interview"; Pröhle was Secretary of State at the Ministry of National Cultural Heritage and in charge of the Hungarian exhibition at the Frankfurt book fair).

The selection of the authors for the book fair was deemed by the government to be "too one-sided" and "not really Hungarian," it was said, because the previous government preferred only the "one-sided liberal spirit of Budapest" and the writers close to it. Csurka, the leader of the right-wing radical Party for Hungarian Justice and Life—represented for the first time in Parliament between 1998 and 2002—wrote that "The Jewish literature of Budapest appears in the name of Hungary" (Csurka). The writer György Dalos—living in Berlin and who was the Hungarian organizer of theme for the book fair until the summer of 1999—commented on the conflict writing that "It was simply an insinuation with a political agenda that the so-called authentic national authors were excluded." And as the new anti-Semitism is expressed by these people, by these members of parliament, he compared the fact that some authors could not appear in Frankfurt with their books to the burning of books by the Nazis" (qtd. in Marsovszky, "Urbane oder Voksnationale?"). Kertész replied to his critics in a public letter as follows:

> If I understand it properly, it is held against me that I would like to shine at the Frankfurter Book Fair in the name of Hungarian literature. . . . No doubt, there are foreign ignoramuses who like my books and in such cases they might think they read Hungarian literature. But these days I hasten to declare in all my foreign interviews . . . that I do not represent anyone but really no one in the whole world, whether an ideal or a religion or a people or a race or a literature, least of all a national literature maintained on an official list, be it Hungarian or anything else. . . . At the Frankfurt Book Fair I will be the guest of my German publishers; the Hungarian state . . . contributed nothing finan-

cially to the German translation of my books. . . . This also means . . . that my appearance at the Frankfurt Book Fair does not cost a penny for the Hungarian taxpayer. Therefore, the representation that I would have taken the place of another Hungarian writer illegitimately is, to put it mildly, an understatement, or put it bluntly . . . a lie. For the same reason, I refrain from participating in events where it is intended to represent the official image of Hungariannes. I did not even accept the invitation of the City of Frankfurt and of the German book sector to the opening ceremony of the book fair, so that I should not besmirch the Hungarian crown with my presence. . . . More I cannot do. . . . And finally, one more remark: I read that according to the author of the article in *Magyar Fórum* I count as a German writer. Well, that is not a great shame. And should some people regard it as such, then it is not my shame. (Incidentally, my works are published in thirteen languages, Hungarian would be the fourteenth.) Item: In the future I shall react to *Judenhetze* neither pro nor contra. ("Megdöbbenés" 8)

Other examples of attacks and the exclusion of what is considered un-Hungarian include the protests in 2003 against the filming of Kertész's *Fatelessness*—the construction of the scene for the shooting of the concentration camp in Buchenwald—on the Pilis hills north of Budapest. The protests were in order to protect the "sacred" location of Pilis, which must not be allowed to be a film location because the Scythians had long ago settled there, followed by the "venerable shamans, the successors of Attila," and, in addition, the protesters declared, the "hill is the energy centre of the Carpathians, where the divine energies are combined" (Illényi 77; on this, see also Aradi; Szörényi). It appears that the social-liberal Medgyessy government was unable to stand up against this psychosis of war. It seems it is powerless against the force, with which the cultural nationalistic right-wing ideology is advancing. The atmosphere is so explosive in the country that political science scholars wonder that it has not yet peaked in a major conflict.

The national-conservative scholar Péter Tölgyessy ponders about a type of leader of a new style:

over the last twelve years, tendencies arose in Hungary which threaten the existence of the republic. Even if there is a proper legal system, these tendencies are hardly accepted by Hungarian society. The normative judicial system is equated with a world of lies. The law is something that one should go around about. When that is the case, however, it is unlikely that a court conviction could evolve according to which the law would provide protection. There is, however, an incredibly great desire in Hungarian society for such protection. So arises the desire for a leader, a *Führer*, who comes and helps and when it becomes necessary to re-establishes law and order . . . The charismatic Fidesz leader [a Hungarian political party], Viktor Orbán, has shown an incredibly good feel for this... for the great desire of the masses for a Hungarian world that is worth living in. There is a great desire for many to be able to express more truths, which one has always spoken about within the

family circle . . . but there were these political systems in which they could
never be expressed openly. . . . These feelings have been allowed to be released by the new right. One can again openly express things, which we had
believed to be true within the family circle. For many, it warms the heart that
what they had always believed to be true they can now read in the papers and
see on television. All that is a tremendous challenge against established law.
(Tölgyessy "A köztársaság állapota")

And the Paris resident historian François Fejtö believes that "there is a civil war in
Hungary which luckily has not yet been expressed in bloody fighting, in which
there has not yet been armed violence. From the outside, the country seems calm
and stable, yet when you know the situation, you perceive how explosive the atmosphere is" (Fejtö "Interview"). Fejtö blames the constellation that is referred to
in Hungary as the political right which, however, cannot be compared with the political right in a West European sense, as it has radicalized itself continuously.

   In my opinion, Hungary is in serious need of an alternative vision—to be
communicated consistently—against the vision of the national-conservative side,
one that could only be the vision of democratic ideals and values. The socialist-
liberal governing coalitions—in power between 1994 and 1998 and since 2002—
have had and do not have an alternative vision and it appears they have not yet
dared to confront the essentialist ethnic notion of culture. Although its understanding of culture is much more democratic, without effective communication its
counter measures have been exhausted in a concept-less gobbledygook. Since anti-
Semitism as a prominent cultural attitude cannot be controlled by legal means, it
should fall within the competence of a democratically oriented cultural policy and
education. However, since the decades of communism, when as an instrument of
power cultural policy was implemented as a strategic function in educating the
"socialist type of man" and prescribed the direction of cultural values and orientation with its monopolistic violence, cultural policy has not been democratized.
Fearing that a value-oriented cultural policy would lead to the continuation of a paternalistic communication by the state, whereby the public would be told what it
had to think) , the government trusts the "healing" forces of the market (on this, see
Horváth). This thinking renounces a creative cultural and media policy and in the
name of the freedom of the press it leaves room even for the worst of right-wing
and radical views. In the meantime, the national conservatives are enabled to
communicate their vision effectively, thereby strengthening their influence on society and the media.

   The radicalization of Hungarian society is surely to be traced to a deficit of
democratic values. Yet, it can also be associated with the fact that over the last few
years largely German and American multinational companies strong on capital
bought up entire industries and, short of a local civil society and proper representation of interests, they did much for the creation of a "wild" capitalism (on this, see,
e.g., Szalai). The UK-based scholar of nationalism and member of the European

Parliament, George Schöpflin (who as a dual British and Hungarian citizen represents Hungary), believes that "the way in which integration has been carried out to date has not only not contributed to the process of democratization in Central Europe but it has even impeded it and provided the opponents of integration with additional arguments" (Schöpflin 5). Because "local discourse was neglected, without conducting a normative dialogue, the candidate countries were given ideas, rules, values and concepts which they accepted but did not internalize and did not integrate. In addition, the West supports certain paternalistic attitudes in relation to Central Europe, so the question arises whether the ways and means whereby the European Union has negotiated the enlargement with the candidate countries would not lead to the export of the democratic deficit of the Union and whether the EU does not unconsciously contribute to the maintenance of the liminal condition of post-communism" (Schöpflin 5). Schöpflin warns that "integration will certainly be concomitant with a cultural shock. In some cases, it will appear in the form of xenophobia and in the rejection of anything new—that is, in an increase in the activity of the new radical right" (Schöpflin 5). It appears that history is repeating itself: every now and then the EU condemns Hungarian anti-Semitism, but it fails to take into account what is really happening in Central Europe.

Under such conditions of radical political polarization, as in Central Europe today, the question must be asked whether the tendencies towards exclusion, such as the "core Europe" concept promoted by European public intellectuals such as Jacques Derrida, Jürgen Habermas, and Adolf Muschg would help, and whether it would not be time, finally, for West Europe to begin with a dialogue with its own Eastern half about democratically oriented cultural policy. The case of Kertész demonstrates poignantly the emotional as well as intellectual pitfalls of a society where democratic values have not been adopted and exercised sufficiently.

Works Cited

Anonymous. "A magyar irodalom ünnepe" ("Celebration of Hungarian Literature"). *Magyar Hírlap* (11 October 2002): 5.

Aradi, Lajos. "Pilis kultikus helyei" ("The Cultic Locations of the Pilis"). *Vasárnapi Újság*. Budapest: Kossuth Rádió (4 January 2004): 06:00.

Balibar, Etienne. "Rassismus und Nationalismus und die Nation-Form: Geschichte und Ideologie." *Rasse, Klasse, Nation. Ambivalente Identitäten.* Ed. Etienne Balibar and Immanuel Wallerstein. Hamburg: Argument, 1990. 49–84.

Balibar, Etienne. "Die Nation-Form: Geschichte und Ideologie." *Rasse, Klasse, Nation. Ambivalente Identitäten.* Ed. Etienne Balibar and Immanuel Wallerstein. Hamburg: Argument, 1990. 107–39.

Barclay, Craig R. "Autobiographical Remembering: Narrative Constraints on Objectified Selves." *Remembering Our Past: Studies in Autobiographical Memory.* Ed. David C. Rubin. New York: Cambridge UP, 1996. 94–125.

Bartus, László. "Jobb magyarok. A szélsőjobb útja a hatalomhoz 1990–2000" ("Better Hungarians: The Way of the Extreme Right to Power 1999–2000"). Budapest: Selfedition, 2001.

Bibó, István. "Levél Borbándi Gyulához 1978" ("Letter to Gyula Borbándi 1978"). *Bibó István összegyüjtött munkái* (Collected Works of István Bibó). Ed. István Kemény and Mátyás Sárközi. Bern: EPMSZ, 1983. Vol. 3, 822–66.

Borcza, Ágnes Z. "Egy Nóbel-díj margójára" ("On the Margins of a Nobel Prize"). *Magyar Nemzet* (5 November 2002): 6.

Chiantera-Stutte, Patricia, and Andrea Pető. "Cultures of Populism and the Political Right in Central Europe." *CLCWeb: Comparative Literature and Culture* 5.4 (2003): <http://clcwebjournal.lib.purdue.edu/clcweb03–4/chiantera&peto03.html>.

Csoóri, Sándor (1990): "Nappali hold 2" ("Daytime Moon 2"). *Hitel* 18 (1990): 4–7.

Csurka, István. "A frankfurti zsarnokság" ("The Frankfurt Tyranny"). *Havi Magyar Fórum* (August 1999): <http://www.c3.hu/~tovidek/frankf2.htm>.

Enzensberger, Hans Magnus. "Ungarische Wirrungen (1985)." *Ach Europa! Wahrnehmungen aus sieben Ländern. Mit einem Epilog aus dem Jahre 2006.* By Hans Magnus Enzensberger. Frankfurt: Suhrkamp, 1989. 121–76.

Eörsi, István. *Erinnerung an die schönen alten Zeiten.* Hamburg: Rowohlt, 1991.

Eörsi, István. "Der Schock der Freiheit." *Ungarn auf dem Weg in die Demokratie.* Ed. József Bayer and Rainer Deppe. Frankfurt: Suhrkamp, 1993. 67–76.

Erős, Ferenc. *Az identitás labirintusai. Narratív konstrukciók és identitásstratégiák* (The Labyrinths of Identity: Narrative Structures and Identity Strategies). Budapest: Janus-Osiris, 2001.

Fejtö, François [Ferenc]. Interview. *168 óra.* Budapest: Kossuth Rádió (1 February 2004): 16.00.

Francis, Emerich. *Ethnos und Demos. Soziologische Beiträge zur Volkstheorie.* Berlin: Duncker & Humblot, 1965.

Gellner, Ernest. *Nationalismus. Kultur und Macht.* Berlin: Siedler, 1999.

Dalos, György. "Kein Ausrutscher. Warum ungarische Autoren den Schriftstellerverband verließen." *Frankfurter Rundschau* (16 March 2004): 15.

Derrida, Jacques, and Jürgen Habermas. "Nach dem Krieg. Die Wiedergeburt Europas." *Frankfurter Allgemeine Zeitung* (31 May 2003): 33–34.

Haklik, Norbert. "Kertész Imre Nobel-díjat kapott" (Imre Kertész Received the Nobel Prize). *Magyar Nemzet* (11 October 2002): 1.

Haklik, Norbert. "Doronggá alázott Nobel-díj" (Nobel Prize Degraded to a Bludgeon). *Magyar Nemzet* (21 October 2002): 7.

Heller, Ágnes. *Auschwitz és Gulág* (Auschwitz and Gulag). Budapest: Múlt és Jövő, 2002.

Holz, Klaus. *Nationaler Antisemitismus. Wissenssoziologie einer Weltanschauung.* Hamburg: Hamburger Edition HIS Verlagsgesellschaft mbH, 2001.

Horváth, János. "Az igazi Közszolgálat" (The Real Public Service). *Közszolgálatiság a médiában. Ábránd vagy realitás?* (Public Service in the Media: Illusion or Reality?). Ed. Tamás Terestyéni. Budapest: Osiris, 1995. 45–51.

Illényi, Balázs. "Szent hegy" (Sacred Mountain). *Heti Világgazdaság* (17 September 2003): 77.

Kaposi, Dávid. "Narratívátlanság. Kulturális sémák és a *Sorstalanság*" ("Narrativelessness: Cultural Schematas and *Fatelessness*"). *Az értelmezés szükségessége. Tanulmányok Kertész Imréről* (The Necessity of Interpretation. Studies on Imre Kertész). Ed. Tamás Scheibner and Zoltán Gábor Szücs. Budapest: L'Harmattan, 2002. 15–51.

Kertész, Imre. *Sorstalanság (Fatelessness)*. Budapest: Szépirodalmi, 1975.

Kertész, Imre. *Fateless*. Trans. Christopher Wilson and Katharina M. Wilson. Evanston: Northwestern UP, 1992.

Kertész, Imre. *Ich—ein anderer*. Trans. Ilma Rakusa. Berlin: Rowohlt, 1998.

Kertész, Imre. "Megdöbbenés, csupa megdöbbenés . . ." ("Astonishment, Nothing But Astonishment . . ."). *Élet és Irodalom* (8 October 1999): 8.

Kertész, Imre. "A végső kocsma. Feljegyzések" (The Ultimate Pub. Notes.). *Élet és Irodalom* (21 December 2001): 3–4.

Kertész, Imre. *Fatelessness*. Trans. Tim Wilkinson. New York: Vintage, 2004.

Kovács, András. "Az antiszemitizmus mint társadalomtudományos probléma" ("Anti-Semitism as a Problem of the Social Sciences"). *A modern antiszemitizmus* (Modern Anti-Semitism). Ed. András Kovács. Budapest: Új Mandátum, 1999. 9–37.

Kőbányai, János. *Jób díja. Háttér és recepció* (The Prize of Hiob: Background and Reception). Budapest: Múlt és Jövő, 2003.

Kőbányai, János. *Az ember mélye. Írások Kertész Imréről a Múlt és Jövőben* (The Depths of Man: Writings on Imre Kertész in *Múlt és Jövő*). Budapest: Múlt és Jövő, 2003.

Kulcsár Szabó, Ernő. *A magyar irodalom története 1945–1991* (History of Hungarian Literature). Budapest: Argumentum, 1995.

Langer, Lawrence L. "Interpreting Survivor Testimony." *Writing the Holocaust*. Ed. Berel Lang. New York: Holmes & Meier, 1988. 26–40.

Lovas, István. "Napi sajtószemle" (Daily Press Review). *Magyar Nemzet* (19 October 2002): 9.

Lukács, John. Interview. *16 Óra*. Budapest: Kossuth Rádió (24 March 2001): 16:00.

Magyar Ház. "Dokumentum összeállítás" ("Sum of Documents"). *Kritika* (June 1994): 12–16.

Marsovszky, Magdalena. "Urbane oder Volksnationale? Die gespaltene Literatur Ungarns. Ein Gespräch mit den Schriftstellern Sándor Csoóri, György Dalos und Tibor Zalán." Saarbrücken: Saarländischer Rundfunk, SR2 KulturRadio, Bücherlese (16 Oktober 1999): 15:04.

Marsovszky, Magdalena. "Aus der Rezeption des Nobelpreises für Imre Kertész in Ungarn. 'Geschmacksterror einer Minderheit.' Dokument der Kultursendung 'Éjjeli

Menedék' des öffentlich-rechtlichen Fernsehens, MTV1 22.11.2002. 22.55 Uhr."
haGalil.com: Culture & News from Central Europe (6 December 2002): <http://
www.klick-nach-rechts.de/gegen-rechts/2002/12/kertesz.htm>.

Marsovszky, Magdalena. "The Ethnic Conception of Culture in Hungary." *Culture
Europe* 38.12 (2002): 18–19.

Marsovszky, Magdalena. "Die Gefahr der Homogenisierung der Kultur." Lecture at the
conference *Die Gleichzeitigkeit des Ungleichzeitigen*. Institut zur Erforschung und
Förderung österreichischer und internationaler Literaturprozesse. Vienna, 6–8
December 2002.

Muschg, Adolf. "Kerneuropa. Gedanken zur europäischen Identität." *Neue Zürcher Zeitung* (31 May 2003): <http://www.nzz.ch/2003/05/31/fe/page-article8VX08.html>.

Nowotny, Stefan. "'Ethnos oder Demos?' Ideologische Implikationen im Diskurs der
'europäischen Kultur'." *Kulturrisse: Kulturpolitische Viertaljahreszeitschrift der
IG Kultur Österreich* (2000): 32–34.

Pröhle, Gergely. Interview. *Vasárnapi újság*. Budapest: Kossuth Rádió (19 December
1998): 6:00.

Radnóti, Sándor. "Ethnosz és démosz" ("Ethnos and Demos"). *Holmi* (June 1992):
868–73.

Radnóti, Sándor. Interview. "Áldjuk a Jóistent, hogy nekünk adott tanút" ("Bless the
Good Lord for Having Given Us a Witness"). *Beszélő* (January–February 2003):
30–36.

Ránki, Vera. *Magyarok—Zsidók—Nacionalizmus. A befogadás és a kirekesztés
politikája* (Hungarians—Jews—Nationalism: The Politics of Inclusion and Exclusion). Budapest: Új Mandátum, 1999.

Sándor, Iván. "Mi a magyar (író) most? A Nobel-díj-szindróma" ("What Does It Mean
to Be a Hungarian [Writer] Now? The Nobel Prize Syndrome"). *Élet és Irodalom*
(21 February 2003): 5.

Sándor, Zsuzsanna. "Nobel-díjas magyar" ("Hungarian with Nobel Prize"). 168 óra (17
October 2002): 24–25.

Scheibner, Tamás, and Zoltán Gábor Szücs, eds. *Az értelmezés szükségessége. Tanulmányok Kertész Imréről* (The Necessity of Interpretation: Studies on Imre
Kertész). Budapest: L'Harmattan, 2002.

Schöpflin, György. "Úton az európai kulturális identitás felé? Közép-Európa és az EU"
(On the Way to the European Cultural Identity? Middle-Europe and the EU). *Élet
és Irodalom* 07. (February 2003): 5.

Solymosi, Frigyes. "Öröm és Üröm" ("Joy and Bitterness"). *Magyar Nemzet* (22 October 2002): 7.

Spiró, György. "Non habent sua fata. A *Sorstalanság*—újraolvasva" ("Non habent sua
facta. *Fatelessness*—Reread"). *Élet és Irodalom* (29 July 1983): 5.

Spiró, György. Interview. *Háttér* (Background). Budapest: Kossuth Rádió (11 October
2002): 18.30.

Spiró, György. "Örüljünk!" ("Let Us Rejoice!"). *168 óra* (17 October 2002): 26–27.

Széchenyi, Ágnes. "Most hirtelen téli mesék rémei kielevenednek. Beszélgetés Radnóti Sándorral" ("Suddenly, the Monsters of Winter Tales Arise: A Conversation with Sándor Radnóti"). *Kritika* (June 1992): 6–10.

Szirák, Péter. *Kertész Imre. A pesszimizmus: bátorság* (Imre Kertész. Pessimism: Courage). Bratislava: Kalligram, 2003.

Szörényi, Levente. Interview. "Pilis szakrális hely" ("The Sacred Pilis"). *Magyar Nemzet* (28 August 2003): 14.

Tamás, Gáspár Miklós. ". . . ahogyan az ember forgószélben viselkedik . . ." (". . . As One Behaves in a Whirlwind . . ."). *Valóság* (April 1992): 79–92.

Tamás, Gáspár Miklós. "A haladó ifjúság példaképe II." ("The Paragon of Progressive Youth II."). *Magyar Hírlap* (1 September 2003): 3.

Tölgyessy, Péter. "A köztársaság állapota" ("The State of the Republic"). *16 Óra*. Budapest: Kossuth Radio (8 March 2003): 16:00.

Tötösy de Zepetnek, Steven. "Imre Kertész's Nobel Prize in Literature and the Print Media." *Imre Kertész and Holocaust Literature*. Ed. Louise O. Vasvári and Steven Tötösy de Zepetnek. West Lafayette: Purdue UP, 2005. 232–46.

Ungvári, Tamás. *Ahasvérus és Shylock. A "zsidókérdés" Magyarországon* (Ahasver and Shylock: The "Jewish Question" in Hungary). Budapest: Akadémiai, 1999.

Vári, György. *Kertész Imre. Buchenwald fölött az ég* (Imre Kertész: The Sky above Buchenwald). Budapest: Kijárat, 2003.

Vásárhelyi, Mária. "Nobel-díj—történeti keretben" ("The Nobel-Prize in a Historical Setting"). *Élet és Irodalom* (18 October 2002): 6.

Volkov, Shulamit. *Antisemitismus als kultureller Code*. München: Beck, 2000.

Wehler, Hans-Ulrich. *Umbruch und Kontinuität. Essays zum 20. Jahrhundert*. München: Beck, 2000.

Young, Judy. "The Media and Imre Kertész's Nobel Prize in Literature." *Imre Kertész and Holocaust Literature*. Ed. Louise O. Vasvári and Steven Tötösy de Zepetnek. West Lafayette: Purdue UP, 2005. 271–85.

Imre Kertész's Aesthetics of the Holocaust

Sára Molnár

In his fiction, Imre Kertész sets himself the task of (re)presenting aesthetically both Nazi and Soviet and communist totalitarianism and he comments often on the fact that for him, as compared with other Auschwitz survivors, such as Paul Celan or Jean Améry, who committed suicide, the notion preventing him from committing suicide was his experience of disillusion with "freedom" and democracy in the communist Hungary. After surviving the concentration camp, Kertész faced another totalitarianism, a fact which helped him get rid of his humanistic illusions, if any remained after Auschwitz. As he declared in his Nobel address, he could not have written his novel *Sorstalanság* (*Fatelessness*) in a free Western society (see at *Nobel Prize in Literature* <http://www.nobel.se/literature/laureates/index.html>). To me, when reading Kertész, it is important to realize that he is writing from the specificities of the Central European context, a context of particular relevance to the history of Jewry and the culture of the region (on the Central European context of Kertész's work, see Tötösy de Zepetnek, "And the 2002 Nobel Prize"). In Hungary, Soviet and communist rule followed Nazism and these historical events forced Kertész to recognize totalitarianism as a general social and human condition. For Kertész, Auschwitz was not a coincidence but a logical and unavoidable consequence of modern European culture and Auschwitz—in a reversal of morals—came to represent the power of "god" and the "father," in turn, symbolizing the collapse of Greek-Christian culture.

The fact that Kertész is the first Hungarian to win the Nobel Prize in Literature generate(d) much debate in the Hungarian media as well as in scholarship about the reasons of the neglect of Hungarian literature within Western literature and why Kertész's work did not attract as much attention in Hungary as it did in some other countries such as in Sweden and Germany (on this, see Marsovszky; Tötösy de Zepetnek, "Imre Kertész's Nobel Prize"; Young). There were some good and illuminating observations in the Hungarian media about the rationale for this double neglect including the incapability of Hungarian society to confront its proto-nazi and fascist history, the role of Hungarians' in the genocide of Hungarian Jews in 1944, and the existence and continuous re-occurrence of anti-Semitism (on this, see, e.g., Braham; Kovács; Ozsváth). Kertész deals with inconvenient subjects, indeed: The Holocaust, the distortion of human integrity, the loss of language and identity during the communist dictatorship (see, e.g., *A kudarc* [The Failure]), the unresolved problems and hatred in Hungarian society after the end of Soviet and communist rule in 1989 (see, e.g., *Valaki más* [Someone Else]), the illusion of freedom, the old structures which survived totalitarianism, the persistence of unlawful laws, and defenselessness, the "system" of authority, as Kertész mentions in one of his interviews and its impact on people of the post-communist countries (see Szilágyi). While these themes are relatively common in Central European culture and literature, in Kertész's work we find a unique language and narrative position. In *Sorstalanság*, for example, there is no retrospective point of view, no explanation of what happened, and no release even for the so-called "victims," Hungarians under German occupation in 1944. In his Nobel address, Kertész declares this point strongly: "Nothing has happened since Auschwitz that could reverse or refute Auschwitz" (Kertész <http://www.nobel.se/literature/laureates/index. html>).

The lack of responsibility towards the Holocaust in Hungarian society could be one reason why many readers, critics, and scholars do not understand or do not want to understand and take offence at the irony and self-irony in Kertész's prose, one of the important poetical features of his fictional narrative. Failing to realize the self-irony and self-reflexivity of the narrator, critics are also unable to differentiate between the text types and narratives of the documentary (autobiography) and fiction. Although *Sorstalanság* is a novel, many critics and scholars were more interested in the life story of its author than in the the poetical and narrative characteristics of the text. In fact, this misguided critical stand was extended to the literary reception of *A kudarc*, Kertész's second novel. The tendency of reducing *A kudarc* to the author's (auto)biography is even more curious, as can be seen in the case of a roundtable conversation about *Valaki más* published in the journal *Beszélő*. *Valaki más*, a text on the boundaries of essay, diary, and fiction, received an ambivalent literary reception: Some critics say that Kertész is vague or possibly wrong with respect to his description of "paranoid" and "apocalyptic" reality and that he does not describe Hungary faithfully. *Valaki más*, as do most of Kertész's books, has strong emotional impact on both readers and critics who seem to forget that it is not a documentary, on the one hand, and on the other, that the narrator speaks ironically of his own role as a "prophet" of the truth while presenting the apocalypses of our day, thus showing that this is only one, although a valid and very personal point of view. Most curious to me is why Kertész's irony is so misunderstood when irony has been for a long time and still is one of the main features of Hungarian—and Central European—literature and public discourse, in general.

Another frequent manner of interpreting Kertész's books in Hungarian literary reception is that the commentators identify with one of the author's heroes, or with the author himself and "correct" what is being said, or argue with their views, as if the work were a philosophical study instead of fiction. One example is the discussion of *Kaddish*: The critic-scholar Sándor Radnóti in his otherwise competent review of the novel criticizes the narrator's "inconsequent" and "pathological" pride, that he does not let anyone, not even his wife, interrupt him in his monologue. Péter Szirák, another reviewer, also objects to the unavoidable veracity of the narrator's voice and points out that the author never lets himself to be interrupted, thus claiming truth without allowing the other characters to agree or disagree. For this reason, Szirák considers *Kaddish* a failure in a sense that the confessional and theoretical voice cannot find its own adequate form. In my opinion, this kind of literary criticism shows a surprising lack of sophistication even among the most competent critics because they do not argue from a neutral point of view. Instead of poetic and aesthetic points of view and appreciation, they assert their own resentment and incomprehension regarding Kertész's subject and language. Some of them claim that they have had enough of his pessimism, or as one reviewer, Sándor Bazsányi, calls it, a "rhetoric of unhappiness" (1744). Péter Dávidházi, another prominent critic, asks for a happier and untroubled work after the gloomy ones (351) and Radnóti calls Kertész's book "monomaniacal" (12). These critics appear to be profoundly uneasy being confronted by the voice of the single narrator on the novel and, surprisingly, are unable to evaluate the novel as a text of that particular type of fictional narration.

In Kertész's novels, most characteristically in *Kaddis a meg nem született gyermekért* (*Kaddish for a Child Not Born* 1997, *Kaddish for an Unborn Child* 2004), polyphony appears in the language of one narrator, which is not only confessional or theoretical, but also ironic towards his own truth as we can read in the so-called "monologue" in the text, a prayer of a potential father commenting on the impossibility of having a child after surviving Auschwitz. Considering the fact that Jacques Derrida, for instance, compares in *Envois* the desire for a child to the desire for universal truths, in a sense that both of them represent a chance to avoid death and finitude, makes it easier to understand why the narrator of the *Kaddish* says no to a child and, at the same time, no to the language of power and authoritative statements by means of irony towards his own truths. The polyphony of the narrator's statements and the discontinuity of his stream of consciousness can be followed in the following passage from *Kaddish:* "And if in the final analysis survival isn't achieved, which of course can only be achieved at a higher level (Dr. Oblath), then (we both together) there are not only the slightest indicators for this idea but its opposite appears to be the case, namely the collapse into ignorance . . . And so on, and so on we blew the false notes of the English horn" (*Kaddish for a Child Not Born* 10). The other voices in the narration, the hero's wife and the character Dr. Oblath, accomplish only what the ironic voice of the narrator has already started: the decomposition of his own truth and, thus, the use of any authoritative and totalitarian language. The "I"-narrator has the faculties of a comic or fool who, in Baudelaire's terms, is able to be both himself and somebody else at the same time. If we consider Kertész's essays and lectures as a context and intertexture of his novels—and this interpretation seems to be correct because of the mutual and

continuous connotations of the texts—"the false notes of the English horn" could
be interpreted as the self-irony of the essayist Kertész, the irony of a static and
moralizing attitude towards the Holocaust. In *Kaddish*, Kertész creates a language
which displays the fragility and sometimes the impossibility of talking generally
and without responsibility about the Holocaust.

Another reason for the widespread critical dismissal of Kertész's work could
be that literary theorists were focused on the so-called "turn of the 1980s" in Hungarian literature and on how the contemporary Western European forms of literary
expression and post-modernity appear in Hungarian literature. In my view, it can
be construed that it might not have been fashionable to write about an author
whose plots and heroes do not encompass the movement toward modernity, by his
refusal to banish the coverage of reality, personal confession, and ethical relations
from his prose. For example, this view could be one reason for the fact that Ernő
Kulcsár Szabó did not mention Kertész in his *History of Hungarian Literature between 1945–1991*. While the personality of the author is very important in
Kertész's work, this "author" cannot be identified with Kertész himself: Such an
identification is a gross simplification and neglect of the fictional character called
into life by the narrative. In fact, when one considers the autobiographical aspects
of Kertész's prose, the interpretation of his oeuvre becomes even more complicated
and multi-layered. In *Az angol lobogó* (The English Flag), the narrator of Kertész
himself talks about the insufficiency of literary formulation when describing the
experience of totalitarianism and its destructive impact on personality. He declares
that the only acceptable form of expressing the experience of the Holocaust would
be the evidence given by the witness, the testimony as a form of literary expression. Although Kertész is not a moralist and he never judges, his description of Nazism and communism conveys the concept of a testimony, in a literary form with
both aesthetic and strong ethical connotations.

Kertész, of course, is not the only one who struggles with the incommunica-
bility of the Holocaust on one hand, and the fear of forgetting on the other, by urg-
ing a new language and a new way of thinking. Others such as Yosef Hayim
Yerushalmi in his book *Zachor*, talking about the relation between Jewish history
and memory, declares that historiography cannot replace collective retrospection.
Furthermore, Yerushalmi claims that despite considerable historical research about
the Holocaust, it was not the historian, but the writers who could form a real notion
of the concept because of the fact that with the Holocaust, history became incommunicable. Hayden White, examining Nazism and the *Endlösung*, tries to find an
answer to the question of whether historical realities or the form of narrative determine their own genre, which would mean that even the Holocaust could be interpreted in many different ways without any restriction. White takes the notion of
"intransitive writing" from Roland Barthes, a discourse in which the subject (the
author) is not independent from its object: as the writer writes about himself, and
thus, he transforms writing into a means of seeing and self-understanding. This

style of writing is, in White's opinion, the only possible way to write about the Holocaust, where giving up all our previous ideas about realistic description is necessary in order to be able to confront the experiences of the twentieth century. White goes even further and suggests that all the Jews should tell about the genocide of their own people in the same way as they were commanded by God to tell the exodus from Egypt to their children, as if it happened to themselves. This is one reason that in Holocaust literature the traditional distinction between autobiography and fiction should be suspended, or at least in view of Kertész's and other Holocaust writers' prose be reinterpreted.

It is not seldom that Holocaust writers choose the first person singular. For instance, Tadeusz Borowski, like Kertész, has an "I"-narrator while writing about the concentration camp. While Borowski's text might give the illusion of an autobiography or a simple diary and while his readers identify the author with his hero, in fact his stories show how impossible the concept of identity of the "I" is in the concentration camp. In his short stories, such as in *This Way for the Gas, Ladies and Gentleman*, Borowski describes the loss of identity, the total assimilation of the "I"—the hero of autobiographies—to the conditions of the concentration camp. Through this process to shock we can see only a lucky survivor without any moral problems, who is absolutely loyal to the rules of annihilation in the camp. And the concentration camp appears not as something unnatural but as a place where it seems easy to get accustomed to the rules. And for Borowski there is no big difference between the prisoners' lives before and after the camp. For him, then, this is the most realistic, yet the most shocking way of describing the concentration camp and the only true remembering of the millions of victims. In the case of Kertész and before him with Borowski, the first person singular narrative was obviously intentional: It helps to lay bare all kinds of ideologies and myths about the narrative of the Holocaust. One good example of this is that they both describe the football field in Auschwitz as an important aspect of the camp, for example, an aspect that seems to downgrade conventional narrative patterns about Auschwitz. It is just as unconventional as the nostalgia of Kertész's hero in *Sorstalanság*, Gyuri (George) Köves, for the evenings of the concentration camp and his longing to be back in the camp again. At the end of the novel, Köves says that, should he ever be asked, he will talk about happiness in the concentration camp, a happiness which in this case is understood as a trap by himself, an absurdity that makes Köves continue his life even if it is not possible.

Kertész, who regards Borowski a true witness of the Holocaust, proposes in his work the necessity of a new language which describes this new experience of reality, one that overwrites our moral and ethical categories and cultural concepts. Celan, too, tried to find an answer for the Holocaust experience by rethinking poetry and poetic language (on this, see, e.g., Ozsváth). Kertész calls this new way of speaking the "language of exile," the language of atonality, which also means the impossibility of identifying with the existing conditions in a dictatorship. In his texts, this atonality, or the lack of harmony, is represented by irony, a clear and lin-guistically formulated distance and objectivity together with the nearness of the witness. This double tone and point of view can be observed particularly well in *Sorstalanság* and in *Kaddish*, where the touching monologue of the narrator is of-ten interrupted by his own doubt and skepticism, allowing no place for sentimen-talism. One good example is the last passage of *Sorstalanság*, a typical Kertész sentence of irony and contingency which makes any moral lesson impossible: Köves plans to talk about the happiness of the camp if anyone asks him and if he does not forget it himself....

One difference is quite clear between Kertész's *Sorstalanság* and Jorge Semprún's *The Long Journey*, another representative work in Holocaust literature (on this, see Peguy). While Semprún's hero talks much about love, solidarity, and friendship, which helps him bear the tortures and accept even the death of his friends, in *Sorstalanság* there is no presence of such human assets. The initializa-tion of Köves takes place in a totalitarianism that transforms not only the outside world, but also the inner and most personal world of people around him. This is why the description of even the deepest feelings in this novel seems to be a deeply ironic farce: the Holocaust did not have any heroes. As Kertész declares in a con-versation about *Schindler's List*, Spielberg's film presents only a rare exception of solidarity, of people who had the chance to do something good (Mihancsik 24). In Kertész's opinion, Spielberg hardly knew anything about the real nature of the Holocaust, least of all that it meant the collapse of European culture (qtd. in Mi-hancsik 24). Semprún knows much more about this than Spielberg, of course, but he is still creating myths of friendship and solidarity, as if he were trying to avoid total hopelessness.

Another important Holocaust text of memory is Zvi Kolitz's "Joszl Rakover Talks to God," an intensely confessional text in the first person singular. The narra-tor was supposed to be one of the last fighters of the Warsaw ghetto uprising, writ-ing his diary and praying to God on the last afternoon before he dies. Kolitz's text was often taken by his readers for real testimony, a documentary from the ghetto, although the author, in fact, was not in Warsaw during the war. His story presents a rabbi who lost everything he had, his properties, his large family, and his friends, but not his faith and loyalty to God. And this is why Joszl Rakover's personal in-tegrity and dignity was not annihilated. In Kertész's oeuvre things are different: He presents a totalitarian world where nothing remained untouched and stable, not even the human soul. If there is no fate, there is no worthy death. Köves does his best to adapt to this world, which seems to be the most natural and acceptable world known to him, and he even tries to understand his murderers. Good, on the contrary, has the most irrational effects in the concentration camp. The narrator of *Kaddish* tells a story about a teacher in the sense of a traditional rabbi who is also a teacher in the context of service to a community who holds the food portion of ten prisoners and risks his own life in order to bring the food ratio to the boy (the narrator himself) laying on a stretcher. However, he is not presented as a hero, but as a prisoner who has other rules to obey than the rules of the camp, but, for this reason, precious little chance to survive: "I wanted to say something, and it seems that my total surprise screamed unabashedly from my face, because as he quickly headed back—if they didn't find him in his place they'd kill him—he replied with recognizable disgust on his moribund face: 'Well, what did you expect!'" (33). In each of his books, Kertész creates a special linguistic expression and context of irony, either of confession such as in *Kaddish* or the impersonal as in *Fatelessness*, strategies of narration which oppose pathos or self-pity. Thus, the results of his narrative strategies give us a more realistic and extensive picture of the Holocaust, a disclosure of this "negative revelation" with all its consequences than either Semprún or Kolitz (see Szántó 35).

László Márton, a contemporary Hungarian writer, in his novel, *Árnyas főutca* (Main Street with Shadows) (1999), attempts to give an account of the Holocaust in Hungary, and like Kertész, comes to the conclusion that something irreparable had happened, the evident signs of which are the loss of identity and the language of all those who survived, victims, the offenders, and unconcerned spectators. His omnipotent narrator makes up a story about the imaginary persons of a photographic collection, the only records that remained of the Jews who had lived in a small Hungarian village and were deported in 1944. The narrator is trying continuously with utter futility to find a chance to save the lives of his heroes. There were no people around helping the Jews, not even their own neighbors in the village. There is only one heroine who survives 1944 and tries to live in the same society which had let her family die. Márton's Jewish-Hungarian heroine surviving the loss of her family can find no continuity in her identity before and after the war; she is no longer the same person, although the world around her tries to be the same again, as if nothing has happened. The narrator also comes to the conclusion that for those who survived the discrimination and mass murder of the Jews, there is no continuity of the "I" before and after the Holocaust. The world is irrevocably different and this is why people who want to relate this experience have to find a new and authentic language.

In sum, my argument is that Kertész's texts are best analyzed in the specific context of Central European history and culture by attention to the region's political, social, and cultural conditions as resulting from several types of totalitarianism and conditions of post-totalitarianism, as well as within the context of European Holocaust literature in toto, represented by such authors such as Borowski, Lévi, Améry, Celan, etc. At the same time, I contend that Kertész is not a "regional" writer as per his minority status based on the limited appeal of Hungarian literature and culture, nor should he be categorized as "Holocaust writer," a label that would imprint his texts emanating from a subject matter rather than emanating from his skills as a writer of fiction. In my view, such localizations of Kertész's work result precisely in the simplifications which generated misunderstandings and problems around the reception of his work in his "home" culture, Hungary. Kertész has found the language to express authentically the most horrific catastrophe of the twentieth century, and thus, he succeeds in speaking to us about many of the important subjects and problems of our time.

Note: This article is an updated version of Sára Molnár, "Nobel in Literature 2002 Imre Kertész's Aesthetics of the Holocaust," CLCWeb: Comparative Literature and Culture 5.1 (2003): <http://clcwebjournal.lib.purdue.edu/clcweb03–1/molnar03.html>.

Works Cited

Bazsányi, Sándor. "A boldogtalanság retorikája" ("The Rhetoric of Unhappiness"). Holmi 12 (1998): 1744–47.

Braham, Randolph L. The Politics of Genocide: The Holocaust in Hungary. New York: Columbia UP, 1981. 2 vols.

Dávidházi, Péter. "Hányatott múlt az utószerkesztés jegyében" ("Past Ups and Downs in Terms of Post-Editing"). Per passivam resistentiam. Változatok hatalom és írás témájára (Per passivam resistentiam: Variations on the Theme of Power and Writing). By Péter Dávidházi. Budapest: Argumentum, 1998. 344–51.

Kertész, Imre. Sorstalanság (Fatelessness). Budapest: Szépirodalmi, 1975.

Kertész, Imre. Gályanapló (Galley Boat-Log). Budapest: Magvető, 1992.

Kertész, Imre. Jegyzőkönyv. Kertész Imre Esterházy Péterrel (Sworn Statement: Imre Kertész with Péter Esterházy). Budapest: Magvető, 1993.

Kertész, Imre. A kudarc (The Failure). 1988. Budapest: Századvég. 1994.

Kertész, Imre. Kaddish for a Child Not Born. Trans. Christopher C. Wilson and Katharina M. Wilson. Evanston: Northwestern UP, 1997.

Kertész, Imre. Valaki más. A változás krónikája (Someone Else: A Chronicle of a Change in Régime). Budapest: Magvető, 1997.

Kertész, Imre. Az angol lobogó (The English Flag). Budapest: Magvető, 2001.

Kertész, Imre. Fatelessness. Trans. Tim Wilkinson. New York: Vintage, 2004.

Kertész, Imre. Kaddish for an Unborn Child. Trans. Tim Wilkinson. New York: Vintage, 2004.

Kolitz, Zvi. "Joszl Rakover beszél az Istennel" ("Joszl Rakover Speaks with God"). Trans. László Kúnos. 2000 5 (2000): 16–21.

Kovács, András. "The Historians' Debate about the Holocaust in Hungary." Imre Kertész and Holocaust Literature. Ed. Louise O. Vasvári and Steven Tötösy de Zepetnek. West Lafayette: Purdue UP, 2005. 138–47.

Kulcsár Szabó, Ernő. A magyar irodalom története 1945–1991 között (History of Hungarian literature between 1945–1991). Budapest: Argumentum, 1993.

Marsovszky, Magdalena. "Imre Kertész and Hungary Today." Trans. Eszter Pásztor. Imre Kertész and Holocaust Literature. Ed. Louise O. Vasvári and Steven Tötösy de Zepetnek. West Lafayette: Purdue UP, 2005. 148–61.

Márton, László. Árnyas főutca (Main Street with Shadows). Pécs: Jelenkor, 1999.

Mihancsik, Zsófia. "Spielberg bárkája" ("Spielberg's Boat"). *Filmvilág* 4 (1995): 24–30.

Nobel Prize in Literature, The. Laureates (2002): <http://www.nobel.se/literature/laureates/index.html>.

Ozsváth, Zsuzsanna. "Radnóti, Celan, and the Aesthetic Shifts in Central European Holocaust Poetry." *Comparative Central European Culture.* Ed. Steven Tötösy de Zepetnek. West Lafayette: Purdue UP, 2002. 51–69.

Peguy, Marie. "The Dichotomy of Perspectives in the Work of Imre Kertész and Jorge Semprún." *Imre Kertész and Holocaust Literature.* Ed. Louise O. Vasvári and Steven Tötösy de Zepetnek. West Lafayette: Purdue UP, 2005. 171–81.

Radnóti, Sándor. "Auschwitz mint szellemi életforma" ("Auschwitz as a Spiritual Form of Life"). *Holmi* 3 (1991): 370–78.

Radnóti, Sándor. "Kertész Imre: *Gályanapló*" ("Imre Kertész: Galley Boat-Log"). *Könyvvilág* 5 (1992): 12.

Szántó, Gábor T. "Interjú Kertész Imrével" ("Interview with Imre Kertész"). *Szombat* 4 (1994): 35.

Szilágyi, Ákos. "2000-beszélgetés Kertész Imrével (1995)" ("2000-Conversation with Imre Kertész [1995]"). *2000* 11 (2002): 5–11.

Szirák, Péter. "A szűk az most tágasabb" ("The Narrow Is Wider Now"). *Kortárs* 11 (1992): 96–100.

Tötösy de Zepetnek, Steven. "And the 2002 Nobel Prize for Literature Goes to Imre Kertész, Jew and Hungarian." *CLCWeb: Comparative Literature and Culture* 5.1 (2003): <http://clcwebjournal.lib.purdue.edu/clcweb03–1/totosy03.hml>.

Tötösy de Zepetnek, Steven. "Imre Kertész's Nobel Prize in Literature and the Print Media." *Imre Kertész and Holocaust Literature.* Ed. Louise O. Vasvári and Steven Tötösy de Zepetnek. West Lafayette: Purdue UP, 2005. 232–46.

White, Hayden. "Historical Emplotment and the Problem of Truth." *Probing the Limits of Representation.* Ed. Saul Friedländer. Berkeley: U of California P, 1992. 37–53.

Yerushalmi, Yosef Hayim. *Záchor. Zsidó történelem és zsidó emlékezet* (Zakhor: Jewish History and Jewish Memory). Trans. György Tatár. Budapest: Osiris, 2000.

Young, Judy. "The Media and Imre Kertész's Nobel Prize in Literature." *Imre Kertész and Holocaust Literature.* Ed. Louise O. Vasvári and Steven Tötösy de Zepetnek. West Lafayette: Purdue UP, 2005. 271–85.

The Dichotomy of Perspectives in the Work of Imre Kertész and Jorge Semprún

Marie Peguy

Translated from the French by Tonin Baltus

What Imre Kertész and Jorge Semprún have in common is first and foremost the experience of the concentration camp, to which they were deported in 1944: Kertész was then fourteen years old, Semprún nineteen. The difference of five years in their ages is significant because while Kertész is a teenager, Semprún is on the threshold of a certain maturity, intellectually and politically. In my paper, I analyze aspects of the two authors' works in the context of autobiographical fiction. What does Kertész tell us in his writings about his fictional alter ego? In *A kudarc* (*Le Refus*/The Failure)—a text engineered much like the interplay of mirror reflections and the intermingling of fiction with reality—the narrator, nicknamed "the old man," conjures up memories of the child he used to be and whose birth is straightaway tantamount to futility, an individual who is not a Jew, brought into a world in crisis, at the very time when a political party leader named Hitler releases *Mein Kampf,* and when anti-Semitic laws are decreed in Hungary. His family story—parents who do not love each other any more and who sued for divorce have sent him to a boarding school—makes him say that already, "on the quiet, some plot was being woven against [his] life" (*Le Refus* 87; all translations from the French, incl. quotations from Kertész's texts in French translation, are by Tonin Baltus). Nothing pointed then to his becoming a writer and he can only manage to define himself through negativity: "I am not . . . , I have not . . . I know not . . ." (87). When in the same text he alludes to his arrest, it is "in the wake of an ever so stupid mesh of circumstances" (21) whose meanings he does not grasp. He states this thorough incomprehension in *Sorstalanság* (*Être sans destin*/*Fatelessness*), in which he is called upon to play a part he has not really made his own.

Françoise Nicoladzé, in her *La Deuxième vie de Jorge Semprun*, discusses Semprún's entry into the French Resistance and she explains that in Semprún's family it was his father who introduced the ethic of resistance and the value of "siding with the humiliated and the underdog" (Semprún, *Autobiographie de Federico Sánchez* 31). The forced exile of the family in 1936 is perceived as abandonment

171

by the child who vows, as he has written in *Le Grand voyage*, "to fill the gap, to make up for lost time" (240). As Nicoladzé puts it, Semprún has left behind an unfinished fight. The future of the Semprúnian narrator, on whose mind a tragic and traumatizing vision of the world is impressed, seems henceforth to be mapped out. With the aim of reversing the trend of things, considering both the possibilities and the pitfalls that History will lay in his path, he will take part in "the Fight of man in the City" (Nicoladzé 25). Later on, his studies in philosophy at the Lycée Henri IV would afford him the possibility to thoroughly think out what was so far only developed in theory: Marxism discovered during the talks with his friends portends the shifting from intellectual commitment to action. The narrator's knowledge of Hegel leads him to see in life the assertion of autonomy through choices. In this case, the identity of the narrator is being built up in the fulfillment of "a vow as ancient as it is ardent" (*Autobiographie* 121). At nineteen the Resistance enabled Semprún to find the means to this dreamt-of form of resistance. Concerning his emotional life, although the untimely death of his mother (for him a rebellious figure) is a profound hurt, the female characters that come his narrators' way in his novels, unattainable and evanescent as they are, keep her memory brilliant. At the same time, the finely chiseled shadow of the father, a humanist and a Christian, testifies to the genuine, deep-rooted identity of the narrator. Thus, although the episode of the deportation is obviously going to destroy the constitutive elements of his identity, still there remain within him the tools adequate to undertake the reconstruction: his political commitment and his authorship, one supplementing the other in the ideal world of a man with a purpose.

One of the major differences between Semprún and Kertész lies in their status in the concentration camps, where Semprún is deported as a resistance fighter and Kertész as a Jew. Semprún finds effective support in the communist network that is in control of the Buchenwald camp: He recounts how his comrades looked after him for two years. He owes having survived to his friends, who were in charge of the secret military organization and who intercepted a note which had put his life in jeopardy, or, again, to the same friends' organizing his pretend death and finding the right corpse for the purpose. What is more, Semprún spoke German; in command of the language of the oppressors, in the concentration camp he is able to wage a war of survival, which places him a cut above many inmates. Finally, and nevertheless, it is sheer luck which allows the Semprúnian narrator to account for his survival. Kertész, although at the time of his deportation not self-identified as such, is deported as a Jew and gradually begins to understand what it means to be a Jew. In *Sorstalanság*, one of the characters in the novel, Uncle Lajos tells the protagonist, George Koves, "from now on you share the fate of the Jewish people" and reminds him that this fate "had for decades been an uninterrupted succession of persecutions," that the Jews had nevertheless to "accept with patience and resignation" (30). George perceives that being Jewish brings him nothing, neither fraternal help nor spiritual comfort. He says he is baffled at the attachment of the members of this community to a status that only brings them inconvenience, "much more loss than profit" (193). The uneasiness he feels when amongst Jews he construes as the strange sensation of being a Jew, an apparent paradox that expresses itself in the narrator's discomfort in front of the other men. Belonging to the Hungarian community does not give him a sense of identity either (on this, see Cohen). He is not exactly acknowledged as a Jew, while the Hungarians are disdained by other Central and East Europeans in the camp. George expresses the pariah status of his character by that haunting irony which makes him find the Germans and their methodical organization simply "beautiful" and "worthy of admiration": He ends up feeling a real complicity and an almost brotherly intimacy with the torturer who sees to him personally by loading him with bags all day long. This is the moment in the story when the totalitarian process has come full circle: The metaphorical train comes to a halt for the character, who can no longer cope with the changes that occur in himself. He considers those inmates nicknamed *Muselmann*-s, those who have lost the desire to live, those figures shaped like "question marks" (*Être sans destin* 191), whose existence puts into question the very meaning of humanity, a disorderly procession he realizes he is joining gradually (*Muselmann* was a term used by inmates for inmates who had been broken psychically and physically by life in the concentration camp).

The perspectives of the protagonists in Kertész's and Semprún's writing represent a dichotomy; the latter insist on siding with humanity and on preserving a political link with the world they knew before. Poetry and fraternity unite to overcome horror. With Kertész there is no sublimation whatsoever, but rather a narrator who "naturally" inches his way towards inhumanity, to which he offers no resistance because to Koves, "the train" which takes man towards his destination halts at the camp at Zeist. All of a sudden the train progresses no more, has no further destination, reduces the future to a tomorrow which is identical to today. Then, little by little, the narrator lives this ultimate experience, by himself turning into a *Muselmann*, so abhorrent to those who keep on fighting, those who are still provided with "obstinacy." We are dealing with a kind of passive resistance, which never materializes into any kind of action. Sometimes it is reduced to "a will to live," which the shadow-like *Muselmänner* have renounced. In the longest, hallucinatory chapter of the novel, the narrator is reduced to lying beside the corpse of another inmate, whose rations he is thus able to get, and he feels a kind of comfort lying next to him; he finds himself suddenly at peace, in the proximity of cadavers, the vermin, the putrefaction gnawing at him, and the spasm of his bowels. There is no fight left in him any more. Nothing seems to survive of his personality, bereft of hope. Neither does despair, only a kind of sense of well-being and the conviction of being still alive. If the determination to live abandons the character, it is ready to resurface in the most surprising ways.

In *Le Grand voyage*, Semprún, too, describes the degradation of the narrator's body under the effect of pain: "all the broken and bruised parts of my body strew the floor to the confines of the poky compartment, all that I have left really in my possession, within myself, is that spongy burning fireball somewhere behind my eyes, where seem to reverberate, sometimes dull, but all of a sudden the pain emanating from a broken body scattered around me" (147). Feeling one's body dislocated jeopardizes, obviously, the notion of identity, but in Semprún's view the oneness of the *self* prevails and persists in the repeated hints at the foregoing person, symbolized by the "fireball" who keeps on centralizing sensations. By the same token, in *L'Écriture ou la vie*, a story in which the writer speaks on his own behalf, torture causes a shock in the individual perceptible in a few words, which echo those of Kertész: "Each day I held my tongue was a victory over the Gestapo; if it separated my body—a gasping envelope—from me a bit more, it reconciled me with my real self" (148–49). Still, in the very formulation of that feeling there exists in Semprún the evidence of a confrontation from which he finally emerges a victor. The buffeted self recovers in the glow of the fight, which reconstructs the identity of the "myself." The difference in the way of reporting what extreme suffering contributes towards the perception of the *self* is also there in the evocation Semprún makes of torture in his *Autobiographie de Federico Sánchez*, in which he tells of his years "underground," fighting Francoism. To a combatant, torture becomes a means to conquer the freedom of the person who has been arrested, resists, gives nothing away, and preserves the freedom of others by keeping silent. And there comes to the narrator a senseless desire to be arrested "so that the freedom of his comrades may depend on [his] resistance: not to yield equates to be free" (61). Pain and physical suffering vanish in the face of those values which give a meaning to his existence.

Semprún's political struggle ends up in disappointment in his ideals, in continuous disillusionment: The German-Soviet Pact, all those trials under Stalin, the Prague ones particularly, the existence of the Soviet camps on the very sites of the Nazi horrors, the Khrushchev report, and, finally, his expulsion from the Communist Party in 1964 prompted him to opt for a different type of struggle. Literature, which his militant action had overshadowed, now constitutes his fight against oblivion. And when Semprún begins to write again, his writing proves to go hand in hand with the meandering nature of the flux of memory, against which he had fought earlier because of his experience in a concentration camp. Thus we discover that Semprún was leading twin struggles: One in broad daylight, as it were, against an outward, quite identifiable enemy, the Francoist dictatorship; and a second one, obscure, interior, against both the past and his memories and whose origin is to be traced back to his encounter with Nazi totalitarianism in its most sophisticated form, the concentration camp. It seems as if the fight in the city is helping to keep at a distance the other battle, in which it is so difficult to find a transcendental ideal because one of the characteristics of a totalitarian regime is to suppress the very notion of resistance. If Semprún, the intellectual, is affected deeply and irreversibly by the malicious power of totalitarianism, the politician he is can come up with a rational system of explanation that saves him from nonsensicality. This may explain why, after the episode of deportation, he is able solely through political struggle to build a system of explanation and values that can protect his damaged identity. That is why, when political struggle no longer proves viable, Semprún finds that his long pent-up need to write takes hold of him, with all its attendant suffering. In her analysis of Semprún's work, Nicoladzé shows that Semprún is able to recover his identity through confessing and repenting his ideological blindness through his writing. In the same way, Semprún deals with the delicate issue of his survivor's conscience and guilt, all the more delicate as he owes his life to his communist comrades.

With Kertész, writing also involves re-conquest, to begin with, of one's destiny. Narrative, which evolves following the movement of a character, most often the narrator, is the appropriate way to undertake that adaptation. In *Valaki más. A változás krónikája* (*Un autre. Chronique d'une métamorphose*/Someone Else: A Chronicle of the Change in Régime) it is the form of the chronicle in which the narrator covers a space in a Europe "suddenly larger" (38). In the second part of *A kudarc*, Koves comes back home after a long absence and finds himself confronted with a new political order. In *A nyomkereső*, the character-narrator comes back to places tied to his experiences and which we guess have to do with the deportation. In these texts the displacement of the narrators enables us to show History on the move. But *Sorstalanság* is the tale that initiates and shapes this meaningful linearity. Koves goes through the narrative, progresses step by step, and towards the end of the text lets it be known that he is not ashamed of that narration, which he refuses to consider as a series of fortuitous events he just had to undergo. Then he begins finally to understand what it means to be a Jew: perhaps nothing more than to be a person, an individual. Autobiographical fiction, which builds on the linear progress of the narrative, becomes the appropriate form to re-conquer one's self, together with one's history. Only the transcription of this progression, the linear passing of time day after day, minute after minute, is able to show actually how totalitarianism destroys an individual little by little. And only writing can help one return to the wellspring of one's self and minister to its reconstruction. Kertész challenges us to do no less than accept Auschwitz, taking up a position which is difficult to bear and whose only form—his narrative—makes it tolerable, whereas the words of the survivor himself are denied. This denial is highlighted in the closing phase of the narrative when the two old Jews, Fleischmann and Steiner, friends of the family, advise him to forget these atrocities and to live in freedom. Thus, Kertész shares this fate; it is not his choice, but by accepting it he can behave as if he were a free agent distancing himself from the attitude of quite a number of Jews who find in their religion a justification for the sufferings they endure, and who willingly fall in line with the martyrs and swell their ranks. Kertész's Koves refuses the status of a victim.

There is a grey stone in *A kudarc:* It is used as a paperweight on top of a grey dossier containing the manuscript of the refused novel, a grey irregular stone which "directs our bankrupt imagination towards origins, destinations, densities, and final units . . . in order to send us back, finally, to our helpless ignorance" (*Le Refus* 19). The shapeless and colorless stone, which helps the imagination of the writer to unfold and links origin and finalities, is much like Koves's image as it appears to the reader. The narrator-character exists through this image, whose peculiarity lies in the events' being so familiar that every emotional charge is neutralized. Koves's story gathers substance with that petrified vision. In a previous chapter which described the scission of the character forfeiting his body and his feelings, Koves's gaze captured only what entered his view "without any superfluous motion or strain" (257). The human being takes the appearance of a misshapen object: "Two sharp accessories—the nose and the chin" (257). The image becomes neutral, a fixed *ciné-camera* that no one operates and that in this morbid fixity undresses the world and exposes it. The man it sees is no longer a man, just a number of accessories, of objects, neither alive nor dead. How then can this disembodied eye transmit any vision? Here, too, the text is explicit because this unsubstantial eye exists only because another eye gives it its substance. It is a look from above, "the mystery of a depth" (257), a look he likens to that of the doctor in charge of the selection at Auschwitz, for whom he had straight away had "a feeling of trust" (120). One cannot but see here a sign representing destiny, "the preposterous order of fortune" ("Heureka!" <http://www.nobel.se/literature/laureates/2002/kertesz-lecture.html>), because Koves actually owes his survival to this man. It is because the doctor believed that he was two years older than he actually was, and hence he declared him to be a worker instead of a boy that he is still alive today. In the evocation of the "ray of light" he saw, numbed, on the threshold of death, the narrator recalls the fits of mysticism, those that throw light upon the saints and the martyrs who then become the eyes and the voice of God. In *Valaki más* the writer speaks of that gaze/image and of that relation to God. He wonders about the part that "fate" cast for him: Is he a kind of prophet or a simple "chronicler"? Did God entrust him with the mission to register signs all about the world, limiting his existence to this humble yet essential task? But is he not he overcome by hubris when he evokes "The answers to the questions that God didn't ask him" or "the questions to the answers that God kept dark" (*Un autre* 86)? Likewise, in his Nobel speech in Stockholm, he declares: "I feel behind me the searching look of a stolid observer" ("Heureka!" <http://www.nobel.se/literature/laureates/2002/kertesz-lecture.html>). And this look sends him back to the humility of his condition: "I rather tend to identify myself with that stolid witness than with the writer suddenly made famous before the whole world" ("Heureka!" <http://www.nobel.se/literature/laureates/ 2002/kertesz-lecture.html>). The question he then singles out as being the most important is the one found at the end of *Az angol lobogó* (The English Flag) and which he reiterates in his chronicle: "Who sees through us" (*Un autre* 86). And this someone sees not only through our eyes but also through our lives. Then we must live; and to the writer, to live is to work—or rather to *be* is to work, because without this work, which occupies all our time, we would have to exist. At that point the loop is looped: writing is to allow this vision to feed on a life devoted to watching, not to existing. To write is not to exist, it is to live.

With Kertész, by writing he can take control of his own destiny. Yet his stance is not that of a combatant: Kertész did not choose action, he chose to be an observer. The Stalinist regime he is up against, which keeps deepening the furrows left by what he experienced in the concentration camp, makes it possible for him to conquer another form of freedom, which is his constrictive newfound prison, an apartment that looks like the old man's in *A kudarc*, a precarious temporary habitat, a provisional that lasts, much like the existence of himself, who has outwitted death "so far" (*Le Refus* 13). The only path to freedom runs through seclusion, a voluntary one this time, an inward exile, even if it begets suffering. In any case, he who has experienced life in prison only feels at home in prison: "You can't live your freedom on the scenes of your former captivity" (11). The stigma is twofold; it affects both the person and the place. But this refusal becomes something you claim and not only suffer: "the old fellow" chooses or, rather, demands this seclusion, which is the only guarantee of moral and intellectual freedom, because the freedom of an artist does not thrive in the same spaces as the ordinary person's. And so Kertész becomes this weaponless resistance fighter.

Kertész's resistance is based on a stubborn "No." It can take on the form of a trifling *kaddish* chanted by a pathetic rabbi who clings to it, fully aware of its futility. A stubbornness "both compulsory and futile" (*Kaddish* 223), which, despite his physical decay, transfigures the rabbi into a triumphant being. Is it language that informs a person's resistance? And the narrator, before the spectacle offered by the rabbi and the expression of that "stubbornness," becomes suddenly aware of something missing; he who does not pray does not know the words that connect with God, the set of questions and answers that he would only learn to make later on. We understand better why the *kaddish* becomes, a few years later, a way of asserting this "No," thanks to which the writer re-appropriates his history, in a process of acceptance. In *Kaddish* Kertész shows that he has filled the void he felt and described in *Sorstalanság:* His assertion is definitely "obstinacy" in one's refusal— the refusal to place oneself in a future which stopped on the day when that train pulled up at Zeist, and broadly speaking, in Auschwitz, in Europe, in the world as a whole. The way of speaking has changed and dialogue has become the means to pray, because, he says, to write is to have a dialogue with God. Yet, as God no longer exists, there remains a dialogue with man and with himself. Thus the text reflects the obstinacy of this muffled speech, which can only go on twisting around itself, within the relentless unwinding of a continuous linearity. The only blanks in the text—when the readers, dragged along as they are by the intense rhythm of these never-ending sentences, can at last get their breath back—are created by the

No's. In *Kaddish*, Kertész asserts this will not to exist, bearing out the stance described in *A kudarc*, a fiction which once more weaves reality with echoes. This augural "No," reiterated in the text itself, is that of "the instincts at work against our instincts" *(Kaddish* 7). Kertész's battle is set there, in the intimate confrontation of vital forces, the instinct for survival, for procreation, quasi animal, coming up against another one, rooted in History, recognizable by its refusal to follow the herd towards a fate which might be similar to Auschwitz. Writing is a saving act, it is a fight for freedom; "in the morass of this consensus, only one alternative was left: either giving up fighting for good, or looking for the winding road of interior liberty" ("Heureka!" <http://www.nobel.se/literature/laureates/2002/kertesz-lecture. html>).

In an interview, Kertész mentions Semprún and *Le Grand voyage*, in which which he says he saw an example of what he did not want to do, namely, in dealing with Auschwitz "sticking strictly to the epoch" (see Kertész, "Mon œuvre"). Semprún's work centers on the confrontation of the subject with a destructive experience and reveals this confrontation of his self with his history, his past, his memories. The characters are occurrences of that self which arrive at reconstruction through writing: The Semprúnian stories are really planting their roots in a dated, located, peopled universe, which gives them an autobiographical dimension even in his most unbridled fiction, *The Algarabie*. To Semprún, the characters are so many doubles of the writer, who gets reconstructed in this diffraction. Semprún's style rests on subjectivity, whereas Kertész strongly opposes this dimension: The character-narrator in *Sorstalanság*/*Être sans destin* has no memory, no past, and exists only through a seeing. All the narrators in Kertész's stories are indeed avatars of that Koves, who himself, being saddled with a real-life experience, is conceived in reference to the author's experiences. Personal life is a stepping stone to the observation of the world but is not important in itself. Hence the title *Être sans destin:* Without a destiny, and so without an existence of one's own. It is the reason why with Kertész the characters receive no light from within; they lack fictional consistency, have no psychological depth—often just nicknames, such as "the Unlucky," "the Smoker," etc.—and to describe them the author resorts to caricature, uses methods which partake of metonymy and animalization and which tend to depersonalize (on this, see also Várnai). In *Kaddish*, the narrator is just a voice. In *Un autre*, the chronicle helps to restore an autobiographical dimension to the text, but the record of the author is a confirmation of the sort indicated in the subtitle: describing the European space after an itinerary comparable with a journey of initiation. Kertész conjures up Semprún and an excerpt of *Le Grand voyage* and by quoting Semprún, he shows that his representation of the character called Ilse Koch reaches an allegorical dimension through an aesthetic of concentration: "Here you are, blood, the pleasures of the flesh, and the devil, concentrated in one character" (*Le Refus* 48). This figure also conjures up—according to the cultural references of the reader—a number of historical characters that literatures have magnified in their perversity, and makes horror an aesthetic object. Yet the literary creation whose object the character is meant to be, is a risky enterprise because it obscures the environment in which he/she is placed, in "a world organized to kill" (*Le Refus* 52). The tragic character, Ilse Koch—or Larréa, in Semprún's *La Montagne blanche*—for whom suicide confers a sort of mythic eternity, stands, in Kertész's view, for the very essence of the matter at hand; the totalitarian universe is historical and determined by situations, and the character is the outcome of it all. The participant simply bears out the logic of the concentration camp, becoming neither an exception nor an act of transgression.

Semprún, in *L'Écriture*, makes himself clear about these choices, which find their justification in the difficulty telling a story: It is true that one is able to say everything, because words are able to express all the components of human experience, both the "good" and the "evil." Yet a never-ending tale is likely to tax the patience of the reader. The terrified looks the officers cast on the narrator at the liberation of the concentration camp show him the limits of receptiveness: "Only the artifice of a well-mastered tale will manage to convey partly the reality of the evidence" (*L'Écriture* 166). Semprún writes to testify and ponders over the question of receptiveness. The Semprúnian text does not speak of the camp but of the souls that flit about it, the narrator's, the writer's, the fictional characters'; in fact, the text claims a place for subjectivity in experience, which is, in his opinion, the only truth, the essential one, the one that no description, no analysis can ever exhaust: "What is at stake isn't the description of horror . . . but the exploration of the human soul at grips with the horror of Evil" (170). It is perhaps a means to keep away from that life in the camp, which, for the intellectual he is, cannot be accounted for.

Primo Lévi, in *Se questo è un uomo*, describes a scene in which the *Divine Comedy* acts as the fraternal link, which abolishes the frontiers of language and temporality, allowing the world without, the former world, to find its place in the camp. This break represents a moment's grace, a sunny day, a fatigue, which takes the two prisoners away from the concentration camp proper, an exceptional moment. Are the last words of François, the young *Muselmann* dying by his side, really Seneca's? "There's nothing after death, death itself is nothing" (Semprún, *Le Mort qu'il faut* 208). Are these words not those that, according to the narrator, express the essence of experience, give it a meaning and keep it from lapsing into nonsensicality? Is it opposition, on the part of the intellectual, to the disappearance from the camp, a universe of transcendence, whatever its form, experienced or fabricated, in a bid to transmit the essence of real-life experiences? In fact, it does not matter, because it is with humanism and fraternity that Semprún's work is built. With Semprún, writing becomes necessary when it is no longer possible to go forward and fight. He is, therefore, confronted by the past and what he considers to be his death. The lack of memory indicates a broken identity, and the act of writing forces him to remember, which in turn allows him to reconstruct himself. His lyricism becomes a worthy witness and helps him put his real identity back together.

With Kertész, observation is not a choice, but the only attitude possible to preserve the ego from fraying. Writing is a reaction, almost an instinctive one, a will to live and survive in the face of destruction, something that echoes incessantly, reminding him of the trials of his experience in the concentration camp. But individual experiences are not the heart of Kertész's work; rather, its subject is a springboard to a view of a modern world as frightening as that of the past. Ultimately, we can understand his sacrifice of the ego to the "stolid observer" as a sort of moral conscience which authorizes living and suggesting that what happened at Auschwitz is permanent and irreversible both for him and for humanity.

Works Cited

Cohen, Sara D.. "Jewishness in Hungary, Imre Kertész, and the Choice of an Identity." *Imre Kertész and Holocaust Literature.* Ed. Louise O. Vasvári and Steven Tötösy de Zepetnek. West Lafayette: Purdue UP, 2005. 24–37.

Kertész, Imre. *Az angol lobogó* (The English Flag). Budapest: Holnap, 1991.

Kertész, Imre. *Un autre. Chronique d'une métamorphose.* Trans. Natalia Zaremba and Charles Zaremba. Arles: Actes Sud, 1999.

Kertész, Imre. *Le Chasseur de traces.* Trans. Nathalia Zaremba-Huzsvai et Charles Zaremba. Arles: Actes Sud, 2003.

Kertész, Imre. *Être sans destin.* Trans. Natalia Zaremba-Huzsvai and Charles Zaremba. Arles: Actes Sud, 1996.

Kertész, Imre. "Heureka!" *The Nobel Prize in Literature 2002.* Stockholm: Svenska Akademien, 2002. <http://www.nobel.se/literature/laureates/2002/kertesz-lecture.html>.

Kertész, Imre. *Fatelessness.* Trans. Tim Wilkinson. New York: Vintage, 2004.

Kertész, Imre. *Kaddish for an Unborn Child.* Trans. Tim Wilkinson. New York: Vintage, 2004.

Kertész, Imre. *Kaddish pour l'enfant qui ne naîtra pas.* Trans. Natalia Zaremba-Huzsvai and Charles Zaremba. Arles: Actes Sud, 1995.

Kertész, Imre. *Kaddis a meg nem született gyermekért* (*Kaddish for an Unborn Child*). Budapest: Magvető, 1990.

Kertész, Imre. *A kudarc* (The Failure). Budapest: Szépirodalmi, 1988.

Kertész, Imre. "Mon œuvre *Être sans destin* est une métaphore du régime de Kádár." Interview by Eszter Rádai. Trans. J. Fühling. *Bulletin Trimestriel de la Fondation Auschwitz* 80–81 (2003): 209–19.

Kertész, Imre. *Le Refus.* Trans. Natalia Zaremba-Huzsvai and Charles Zaremba. Arles: Actes Sud, 2001.

Kertész, Imre. *Sorstalanság* (*Fatelessness*). Budapest: Szépirodalmi, 1975.

Kertész, Imre. *Valaki más. A változás krónikája* (Someone Else: A Chronicle of the Change in Régime). Budapest: Magvető, 1997.

Lévi, Primo. *Se questo è un uomo.* Milano: Einaudi, 1947.

Nicoladzé, Françoise. *La Deuxième vie de Jorge Semprun: Une Écriture tressée aux spirales de l'histoire.* Castelnau-le-Lez: Climats, 1997.

Semprún, Jorge. *Le Grand voyage.* Paris: Gallimard, 1963.

Semprún, Jorge. *Autobiographie de Federico Sánchez.* Trans. Claude and Carmen Durand. Paris: Seuil, 1978.

Semprún, Jorge. *L'Algarabie.* Parie: Fayard, 1981.

Semprún, Jorge. *La Montagne blanche.* Paris: Gallimard, 1986.

Semprún, Jorge. *L'Écriture ou la vie.* Paris: Gallimard, 1994.

Semprún, Jorge. *Le Mort qu'il faut.* Paris: Gallimard, 2002.

Várnai, Paul. "Holocaust Literature and Imre Kertész." *Imre Kertész and Holocaust Literature.* Ed. Louise O. Vasvári and Steven Tötösy de Zepetnek. West Lafayette: Purdue UP, 2005. 247–57.

Imre Kertész and the Filming of
Sorstalanság (Fatelessness)

Catherine Portuges

As we continue to celebrate Imre Kertész's *Sorstalanság* (*Fatelessness*), the first
Hungarian-language novel to win the Nobel Prize for Literature, we also com-
memorate the sixtieth anniversary of the Holocaust in Hungary on the eve of the
enlargement of the European Union in 2004. The confluence of these major events
cannot fail to evoke the memory of the massacre of the country's Jewish population in the last months of 1944, the most intensive process of extermination in the
Second World War (see, e.g., Braham; Lendvai). Yet, the proliferation of recent
publications on these subjects should not be allowed to obscure the silence that
once surrounded (and in fact nearly obliterated) the discourse of the Shoah in Hungary after 1948 (see Kende; Lanzmann; Resnais). In order to account, albeit
briefly, for the stages that led to the breaking of that silence, it is useful to consider
for a moment a major development in the realm of artistic creativity: Over the
course of the 1970s, Holocaust memory appeared to return to the public scene primarily in the form of literary texts produced by a generation of writers who had
experienced personally this persecution as children or as adolescents (see, for example, Delbo; Dénes; Handler and Meschel; Márai; Suleiman; Szép; Wiesel; on
English-language Central European Jewish memoirs, see Tötösy de Zepetnek).
Among them was Imre Kertész, whose interrogation of the role of the Holocaust in
Hungarian literature continues today. In "Long Dark Shadow," an essay from his
collection, *A holokauszt mint kultúra* (1993) (The Holocaust as Culture), he suggests that "nothing would [appear to] be simpler than to collect, name and evaluate
those Hungarian literary works that were born under direct or indirect influence of
the Holocaust. . . . However, in my view that is not the problem. The problem, dear
listeners, is the imagination. To be more precise: to what extent is the imagination
capable of coping with the fact of the Holocaust? How can imagination take in, receive, the Holocaust, and, because of this receptive imagination, to what extent has
the Holocaust become part of our ethical life and ethical culture…This is what we
must talk about" (171). In this essay, published in English in Suleiman and Forgács's collection, *Contemporary Jewish Writing in Hungary*, Kertész attempts to
explain why, during forty years of Stalinist rule in Hungary, the genocide of the

Jewish people and the complicity of so many Hungarians in that genocide went unacknowledged.

Kertész was honored by the Nobel Prize in 2002 for his novel *Sorstalanság*, first published in 1975, for writing that "upholds the fragile experience of the individual against the barbaric arbitrariness of history," and that admittedly has drawn upon the "barbaric arbitrariness" of his own tragic experience as a fifteen-year-old Hungarian Jew in Auschwitz (*Nobel Prize in Literature: Laureates* [2002]: <http://www.nobel.se/literature/laureates/index.html>). In the aftermath of the Nobel, and following years of relative invisibility, Kertész was catapulted into the forefront of media attention, generating acclaim as well as ambivalence and hostility (on this, see, e.g., Nádas). Born in Budapest, he considers himself to be part of a generation whose lives were marked by momentous historical turning points—1944, 1945, 1948, 1953, 1956. After his liberation from Buchenwald, he was both a factory worker and journalist in Budapest before publishing his collected works in Germany in 1999. Nonetheless, at present, only *Fatelesnesss* and *Kaddish for a Child Not Born* (Wilson and Wilson) have been translated into English, in what the author considers to be "a disgracefully bad English translation, a fact I consider utterly unethical . . . [and that has] . . . nothing to do with what I wrote. The language, yes, that's all that connects me to Hungary. . . . How strange. This foreign language is my mother tongue") ("A Nobel-díjat" 47–48; subsequent translations from the Hungarian are mine unless noted otherwise; it should be note that the 2004 translation by Tim Wilkinson, *Fatelessness* and *Kaddish for an Unborn Child* have been approved by Kertész).

Although *Sorstalanság* was written between 1960 and 1973 and published in a censored form in 1975, it received wide recognition only after 1990 (e.g., the novel was named one of *Publisher's Weekly*'s Best Books of 1992). Kertész's earlier, mesmerizing novel of identity and memory, *Kaddish for a Child Not Born* (1999) was published on the fiftieth anniversary of the liberation of Auschwitz. Set in the context of a writer's retreat where a middle-aged Holocaust survivor engages in an interior monologue, *Kaddish* reflects on the narrator's failed literary career and his inability to bring a child into a world in the shadow of the fear of another future Holocaust: "Auschwitz must have been hanging in the air for a long, long time, centuries, perhaps like a dark fruit slowly ripening in the sparkling rays of innumerable ignominious deeds, waiting to finally drop on one's head" (*Kaddish* 32). In interviews, however, he has characterized himself as "a non-believing Jew. Yet as a Jew I was taken to Auschwitz, as a Jew I was in the death camps and as a Jew I live in a society that does not like Jews, one with great anti-Semitism. I always have the feeling that I was obliged to be Jewish. I am Jewish, I accept it, but to a large extent it is also true that it was imposed on me" ("A Nobel-díjat" 47). Kertész clarifies this ambivalent positioning stating that

> Germany was from the very first moment forced to confront its past and could not do so in any way other than self-examination. This was not an easy process—it lasted a long time, and actually only after the student movements of 1968 . . . did the breakthrough take place . . . In Hungary as well, after the war some kind of clarification began, but soon afterwards this whole group of issues was suppressed. So Hungary has not yet had its turn in coming to terms with the past. It is true that Hungary indeed suffered a great deal of national pain, it was a threatened country, and one has to understand that it is more sensitive to suffering. But the time will come, even if the nation does not yet have the power or generosity to complete the process . . . Membership in the European Union now gives the country *carte blanche* to do so. ("A Nobel-díjat" 48)

While *Fateless* (1992; *Fatelessness* 2004) was praised by the Swedish Academy, the book's "lack of moral indignation" was also considered disturbing, a response that perhaps has more than a little to do with its specifically Central European meta-language, a style that resists deconstruction and interpretation by readers who might not benefit from the requisite comparative cultural context. Indeed, Kertész might well have been anticipating this aspect of the Academy's response in an interview broadcast on Hungarian radio in 1991 when he declared:

> I was not brought up as an observant Jew and I did not become a believer later on; at the same time, I find that Judaism is an absolutely decisive moment of my life, one I am attached to because, on account of it, I lived through a great moral test. But is it possible to rise above the experiences one lives through in such a way that we don't exclude them and at the same time manage to transpose them to a universal level?...My country has yet to face up to the skeleton in the closet, namely awareness of the issue of the Holocaust, which has not yet taken root in Hungarian culture, and those writing about it [still] stand on the sidelines . . . I think it is a success if my book has made even a slight contribution to this process. (qtd. in Riding A7-A8).

A significant gesture toward the ongoing process of re-inscribing Hungarian Holocaust memory was made by the Hungarian Motion Picture Foundation's February 2003 decision to provide funding for a film adaptation of *Fatelessness*—the very Foundation that, two years earlier, had allocated the majority of its budget to productions considered by many to be nationalist epics, *Bánk Bán* (2003) and *Hídember* (2003). That a new film from such a different perspective and sensibility is currently in production, based on the author's screenplay published in both Hungarian and German, would seem to suggest that both Kertész and the Hungarian government embrace the opportunity afforded by the visibility of his status as a Nobel Laureate to make just such a contribution. The production in fact marks the directorial debut of Lajos Koltai, the renowned cinematographer and veteran of more than seventy features including such acclaimed films as István Szabó's Oscar-winning *Mephisto* (1982) as well as his Oscar-nominated *Bizalom* (Confidence), *Colonel Redl, Hanussen* (1988), *Meeting Venus* (1991), *Taking Sides* (1999), and *A napfény íze* (*Sunshine*) (1999). Nonetheless, given Kertész's much-publicized critique of published translations of his books in English, one wonders whether his personal invitation to Koltai to direct the adaptation—which is also a form of translation—from book to screen will meet a more auspicious fate. Koltai discusses his perspective in a new documentary, *Koltai napló* (The Diary of Lajos Koltai) screened at the Hungarian Film Week, known as the "Szemle," in February 2004. In one sequence, Kertész expresses his reservations concerning previous Holocaust-related films:

> Many directors have tried to deal with the theme of the concentration camps. But few have done so in an authentic way. After the war, in 1946–47, I saw a film about Auschwitz by a Polish woman director, which I found stunning [Kertész is referring to Wanda Jakubowska's 1948 film, *The Last Stage*]. The first few scenes are astonishingly authentic: it is raining, early morning in Birkenau. The women prisoners are very tired, they start to move slowly back and forth, in a totally credible way. What Spielberg does [in *Schindler's List*], in contrast, is inauthentic: inmates call to each other across barbed wire...this would have been totally impossible...the whole picture lacks credibility. (qtd. in *Koltai napló*).

One might suspect that the ever-increasing production of Holocaust-related film narratives may in fact be attributable to the 1993 release of *Schindler's List*; among other factors, the public debate surrounding the film led to the creation of Spielberg's "Survivors of the Shoah Visual History Foundation," which has since become a major site of international archival, oral history, film, video and digital research, and preservation.

In my first interview with Koltai in February 2003, and again a year later, in Budapest, the director referred to numerous failed attempts to secure funding for the project, long before the Nobel Prize was awarded, for the first time in its history, to a Hungarian writer. Koltai began our conversation by asserting that: "this has been a living project for years, and not merely a sudden urge to capitalize on the Nobel." Explaining that his preparation of the film is based on the author's own scenario, he conceptualizes it as "a Hungarian work of art . . . a Central European co-production involving slightly more than fifty percent Hungarian funding" (Personal interview, Budapest, 8 February 2003). The film's total budget is expected to be $11.7 million (2.5 billion Forints), the largest in history allocated for a Hungarian production. The director agrees with Kertész that, in Koltai's words, the story "would not be worth making into a film except under the most perfect conditions . . . the best advertisement for the film would be the star quality of Kertész himself . . . when, the other day, he read aloud to me some parts of his latest novel, I saw again that not only is he a highly unique thinker but also a great performer" (Personal interview, Budapest, 8 February 2003).

The film is to be released in Hungarian and dubbed or subtitled in English and German, (delete following: The film, Koltai adds, will be shot in color "but completely matte on the screen; although it might be adequate in black-and-white, that technique was already used by Spielberg in *Schindler's List*. I will try for an effect somewhere between color and black-and-white" (Personal interview, Budapest, 8 February 2003). Koltai's vision invites comparison with the visual strategies of other recent large-scale Holocaust-centered films such as Roman Polanski's *The Pianist*, based on the memoirs of Ladislaw Szpilman, a young musician in the Warsaw Ghetto. That film's star, Adrien Brody, won the Oscar for best actor, as did Polanski himself for best director, at the 2003 Academy Awards for a work that also addresses Polanski's own experience as a child of the Holocaust, as he admits: "I had searched for decades for a model parallel to my life, which I couldn't film myself . . . Szpilman's book was the text I was waiting for—a testimony of human endurance in the face of death, a tribute to the power of music and the will to live, and a story told without the desire for revenge" (Personal interview, Budapest, 8 February 2003). Films as diverse in approach and conceptualization as Liliana Cavani's *The Night Porter* (Italy, 1974), Roberto Benigni's *Life Is Beautiful* (Italy, 1998*)*, and Claude Lanzmann's *Shoah* (France, 1985) continue to elicit debate with regard to representational strategies adequate to convey what many survivors consider to be un-representable (see Colombat; Lévi).

Koltai has re-created a simulacrum of the camps on location near the Hungarian capital in order to re-imagine the texture and look of Auschwitz, Buchenwald, and Zeitz: the film "will be linear, with no major dramatic point, tracing the path of a boy who, in the end, is destroyed by his experience. The opening sequence will be set in the beautiful colors of a magnificent central European autumn, and gradually fade to black-and-white over time as we see the consequences of his experienced inscribed in his psyche" (Personal interview, Budapest, 8 February 2003). The complex logistics include the deployment of 150 actors and 12,000 extras and the use of digital technology to graft the protagonist onto authentic wartime archival film footage. Koltai has been inundated with offers of help from Hungarian Holocaust survivors, one of whom presented a collection of previously unpublished photographs taken inside the camp with a hidden Agfa camera. A quite different response to the production was noted by the Hungarian daily *Népszabadság* concerning public reaction to the location shoot:

> Scenes from the Nobel prize-winning novel by Imre Kertész that take place in the Buchenwald concentration camp will be shot at a location that is under the control of the interior ministry. The people of Piliscsaba themselves offered this opportunity to the director. However, the daily *Magyar Nemzet* accounted for protests there to the effect that Pilis is a sacred location, an ancient, protected, and endangered site, suggesting that it might disturb the peace of the landscape if a death camp were to be built there. One protestor drew a parallel between the construction of this set and the Israeli prime min-

ister Sharon's visit to the Temple Mount . . . but he did not say exactly what kind of conflict might erupt in twenty-first-century Hungary . . . some seem to detect a hidden anti-Semitism behind these published objections. (*"Sorstalanság*: viszály a díszlet" 11; my translation in consultation with László Dienes)

This reaction brings us to the question of witnessing and testimony: to what extent are there differences between films that are written and directed by those who were direct witnesses and victims, and those based on memoirs, archival materials, historical accounts, photographic documents or the much-debated status of fiction or semi-autobiographical novels, adapted or "translated" to another medium by those who did not experience the Holocaust first-hand? While a full analysis of this important issue lies far beyond the scope of this paper, we must take into account the ways in which the internal, often inchoate language of psychological experience is translated into the more specific, graphic language of cinema. The case of *Sorstalanság* is complex, involving as it does on the one hand a witness / victim—Kertész, the writer and screenwriter—and a second-generation non-witness, Koltai, the director/translator/friend. Such a project—a cinematic meditation on fate and its absence, on the trauma survived by a young protagonist—disposes of a variety of modalities, depending upon the protagonist's (and the filmmaker's) conception of the term: it may be represented as dramatic or quotidian, random, inevitable or pre-ordained, in narrative and experimental genres, as documentary or fiction, in feature-length or short formats. Likewise, as has been theorized in psychoanalytic and structuralist film scholarship, the film medium is supremely capable of evoking a sense of immediacy and intimacy, of recurrent temporality, or repetition and timelessness. In genres varying from tragedy to melodrama to comedy, cinematic fate has variously been portrayed as a universal existential condition common to all human beings, as in the cruelty of Robert Bresson's French provincial protagonists depicted in his Jansenist-influenced *Mouchette* (France, 1967) or the existential awareness of the prisoners portrayed in his *Un condamné à mort s'est échappé* (A Condemned Man Escapes) (France, 1956), or in the ennui of Michelangelo Antonioni's upper-middle-class urban Italians in his *L'Avventura* (1961). One of Hungary's most innovative directors, Béla Tarr, visualizes fate "as emanating from below, so to speak, rather than from above," according to András Bálint Kovács, as in Tarr's seven-hour masterpiece, *Sátántangó* (Satan's Tango) (1994) and his surreal epic *Werkmeister harmoniák* (2001), insuring that "no one may claim that [my] films represent only the misery of the poor . . . In Tarr's world deconstruction is slow but unstoppable, and finds its way everywhere. The question therefore is not how to stop or avoid this process, but what we do in the meantime" (Kovács n.p.). As director, Koltai must also invite the audience to ponder these questions and to do so, he will require a filmic sense of temporality adequate to Kertész's literary style through which the viewer, like the reader, follows his protagonist's odyssey into the univers concentrationnaire.

The trajectory of *Sorstalanság*, as Hungary's first Nobel Prize in Literature invites comparison with other Hungarian films that have thematized this profoundly challenging subject, opening a space for discussion of cinematic representation of the Holocaust in Hungary, sixty years later. Production documents, interviews with the writer, director, producer, and literary and film historians thus become part of a public text-in-the-making, which is framed inescapably by the small but important genre of Hungarian films that—whether semi-autobiographical or wholly fictional, if indeed such a construct may be said to exist—constitute a valuable history of Holocaust representation. For these works at once interrogate and articulate the unresolved question of intergenerational transmission of Jewish identity and its traumatic sequellae upon successive generations (see Hirsch). The debates surrounding *Fatelessness* may be illuminated in part by the concept of postmemory which has proved useful in theorizing visual representation as a powerful medium through which connection to an object or source is mediated not through recollection but through imaginative investment and re-creation, a kind of empathic projection that characterizes the experience of those whose own stories are experienced as being of lesser importance to the subjects than those of a previous generation shaped by traumatic events (see Portuges, Review of *The Pianist*). The reader's engagement with the text, like that of the film viewer with the screen image thus becomes part of a dialectical process in which the necessary work of mourning can take place (Portuges, "Home Movies"; Hirsch).

Let us return for a moment to Koltai's statement that "this film will be different from other Holocaust movies" by recalling selected titles from the archives of Hungarian films, both semi-autobiographical and wholly fictional, produced during the post-Holocaust period. One of the most relevant to this discussion is István Szabó's 1966 *Apa* (Father) which focuses on a twenty-year period from the early 1940s to the early 1960s, deploying a narrative technique based on flashbacks in which factual and imaginative material are interspersed in what has become familiar as a modernist cinematic approach. *Hideg napok* (Cold Days) (1966) directed by András Kovács, is a fictionalized version of a much-debated historical event—the massacre, by Hungarian soldiers, of several thousand Jewish and Serbian inhabitants of Novi Sad in 1942, which may be read today as a courageous filmic intervention at a time when uncomfortable silence had long engulfed the question of Hungary's role in the Second World War (on this, see Petrie 114–20). *Budapesti tavasz* (Spring Comes to Budapest) (1955), directed by Félix Máriássy, reconstructs vividly the last days of the German occupation in 1944, with scenes of horrifying immediacy that include sequences of the mass shooting of Jews on the banks of the Danube, and the defeated Fascists using civilians as hostages against the advancing Russians (on this, see Petrie 185–86). Zoltán Fábri's 1961 feature film, *Két félid   a pokolban* (Two Half-Times in Hell), concerns a group of Hungarians deported to a German labor camp in the Ukraine and ordered to stage—and, not unexpectedly, lose—a soccer match with their guards in honor of the

Führer's birthday. One of the earliest films of this archive is the 1947 *Valahol Európában* (Somewhere in Europe), directed by Géza Radványi, in which a group of children aged from five to eighteen, orphaned by the war or separated from their parents, band together to survive by raiding untended farms and fields. The first half of the film chronicles, quietly and without sentimentality, the process whereby they become progressively hardened and anarchic, stealing boots from the bodies of men hanged by the wayside, and eventually even accepting death and deprivation as their normal lot in life (see Petrie 10–11). Finally, one must reference a Polish production I mentioned previously, *Otatni etap* (*The Last Stage*) (1947), directed by Wanda Jakubowska, herself a survivor of Auschwitz, which was shot on the exact locations where the filmmaker herself had been a deportee, a courageously groundbreaking film that has influenced others of this genre (see Löewy).

Szabó's *Apa* illuminates, through the monologue of a young female protagonist—similar to Kertész's profoundly conflicted and ambivalent stance toward Jewish identity and assimilation—a particularly complicated stance that is characteristic of Jewish-Hungarian writers, artists, and intellectuals. The film, a compelling tribute of a son, Takó, active as a student in the uprising of 1956, to his father, who died in the Second World War, begins with the inscription: "I confront your failure, you who look human." In one powerful scene, a teacher asks his class of young boys how many have lost a father during the war; nearly three-quarters of the class stand up in a silent testimony to the toll of the war on Jewish families. A later sequence addresses the question of Jewish identity somewhat more directly when Takó, now a university student, walks along the Danube with Anni, a student friend, who confesses to him:

> It's awful, you know. For years I denied that my father died in a concentration camp. I'd make up a story rather than admit I was Jewish. I finally realized the futility of it and I faced reality. I even went to Auschwitz with an excursion group and I took pictures. All I got were pictures of well-dressed tourists milling around. Sometimes I still feel ashamed and pretend not to be Jewish. I am Hungarian, am I not? The forgotten past of my ancestors doesn't count. And I can't overcome it. I want to be proud of that Jewish past for which my parents gave their lives. I simply can't behave normally. I just don't know where I belong, where I want to belong, what I am, or where I should belong. The Pope at last forgave the Jews for their sins. That means that they were guilty of crucifying Christ 2000 years ago. And those who twenty years ago let six million Jews be gassed and burned? How soon will they be absolved? You see how maddening this can be, and how idiotic this Auschwitz thing is! Part of me is there. My parents and relatives perished there. But I can't go on harping on it just to get sympathy. I feel ashamed for belonging to those who were slaughtered like sheep. I always feel as if I had to prove something. . . . (*Apa*).

It is all the more remarkable that this incisively nuanced monologue was produced in 1966 when such questions were far from commonly addressed in Hungarian or, for that matter, Central and Eastern European cinema. Clearly, both documentary and narrative cinema have proved to be powerful means of enacting memory and mourning, enabling filmmakers and viewers alike to engage in processes of working through trauma. Both are forms of witnessing and testimony, and both are capable of addressing voyeurism, violence, comedy, and propaganda, as well as historical research. Since 1989, Hungarian cinema has undergone dramatic and traumatic changes in, among many other aspects, filmmakers' sense of obligation with respect to their audiences. A number of films of the 1990s have, whether directly or obliquely, invoked the Holocaust in Hungary, including *Eszterkönyve* (The Book of Esther, dir. Krisztina Deák, 1990), *Sose halunk meg* (We'll Never Die, dir. Robert Koltai, 1994), *Tutajosok* (The Rafters, dir. Judit Elek, 1990; *Ébredés* (The Awakening, dir. Judit Elek, 1994), to mention only a few (see my review of these films in Portuges, "Jewish Identity"). These past fifteen years have thus witnessed the return of the history of Hungarian Jews to the center of the cinematic stage through ambitious historical frescoes as well as intimate, moving narratives. Where once Hungarian cinema was seen as "the most important art" (Lenin) whose purpose was to bear witness to political realities, today's industry is far more dependent upon profits and market share, although recently enacted legislation of a new Hungarian Film Law, approved in January 2004, promises to restore much-needed stability to Hungarian film production by assuring foreign investors of appropriate revenues, thus enabling international co-producers to benefit from their investments. That the producers of *Fateless* were allocated half the national film budget by the Hungarian government, with the balance to come from international co-producers in Holland, Germany, and Italy, suggests at the very least an opportunity to make use of Kertész's recent celebrity in the interest of promoting and interrogating national narratives of the Holocaust.

In spite of the financial support the film has received, Koltai's task is monumental, perhaps not unlike that faced by Art Spiegelman with regard to his Pulitzer prize-winning illustrated book, *Maus*, a highly sophisticated representation of the interplay of animal figures with masked humans, a strategy through which the author conveys aspects of Holocaust events and memory without showing them directly—depicting, as he suggests, the masking of these events in their representation. National stereotypes are deployed and cultural norms intentionally subverted in the multiple narratives and other textual portrayals of the protagonists as cats (Nazis), pigs (Poles), mice (Jews); such intentional condensation serves to illuminate the dynamics of devaluation and reduction typical not only of Nazi practices but also arguably of certain oversimplifications of the Holocaust by Hollywood cinema and other literary representations (on this, see *Imaginary Witness;* Leventhal). As Saul Friedländer comments with regard to *Maus:* "Whether commentary . . . is built into a structure of a history or developed as a separate, superimposed text is a matter of choice, but the voice of the commentator must be clearly heard. The commentary should disrupt the facile linear progression of the narration, introduce alternative interpretations, question any partial conclusion, withstand the need for closure. . . . Such commentary may introduce splintered or constantly recurring refractions of a traumatic past by using any number of different vantage points" (42). These concerns might well address the responsibilities of present and succeeding generations through their exhortation to measure up to the psychological and historical challenge posed by those who survived and subsequently sought, often at great personal cost, as in the case of Kertész, representational strategies that would somehow prove commensurate to a seemingly impossible project.

The film *Sorstalanság* is to be produced by the Budapest-based production company, MagicMedia and the producer, Péter Barbalics, who have held the rights to Kertész's screenplay adaptation of his novel for a number of years. Earlier plans to shoot it in English were abandoned, according to the director, after he realized that a central element of the narrative lies in the linguistic confusion and isolation of the Hungarian Jews upon their arrival in camps that were largely populated by Polish inmates. Reference to Wanda Jakubowska's *The Last Stage* is useful in resolving such linguistic concerns: for the main protagonist in the Auschwitz Jakubowska foregrounds is a translator who serves as a cornerstone for the multilingual inmates whose native languages, as indicated in the film, include Polish, Greek, Hungarian, French, Portuguese, and many others (see Löewy). Koltai gives the impression of having a passionately committed—if not yet completely articulated—vision of the project. With a score by the award-winning Italian movie composer Ennio Morricone and a shooting schedule of seventy days, the film was scheduled to complete production by the end of March 2004 and meant to premiere in conjunction with Hungary's accession to the European community this year, thereby marking the Hungarian film industry's début as a European entity. However, production delays have resulted in postponement of the film's release.

By linking Koltai's contemporary project with earlier films, I hope to suggest that cinematic representations of the Shoah are in some sense always already readable in light of earlier endeavors. This speculative mode of analysis invites us as potential spectators and engaged witnesses to participate in a kind of interactive, imaginative exercise with the work in progress, an inter-textual dialogue with the multiple discourses of individual and collective memory. My wish is at once to honor and, in some sense, facilitate Koltai's and Kertész's interest, and that of the production, in communicating with survivors and others who may have experiences, ideas or materials to contribute to their project. Post-Nobel interest in Kertész is enhanced undoubtedly by a number of factors, not least of which is the desire to bring to light a great national literature that has suffered from a perception of linguistic isolation that too often has relegated it to minor or marginalized status. The Nobel Laureate's current novel, *Felszámolás* (*Liquidation*), is the story of a literary editor's struggle to survive after the collapse of communism and the suicide of his close friend soon afterward, set in Budapest in the aftermath of the fall of the Iron Curtain, about which he has remarked, "This book will be the last glance I will personally cast on the Holocaust" ("Hungary's Kertesz" <http://www.eubusiness.com/afp/040420021357.cv0awuut>). Such a statement, while understandable in terms of the vast literature of the Shoah, nonetheless gestures toward the layered process of remembrance characteristic of those who have made writing—and film-making—their duty in order to bear witness and memorialize. One can hope that the retrospective glance cast by the film version of *Fatelessness* will be mapped onto the topography of cinematic representations that sustain the intergenerational work of memory transmission at a time when the desire to forget—the very gesture *Fatelessness* rejects so persuasively—is too often the order of the day.

Works Cited

Apa (Father). Dir. István Szabó. Budapest: Filmstudió, 1966.

Bánk Bán. Dir. Csaba Káel. Budapest: András Werner Productions, 2002.

Braham, Randolph. *The Politics of Genocide: The Holocaust in Hungary*. New York: Columbia UP, 1981.

Colombat, André Pierre. *The Holocaust in French Film*. London: Scarecrow P, 1993.

Dénes, Maga. *Castles Burning: A Child's Life in War*. New York: Touchstone, 1997.

Delbo, Charlotte. *Auschwitz and After*. New Haven: Yale UP, 1995.

Friedländer, Saul. "Trauma, Transference, and Working-Through." *History and Memory* 4 (1992): 39–55.

Handler, Andrew, and Susan V. Meschel, eds. *Young People Speak: Surviving the Holocaust in Hungary*. New York: Franklin Watts, 1993.

Hirsch, Joshua. *Afterimage: Film, Trauma and the Holocaust*. Philadelphia: Temple UP, 2004.

"Hungary's Kertesz Writes about Survival under Communism." *EUbusiness.com* (20 April 2004): <http://www.eubusiness.com/afp/040420021357.cv0awuut>.

Imaginary Witness: Hollywood and the Holocaust. Dir. Daniel Anker. New York: Anker Productions/Films Transit/AMC, 2004.

Kende, Péter. *Le Défi hongrois. De Trianon à Bruxelles*. Paris: Buchet Chastel, 2004.

Kertész, Imre. *Fateless*. Trans. Christopher C. Wilson and Katharina M. Wilson. Evanston: Northwestern UP, 1996.

Kertész, Imre. *Kaddish for a Child Not Born*. Trans. Christopher C. Wilson and Katharina M. Wilson. Evanston: Hydra Books, 1999.

Kertész, Imre. *Sorstalanság. Filmforgatókönyv* (Fatelessness: Film Script). Budapest: Magvető, 2001.

Kertész, Imre. "Long Dark Shadow." Trans. Imre Goldstein. *Contemporary Jewish Writing in Hungary: An Anthology*. Ed. Susan Rubin Suleiman and Éva Forgács. Lincoln: U of Nebraska P, 2003. 171–77.

Kertész, Imre. "A Nobel-díjat zavaró repülésnek éreztem" ("I Felt the Nobel Prize to Be a Distracting Flight"). *Heti Világ* (6 September 2003): 47–48.

Kertész, Imre. *Fatelessness*. Trans. Tim Wilkinson. New York: Vintage, 2004.

Kertész, Imre. *Kaddish for an Unborn Child*. Trans. Tim Wilkinson. New York: Vintage, 2004.

Koltai napló 2001–2003. Dir. András Muhi and Klára Muhi. Budapest: Muhi Productions, 2004.

Kovács, András. "The World According to Béla Tarr." MOMA retrospective of Béla Tarr. Catalogue Essay. New York: Museum of Modern Art, 2000. n.p.

Lanzmann, Claude. *Shoah: An Oral History of the Holocaust. The Complete Text of the Film*. New York: Pantheon Books, 1985.

Last Days, The. Dir. James Mol. Los Angeles: Survivors of the Shoah Foundation, 1998.

Last Stage, The (Otatni etap). Dir. Wanda Jakubowska. Warsaw: Polart Films, 1948.

Lendvai, Paul. *Anti-Semitism without the Jews: Communist Eastern Europe*. New York: Doubleday, 2002.

Leventhal, Robert. *Art Spiegelman's MAUS: Working-Through the Trauma of the Holocaust* (1995): <http://www.iath.virginia.edu/holocaust/spiegelman.html>.

Lévi, Primo. *Survival in Auschwitz: The Nazi Assault on Humanity*. New York: Collier, 1978.

Long Way Home, The. Dir. Mark Jonathan Harris. Los Angeles: Warner Bros., 1997.

Löewy, Hanno. "The Mother of All Holocaust Films? Wanda Jakubowska's Auschwitz Trilogy." DEFA Film Library Lecture. Amherst: U of Massachusetts Amherst, September 2003.

Márai, Sándor. *Memoir of Hungary, 1944–1948*. Trans. Albert Tezla. Budapest: Corvina / Central European UP, 1996.

Nádas, Péter. "Imre Kertész's Work and His Subject." *The Hungarian Quarterly* 168 (2002): 38–41.

Nobel Prize in Literature, The. Laureates (2002): <http://www.nobel.se/literature/laureates/index.html>.

Petrie, Graham. *History Must Answer to Man*. Budapest: Corvina, 1978.

Pianist, The. Dir. Roman Polanski. Warsaw/Paris: Canal Plus/Studio Canal, 2002.

Portuges, Catherine. "Jewish Identity in Post-Communist Hungarian Cinema." *Assaph-Kolnoa Studies in the Cinema and Visual Arts* 1.1 (1998): 83–101.

Portuges, Catherine. "Home Movies, Found Images, and Amateur Film as a Witness to History: Péter Forgács' *Private Hungary*." *The Moving Image: Journal of the Association of Moving Image Archivists* 1.2 (2001): 107–24.

Portuges, Catherine. Review of *The Pianist*. *American Historical Review* 108 (2003): 2.

Portuges, Catherine. "Intergenerational Memory: Transforming the Past in Post-communist Central European Cinema." *Quo vadis, European Cinema?* Ed. Luisa Rivi. Special Issue of *Spectator* 23.2 (2003): 44–52.

Portuges, Catherine. Personal Interviews with Lajos Koltai, Budapest, 8 February 2003 and 10 February 2004. Budapest: Magyar Filmszemle/Hungarian Film Week.

Private Hungary/Privát Magyarország. Dir. Péter Forgács. Budapest/Amsterdam: Lumen Films, 1990–2004.

Riding, Alan. "Nobel for Hungarian Writer Who Survived the Death Camps," *New York Times* (11 October 2002): A7-A8.

Schindler's List. Dir. Steven Spielberg. Los Angeles: Amblin Entertainment/Universal Pictures, 1993.

Shoah. Dir. Claude Lanzmann. Paris: Les Films Aleph, 1985.

Sorstalanság. Dir. Lajos Koltai. Budapest: MagicMedia, 2004. In production.

"*Sorstalanság*: viszály a díszlet miatt" ("Fatelessness: Conflict over the Set Décor"). *Népszabadság* (3 August 2003): 11–12.

Spiegelman, Art. *Maus: A Survivor's Tale.* New York: Pantheon, 1985.

Sunshine / A napfény íze. Dir. István Szabó. Budapest: Lantos/Hamori Productions, 2000.

Szép, Ernö. *The Smell of Humans: A Memoir of the Holocaust in Hungary.* Trans. John Bátki. Budapest: Corvina / Central European UP, 1994.

Tötösy de Zepetnek, Steven. "Comparative Cultural Studies and the Study of Central European Culture." *Comparative Central European Culture.* Ed. Steven Tötösy de Zepetnek. West Lafayette: Purdue UP, 2002. 1–32.

Wiesel, Elie. *Night.* New York: Avon, 1960.

Danilo Kiš, Imre Kertész, and the
Myth of the Holocaust

Rosana Ratkovčić

Translated from the Croatian by Irina Krlić

In this paper, I present an analysis of how two Central European authors, Imre Kertész and Danilo Kiš, relate to the Holocaust myth, what their reconsiderations about the myth are, and how they, with their work, become involved in the myth and inscribe themselves in it. I investigate what the points of reference in their different experiences and different literary interpretations of the Holocaust are. There is a need to express and present the inexpressibility and incomprehensibility of the deliberate and systematic persecution and destruction of European Jewry, as well as of other groups, who did not fit the a Nazi ideal of a "pure" Aryan race with its notions of ethnic, racial, or religious affiliation, physical or mental abilities, or sexual orientation. I propose that one way in which this expression can be achieved is the construction of an alternative myth. Of course, I do not use the term "myth" in a revisionist sense of negation or denial of the Holocaust. However, I should like to point out that the use of the notion of "myth" in the context of the Holocaust does not relate well to Roland Barthes's definition, namely that modern myths are a powerful means of ideological modifications of daily signs via which we erase their historical conditioning. By using the notion of the "myth of the Holocaust" I emphasize, rather, that the Holocaust became an untouchable topos in the imaginary of European culture and civilization. Instead, I employ the notion in the context of the work of C.S. Liebman and E. Don-Yehiya, who use the term "the Holocaust myth" in their study of Israeli civil religion, by stressing that "by labeling a story a myth we do not mean it is false," but that "a myth is a story that evokes strong sentiments and transmits and reinforces basic societal values" (Liebman and Don-Yehiya 7).

In his book *Selling the Holocaust*, Tim Cole points out that "the term myth of the 'Holocaust'—for all its problematic connotations—is useful for distinguishing between the historical event—the Holocaust—and the representation of that event—the myth of the 'Holocaust'" (4). Cole draws our attention to this distinction, as noted by Lawrence Langer, who points out that "the two planes on which the event we call the Holocaust takes place in human memory are the historical and the rhetorical, the way it was and its verbal reformation, or deformation, by later commentators" (33). Furthermore, Cole quotes P. Lopate, who writes that "in my own mind I continue to distinguish, ever so slightly, between the disaster visited on the Jews and the 'Holocaust'" (Lopate qtd. in Cole 56). Cole stresses that "the myth of the 'Holocaust' may have drawn on the historical Holocaust, but it now exists apart from that historical event" (Cole 4). The inability to distinguish strictly between mythical and non-mythical discourses about the Holocaust is conditioned by the complex nature of passing on of what was experienced to the verbal medium, of the inter-relationship of immediate and mediated historical experience, of individual and collective history, and of historical and cultural memory. Simultaneously, the creation and acceptance of a myth includes the immediate danger of losing interest in it. The danger that a myth in its givens and invariability loses a connection with events that are its starting point and, thus, the meaning of the Jewish and other's tragedy, people who Nazi ideology established as unacceptable for life in a "pure" state that they aspired to. Therefore, the survival of the Holocaust myth demands its constant reassessment, and at the same time, every attempt of reassessing it becomes a part of it, enriching it with new content and insight, owing to the universality of its acceptance.

The works of Imre Kertész and Danilo Kiš I am dealing with here were first published in the 1970s. Kertész's novel *Sorstalanság* (*Fatelessness*) was published for the first time in 1975, whereas Kiš's *Peščanik* (*Hourglass*) was published in 1972 as the last in his sequel *Obiteljski cirkus* (*Family Circus*), after the novels *Bašta, pepeo* (*Garden, Ashes*) published in 1965 and *Rani jadi* (*Early Sorrows*) published in 1969. At the time these works of Kertész and Kiš were published for the first time, there was a similarity between the Hungarian and Yugoslav socialist ideology about the Holocaust. Both states were discouraging discourse about the Holocaust because they were intent on emphasizing the quantity of their own "ethnic" losses in the war, both from the perspective of the always endangered "little nations." In addition, in both countries there existed latent and "hidden" or, at times even explicit anti-Semitism. For example, Yugoslavia did not even have diplomatic relations with the State of Israel. As David Bruce MacDonald notices in his book *Balkan Holocaust?: Serbian and Croatian Victim-Centered Propaganda and the War in Yugoslavia*, the Holocaust as the universal metaphor of genocidal suffering became apparent in Yugoslavia only as late as the 1980s due to the nationalistically competitive "victim-centered" propaganda via which both Croatia and Serbia wanted to demonstrate the weight and proportions of their own historical suffering. The strength of Kertész's intervention within the myth of the Holocaust was recognized by the Swedish Academy which rewarded him with the Nobel Prize in Literature for the year 2002, confirms the integration of Kertész's questioning of the myth into an already existing myth. On the one hand, the extreme strength of Kertész's intervention could have a long-term influence due to which the myth about the Holocaust may never be the same. On the other hand, it might itself slip easily into myth, as has been the case with the story of Oscar Schindler.

The most important of Kertész's works, *Fatelessness*, is a novel with autobiographical components about a youth's life in Nazi concentration camps, about his liberation from the camp, and his returning to post-war Budapest. The book is written in first person, although the names of protagonists have been changed for the purpose of detaching the narrative from personal experience and universalizing the events described. Clearly, *Fatelessness* is a way of dealing with unbearable events and experiences. That unbearable-ness is determined equally by physical and spiritual suffering during the protagonist's stay at the camp, as well as by his inability to attribute any meaning or purpose to that suffering, when viewing the whole of life and existence. At the same time, it also indicates disagreeing and rejection, a denial of fate, which is contained in the title of the book. A key moment for a re-examination of the Holocaust myth in the novel is when the protagonist meets a journalist and two of his former after his return to Budapest. By their questions and by insisting constantly on their suffering they reveal an already constructed concept of a camp, which is rejected by the main character, as he recalls moments of pleasure that shock the reader of the text, but that represent the sole condition for surviving, as well as the only possible form of resistance. The author passes on this type of experience even earlier on in the book when he states that he "was ashamed of its lack of reason but became more and more insistent: that I would like to live a bit longer at that nice concentration camp" (181). The protagonist's final form of this understanding of his life in the concentration camp is given to the thought at the end of the novel when he speaks of the happiness at the camp and how he would talk about it if he were aver to be asked.

Danilo Kiš was born in 1935 and thus his experience of the Holocaust is that of the second generation, the experience of a child faced with terrifying and incomprehensible events, combined with disappearance of his father from his life. Kiš shaped his experience and search for the lost father character in three interconnected works; *Early Sorrows*, *Garden, Ashes*, and *Hourglass*. This is how Kiš describes his trilogy: "*Early Sorrows*, *Garden, Ashes*, and *Hourglass* comprise an ensemble that you could call 'novels of apprenticeship'—literary apprenticeship. *Early Sorrows* is a collection of short stories, the world seen through a child's eyes, and the vision is deliberately naive. Then there's *Garden, Ashes* where the main character becomes the father; in *Early Sorrows* he appears only on the horizon. There's also a stylistic change in the second volume: the child's naivete is still there, but there's also the perspective of someone writing thirty years later. In the third part, *Hourglass*, the child is no longer a character, the subject becomes more intellectual. In these three volumes you can see the development of a writer. And you can see three different points of view about the same subject: the vanishing world of Hungarian Jews" (qtd. in Lemon 108). Elsewhere, Kiš gives this explanation of his trilogy: "Each book here corrects the earlier one. *Early Sorrows* is written from a child's point of view. *Garden, Ashes* unites this point of view with the commentary by the narrator, a man of about thirty, the two occasionally coexisting in the same sentence. In *Hourglass* I wanted to describe the same world from an objective, external point of view, the view of an author-God, omniscient and omnipresent—the child appears only once, briefly, in the father's letter that ends the novel. It is just as if there was fist a sketch, then a drawing, and finally a painting" (Kiš, *Gorki talog iskustva* 247; all subsequent translations from the Serbo-Croatian are mine unless noted otherwise). The title, *The Family Circus*, chosen by the author for his trilogy indicates an ironic detachment he uses as his way of relating to the myth of the Holocaust.

Kiš did not accept being labeled a Jewish author because he considered that it would be a type of reductionism that could be an obstacle for integrating personal experience into "the generality of human fate" (*Gorki talog iskustva* 183). At the same time, he claimed for himself the title of the only Yugoslav writer (*Gorki talog iskustva* 255, 260) by locating himself in the even narrower circle of complete exclusiveness. This also entails the antagonism present in his literary work, where he writes about events of universal meaning and influence from the position of his own experience as a child. Kiš's relationship with the Holocaust as a myth is reflected in his response to the question about Adorno's well-known statement about the impossibility of writing literature after Auschwitz. Kiš responded that for him it was not a question of morality but a question of style, a question of finding the right form and possibility of introducing irony as means of freeing the topic of the Holocaust from pathos and banality that are associated with it (see *Gorki talog iskustva* 235). I would compare Kiš's ironic detachment and avoidance of pathos he aims for in his *Family Circus* trilogy with Kertész's lack of acceptance of the established discourse about concentration camps at the end of his novel *Fatelessness*, when meeting former neighbors who survived. I perceive this act as a rejection of speaking about the Holocaust in clichés and the search for the expression that would properly reflect the camp experience.

Unlike Kertész, who describes his own experiences in concentration camps in the first person and without a narrator's comments, Kiš writes about the Holocaust as part of childhood memories about his father's experience using complex narrative procedures. Guido Snel understands Kiš's writing, "As readers proceed in the trilogy, they face increasingly complex narrative forms: plain fictional autobiography, narrated in the first person in *Garden, Ashes*, a mix of first and third person narration in *Early Sorrows*, a combination of fictional autobiography and fictional biography in *Hourglass*" (393) and Ivana Vuletić defines the genre of the novel *Garden, Ashes* as pseudo-autobiographical, as "an autobiographically based work that imitates the autobiography in all respects but one: its author and narrator are not the same person" (40). With these complex narrative procedures, Kiš establishes a multiple and recurrent relationship with events he participates in and that had a powerful influence on him, but that he did not or could not understand at the time of their occurrence. *Garden, Ashes* opens with Kiš's detailed description of a tray "as though offering his enormous talent on it" (Hemon <http://www.centerforbookculture.org/context/no9/hemon.html>). The narrator's mother carries the tray, with a jar of honey and a bottle of cod liver oil, along with "the amber hues of sunny days, thick concentrates full of intoxicating aromas" (8). Kiš goes beyond the content, as it were, and gives us a nearly microscopic description of the form of the tray, with "a raised rim" (7) along its edges and flaky patches of nickel that look like "tin foil pressed out under fingernails" (7). There are "tiny decorative protuberances—a whole chain of little metallic grapes" (7) on the outer edge of the rim, which can be felt "like Braille letters, under the flesh of the thumb" (7) and around those grapes "ring-like layers of grease had collected, barely visible, like shadows cast by little cupolas" (7). Discussing the vigilance of Kiš's in describing little details, Aleksandar Hemon stresses that "the patience with which Kiš goes deeper into the tray, looking for a more precise detail, betokens his conviction that the exactness of the detail, as miniscule as it may be, opens doors into whole new worlds. Choosing a unique specific detail, Kiš implies that the world and human life consist of an infinite number of details, and that the writer's job is to uncover them, to expose them to the reader's eye" (Hemon 1). The tray at the beginning of the novel *Garden, Ashes* represents a palpable world as the only thing we can comprehend in the world of amazing and incomprehensible happenings: "By insisting on the material . . . along with giving the narrative voice to the boy, Andi Sam, Kiš instantly dismisses the ambition of explaining the Holocaust—the most we can hope for is experiencing it, our experience admittedly limited to the barely visible, but all the more true because of that" (Hemon <http://www.centerforbookculture.org/context/no9/hemon.html>). Finally, Hemon stresses that "Kiš's ability to infuse detail with the material, cosmic, literary, cultural, self referential, historic, structural and philosophical, and to do it with self-effacing ease, makes him one of the greatest twentieth-century writers. This is a sign of poetry at its purest—the ability to condense the world and concentrate experience, whereby the language is not a mirror, but a magnifying glass, or indeed a prism. No wonder that Joseph Brodsky considered *Garden, Ashes* 'the best book produced on the Continent in the post-war period'" (Hemon <http://www.centerforbookculture.org/context/no9/hemon.html>). After a narrative of complex personal and family histories, the novel finishes at dusk of another day when the impoverished family is collecting cones in the forest for making a fire, with the mother's telling words, "Lord, how quickly it gets dark here" (*Bašta, pepeo* 228). After dusk, when *Garden, Ashes* concludes, night falls when *Hourglass* begins. This night represents the dark age of the Holocaust as well as the darkness of ignorance about the father's mysterious character that Kiš is trying to embrace in this novel. After the tangible reality of the tray with which *Garden, Ashes* commences, this darkness represents the spiritual state of intangible reality. Through the darkness at the beginning of *Hourglass*, there are weak rays of light coming from an oil lamp. They are like guidelines in the darkness indicating the end of a novel that takes place in the course of one night and finishes in the morning, at daylight. At that same time the letter is finished; the very same letter that brought us the insights that shed light on the darkness.

A connection is established by introducing the oil lamp that belongs to the world of objects at the beginning of *Hourglass* with the tray from the beginning of *Garden, Ashes*. When Kiš describes the oil lamp, he does not give its physical, tangible characteristics, unlike with the description of the tray, but its characteristic of creating and giving light. The description of the light's reflection in the mirror introduces the hourglass which provides the title of the novel. The hourglass is a measure of time, a place where time reflects in itself, and here lies its connection with the mirror. In *Hourglass*, Kiš uses the father's only saved letter in order to reconstruct a night in his life and to explain to himself the father's mysterious character. This letter appears at the end of the novel about the traces its readers followed when reading the novel. When asked why he introduced father's letter at the very end of the novel, Kiš explained that "I reversed the normal order because I wanted to unveil the subject very slowly throughout the novel. I saw the relationship between the novel and the letter in the following manner: as the story opens, a man enters a small, badly-lit room late at night and begins to write a letter. I wanted the reader to travel bit by bit from that darkened room towards a final 'illumination'; the novel would be a mosaic of images that finally became clear for those with a little patience. The following morning the father would have gained his letter, the writer his novel, and the reader his revelation" (qtd. in Lemon 109). This transition of reality and literature is a transition of time and sand when turning the hourglass; the relation between a face and its reflection in the mirror.

The motive of a mirror is frequent in art as a symbol of soul-searching. It is also present in various interpretations of the Holocaust. A photograph that is at the entrance to the permanent exhibition of the United States Holocaust Memorial Museum in Washington, D.C. portrays American soldiers after the liberation of Ohrdruf—a sub-camp of the Buchenwald concentration camp—shocked at the horrors they encountered. The soldiers are standing at the spot where there are charred corpses of detainees. Their faces are turned towards the camera that caught the expression of disbelief and horror. Facing the camera, they are facing the observer, the exhibition's visitor. The idea behind this is that, after seeing the exhibition and becoming acquainted with Nazi crimes, the observer should recognize his/her horror as a mirror reflection on the faces of photographed, American soldiers. Another example of the motif of the mirror in the context of the Holocaust is in the stage design of a drama, *The Fifth Gospel*, by Slobodan Šnajder and directed by Branko Brezovac. The play was staged in 2004 by the Zagreb Youth Theatre as a joint project with Kampnagel Theaterfabrik Hamburg. It is based on the motives of a novel *Konclogor na Savi (Concentration Camp on the River Sava)* which is a collection of autobiographical notes of a Croatian writer, Ilija Jakovljević, who was interned at the Stara Gradiska concentration camp (Stara Gradiska was a part of a system of camps, its center being at Jasenovac, the largest concentration camp in the "Independent State of Croatia," founded in 1941 under the auspices of Nazi Germany). In the stage design of the play the motive of a mirror represents an invitation to the viewers to soul-search their role, to investigate their own feelings of guilt and innocence, to determine which side they belongs to, to that of the victims' or executioners', persecutors' or the side of the persecuted.

By establishing multiple relations between reality and its mirror reflections, in *Hourglass* Kiš pulls the reader into his world, created on the verge of reality and literature. A part of this narrative strategy is also the motif when the father, at the beginning of his letter, speaks of writing a novel and mentions *Hourglass* as one of potential titles: "Dear Olga! I am answering the short letter you sent me through Babika at some length, because—the Lord be thanked—you have given me something to write about: my dear relations are providing me with ample material for a horror novel of the bourgeois life, which I might entitle *Parade in the Harem* or *Easter Celebrations in a Jewish Castle* or *Hourglass* (everything crumbles, sister mine)" (*Hourglass* 265). A comparison with the published facsimile of the letter reveals a major departure from the original: the third suggested title, *Hourglass*, and the words in parentheses (everything crumbles, sister mine) that follow it have been added by Kiš (on this, see Vuletić 23). Adding the title of the novel that Kiš is writing and that readers are reading at that moment is a way of indicating the narrator's reflection of this novel in the letter and vice versa. The original letter was written in Hungarian (Kiš's father was Jewish Hungarian). Since in the novel Kiš translates it into Serbo-Croatian (the official language of the former Yugoslavia), we can also justify this addition as an intervention on behalf of the translator. Ivana Vuletić points to the difference that exists between father's letter that Kiš publishes in its entirety at the end of *Hourglass* and the detail of the same letter that is listed in the novel *Early Sorrows*, explaining that with the need of the author to take a distance from the strictly factual, as "an attempt to substitute seeing for recognition, to force us to see E.S. or Eduard Kiš as something more than a mere Jewish statistic, to acknowledge him imaginatively as a unique individual rather than classify him routinely as one of the countless victims of the Holocaust" (Vuletić 24). On the other hand, during a conversation with Brendan Lemon, Kiš states that he lost his father's letter during his studies and that when he was writing *Garden, Ashes* he did not have it (see Lemon 109). This might, then, mean that he also did not have it when he was writing *Early Sorrows*. Therefore, the difference between the letter published in *Hourglass* and the detail published in *Early Sorrows* might originate from the fact that in *Early Sorrows* Kiš quotes the letter from memory. Kiš deepens his game of mirror relations between reality and literature also by describing, in a different part of *Hourglass*, what a father's novel might look like:

> *Parade in the Harem*, which comes to us in the excellent low-priced Tábor edition, is Mr. E.S.'s first novel. . . . Behind the deliberate sensationalism of

the title . . . the reader discovers with satisfaction a sensitive, talented writer and an interesting social and psychological theme. Not wishing to reveal the entire contents of the novel to the reader, as certain bugling spoilsports do, we shall only say that the plot does not, as the title might lead one to suppose, unfold in the exotic atmosphere of Oriental courts but in a remote Pannonian small town in our own day. The hero of the novel, a certain E.S., an extremely sensitive and, one might say, unbalanced individual, after having suffered a shattering experience (the Novi Sad raid), is unable to cope with the commonplace, quite bourgeois situations of everyday life. The action of the novel takes place in a single night, from late evening to dawn. During this brief period the hero relives some of his most important experiences, both recent and remote, and settles his account with life. His conflict with the world is in fact a conflict with death, a contest with death, whose approach he senses. We warmly recommend this novel to our subscribers and new readers, to all those who are not after cheap adventure stories and who are convinced, as we ourselves are, that the so-called plot is far from providing the main appeal and the main value of literary work. (*Hourglass* 208-09)

Besides mirror relations of reality and literature that multiply in *Hourglass*—e.g., by mentioning this title in the father's letter as one of possible titles of the novel that the father should write—the title *Hourglass* establishes a relation with a work by Bruno Schulz, *Sanatorium under the Sign of the Hourglass*. Hemon believes that the detailed description of the tray at the beginning of novel *Garden, Ashes* also represents homage to Bruno Schulz: "It is clear that Kiš studied Schulz describing the minutiae of his provincial hometown and family, including everything from neglected back lots to messy morning beds; from the precise hues of sunlight in August to a stamp collection exhilarating a boy. It is in Schulz's work that Kiš saw it was possible to spin a cosmos out of the microscopic. 'Bruno Schulz is my God!' Kiš is known to have said, and that should be understood not as blurry-eyed worshipping, but a statement of awareness of whom he inherited a universe from, who bequeathed him the world simultaneously horrible and beautiful" (Hemon <http://www.centerforbookculture.org/context/no9/hemon.html>).

Even before the *Hourglass* was published, Kiš said in an interview that he was engaged in writing an "anthropological novel," in which on the basis of a "single human bone" he was trying to "reconstruct the entire animal, to put the each bone in its proper place, to clothe those bones with flesh, to make blood circulate through the flesh, to recall the voice of that animal, its cry, to explore the landscape through which that animal moved, what it ate, drank, whom it met, what it said, where and with whom it slept, what it dreamed, what the climate was like in the time of its existence" (*Po-etkika, knjiga druga* 36). The need to reconstruct a chain of details from the father's life and based on the only preserved letter by him is the need of the author to try to bring closer and clarify the father's unknown and mysterious character. Kiš's own father, Eduard Kiš, was murdered in Auschwitz and thus the story about the father's life prior to his disappearance in the concentration camp is simultaneously a story about the Holocaust. It is narrated in such a way that via understanding the tragedy of one victim with all of his human weaknesses, passions, and obsessions we comprehend the tragedy of the whole of the Jewish people. As Kiš himself stated in an interview about the relationship of literature and history: "I think that literature should correct History because History is general, and literature concrete. History is manifold, literature individual. History is devoid of passion, devoid of crime, regardless of numbers: What is the meaning of six million dead if we don't *see* a single individual and his face, his body, his age, and his individual story. Instead of History's lack of specificity we have a specific individual, and the indifference of historical facts is corrected by literature" (*Gorki talog iskustva* 145).

When answering the question about distinguishing between reality and fiction in his books that belong to *Family Circus* cycle, Kiš warns that life cannot be reduced to books, but that neither can books be reduced to life, and explains that as he presented his childhood in a lyrical, unique, and final form, this form became an integral part of his childhood, his only childhood (*Gorki talog iskustva* 181). The sentence with which *Hourglass* ends is also the last sentence of the father's letter and a quote from Talmud; "It is better to be among the persecuted than among the persecutors" (*Peščanik 293*). I refrain from analyzing this narrative characteristic in the present context because it would cast a shadow over its beauty and depth. However, it is advantageous to compare it to the position Kertész chose for himself at the end of his novel *Fatelessess* when, by guarding his own truth, he denies the possibility of attaining reputation and safe material existence that could be made possible by accepting the given and requested discourse about concentration camps.

Works Cited

Barthes, Roland, *Mythologies*. Trans. Annette Lavers. New York: Hill and Wang, 1972.

Cole, Tim. *Selling the Holocaust*. New York: Routledge, 2000.

Hemon, Aleksandar. "Reading Danilo Kis." *Context: A Forum for Literary Arts and Culture* 9 (2001): <http://www.centerforbookculture.org/context/no9/hemon.html>.

Kertész, Imre. *Fateless*. Trans. Christopher C. Wilson and Katharina M. Wilson. Evanston: Northwestern UP, 1992.

Kertész, Imre. *Fatelessness*. Trans. Tim Wilkinson. New York: Vintage, 2004.

Kertész, Imre. *Besudbinstvo (Fatelessness)*. Trans. Aleksandar Tišma. Novi Sad: Stylos, 2002.

Kiš, Danilo. *Po-etika, knjiga druga* (Poetics: Book Two). Beograd: Ideje, 1974.

Kiš, Danilo, *Garden, Ashes*. Trans. William J. Hannaher. New York: Harcourt, Brace and Jovanovich, 1975.

Kiš, Danilo. *Bašta, pepeo (Garden, Ashes)*. Zagreb: Globus, 1983.

Kiš, Danilo. *Peščanik (Hourglass)*. Zagreb: Globus, 1983.

Kiš, Danilo. *Rani jadi* (Early Sorrows). Zagreb: Globus, 1983.

Kiš, Danilo. *Hourglass*. Trans. Ralph Manheim. London: Faber and Faber, 1990.

Kiš, Danilo. *Gorki talog iskustva* (Bitter-sweet Sediments of Experience). Beograd: Beogradski izdavačko-grafički zavod, 1991.

Kiš, Danilo. *Early Sorrows: For Children and Sensitive Readers*. Trans. Michael Henry Heim. New York: Directions Publishing, 1998.

Langer, Lawrence L. *Admitting the Holocaust*. Oxford: Oxford UP, 1995.

Lemon, Brendan. "A Conversation with Danilo Kiš." *The Review of Contemporary Fiction* 14.1 (1994): 107–14.

Liebman, C.S., and E. Don-Yehiya. *Civil Religion in Israel: Traditional Judaism and Political Culture in the Jewish State*. Berkeley: U of California P, 1983.

MacDonald, David Bruce. *Balkan Holokaust? Serbian and Croatian Victim-Centered Propaganda and the War in Yugoslavia*. Manchester: Manchester UP, 2003.

Snel, Guido. "Gardens of the Mind, Places for Doubt: Fictionalized Autobiography in East-Central Europe." *History of the Literary Cultures of East-Central Europe*. Ed. Marcel Cornis-Pope and John Neubauer. Amsterdam: John Benjamins, 2004. 386–400.

Vuletić, Ivana. *The Prose Fiction of Danilo Kiš, Serbian Jewish Writer*. New York: Edwin Mellen P, 2003.

Imre Kertész's *Jegyzőkönyv* (*Sworn Statement*) and the Self Deprived of Itself

Tamás Scheibner

Translated from the Hungarian by Sean Lambert

The themes upon which existing analyses of Imre Kertész's oeuvre have been built would suggest the central problem contained in the author's works to be that of the constructability of personality and attendant questions regarding the nature and existence of freedom. It would be difficult to deny that the answers contained in Kertész's work to these fundamental questions are inconsistent—sometimes even within a single work. One must also consider possible discrepancies between the author's original intentions and the "position" advanced in the finished work. Critics have pointed repeatedly to such inconsistencies in Kertész's work. For example, István Margócsy has discerned that in *Valaki más. A változás krónikája* (Someone Else: A Chronicle of the Change in Régime) although Kertész acknowledges a diminished role of the self, in his text in fact he proclaims a strong sense of individuality (Margócsy 17). The complexity of the matter is evident also in Anna Gács's paper on *Gályanapló* (Galley Boat-Log) (Gács, "Egy különös regény" 857–60) and, more recently, in István Fried's paper on the same work. In brief, one cannot expect complete consistency and an absence of internal contradiction in a book compiled from thirty years of journal entries. This is especially true in the case of an author who, according to one of the entries in his *Gályanapló*, has raised contradiction to the level of poetics: "I am a revolutionary, although I already know beforehand that the revolution has long ago failed. I am the kind of revolutionary who despises the powers in place, but doesn't do a thing to overthrow them. From an 'objective' standpoint, I like the bad, and my thought is not dialectical, but contradictory; and what's more, I find this to be moral, more precisely, my morality" ("Forradalmár vagyok, de már előre tudom, hogy a forradalom rég megbukott. Olyan forradalmár vagyok, aki gyűlöli a fennállót, s mit sem tesz a megdöntéséért. 'Objektíve' a rosszat szeretem, és gondolkodásom nem dialektikus, hanem ellentmondásos; mi több, ezt találom erkölcsösnek, pontosabban az erkölcsömnek") (155; all subsequent translations from the Hungarian are by Sean Lambert unless noted otherwise).

205

Although I have my doubts, it may be possible to detect a certain receptiveness toward the notion of the constructability of the personality in Kertész's work, a category that both includes and excludes *Gályanapló* and *Valaki más*, texts that create and document personality simultaneously. I discuss a less extensive text which, if we believe it to be "the thematical nexus of all Kertész's works . . . one that binds the pieces of his life work into a journal-like stream" (Gács, "Mit számít" 1294), might represent an interesting juncture in his scattered "internal" debate regarding the possibility of the autonomous self. Of all of his works, it is in *Jegyzőkönyv* (*Sworn Statement*) where Kertész proclaims in the most remarkable and explicit manner the duality whose axis is formed from the constructability of the individual. The few studies where an attempt has been made to analyze *Jegyzőkönyv* have all skipped nimbly over the self-interpretation to be found in the first paragraph of the text. In my view, this passage merits an a priori consideration: "The purpose of the following register is to provide a countersignature for that other, although more official, not in the least more authentic, register that has (reportedly) reported information about a certain location, on a certain day, at a certain time, but whose details we consider to be insignificant at this time" ("Az alábbi jegyzőkönyv ama másik: mindenképpen hivatalosabb, ha másfelől korántsem hitelesebb jegyzőkönyvet hivatott ellenjegyezni, amely jegyzőkönyv fel- és (nyilván) nyilvántartásba vétetett bizonyos helyen, bizonyos napon és bizonyos órában, mely részleteket azonban itt mellőzhetőnek tekintjük") (*Jegyzőkönyv* 279). Importantly, the text refers to itself as "countersignature." A countersignature denotes none other than the signing of a document that another or others have endorsed previously in an expression of an accord: a name. Given that the proper noun is conceived commonly as a designation of the self, one may conclude easily that a work that refers to itself as the pronouncement of a name, might embrace the intention of reestablishing the unity of the personality. Thus one might interpret the narrative as an invalidation—if not outright repudiation—of twentieth-century history, whose fundamental characteristic, according to Kertész, was that it "totally obliterates the individual and the personality" ("maradéktalanul elsöpri a személyt és a személyiséget") ("A boldogtalan huszadik század" 12).

Indeed, the text places great emphasis on acts of identity building. The narrative that follows the introductory text revolves around the establishment, definition, and retention of the self. The following elements almost implicitly constitute a redefined notion of the autonomous self, which has just "woken [up] from its long and deep unconsciousness" ("verődött [fel] régi és mély ájulatából") (*Jegyzőkönyv* 281): the informal manner of speech established immediately at the book's anecdotal beginning—this casual discourse is evident even after the initial confrontation with the customs officer, i.e., "What will happen to me? 'My head taken off on a public square in the name of the French people?'" ("Mi történhet velem? 'A francia nép nevében fejemet veszik egy köztéren?'") (293); the sense of arbitrariness (for example, "I could spend at least two, but at the most three days in Vienna" ("néhány, mondjuk két, de legföljebb három napot Bécsben tölthetnék") (280); the emphasis on individual perspective "at least in me" ("legalábbis bennem") (280); and the explicit claim to personal liberty.

It is striking how frequently the motif of awakening, of realization, occurs throughout the rest of the book. Not long after the aforementioned episode the narrator's wife wakes him from a feverish nightmare, then the protagonist rises at dawn on the day of his departure in order to preclude a telephone wake-up call. When he refrains from his reading of Dali's journal as his train passes by the city of Tatabánya and the customs officer announces that his passport will be seized, we read that "suddenly I came to" ("hirtelen magamhoz térek") (292). He displays a similar reaction when the customs officer summons him to get off the train: "I sat there in daze for awhile . . . then I suddenly jumped up" ("Darabig bénultan ülök a helyemen. . . . Aztán hirtelen felugrom") (295). At the border to Austria, at the Hegyeshalom customs office he is roused from his contemplation of the relationship between Dali and Nietzsche in order to look at the customs report, the reading of whose first sentence is likewise presented as an instance of awakening: "At that moment I was gripped, overwhelmed, spellbound by insight" ("E pillanatban megszáll, elönt és lenyűgöz a tisztánlátás") (300). Finally, on the return trip, the train passes back past Tatabánya: "This is the point when I collected my senses" ("Ezen a ponton feleszmélek") (308).

An instance of realization employed to represent self-discovery, under given circumstances that of self-definition *vis-á-vis* others, signifies one of the most decisive acts in the process of constructing the self. This type of contextualization of the self, which at the same time signifies a reinforcement thereof, is present unmistakably at another level as well. If we understand the self to be a system of choices, it may be interpreted as a kind of—although not necessarily literary—canon. It is such a canon that contains these self-constructing choices, which in turn refer back to the self and fortify it insofar as the self recognize itself in these choices. Thus the narrator's citation of the words of his favorite authors to express his own thoughts serves paradoxically to further fix his own self-identity—precisely the same way in which the entire system of intertextual allusion functions (here we might consider e.g., Camus, Esterházy, Thomas Mann, Orwell, and even Wagner). Reference to his earlier works—in this instance *A kudarc* (The Failure) and *Gályanapló* (Galley Boat-Log) (an entry in this is nearly identical to a paragraph in *Jegyzőkönyv*)—represents likewise "The means of self-formation of the individual, the expression of the freedom of individual 'history' writing unconstrained by determination" (Gács, "Egy különös regény" 859).

That Dali's diary emerges from time to time in this work as the object of the narrator's contemplation and nostalgia is owing not only to the fact that it is a journal, but also (and above all) to its supreme affirmation of the notion of the autonomous self, as manifested in its varied declarations of the unique status of the sovereign genius: "With the very first words one is taken down and pinned by the genius of it, a distinctive amalgam of swagger and the free rein of a child's heart" ("már az első szavaknál leteper és maga alá gyűr a zsenialitás, a gyermekszív gáttalansága és a hencegés e különös vegyüléke") (*Jegyzőkönyv* 288) recounts Kertész of his experience; and certainly an author who dares to label Nietzsche a "lightweight" cannot be lacking in self-assurance and -confidence. Nonetheless, it would be worth noting that in addition to the Hungarian (*Egy zseni naplója*), the narrator cites the self-descriptive title in English (*Diary of a Genius)*, which, of course, does not correspond to the original: this gesture may reveal a degree of diffidence corresponding to that of the self-confidence projected in the text, which in turn serves at the same time to reinforce Kertész's own identity. If one accepts the linguistic underpinning of identity construction, one might interpret this indication of the narrator's proficiency in another language to be a manifestation of the ability of the self to become another; while remaining unchanged it is capable of rendering the "foreign" identical to itself which may then quickly become a characteristic, therefore distinctive, trait. According to this logic, placement of this seemingly unwarranted (because it does not satisfy the requisite of clarification in the original language) English-language expression in the Hungarian-language text. The text's final instance of realization-awakening is concealed in the narrator's subsequently articulated conclusion that "I'm dead" ("Halott vagyok") (*Jegyzőkönyv* 308). This statement suggests an end of the self given that the final bastion of his self-identity also appears to be on the verge of ruin; namely, as Kertész writes, the single prerogative of the individual is that "if I have already become irrevocably tired of it . . . I'll put an end to it" ("ha már leküzdhetetlenül megcsömörlöttem tőle . . . véget vessek neki") (*Jegyzőkönyv* 307).

At the same time, the absurdity of the statement itself directs attention toward the problem of linguistic mediation, almost as if the very condition of its being expressed in language might cast doubt upon the story, thereby opening the way for a new meta-level of interpretation. From the perspective of language, the (pen)ultimate sentence of "I'm dead" ("Halott vagyok") (308) refers back to the particularly exciting introductory segment, which plays a key role in *Jegyzőkönyv*. This preface is exceptional in that it does not place itself "above" the body of the text in all respects: it has not established its identity after the fact. This is clearly demonstrated in two ways: first, in the usage of the present-tense of the verb *készül* (to be in the process of doing something), which in this form suggests that the text is in the process of formation; and second, that the narrator speaks of Sworn Statement in the future tense, when he could have very easily omitted the verb "to be" had this word of existence not been of vital importance. He is unsure even of the outcome of his telling of the story, binding it to the proviso of reaching the desired objective; and the outcome is not even certain if this condition is fulfilled: *"perhaps* we might even catch it" ("*tán* utól is érhetjük") (*Jegyzőkönyv* 280, my emphasis). One might say that he seems to be leaning toward the telling of it.

The allegorical quality of the narrative surrounding the customs official serves to accentuate this inclination, establishing a passage toward a genre that attempts to embody experience in the form of a single story. If we view the principle contextual differences in terms of Ágnes Proksza's criteria of the "language of judgment" and the "language of decision," "the decision is always in the present; therefore a text constructed in the language of decision presents rather than represents" and "illustrates the given situation of decision as an event in progress" (Proksza 88), whereas that in the language of judgment is retrospective, associated in all instances with the narration of a story (Proksza 80). Examined from this perspective, we can discern and understand the aforementioned differences in language usage that set the preface apart from the body of the text. This language of decision establishes a present-day condition—in Kertész's works the theme of existential struggle implicit in the metaphor of Auschwitz—and rejects any sort of narrative that would attempt to circumscribe it. Yet the story told in *Jegyzőkönyv* ends apparently in precisely this way, with redemption in the sanctuary of certainty. Numerous aspects of the text would make it difficult to accept without reservation the genre suggested in the title.

The epigraph, the jumbled chronology, the use of anecdote, the lack of objectivity, legal certification, and precise facts (such as the initial omission of the date, a purely symbolic gesture since it is later specified in reference to the "other" register) are not compatible with the conventions of a register. However, it is precisely this disregard for formal requisites of the genre that focus the reader's attention on other attributes typical of a register. The basic characteristic of a register is that it always pertains to a *fait accompli* and that it represents the act that establishes a *fait accompli*. The purpose of *Sworn Statement* is, in fact, none other than to make the relevant events accessible for the purpose of making a decision. This is the point at which the allegory and Sworn Statement converge given that the parable is not only a text that "meets the needs of the recipients of knowledge," but also one representing a sort of closure as the end of the road toward "knowledge" (Elm 82–110).

The explicit reference of the work to itself as a confession, which accentuates likewise the formation and demonstrative completion (accomplished in Catholic liturgy through the act of atonement and the priest's absolution) of a unified narrative, also comes into play here. The act of confession, in addition to bringing an end to a certain phase of life, entails the not insignificant motif of a new beginning. This explains its appeal and the fact that the voice of the preface considers it to be the final matter in which he has faith; it would, of course, be wise for the reader to bear in mind that faith cannot exist without its own prerequisites. As the narrator puts it: "*If only* . . . not in the power of confession" ("*hacsak* . . . a gyónás erejében nem") (279, my emphasis). In addition to its conditionality, there is yet another circumstance that mitigates his faith in the power of confession: the ironic overtone of the preface. That the language of the preface differs greatly from that of the narrative has already been established; however, this is by no means the only difference between them. The language used in the preface nonetheless bears greater resemblance to that of a prayer than to that of a confession. Although this affinity is not unrelated to the fact that the preface is introduced by an excerpt from the Lord's Prayer, it is owing in greater part to its usage of verbs in the third-person plural rather than the first-person singular of the narrative part of the text. This prayer-like quality imparts a distinctly ironic dimension to the preface considering that the text—aside from its professed belief confession, seen in terms of a spiritual exercise—rejects categorically the notion of faith in all forms. Neither is its definition of the "power" of confession completely devoid of derision: "it makes us brothers with our own loneliness" ("testvérévé tesz önmagunk magányának") (279), that is, the self (which, incidentally, is rendered in the plural from the beginning) finds an inseparable companion in Loneliness anthropomorphized. The reader may well take an ironic view of the episode in which the narrator turns to the customs official, not a priest, for absolution of his sins: one is not exempted from this perspective even if he or she is cognizant of the analogy to Matthew (Selyem 94). I return to this ironic dimension later; however I would first like to examine more thoroughly the conspicuous contrast between the preface and story per se.

As I indicated earlier, the narrator's final realization is that he is "dead." In *Jegyzőkönyv*, as in so many of Kertész's works, the narrator is forced to confront the continued reality of Auschwitz. One may catch a glimpse of this presence by way of its clear intertextual dimensions, since this work establishes numerous links to *Sorstalanság* (*Fatelessness*). The mere fact of the narrator's train trip would, in itself, seem to confirm the existence of this connection. The circumstances of security and comfort surrounding his railway travel provide an antithesis to those experienced during deportation. The morbid humor, that familiarity with the author's own past, imparts to the narrator's diagnosis of his *Wanderlust* as a symptom of a childhood persecution complex sharpens this contrast. The reader may find another parallel in the narrator's bargaining with the Hungarian customs official: he is reminiscent of the gendarme, who in *Fatelessness* endeavors to impose an "export duty" on Jews when they reach the Hungarian border on their way to Auschwitz. However, the most obvious similarity may be Kertész's description of the city of Tatabánya as he passes by it on the train: "The doomsday landscape, run down, torn to pieces, rising bleakly, massive concrete smokestacks, pipes, scaffolding splitting the sky crosswise like the stroke of a pen crossing out a bit of writing or a part of a life, undisguised exploitation in every direction, unrelenting expediency, rationality" ("Lepusztult, szétmarcangolt, kopáran meredő, végítéletszerű táj, masszív betonfüstölők, csövek, az eget rézsút hasító állványzat, akár egy szövegrészt vagy életdarabot kihúzó, kemény tollvonás, leplezetlen hasznosítás mindenfelé, ádáz célszerűség, racionalitás") (289). This allusion to the extermination camps would be difficult to miss, especially given that the book's previous sentence evokes the narrator's perception of a stench streaming in through the train window, which is also one of Gyuri Köves's first and most momentous sensations when he arrives to Auschwitz. Further, it is also worth noting that Köves associates the odor of the crematorium smoke with an earlier experience, namely that of the reek drifting in through the streetcar window from the Újpest leather factory (of the Balogh family, who were expropriated by the nazis).

Emerging frequently in Kertész's works is the motif of existence beyond life, which connotes the reality of existence at Auschwitz: the lives of the deportees at the camp are all about self-obliteration—as one who is condemned to death and essentially assumes the duty of the executioner. To be our own assassin: this theme surfaces several times in the course of the narrative. In one scene, for instance, the narrator finds himself on the losing end of a short argument after opening the door of the customs officials' compartment, an incident to which he appends the following commentary: "I've got the feeling that I've drained the cup this time" ("Úgy érzem, a poharat ezzel fenékig ürítettem") (297). One possible interpretation of these words would be to equate the cup with the poisoned chalice, thereby establishing a significant parallel to the death of Socrates that will be expanded upon later in the book. I should like to note that this is not the first of allusion to the death of Socrates in this text; when the mother of the narrator dies, the doctor quotes the final sentence(s) of Plato's *Apology*. The motif of suicide reemerges in more dramatic form in the final paragraph: "This time, as always, I greedily clutch the aggression to which I've been subjected—I can do nothing else—as if it were a dagger, whose blade I turn against myself" ("Az engem ért agressziót—mert nem tehetek mást—most is, mint mindig, tőrként mohón megmarkolom, és a pengét önmagam ellen fordítom") (307). The role of suicide in Kertészian self-analysis is elucidated most clearly in an entry of *Gályanapló*, written during the same period or perhaps even the same month as *Jegyzőkönyv;* that suicide continues to serve as a cornerstone in Kertész's *Weltanschauung* is demonstrated in his "A száműzött nyelv" ("The Exiled Language"), in which he quotes from this entry:

> I began to realize that what had saved me from suicide (from following in the footsteps of Borowski, Celan, Amèry, Lévi, etc.) was the very "society" which, following the experience of the concentration camps, had proven in its so-called "Stalinist" form that there could be no question of freedom, liberation, great catharsis, etc.—everything that intellectuals, thinkers, and philosophers in more fortunate parts of the world not only proclaimed, but evidently believed in as well. This situation guaranteed that my captive life would continue and precluded the possibility of harboring misconceptions of all types. It is for this reason that the rising tide of disappointment, which had begun to lap at the feet of those with a similar set of experiences living in freer societies, eventually reaching their chins in spite of their efforts to stay ahead of it, never reached me.

> Kezdem átlátni, hogy engem az öngyilkosságtól (Borowski, Celan, Amèry, Primo Lévi stb. példájától) az a "társadalom" mentett meg, amely a KZ-

élmény után az ún. "sztálinizmus" képében bebizonyította, hogy sza-
badságról, felszabadulásról, nagy katarzisról stb.: mindarról, amiről szerenc-
sésebb világtájakon értelmiségiek, gondolkodók, filozófusok nem csupán
szavaltak, de amiben nyilván hittek is, szó sem lehet; amely nekem a rabélet
folytatását garantálta, és így mindenféle tévedésnek még a lehetőségét is
kizárta. Ez az oka, hogy engem nem ért el a csalódás ama tengerárja, amely a
szabadabb társadalmakban élő, hasonló élménykörű embereknek, mintegy e
dagály elől szaladó lába körül csapdosni kezdett, majd—hiába szaporázták a
lépést—lassan a torkukig felért. (350)

Earlier, in an interview Kertész says: "I found myself living [after the war] in
a society in which my captivity continued unhindered; therefore there was no possibility of my becoming captive to illusions that I would experience catharsis or
liberation. I was still forced to face the basic question: am I going to survive or not?
This is, in fact, always the question; life is the problem of suicide" ("Egy olyan tár-
sadalomba csöppentem [a háború után], ahol a rabéletem teljes természetességgel
folytatódott; tehát nem lehettem olyan illúziók rabja, hogy katarzisban részesülök,
felszabadulásban, hanem változatlanul szembe kellett néznem az alapkérdéssel:
életben maradok-e vagy sem. Voltaképpen mindig ez a kérdés; az élet az öngy-
ilkosság számára feladott probléma") (Interview with Judit Csáki 25–26). The narrator of Jegyzőkönyv must experience death (an awareness thereof), just as the
above-mentioned mostly Western writers (among many others), precisely because
he has not shunned the "deceptive slogans of deceptive liberty" ("a megtévesztő
szabadság megtévesztő jelszavait") (Jegyzőkönyv 350) the rekindled "illusions of
liberty" ("szabadságillúziókat") (281). And in his essay "A boldogtalan huszadik
század" ("The Unhappy Twentieth Century"), Kertész writes that the "role confusion of everyday survival stems, to no small degree, from the fact that during the
given period of time the survivor had to truly comprehend that which he subsequently finds incomprehensible. This was the price of survival . . . the survivor had
to understand how to survive, therefore he had to understand that which he survived" ("[A] hétköznapi túlélés szerepzavara nem csekély mértékben abból szár-
mazik, hogy adott időszakban a túlélőnek igencsak értenie kellett mindazt, amit
utólag érthetetlennek minősít, hiszen éppen ez volt a túlélés ára . . . a túlélőnek értenie kellett a túléléshez, tehát értenie kellett, amit túlélt") (22–23).

In Jegyzőkönyv the promise of a free world enables the narrator to concentrate on endeavors other than that of mere survival, i.e., on the previous evening he
feels free to go to a concert; on the train he indulges in the diversion of reading
Dali), which he feels unworthy of his attention because "what could happen to
me?" ("Mi történhet velem?") (293). The death experience is a precondition to this
waning attention: he really never understood the world in which he lived—the declared "I don't know" ("nem tudom") of the narrator implies that he no longer recognizes totalitarianism to exist in its role as the adversary of individualism:

The great realization, more precisely, discovery: *every single person* is the creation of God—at the time of Rome's overwhelming expanse, at the time of the medieval epidemics, at the time of totalitarian states. What is power? Truly, in truth? The nothing-ness and nobody-ness of the individual. The fury of power, the passion of fury, the destructive and self-destructive, obsessive comportment of this passion vis-à-vis reason, individual nonconformity, indeed: vis-à-vis *the individual as disobedience*. This fury as a form of government, this form of government as a form of life. And under these circumstances solidarity—affection—as a subculture. And authentic solidarity, authentic affection is always really just this: subculture. Put plainly: rebellion, the only kind of rebellion that pleases God. God's rebellion against defective Creation.

A nagy felismerés, helyesebben felfedezés: *minden egyes ember* Isten teremtménye, a Római Birodalom eltipró nagysága idején. A középkori nagy járványok idején. A totalitárius államok idején. Mi a hatalom? Valójában, valóságosan? Az ember semmisége és senkisége. A hatalom dühe, a düh szenvedélye, e szenvedély pusztító és önpusztító, rögeszmés viselkedése a rációval, az individuális nonkonformmal, egyáltalán: *az individuálissal mint engedetlenséggel* szemben. Ez a düh mint államforma, ez az államforma mint létforma. És ilyen körülmények közt a szolidaritás—a szeretet—mint szubkultúra. És igazából az autentikus szolidaritás, az autentikus szeretet mindig is ez: szubkultúra. Magyarán: lázadás, a lázadás egyetlen Istennek tetsző módja. Isten lázadása a balul sikerült Teremtés ellen. (*Gályanapló* 304)

But this is not the only thing that the narrator forgets: totalitarianism has another trait closely related to the aforementioned. The following will shed light on this: "The essence of our lives, the mere fact of our struggle to sustain them, serve to perpetuate totalitarianism . . . this is a virtually organic, one might say primitive, artifice of human organization" ("Életünk lényegével, már annak puszta fenntartásával is a totalitarizmus fenntartásához járulunk hozzá . . . ez csupán a szervezés úgyszólván önmagától adódó, mondhatni primitív furfangja") (*Kaddis* 112). Here survival becomes perceptible as an *act*, an act that contributes to the maintenance of the very totalitarian order that destroys the individual; thus the act of survival promotes the demise of the actor, and this represents the fundamental experience portrayed in *Sorstalanság*, as expressed in the "everybody continued ahead as long as they could" formula. The continued presence and operative quality of totalitarianism becomes palpable through the concrete act contained in the account of the custom's official. The narrator perpetrates three transgressions in quick succession: he breaks the law, then gets entangled in a lie, and, finally, commits slander. At the same time it is difficult not to notice that Kertész performs these deeds with a complete lack of consciousness: the legal infraction was not a willful act, but the result of his own ignorance; the lie (which proves undoubtedly to be the most serious transgression) leaves his mouth with a spontaneity incomprehensible even to himself; and the ominous slander was a manifestation of a sudden emotional outburst, of a loss of self-control. The language in which the individual presumes to express himself is not his own, it is not part of the terrain of self-identification, but is a totalitarian language that, as Kertész put it in "A száműzött nyelv" ("The Exiled Language"): "with the help of a well-measured dynamic of violence and fear penetrates the consciousness of every person and slowly expels him from it" ("az erőszak és a rettegés jól adagolt dinamikájának segítségével behatol az egyes ember tudatába, és őt magát lassacskán kirekeszti onnan") (279). The sudden "consciousness of death" does not coincide with a "reclamation" of language: in part because it is extremely doubtful that the individual has ever been in possession of language, thus making it impossible to "re"-claim it, but above all because this very realization entails the act of accepting the role that the totalitarian order has thrust upon him. Total acceptance of this role, whose arbitrariness and incompatibility with the narrator's character the text establishes beyond doubt: "I am playing the wrong role this time" ("ezúttal rossz szerepben lépek fel") (*Jegyzőkönyv* 296]), represents the individual's only chance for survival, although—according to "A száműzött nyelv"—"this is the method of total destruction of the personality as well" ("ez a módja a személyisége totális megsemmisítésének is") (280).

This reasoning is based on a deepening and unfolding contradiction: the motif of dual consciousness one encounters so often in the works of Kertész becomes clearly discernable in *Jegyzőkönyv*, the "schizophrenia" that can be described in terms of an oscillation between the autonomous personality and a kind of internalized external determination, or automatism. This rift is best depicted in a sentence of the book in which the narrator analyzes one of his dreams: "The only thing that could have been determined was already obvious: beyond a gesture that would indicate pain at the *root* of a tooth, my deeply-*rooted* bad relations with myself" ("Csak az derülhetett ki, ami nyilvánvaló: túl a *foggyökérben* fészkelő fájdalomra utaló mozdulaton, az önmagammal való *gyökeresen* rossz viszonyom") (283, my emphasis). The appearance of the word "root" twice in one sentence establishes a metaphor that confronts the reader with a self whose physical pain furnishes him with a supreme awareness of his own existence. Here it would be worthwhile to recall the remark Kertész makes upon reading Friedrich Hebbel's (1813–63) journal: "It is really exciting: 'Die Freude verallgemeinert, der Schmerz individualisiert den Menschen—joy renders the individual commonplace, pain individualizes him'" ("Nagyon izgalmas: 'Die Freude verallgemeinert, der Schmerz individualisiert den Menschen—Az öröm az általánosba emeli, a fájdalom individualizálja az embert'") (*Gályanapló* 313). Although it is precisely this pain that prevents him from accepting himself as himself. The un-governability of physiological processes symbolizes this schism in such a way as to transform the previously described automatism into the "physical" component—at once subordinate and dominant—

of the personality, thereby making possible the continued cessation of sacrificial discourse.

It is precisely from this perspective, in terms of the duality of the personality, that the analogy to Socrates gains significance. For Hegel, whom Kertész rejects generally despite exhibiting traces of his influence, the Greek philosopher is an emblematic figure signifying an important evolution in thought. Charles Taylor, in his Hegel monograph, characterizes this transformation as follows: "With Sokrates arises the challenge of a man who cannot agree to base his life on the parochial, on the merely given, but requires a foundation in universal reason" (Taylor 385). This transformation indicates the onset of the process of alienation, which "arises when the goals, norms or ends which define the common practices or institutions begin to seem irrelevant or even monstrous" (Taylor 384). The narrator's attitude toward the law is an extreme example of this process: "I fall asleep immediately if I see legal clauses and paragraphs: I fall asleep especially because in the country in which I happen to live, these legal clauses and paragraphs have been conceived *against me*—often *against my very physical existence*—from my very beginning. Even those which have served nominally to protect me also always turned out to be of potential use *against me*" ("[Ha] paragrafusokat és törvénycikkelyeket látok, tüstént elalszom; elalszom, annál is inkább, mivel az országban, amelyben élnem adatik, e törvénycikkelyek és paragrafusok már kezdetemtől fogva *mindig ellenem*—gyakorta a puszta *fizikai létezésem ellen*—fogantattak, azok pedig, amelyek értelemszerűen netalán a védelmemre szolgálnának, gyakorlatilag úgyszintén *mindig ellenem* fordíthatóknak bizonyultak") (*Jegyzőkönyv* 285–86, my emphases).

Parallel to this increasing alienation, the individual begins to insist with increasing vigor upon defining himself as an individual: "When this [alienation] happens men have to turn elswhere to define what is centrally important to them. . . . Sometimes . . . they strike out on their own and define their identity as individuals. Individualism comes, as Hegel puts it in the *VG* [*Die Vernunft der Geschichte*], when men cease to identify with the community's life, when they 'reflect,' that is, turn back on themselves, and see themselves most importantly as individuals with individual goals" (Taylor 384). In addition to the previously described acts of identity building, Kertész's rejection of society is very characteristic of this condition. In the narration, the "community," that is, other people are portrayed as adversaries from the outset:

> Gangrenous-legged beggars, junk dealers, sly-eyed alcoholics. I scurry forward among them, my hand squeezing the bag hanging from my shoulder, I don't dare to stop, I don't give anything to anybody, I don't take anything from anybody, *I am wary*, there is no affection in me. There is no affection in me. There is a train for me, a railway car with a number, even a seat with a number, right next to the window. *I am secure* for the most part. There is heat. The door closes automatically. The seat next to me is empty: I'm happy because there is nobody sitting next to me, there is no affection in me.

Üszkös lábú koldusok, üvöltő zsibárusok, alattomosan fürkész pillantású
alkoholisták. Iszkolok köztük előre, kezemmel is óvom, szorítom a vállamon
lógó válltáskát, nem merek megállni, nem adok senkinek semmit, nem
veszek senkitől semmit, *bizalmatlan vagyok,* nincs bennem szeretet. Nincs
bennem szeretet. A vonatom megvan, számozott vasúti kocsim megvan,
megvan számozott ülőhelyem is, az ablak mellett. Nagyjából *biztonságban
vagyok.* Fűtenek. Az ajtó automatikusan záródik. A mellettem lévő hely üres:
örülök, hogy nem ül mellettem senki, nincs bennem szeretet. (*Jegyzőkönyv*
287–88, my emphases).

However, the source of the narrator's generalized feeling of dread is not necessarily
to be found in his immediate environment. In a feverish dream the narrator makes
this interesting comment when a blond, unshaven figure rings his doorbell: "he's
probably just putting me to the test and will gauge his behavior to mine"
("valószínűleg csak próbára tesz, és viselkedésemhez méri majd a magáét") (*Jegyzőkönyv* 282). Kertész's presumption proves correct: the customary and logical order of events becomes inverted and he quickly determines that "since . . . I didn't
let him in my door, I began to see him as my murderer" ("miután . . . nem enged-
tem be ajtómon, most már a gyilkosomat láttam benne") (*Jegyzőkönyv* 283). Thus
it is the narrator, himself, who is the source of the hostility of another. Although
one could argue that this logical structure is a distinctive feature in the formation of
dreams, it would nevertheless be worth noting, on the one hand, the degree to
which the text obscures the distinction between dream and reality: "my wife shook
me awake, although I really don't know whether it was out of me sleep or out of
my life since the difference between the two is so delicate" ("a feleségem felrázott,
de valójában nem tudom, hogy az álmomból-e vagy az életemből, hisz oly
törékeny a különbség") (*Jegyzőkönyv* 283) and, on the other, that the narrator interprets his dream to be an *omen.* Viewed from a Hegelian philosophical perspective,
Socrates represents a dichotomy, simultaneously espousing *Sittlichkeit*—the principle of compliance with the law—and encouraging skepticism toward the law.
Naturally, the circumstances of the narrator in the *Jegyzőkönyv* differ radically
from those of Socrates—the very notion of *Sittlichkeit* is completely foreign to
Kertész; nonetheless, in addition to the historical rationale that can be traced to
Hegel, it is this duality in Socrates's thought, in which the laws of society constitute both the contrasting "exterior" and part of the integral interior of the constructed individual, that would justify drawing this analogy.

The narrator's declaration, "I'm dead," exposes the schizophrenic duality existing between the autonomous personality and the internalized external determi-
nants. This phrase reflects the narrator's evaluation of his own existence—
obviously, it cannot be interpreted in any other way: it cannot be understood to de-
note literally his death and therefore it must be construed to be a metaphor. Yet the
final sentence of the penultimate paragraph rejects explicitly a metaphorical interpretation of the statement in question: it is absolutely clear that the reference here is

to physical death seen in the context of the final bastion of the person. It is precisely this contrast between literal and metaphorical death that makes it possible for the individual to retain a modicum of autonomy *vis-à-vis* the totalitarian system. The last paragraph of the book muddles this opposition since the essence of the aforementioned realization represents the total obliteration of the personality, that is, the elimination of the possibility of physical death. The thought that prompted this realization was not coincidental: the narrator's enlightenment is the product of his contemplation of suicide, which questions, then eliminates, this possibility. The impossibility of physical death can exist under only one circumstance: if the condition of physical death has already established itself—likewise an impossibility. One needs a tongue to speak a language. The phrase "I'm dead" is one form of the Epimenides paradox, which makes the absurdity of the entire narrative palpable: the collapse of that text which exposes the impossibility of narrating the story of the individual self deprived of itself. The failure manifests itself in the most direct manner possible in this phrase. I do not, however, exclude the possibility that this reading obscures patterns established in certain interpretations of Kertész's other texts, and that an—even more?—essentializing critique might detect in the "I'm dead" remark a permutation of the personality that would promote the continued survival of the individual, although such a reading would have to account for a lack of linguistic consciousness whose breadth I would find difficult to imagine in Kertész. Although we cannot to look to other works in Kertész's so seemingly unified *oeuvre* to provide conclusive evidence in regard to this question, it would be useful for us to consider how foreign the narrative of triumphant survival would be to this author.

This turn of events, implemented in such a way as to investigate the nature of language itself, as I mentioned earlier, leads back to the introductory portion of the text. There we encounter an entirely different conception of language than that which manifests itself in the narrative: one finds in every sentence a totally ironic linguistic element that serves to underscore the intermediary role of language, be it a play on words whose striking contextual impropriety and incongruity ("[reportedly] reported" ("[nyilván] nyilvántartásba vétetett") (*Jegyzőkönyv* 279) places the automatism of the text in the foreground or a statement that comes close to questioning the validity of its own foundations. An example of the latter would be the passage according to which this "sworn statement wasn't produced as if we wanted to change the facts" ("jegyzőkönyv nem azért készül, mintha helyesbíteni akarnánk a tényeket") (*Jegyzőkönyv* 279). This remark implies the possibility of correcting a fact, whereas a "fact" is, *per definitionem*, immutable, uncorrectable. It is, nevertheless, beyond doubt that the narrator's perception that "I'm dead," which takes place in the narrative portion of the book, represents the "ultimate realization" presaged in the introduction; the reader is also compelled to acknowledge that the realization which he or she ultimately identifies as the "ultimate realization" can only take place following this ultimate realization. In this sense it might be justifiable to argue that the introduction is couched in language that is at once anticipatory and retrospective, in this way placing itself outside the bounds of narration, speaking, in Kertész's words, "from the direction of death (from beyond the abyss)" ("a halál felől [a szakadékon túlról]") (*Gályanapló* 326) an abyss that lies between the two—previously introduced—forms existence of the individual.

The second part of the circumlocution that concludes the introductory section, enigmatic at first glance, establishes the following connotative sequence: I-ultimate realization—a name—a lamb dashing before us. The "ultimate realization," into which the act of confession "shapes" (that is, to which it renders identical) the individual, becomes accessible through a frightful name. However, the ultimate realization only becomes recognizable as such when the name transforms into the pursued lamb, thus the name serves merely to conceal. If we understand the lamb to symbolize Christ, then this portion of the text foreshadows the narrator's discovery of his own personality: "We don't believe in anything anymore—so to say—if not . . . in the power of confession, which . . . shapes us into the ultimate realization whose frightful name changes suddenly into the sheep running before us, a sheep that—we only now become aware of it—we have long since been following; and this time, perhaps, if we don't give an ounce on our perseverance, we might even catch up with it" ("Mi már semmiben sem hiszünk—szól a mondat—hacsak . . . a gyónás erejében nem, amely . . . belesimít minket legvégső felismerésünkbe, aminek rettentő nevét egyszerre az előttünk szaladó báránnyá változtatja, amelyet—csak most ébredünk rá—már réges-rég követünk; s ezúttal, ha következetességünkből jottányit sem engedünk, tán utol is érhetjük") (*Jegyzőkönyv* 279–80). In this instance the catching of the lamb would signify the attainment of the Christlike condition—summed up in the formula *ego sum via, veritas et vita*—that comes with an ultimate certainty in the personality. Here the possibility emerges that the individual will identify himself as one with totalitarianism. However, the uncertain "perhaps" leaves open the question of whether this process has really been completed. In my opinion, however, the lamb should not be viewed as a mere component of the Christ motif that surfaces in *Jegyzőkönyv*, but, correlating to early Christian symbolism, refers also to the condition of the soul after death. That which the name conceals is nothing other than the ultimate realization of "I'm dead."

The stating of the name represents the moment of disclosure and it is for precisely this reason that this certain name—that of the narrator, himself—is "frightful," because it is revealed as the synecdoche of totalitarianism. The real twist in the narrative occurs at this point, because Sworn Statement, as an endorsement of agreement, indicates both an acceptance of the customs authority's register and, in spite of the countersignature, a rejection thereof, since the narrator's own name ceased to become a designator of the individual when it assumed the figure of totalitarianism. In other words, we are witness to the simultaneously intentional and automatic operation of an act, which is left unresolved and undecided from both perspectives. In my view, Kertész's subtle and tension-filled portrayal of this conjunction is a belletristic construct that places *Jegyzőkönyv* among his more significant works and makes it worthy of consideration as one of the author's masterworks as well as one of the most significant works of Hungarian literature in the past few decades.

Works Cited

Elm, Theo. "Die Parabel—eine 'hermeneutische' Gattung." *Die moderne Parabel. Parabel und Parabolik in Theorie und Geschichte.* By Theo Elm. Darmstadt: Fink, 1982. 82–110.

Fried, István. "A naplóíró Kertész Imre" ("Imre Kertész, Journal Writer"). *Irodalomtörténet* 91.3 (2003): 337–47.

Gács, Anna. "Egy különös regény. Kertész Imre: *Gályanapló*" ("A Peculiar Novel: Imre Kertész's Galley Boat-Log"). *Jelenkor* 35 (1992): 857–60.

Gács, Anna "Mit számít ki motyog? A szituáció és autorizáció kérdései Kertész Imre prózájában" ("What Does It Matter Who Is Mumbling? Questions about Situation and Authorization in the Prose of Imre Kertész"). *Jelenkor* 45.12 (2002): 1280–95.

Kertész, Imre. *Sorstalanság (Fatelessness).* Budapest: Magvető, 1975.

Kertész, Imre. *Kaddis a meg nem született gyermekért (Kaddish for an Unborn Child).* Budapest: Magvető, 1990.

Kertész, Imre. *Gályanapló* (Galley Boat-Log). Budapest: Holnap, 1992.

Kertész, Imre. Interview with Judit Csáki. *Kritika* 20.3 (1992): 25–26.

Kertész, Imre. *Jegyzőkönyv. Kertész Imre Esterházy Péterrel* (Sworn Statement: Imre Kertész with Péter Esterházy). 1993. Budapest: Magvető, 2001.

Kertész, Imre. *Valaki más: A változás krónikája* (Someone Else: A Chronicle of the Change in Régime). Budapest: Magvető, 1997.

Kertész, Imre. "A boldogtalan huszadik század" ("The Unhappy Twentieth Century"). *A száműzött nyelv* (The Exiled Language). By Imre Kertész. Budapest: Magvető, 2001. 11–44.

Kertész, Imre. "A száműzött nyelv" ("The Exiled Language"). *A száműzött nyelv* (The Exiled Language). By Imre Kertész. Budapest: Magvető, 2001. 274–97.

Kertész, Imre. *Fatelessness.* Trans. Tim Wilkinson. New York: Vintage, 2004.

Margócsy, István. ". . . valami más . . ." (". . . something else . . ."). *Élet és Irodalom* (6 June 1997): 17.

Proksza, Ágnes. "Döntés és ítélet. Kertész Imre: *Sorstalanság*" ("Decision and Judgement: Imre Kertész's *Fatelessness*). *Az értelmezés szükségessége* (The Necessity of Interpretation). Ed. Tamás Scheibner and Zoltán Gábor Szűcs. Budapest: L'Harmattan, 2002. 77–102.

Selyem, Zsuzsa. "Irodalom és irodalom—A mellérendelés etikája" ("Literature and Literature: The Ethics of Co-ordination"). *Pannonhalmi Szemle* 9.3 (2001): 75–97.

Taylor, Charles. *Hegel.* Cambridge: Cambridge UP, 1975.

Imre Kertész's *Kaddish for a Child Not Born*

Eluned Summers-Bremner

Discussing the work of artist Jochen Gerz, Gérard Wajcman notes that its subject matter is memory, "much as others erect edifices in concrete or in iron" (187). In Gerz's work, Wajcman claims, the material and the meaning, or substance and subject, are one and the same, and this oneness—albeit a oneness charged with ambiguity—is visible in the way the works each put forward "nothing to see" (Wajcman 187). Gerz's Anti-Fascist Memorial in Hamburg, created in collaboration with Esther Shalev-Gerz, for instance, consists of "a square cut column, 40 feet high . . . by 3 feet wide on each of its four sides . . . entirely wrapped with sheets of blank lead" (Wajcman 187). Instructions in eight different languages on a nearby wall invited passers-by to etch their names on the monument, which was made so as to sink gradually into the ground by about six feet each year. Six years after its unveiling in 1986, then, all trace of the monument had vanished. The *modus operandi* containing the instructions finishes with the phrase: "Since nothing can stand up for us against injustice" (Wajcman 187).

Another monument in Saarbrücken, the 2146 stones-monument against racism (see Gerz), was constructed in an alley which leads from the centre of the city to the castle, where the Gestapo was stationed during the Second World War. Of the eight thousand paving stones that line the alley, the artist picked 2146 of these at random, "the figure correspond[ing] to the number of Jewish cemeteries existing in Germany prior to 1939" (Wajcman 187). Each cobblestone was engraved with the name of one of these, then replaced in the alley, its inscription facing the ground. Once again, with time, the appearance of the alley was unchanged. Wajcman informs us that, "since Gerz disposed of the planting map, no one knows where the engraved cobblestones lie." The monument is marked only by a street plate: the "Square of the Castle" has become the "Square of the Invisible Monument" (Wajcman 187–88).

What do these disappearing monuments have to do with Kertész's searing novella *Kaddish for a Child Not Born*? On the face of it, nothing. However, the book, no less than Gerz's material testaments to transience, is consumed with the question of what nothingness, after the Holocaust, means (Carson 118). It begins with the narrator, a writer like Kertész himself, who is staying at a writers' retreat, being accosted by one of the other guests, a philosopher, while on an afternoon

walk. We enter the story mid-conversation, at the point of the narrator's exclama-
tory "No," which leads onto a theme that will become familiar, namely the way
"our instincts actually work against our instincts" (1), evidenced by the narrator
himself as he "expound[s] to the philosopher with that disgusting . . . and yet irre-
pressible urge to speak" which "seizes" him when he has "nothing to say" (2).
While Gerz's monuments, as Wajcman claims, deprive their viewers of "a long
aesthetic debate" (188), Kertész's short novel pitches us instantly into the mael-
strom of its narrator's state of mind. At the same time, Gerz's disappearing monuments have a peculiar relevance to the Hungarian situation and this resides not so
much in the way they set in train a process in which names and stones revert to
"nothing to see" but in the way they return to their beginnings through a process of
incorporation. On the second page of the novel we learn that the writers' retreat in
which the narrator is staying is "in the lap of Hungary's mountains" (2); the rest of
the book will detail how geographical and historical positioning—namely the narrator's status as a Hungarian Jew whose Jewishness was brought home to him
through the traumatic events of the Holocaust—has barred access to words as a
comfort, making retreat from the world both desired and impossible (34). It is not
only words, of course, that have been placed under suspicion by traumatic events,
but the prior condition of life itself. In this sense, the house in the lap of Hungary's
mountains—"let's call it a resort," says the narrator, "even though it would also do
for a place of work" (2)—is a place of last resort or death that is intimately related
to the term "lap"'s other meanings. There is the pen that the narrator characterizes
repeatedly as a spade with which he is digging compulsively a grave or declivity in
the earth or air, like that between mountains, a kind of death work or counter-
instinctual forced labor, and the maternal lap whose comforts he cannot in any respect entertain. For his emphatic "No" is, it emerges, directed not only to the philosopher and to the reader but to the narrator's former wife and the possibility, first
raised by her, of the couple's giving birth to and bringing up a child.

If we think of Gerz's monuments sinking or facing down into the earth
alongside Kertész's narrator's lament, his *Kaddish* or mourning prayer for the impossibility of his unborn child, and of his situation as a Hungarian who was made
to answer, retrospectively, to the fact of his Jewishness from within his place of his
birth, then the theme of incorporation is at least as important as that of nothingness.
Indeed, incorporation might be described as the Hungarian national dilemma, one
that achieved particular significance during the Second World War, when the
country's alliance with Germany occurred. This was partly the result of the failure
of the post-war Trianon Treaty negotiations in 1919, in which Hungary was unable
to reconcile its claims with those of its minorities in outlying regions (see Cohen,
"History" 14). As a result, the country "lost 60% of its territory and population"
(see, e.g., Tötösy de Zepetnek <http://clcwebjournal.lib.purdue.edu/clcweb03–1/
totosy03.html>), so that alliance with what would become Nazi Germany was
grounded in a sense of righteous loss. Yet the Second World War resulted in the

culling of Hungary's Jewish and minority populations to an extent surpassing the prior loss of its land, because as well as residing in its outlying, now contested regions, they were active contributors to Hungarian identity from within its cosmopolitan heart. As Zsuzsanna Ozsváth puts it: "For many years, most Hungarian Jews had participated in and benefited from, the fast-spreading emancipation and assimilation processes initiated in nineteenth-century Hungary . . . masses of Hungarian Jews assimilated to the Hungarian way of life and became passionately patriotic" (Ozsváth 52–53). Jews were also, as elsewhere, driven into the urban bourgeois professions of banking, artistic, and intellectual work because they were forbidden to own landed property (see Tötösy de Zepetnek <http://clcwebjournal. lib.purdue.edu/clcweb03–1/totosy03.html>). So they were stigmatized for their adaptation to, and embrace of, the very conditions on which they were granted the right to belong.

Péter Nádas makes a fascinating connection between the Hungarian linguistic predicament and Kertész's artistic treatment of the Holocaust. The Hungarian language, as is widely known, presents difficulties for non-Hungarian speakers because it resembles no other language, having only a distant relation to the Altaic-Uralic branches that include Turkish, Finnish, and Mongolian (Cohen, "Language" 27). In describing the philosophical dimensions of Kertész's work as having been obscured by the controversial nature of his subject, that is, the Holocaust, Nádas identifies Hungarian as having "barely been scratched hitherto by any spadework of philosophical scrutiny," and as having, therefore, "no self-sufficient philosophy of its own" (40). Nádas claims that Kertész, however, has "turned this drawback, a near-general absence of analyzed and fixed conceptual substance, into an advantage. He has fashioned the surfaces of a dispassionate way of viewing things from the material of the Hungarian language. In hindsight, it can now be seen that the malleable sentence structure of Hungarian gives the language the ability to adopt a dispassionate view. In the pause of a feeling charged by two commonplaces . . . Kertész's sentences take note of painful reality" (40). "In the pause of a feeling charged by two commonplaces": This could almost be a description of Hungary's wartime position between two larger and more easily defined blocs of power. For the commonplace is that which has achieved such precedence that we no longer notice it rather than that which functions as the site of real community. If Kertész has used the Hungarian language to express Hungary's own assimilative tendencies in their resultant brutality then we might say he has performed, in language, an act not dissimilar to those involved in Gerz's monuments, made of material on which we depend without thinking—the stones or earth we walk on, the words we speak—but with an even harsher message. For if he "has fashioned the surfaces of a dispassionate way of viewing things from the material of the Hungarian language," as Gerz has made it impossible for passers-by to identify the meaning and exact location of the names of the dead on which they walk, or to find their own names, then Kertész has made his Hungarian readers complicit in his suffering. He has taken the material marker of Hungarian difference *par excellence*, the language that is unlike any that others speak, and demonstrated its deathly potential. With this dies the possibility that a language, like a people, can ever really be neutral, leaving us with the question of the ethical responsibility arising from its historical effects.

While I cannot attest to the linguistic effectiveness of the manoeuvre Nádas identifies in Kertész's work, in my opinion it is very powerful symbolically. A passage at the centre of *Kaddish* provides the first clear mention of the narrator's Hungarian situation, and it is a harsh judgment. Speaking of the work that became the means of the narrator's meeting his future wife, the narrator describes its conditions of birth or production. Noting that "it didn't appear without all the ugly and trying prior complications" and designating it a "modest, futile appendage" that "belongs entirely to the Hungarian literary scene," the conditions of publishing in this scene are said to make the book a "crucifying, humiliating occurrence thriving on exclusion and privilege," resulting in the "shameful and embarrassing literary event" at which the narrator and his wife-to-be meet (57). This situation complicates matters for them both. Of course, the narrator's experience of the Hungarian literary scene is not only to do with the status of his Jewishness but with the complex overlaying of this reality with that of literary production under Communism (see Molnár; Davis). We learn that this history has made him into "an outside observer" alienated from what is called literature and that the narrator of the book in question is similarly marked. The passage preceding gives the narrator of *Kaddish*'s response to a question from his future wife regarding whether he continues to suffer from his Jewishness in addition to the sufferings of the past. His response brings up another of *Kaddish*'s recurrent themes, that of a lingering shamefulness:

> I have felt that some sort of awful shame is attached to my name and that I have somehow brought this shame along from somewhere, from somewhere I have never been, and that I have carried this sin as my sin even though I have never committed it . . . . I think, though, I said, that not everything is necessarily a direct result of my Jewishness, it could simply be a result of myself, my being, my personality . . . or the result of others' behavior toward me, my behavior toward others, my and others' general behavior and mutual treatment of each other . . . because, as I said, *judgment doesn't come suddenly; process gradually becomes judgment,* as was written. (56–57; emphases in the original)

This passage, preceding the first mention of the narrator's feelings about his placement within the Hungarian literary scene, may be read as a description of the historical conditions that predate it, and which produce the figure of the Jew as the outlawed instance of the Hungarian national character: at once assimiliatory and distinctive. That the source of the narrator's shame is un-locatable is not surprising, since the only condition of life as a Hungarian Jew was, historically, exclusion or

assimilation. In this respect, Kertész makes clear that the Jewish-Hungarian Holocaust survivor's predicament is, in a seldom noticed way, identifiable in its structure, if not in kind, with that of non-Jewish Hungarians. This is a judgment that
many refuse to recognize. As Nádas observes, "it is a painful insight to see continuity where others wish, at best, to see only a short-circuit in civilization, the inexplicable workings of evil, or a product of chance" (40). The sense in which everyone
is both a product of their nation or historical context and an instance of non-
historicizable uniqueness is particularly charged in Hungary. Nádas's claim that
Kertész has turned an absence of "fixed conceptual substance" in the language
"into an advantage" (40), highlights the strangeness of that context before the question of Jewishness is even introduced. For this is a culture of assimilation with,
ironically, if we are to believe Nádas, an absence of fixed ideas in its language owing to its linguistic uniqueness. Or, it is a culture whose sense of historical distinct-
iveness is so pronounced that it allowed itself to be divested of a large part of its
population. *Kaddish*'s narrator is made to know that his shame belongs to his history, to his race, but this is not located anywhere. Despite his having brought it
along from somewhere, it comes from "somewhere [he] ha[s] never been" (57).
The narrator's inability to attribute his retrospective shame to his Jewishness is the
result, not only of the history of Hungarian Jewish assimilation, but also of Hungary's own relation with the powers that surround it, within which the Jewish question is at once both dispersed and secretly located or buried.

To put this in more general terms, the exceptionality of the Hungarian language is made to bear, if Nádas's reading of Kertész is correct, the historical truth
of Hungary's too-quick assimilation within the policies of Nazi Germany as well as
the more damning about-turn through which it disowned, or buried, its own best
assimilators, the Jews. The words "as was written" following the above claim
about judgment echo the sounds of Jewish prophetic tradition (derivatives recur often in the Hebrew scriptures). At the same time they suggest that the narrator has
only written about what really happened. That is, a process occurred in which there
was no sudden judgment which might have been remarked, if not resisted, but instead the recasting of the historical conditions—the process—of Hungarian Jewish
belonging and achievement as the very reason for the murder of the nation's Jews
and for their shame. In this respect Kertész's writing as digging, using the linguistic
tools Nádas identifies as being hitherto untouched by the "spadework" of "philosophical scrutiny," works back through this history of assimilation, the soil of nationalist sentiment, uncovering its dispassionate and potentially murderous heart. Of
Fatelessness, the novel for which Kertész was awarded the 2002 Nobel Prize and
which is the first book in the trilogy of which *Kaddish* is the last, Kertész has said:
"It is a proud work. Because of that, people will never forgive either the book or
me" (qtd. in Gustafsson <http://www.nobel.se/literature/articles/gustafsson/index.
html>). *Kaddish*, too, is a proud work that goes further back in time and space than
Fatelessness in order to raise implicitly the question of a Hungarian-Jewish future

in light of the process through which Hungary's Jews were made, first to exist, and then to die as if they had never been born.

As the passage quoted above demonstrates, Kertész has not begun, as is common in Holocaust writing, with the question of the uniqueness of the Holocaust or of the Jewish people's situation but with its opposite, arguably more relevant in Hungary. This is the question of whether, or how, one can know the composition of one's origins and history at all. And while Nádas's claim is borne out in the structure and imagery of *Kaddish for a Child Not Born*, I think this bleak aspect of the novel is also linked, perhaps unconsciously, to the work of another Jew obsessed with death, one who might himself, but for the shifting of borders and renaming of lands, have been a Hungarian of another sort, Sigmund Freud. We know that Kertész, who after the war performed a number of menial jobs before proceeding first to literary translation and then eventually to other writing, including fiction, translated the work of Freud. And the question of the inseparability of death and birth underwrites the quintessentially Freudian notion that "our instincts . . . work against our instincts," to put it in the words of *Kaddish*'s narrator on the book's opening page. It was in the aftermath of war that Freud advanced this idea in *Beyond the Pleasure Principle* of 1920, incidentally just after Hungary's loss-inducing Trianon Treaty was signed. Freud was provoked into revising his theories to date at this point, not only by the death of his daughter as has been claimed (Bronfen 15–18)—a near parallel with *Kaddish*'s narrator, who mourns a child's life unlived—but also by observing the traumatic effects of war on homecoming soldiers. While a drive toward life might be deduced from the desire to repeat or experience again particular human pleasures, the insistent return to a traumatic event shown by such soldiers indicated a dimension "beyond" or prior to the pleasure principle: a senseless, fated quality. The essence of this fatedness, however, was resistance and conflict.

At times, especially in its closing pages, *Kaddish* appears to be invoking this idea directly, as the narrator rails against his wife for choosing life rather than allowing herself to be sacrificed to his ongoing destruction. Three pages from the end he offers us an instance of his complete identification with his suffering, his symptom, with the shocking statement—as much so as the one that ends *Fatelessness*, where affection is given as an appropriate response to the Holocaust, that: "Being a Jew does undoubtedly have a large advantage . . . exclusively in this respect do I consider it lucky . . . even a blessing not that I am a Jew . . . but the fact that, labeled a Jew, I was allowed to be in Auschwitz and that on account of my Jewishness I experienced and survived something and faced something . . . something that I won't let go of, will never let go of, I shouted" (*Kaddish* 93).

On the evidence of *Fatelessness* and *Kaddish* I would count Kertészas one of Freud's more perspicacious readers in that he has drawn from his experience and allowed to resonate in both works not only one of the more troubling aspects of surviving trauma—that one is always in some sense bound to the traumatic event—but one of the most troubling aspects of human reality. This is the tendency to be satisfied by repeated experiences of suffering in a way that is at odds with a person's or a culture's stated ideals. It is this that makes *Kaddish*, for me at least, resonate also with the work of the French psychoanalyst Jacques Lacan, who in the last period of his scholarship, confronted the same problem as the later Freud, namely, the attachment people form to their symptoms, the way an affective or libidinal consistency—a state of mind we know and return to—is often given primacy long after its felt benefits or delivery of pleasure have worn down. Lacan relates this problem directly to the work required of human beings as subjects of language, which exiles us effectively from the land of instincts that is the animal domain (see Lacan; Rodriguez 194; Cantin 35). For humans do not only need to eat, sleep, and reproduce but experience all these things and more in the shadow of unanswerable questions regarding the meaning of our lives. Language, moreover, which is held in common, cannot say everything, since the history and desire of each of us marks an exception to its general laws (Levy-Stokes 101). While language institutes a lack of fit or completeness between the drive—the human version of the instincts—and the object around which it circles, this very failure produces the impetus to repetition.

This situation is in one respect a rationale for the above mentioned divergence between human ideals and the history of barbarous or self-destructive activities—unhappiness is at least familiar to us, while hope and joy are much more difficult to control. But it is also literalized and over-complicated in the life of a Jewish death camp survivor. For in addition to having one's human appetites, in the concentration camps, reduced to a level of satisfaction below that of many beasts, there is a corresponding surfeit of non-meaning. This might take the form of confusion regarding the purpose of the camps or, alternatively, the inability to completely quash in oneself some expectation that things might improve. When he is about to describe a particularly inscrutable act of generosity towards him that occurred in Auschwitz, the narrator of *Kaddish* begins: "First and foremost, I couldn't feed my eternal torturer, hunger," but in the course of the sentence hunger—which is not only instinct but also desire—becomes "that estranged, angrily demanding beast, hope, which up until now continued to drum . . . that in spite of everything there was still a chance for surviving" (32). Indeed, it is the inseparability in humans of the instinct that connects food with survival and the excessive, enigmatic elements to do with meaning—the way hunger can never be divorced from hope—that almost exacerbates the suffering here. Certainly, it does not appear to diminish it. It would help greatly if, when we are faced with suffering, we could somehow be released from the need or desire to understand it, but it is doubtful that any human being who is conscious can achieve this. A crying baby, for instance, may well learn that crying engenders the prospect of food but neither the baby nor the caregiver can really decipher the meaning of the tears. Hunger and food together satisfy the instinct for survival in us, but it is the leftover part, the wondering or hope or enigma, that at times appears to increase, while at others it can soothe and alter, one's private suffering and pain.

Since, as Sára Molnár points out, Kertész's work as a whole indicates that the Holocaust continues with us rather than residing in a specific instance of historical conditions (see Molnár; see also Gustafsson <http://www.nobel.se/literature/articles/gustafsson/index.html>), it seems reasonable to assume that this enigmatic occasion says something, not only about death camp conditions, but about humanity itself. The act of inexplicable kindness is performed by an older man at Auschwitz whom the narrator names "the Professor." About to be transported as one of the sick to a new location, the narrator lies on a stretcher and his food ration, which must last for several days, is held by the Professor who is described as "a skeleton" (*Kaddish* 32). The Professor seeks out the narrator unsteadily and gives him his due portion of food. The narrator's surprise, which, he says, "must have screamed unabashedly from my face," elicits a corresponding "disgust" on the Professor's, as if to say: "Well, what did you expect?" (33). The narrator continues: "That's it for the story, and even if it's true that I don't wish to view my life merely as an arbitrary chance of birth followed by a series of other arbitrary chances . . . I want to view my life even less as a series of attempts to keep me alive . . . yet it is a fact that . . . the Professor did what he did in order to keep me alive. . . . And this here is the question, this is what I'd like you to answer if you can: why did he do it?" (33). Kertész's familiarity with the literature of existentialism by Camus and others is evident here, as the act assumes momentarily the burden of meaning of the entirety of human existence. Caught between two equally unpalatable views—that the event, like a person's birth, means nothing and that by contrast it was already written or fated—he responds by asking the reader a question. The question itself is a kind of excess, for while the reader was not present at the event we can only interpret the question in unwieldy or inappropriate ways. "It's the good in human nature," we might say, or: "the worse things are, the more important it can feel to act otherwise," but in their generality these answers will always have a ring of falseness.

I would go so far as to suggest that the professor's enigmatic act of kindness is a stand-in for the prospect of the narrator's unborn child. It is an instance of senseless life and goodness within the hate-filled monologue that is *Kaddish*, and, like a child, it has no real rationale. The narrator attempts to understand Auschwitz by pointing out, not only the commonality all humankind shares with its perpetrators, but the way this is masked by reliance on reason: "When a criminal madman ends up not in an insane asylum . . . but in the Chancery . . . you immediately start to search for some meaning, you start to look for the original, the extraordinary, the—you don't dare say it aloud but in secret—for the greatness in him so that you won't be forced to see yourselves as dwarfs and world history as incomprehensible . . . you do this so that you can see the world rationally and be seen by the world rationally" (29–30). For a rational world is a "sufferable world," he claims (30). And

yet, this condition with which he charges others is also his own condition, for he
has no knowledge of himself as a Jew apart from that senselessly wrought in him
by the events of the Holocaust, just as he and others have no knowledge of themselves as potential murderers. Kertész's words about his own Jewishness are relevant here: "What kind of a Jew is somebody who never received a Jewish upbringing, does not speak Hebrew, barely knows the sources of Jewish culture and does
not live in Israel, but in Europe? Someone who derives his primary Jewish identity
perhaps exclusively from Auschwitz, in a certain sense, should not be called a Jew.
He is the 'non-Jewish Jew,' of whom Isaac Deutscher speaks, the uprooted European variety who barely find[s] a personal connection [with his] imposed Jewishness" ("Jerusalem, Jerusalem" <http://www.logosjournal.com/kertesz.htm>). Thus
the narrator is faced with an impossibility. The question that troubles all human beings—"who am I for the Other (parents, lovers, employers, and so on)?"—
consumes him but his experience has taught him that there is no answer. While
Jewishness is given as the rationale for his incarceration in Auschwitz, all that he
has to hang it on is his history of assimilation into Hungarian life, a history in
which Jewishness now has no place. Where formerly his life appeared to be no different to those of non-Jewish Hungarians—after all, assimilation combined with
(linguistic) difference was the Hungarian *raison d'être*—this very assimilation was
then switched into its opposite: ejection from society based on belonging to the dis-
tinctively shaming category of the Jew. The narrator's Jewishness, with which he
can form no identification, becomes the hateful point of exception within his prior
Hungarianness (*magyarság*), just as a child is the point of exception within its parents' history and desires.

The narrator appears to recognize something of this, albeit in the enigmatic
way that knowledge of one's historical truth must always arrive, carried by the dis-
torting dynamics of language. Of the address to the reader regarding the Professor's excessive act of kindness he admonishes: "But don't try to answer in words,
for we all know that under certain circumstances at a particular temperature, meta-
phorically speaking, words lose their form, their context, their signification; they
simply turn to naught; so that in this vaporized state only deeds, sheer deeds show
any tendency to remain concrete" (33). The narrator muses on the fact that the Professor, who was carrying his own portion of food, as well as the narrator's at the
time of his act of kindness, was in fact giving up something greater than a simple
portion of food, for "he was given two chances for survival and . . . he threw away
this double chance . . . the chance beyond his chance" (34). Fascinatingly, however, the narrator suggests that if the Professor had taken this chance and eaten the
extra portion himself he would have effectively "assimilated the only chance he
had enabling him to live and survive" (34), he would have caused to die something
that carried hidden but significant meaning. The double chance, in other words,
that offered the hope of surviving could not but be visible within the wastes of
camp "life" at this moment as a saving instance, as something much more than a

mere extra portion of food. It is the act of giving this chance away that causes the death-identifying narrator such perturbation and that registers in his involuntary shock of surprise and in the Professor's disgust, as though the only possible response to this inexplicable life-chance, for both parties, is an affective lurch or grimace.

The narrator claims that this second chance which was passed on to him testifies that "there exists a pristine concept untainted by all . . . material circumstances . . . an idea that exists in the minds of all of us" but he begs his readers not to try to name it and concludes only that it is "not rational" (34). The story is an opening onto the mystery of why human beings do, at times, embrace their suffering, will sometimes sacrifice themselves for a cause or meaning, even a meaning with such fragility as this. In giving away his extra chance of living, the narrator concludes, the Professor gave something belonging to his humanity—namely desire in the form of hope, an unlooked-for opportunity—but in doing so he also instantiated that humanity anew. He passed it on, in other words, just as the narrator is passing the story onto us, the readers, and as children pass on to future generations in their being the histories of their ancestors that they themselves can never really know. Because he knows he will never be able to grasp this "untainted concept" at the same time as his life continues in its debt, and because it was given from within Auschwitz, or life-as-death, the narrator cannot contemplate giving birth to children. For him, the terms of life have been inverted, so that a superficially meaningless event like another skeleton holding one's food ration for a moment, which ought in the normal way of things to mean nothing but the proximity of death, instead shines with hope against it, provoking writing as the lifelong endeavor to bear it witness: "It is my duty to tell [my stories]," he declares, "albeit I don't know why" (34). In view of this, the refrain directed by the narrator towards his unborn child, "my life's existence viewed in the light of your potential existence . . . your nonexistence viewed in light of the necessary . . . liquidation of my existence" (55), serves paradoxically something of the function of the kaddish in Jewish tradition. For the kaddish, the prayer that it is incumbent upon orphaned sons to recite in the synagogue three times a day for the first year of mourning, has nothing, on the surface, to do with mourning. On the contrary, it is a prayer of praise (see, e.g., Heilman 164).

Leon Wieseltier observes that connection between the kaddish and the funeral resides traditionally in the way "the study of Torah is cancelled for the sake of a funeral or a wedding," and so is required to make good the disruption of the natural—that is, in this context, the scriptural—order of things (32). The kaddish is not recited at a wedding because the people come together with the sole purpose of celebrating a marriage. At funerals, by contrast, verses from Scripture concerning the Judgment are uttered, and the kaddish is then required to mark the disruption, caused by the funeral, to the study of the Torah that is of the same order as these. In this respect the mourner's kaddish is not so different from the Auschwitz Professor's inexplicable act of kindness, a disruption to Auschwitz itself that continues as an unresolved question within Kertész's *Kaddish* narrative. Paradox is the essence of the mourner's kaddish, a statement of praise that, through its ritual utterance by a bereaved son in the synagogue, marks desolation and community at one turn. While Kertész's *Kaddish* is a lament for a child unborn, its function as an outcry at odds with its subject, issuing forth to a community of readers, means that it shares the kaddish's paradoxical movement, even though the father/son relationship has been reversed. For if there can be no more life after Auschwitz, why does the narrator of *Kaddish* continue speaking to us, the readers? Why does he seek to share his burden? Or as Wieseltier puts it: "I conclude that the liturgical function of the kaddish has nothing to do with its content; and that the kaddish at the funeral has nothing to do with the mourner's kaddish; and that the mourner's kaddish has nothing to do with mourning. So what exactly is this exclamation whose servant I have become?" (32–33).

In fact, as Wieseltier remarks later, the function of the kaddish hangs on a further reversal: "that the dead are in need of spiritual rescue; and that the agent of spiritual rescue is the son; and that the instrument of spiritual rescue is prayer; notably the kaddish" (127). It is the bereaved son who bears the responsibility to assist the departed to find solace, a responsibility whose form—the kaddish—is inexplicable within the mortal context. So Kertész's *Kaddish* becomes the instance of excess that makes the reader wonder, just as the Professor's act delivered to him the injunction to wonder in his turn. It is strange indeed that the dead should be rescued by the grief of an orphan. And yet perhaps it is this same orphan, the child who has no father because he will never be born, who is charged with rescuing *Kaddish*'s afflicted narrator, in so far as this child is present in the book that stands in for him, and in so far as this book that stands in for him is the enigmatic instance of life that we hold in our hands.

Works Cited

Bronfen, Elisabeth. *Over Her Dead Body: Death, Femininity and the Aesthetic.* New York: Routledge, 1992.

Cantin, Lucie. "The Trauma of Language." *After Lacan: Clinical Practice and the Subject of the Unconscious.* Ed. Robert Hughes and Kareen Ror Malone. Albany: State U of New York P, 2002. 35–47.

Carson, Anne. *Economy of the Unlost: Reading Simonides of Keos with Paul Celan.* Princeton: Princeton UP, 1999.

Cohen, Bob. "History." *Budapest.* Ed. Dave Rimmer. London: Penguin, 1999. 5–23.

Cohen, Bob. "Language." *Budapest.* Ed. Dave Rimmer. London: Penguin, 1999. 27–30.

Davis, Robert Murray. "Desperate But Not Serious: The Situation of Hungarian Literature in the Nineties." *World Literature Today* 74.1 (2000): 81–90.

Gerz, Jochen. *2146 Stones: Monument against Racism*. Saarbrücken, Germany, 1990–1993.

Gerz, Jochen, and Esther Shalev-Gerz. *Anti-Fascist Memorial*. Hamburg, Germany, 1986–1993.

Gustafsson, Madeleine. "Imre Kertész: A Medium for the Spirit of Auschwitz." Trans. Victor Kayfetz. *Nobel e-Museum* (2003): <http://www.nobel.se/literature/articles/gustafsson/index.html>.

Heilman, Samuel C. *When a Jew Dies: The Ethnography of a Bereaved Son*. Berkeley: U of California P, 2001.

Kertész, Imre. *Kaddish for a Child Not Born*. Trans. Christopher C. Wilson and Katharina M. Wilson. Evanston: Northwestern UP, 1997.

Kertész, Imre. "Jerusalem, Jerusalem: Reflections Sparked by the Sight of a War-torn City." *Logos* (2003): <http://www.logosjournal.com/kertesz.htm>.

Kertész, Imre. *Fatelessness*. Trans. Tim Wilkinson. New York: Vintage, 2004.

Lacan, Jacques. *Le Séminaire. Livre IV. La Relation d'objet*. Paris: Seuil, 1994.

Levy Stokes, Carmela. "*Jouissance*." *A Compendium of Lacanian Terms*. Ed. Huguette Glowinski, Zita Marks, and Sara Murphy. London: Free Association Books, 2001. 101–19.

Molnár, Sára. "Imre Kertész's Aesthetics of the Holocaust." *Imre Kertész and Holocaust Literature*. Ed. Louise O. Vasvári and Steven Tötösy de Zepetnek. West Lafayette: Purdue UP, 2005. 162–70.

Nádas, Péter. "Imre Kertész's Work and His Subject." *The Hungarian Quarterly* 43.168 (2002): 38–40.

Ozsváth, Zsuzsanna. "Radnóti, Celan and the Aesthetic Shifts in Central European Holocaust Poetry." *Comparative Central European Culture*. Ed. Steven Tötösy de Zepetnek. West Lafayette: Purdue UP, 2002. 51–69.

Rodriguez, Silvia A. "Subject." In *A Compendium of Lacanian Terms*. Ed. Huguette Glowinski, Zita Marks, and Sara Murphy. London: Free Association Books, 2001. 192–27.

Tötösy de Zepetnek, Steven. "And the 2002 Nobel Prize for Literature Goes to Imre Kertész, Jew and Hungarian." *CLCWeb: Comparative Literature and Culture* 5.1 (2003): <http://clcwebjournal.lib.purdue.edu/clcweb03–1/totosy03.html>.

Wajcman, Gérard. "The Absence of the Twentieth Century." *Jacques Lacan: Critical Interventions in Cultural Theory*. Ed. Slavoj Žižek. New York: Routledge, 2003. Vol. 4, 186–98.

Wieseltier, Leon. *Kaddish*. New York: Knopf, 1998.

Imre Kertész's 2002 Nobel Prize for Literature in the Print Media

Steven Tötösy de Zepetnek

In this paper, I discuss aspects of media coverage in German-, Hungarian-, and English-language newspapers and magazines of the 2002 Nobel Prize in Literature awarded to Imre Kertész. The perspective of my analysis is to gauge the importance and impact of media coverage in the three cultural and media landscapes comparatively. Attention to the processes and impact of media coverage of cultural products is of interest because of its obvious importance in the process of canonization, including book sales and general cultural, social, and political discourse (for an example of statistics of book sales after the award in Hungary and Germany, see H.Gy.-T.K.; Young). In particular, what interests me in Kertész's reception in the media are aspects of the convergences of the media and the contents of the message within public discourse, resulting in Kertész's role as a public intellectual. And this is not a given since Kertész pronounces repeatedly that he does not consider himself a public intellectual, while at the same time his works themselves and virtually all media items concerned with his work (or with him personally) he received, as well as his own words in interviews are contextualized in public discourse with special reference to the social responsibility of the writer per se, implicitly or explicitly. The reason for this, I propose, is the latent and since 1989 baffling explicit anti-Semitism with its parallel conservative-nationalist sentiment and, indeed, "program" of culture apparent in public discourse, as well as—in a more sophisticated manner—in government such as the Orbán government of 1998–2002 in Hungary. I should like to note that the publicly displayed anti-Semitism in today's Hungary remains in Europe as well as in North America at best downplayed, as I experience(d) repeatedly in both Europe and North America (Canada and the U.S.).

The reception of Kertész's work in his native and "literary" country, Hungary, in contrast to his position and reception where he feels at home intellectually, namely Germany, contextualizes and locates his own media statements and the public discourse in general in a political and ideological momentum. Kertész, I believe, is a public intellectual *malgré lui* and thus he is of great significance in the context of the above-mentioned problematic of Hungary, Central Europe, and, indeed, of the European Union, with regard to latent and currently explicit anti-Semitism and ethnic essentialism in Hungary: Comparatively, it is here where the media play a crucial role and where their impact is acutely discernable. Of course, the finding itself that Kertész, despite his reservations, is a public intellectual is not particularly interesting. What is interesting and worthy of study is, however, the description of the factors and processes of the controversy surrounding Kertész's Nobel Prize in Hungary in its relationship with the media elsewhere, precisely because of the shrill and sharp anti-Semitic and nationalist discourse present in the country (on this, see Gerő, Varga, and Vince; Marsovszky; Young). In addition, the media reception of the Nobel Prize in the case of a minor language and literature may be of interest to those working in literary as well as in media studies.

An important issue—while not discussed or reflected in the media, is, nevertheless, the "un-writability" of the Holocaust in fiction with regard to Kertész's texts: It appears that most general readers and, indeed, the general public, finds Adorno's dictum about the impossibility of poetry after the Holocaust the status quo, still. Although some—including scholars—would argue that fictional literature about the Holocaust is possible and even desirable and that Adorno's dictum would be a matter not applicable any more, the verdict is not out. Important authors and thinkers such as Elie Wiesel, George Steiner, or Michal Borwicz have stated in forceful terms that "there is no such thing as a literature of the Holocaust, nor can there be" (Wiesel qtd. in Felman 4; see also Taterka 117).

Kertész's work in world literature is established with the Nobel Prize. However, as we know, the majority of writers who receive the Nobel Prize, while thus established in the canon, do not maintain visibility or a readership. In fact, most Nobel Laureates disappear from the landscape of reading shortly after receiving the award and remain, as well, little studied in scholarship. In the case of Kertész, this to-be-expected "disappearance" is the more acute because he writes in Hungarian, a minor language and a minor culture (I do not intend rehash the argument that Hungarian is a most difficult language, that it is un-categorizable and of unclear origins, and that it does not belong to the Indo-European family of languages, etc., but I would like to say that there is something true to these arguments, that is, how the language, because of the reasons mentioned, remains by definition marginal). I understand the Nobel Prize for Kertész as an award based on the particularity and specificity of his work, namely, the description of the terror in and the horrors of the twentieth century, *the* human condition of that century. I would like to add here that in comparison with the importance of the Laureate's texts, among incisive writers in Hungary today, there is an author who deserves our attention, Péter Nádas, an author who writes about the universal human condition with thematics and a narrative in his fiction, which transcend any particularity yet represent perhaps more eloquently linguistically, thematically, and narratively the best of literature of today anywhere. However, Nádas, too, suffers the same problem as Kertész, namely being a writer in a minor literature and minor culture with all all the drawbacks that go with that position. Other Hungarian writers of high currency are at best writers with a provincial or period flavor, such as Péter Esterházy—who received, among other prizes, in 2004 the coveted German Friedenspreis—and whose importance and popularity are based on his playing with a curious Central European type of irony and word play and on his *passé* status of an *enfant terrible*, or György Konrád, who is taken, mistakenly, for a writer of literature when, in fact, in my opinion he is a public intellectual who excels in essay writing—but not as a writer of fiction, or the poet Endre Kukorelly, who, similarly to Esterházy, was important before and shortly after the fall of "real socialism" in 1989 because of the politico-cultural impact and period-location of his writing. To use another example, the highly acclaimed novel of László Márton, *Árnyas főutca* (1999), gives me the impression of an author who wants to be clever: The narrative structure of his novel is not particularly innovative except, perhaps, in Hungarian. It is a copy (or adaptation) of the *Memento* idea (or, and I am not facetious, of the film *Ground Hog Day* with Bill Murray). While the topic of Márton's book, dealing with anti-Semitism in Hungary before and after the war, is, of course, an important one for Hungary and in Hungarian literature, but as *literature* it is not particularly impressive. Kertész's work is.

To begin with the analysis of selected print media, I recapitulate briefly the 2002 Nobel Prize in Literature: Imre Kertész—resident of Budapest and Berlin and citizen of Hungary—received the 2002 Nobel Prize for Literature in October of that year. The Swedish Academy's choice came as a surprise to many and in various ways observers of literary and culture affairs, including many scholars, were taken unawares. In particular, the English-speaking world, including the U.S., knew and still knows little to nothing about Kertész and his work. For example, the MLA: Modern Language Association of America, the principal U.S.-American organization of scholars working in the humanities and of academic institutions in the humanities, was unable to find a U.S.-American expert who would field queries about the author (personal information). U.S.-American and Canadian newspapers in print and on the world wide web contain scant and same-source information (the relatively large number of items on Kertész's Nobel Prize on the web, for example, are more often thank not of the same information drawn on the same source; on this, see also Young). The cavalier and sloppy attitude towards minor languages such as Hungarian prevails even with the Swedish Academy: In the first version of the official web site of the Swedish Academy about the new awardees, *Nobel Prize in Literature: Laureates* at <http://www.nobel.se/literature/laureates/index.html>, the material about Kertész contained several errors in the spelling of names and in titles of books (see Tötösy de Zepetnek "And the 2002 Nobel Prize" <http://clcwebjournal.lib.purdue.edu/clcweb03–1/totosy03.html>).

My brief analysis of the print media with regard to Kertész's Nobel Prize is based on a selection of items in German-, Hungarian-, and English-language newspapers and magazines, as well as some items on the world wide web. The method of sampling I use is "judgement sampling," an extension of convenience sampling, within the main category of the non-probability method of sampling. Thus, while my selection is by no means representative, it is an acceptable sample from a number of culture-oriented canonical newspapers with reports about and discussions of Kertész's Nobel Prize. Also, as my samples are from canonical newspapers I believe they allow for gauging public opinion. It is the general impression of the contents of the selected items that provide us with a gauge of the divergent qualities of Kertész's media presence and, by extension from the tone and language of the coverage, the hypothetical importance of media coverage of Kertész's Nobel Prize.

In German-language media, Kertész and his work have been discussed prominently and positively. This is not surprising considering the fact that it was in Germany where Kertész's work received the most widespread and positive attention and it was the German committee for the nomination of authors for the Nobel Prize that proposed Kertész for 2002. In Iris Radisch's 2002 interview with Kertész in the weekly *Die Zeit*, the interview covers Kertész's personal as well as literature- and writing-related perspectives about love, the Holocaust, central Europe, Hungary, etc. Kertész's views are given well-guided exposure and his thoughts on various matters are stimulating, even if at times surprising. For example, Kertész defends German author Martin Walser's right as a writer to depict in his novel a Jewish literary critic in a negative and disturbing manner and Walser—according to Kertész—has the right to do so because as a writer he should be allowed to dislike *this* particular critic who happens to be Jewish (the interviewer's question relates to the much discussed Walser and Reich-Ranicki affair about the former's novel, *Tod eines Kritikers* (Marcel Reich-Ranicki is one of Germany's prominent literary critics, whose function as a public intellectual is significant). Kertész's opinion is of course that of a writer whose writing has been censored enough, and for long enough, so that this determines his permissive view pertaining to the freedom of expression. The reasons for his view, as Kertész himself explains in the interview, would not stand up to scrutiny were he German (and, interestingly, no interview or other type of publication in the German-language media makes references or allusions to this matter). Nor would his view work for the North American (Canadian and U.S.-American) reader either. Kertész says that Walser's disturbing depiction of a literary critic who happens to be a Jew whom the writer dislikes is allowable because "Why should it be anti-Semitic when this protagonist is unlikable? The protagonist is unlikable and by coincidence he is also Jewish. But in the first instance he is a critic. And most Jews are not critics" (all translations are mine unless noted otherwise) ("Warum soll es antisemitisch sein, wenn diese Romanfigur unansehnlich ist? Die Figur ist unsympatisch, und zufällig ist sie Jude. Aber in erster Linie ist sie Kritiker. Und die meisten Juden sind keine Kritiker") (Kertész qtd. in Radisch 45). The interviewer about the Walser affaire ends the conversation with the remark: "You are terrifyingly pluralistic" ("Sie sind erschreckend pluralistisch") (45). Indeed. And what is of importance here is the fact that what Kertész bases partially his argumentation on not to censor Walser, namely that "And most Jews are not critics" would of course work less in the U.S. and, thus, there, the negative prototype of the Jew as a cultural standard of a Euro-centric world would make Walser's text clearly anti-Semitic. With regard to Ger-man-speaking countries, it is of course well known that in comparison with Canada or even the U.S., the non-acceptance of the foreigner remains a serious problem (see, e.g., Bittner; Terwey). In spite of the importance of the Radisch interview in term of its wide-ranging thematics with regard to Kertész and his work, it did not find its way into either the Hungarian nor the Canadian or U.S.-American media.

Critics in German-language media paid close attention to the question of eth-ics and morality in the work of Kertész and its relationship with the Holocaust (see, e.g., Steinfeld; see also Adorján and Minkmar). With regard to this problematic, of significance is the recognition apparent in media items that Kertész's work is un-derstood as non-moralizing, and this was described in comparison with the work of German Nobel Laureate Günter Grass (see Steinfeld). The non-moralizing aspect of Kertész's work is often developed when he is discussed in the context of other recent Nobel Laureates: The 2001 Nobel Laureate Gao Xingjian (see, e.g., Lee) as well as 2001 Nobel Laureate Naipul represent similar non-political and non-politicizing writing, where the task of a writer is understood as the writing of, foremost, *littérature pure*. But this understanding of writers such as Gao and Naipul is misguided when we take into account the role of media. In the media, the work of Kertész and his persona are perceived clearly as "in-between" and contrary to the status quo, and in this regard he is similar to Gao, to Naipul, to Coeetze, to Jelinek, all awardees in the last years. What the media presence of these authors shows is that while they themselves may point to the importance of a *littérature non engagée*, in the media their writing is inevitably read and discussed often in political and ideological contexts. This locus of in-between and writing contrary appears to be evident in the case of the last several Nobel Laureates. For example, Gao is not accepted as a significant writer in the People's Republic of China (and resides in France) and his Nobel elicited almost nothing but objection there, Naipul often criticizes India in many of his novels (and lives in the United Kingdom), Kertész is considered in his native country by many a non-Hungarian (and resides in Berlin and Budapest), and the 2004 recipient of the Nobel Prize in Literature, El-friede Jelinek, similarly to Kertész with regard to Hungary, criticizes Austria's re-luctance to accept responsibility for the Holocaust, has been for years practically an "enemy of the state" (and she resides in Munich and Vienna).

A further perspective in the work of Kertész discussed in the media, that of its European-ness and, more precisely, its "Central European" cultural perspec-tives, are particularly noteworthy (on Kertész's Central European cultural location, see Tötösy de Zepetnek "And the 2002 Nobel Prize" <http://clcwebjournal. lib.purdue.edu/clcweb03–1/totosy03.html>). It was in the German media where

Kertész's work and its award of the Nobel were discussed as a sign of *Wiederver-einigung* (reunification) in the context of the *Ost-Erweiterung* (expansion to the east) of the European Union (the irony of the term is of course not lost when think-ing in terms of German history) (see, e.g., Müller). At the same time, some German critics with a more than usual knowledge of Central Europe and Hungary, propose that the Nobel Prize for Kertész could or would also mean that Hungarian culture is expanding to and penetrating the West with and through the international recogni-tion of Kertész's work (see, e.g., Müller). The connection of Kertész's Nobel Prize with the May 2004 joining of Hungary with the European Union in media items would of course result in an improvement of latent cultural perceptions about "eastern" Europe.

As I already indicated previously, an important aspect of Kertész's work, as well as of the last several Nobel Prizes, is the notion of periphery and in-between-ness (there is a substantial amount of theoretical as well as applied work on the marginal and peripheral status of Central and Eastern European cultures; see Tötösy de Zepetnek, "Comparative Cultural Studies"). What is interesting with Kertész in the context of the Nobel Prize is the fact that four consecutive laure-ates—Gao, Naipaul, Kertész, and Jelinek—are all "in-between" individuals, writ-ers who live and write located in in-between cultures. This aspect of Kertész and his work has been recognized in the media. For example, critic Uwe Schmidt, in his article "Poeta laureatus. Der Literaturnobelpreisträger 2002," focuses on this specific aspect of Kertész, namely his cultural *Heimatlosigkeit*, but which is to be understood as a construct of culturality that the author has developed to exist in in-between spaces, times, and cultures (see Schmidt). This aspect of existence in-between obtains higher importance in a situation when Kertész publishes in the *Frankfurter Allgemeine Zeitung* his essay "Ich bin der Spuk." The importance of Kertész's thought in the essay—and the forum of its publication in a conservative newspaper—lies in his argumentation to deprive meaning from the cliché that the root of identity resides in the mother tongue. This is the more important because Hungarian nationalism before and now argues for the tantamount importance of language for the maintenance of national identity: "The writer of the Holocaust is, indeed, in a difficult situation. . . . that there is no language of the Holocaust and that there cannot be one. The survivor in Europe is able to tell his/her story only in a European language, yet this language is not his/her language nor is it the lan-guage of the nation from which he/she borrowed it for his/her writing" ("Der Schriftsteller des Holocaust ist also in der Tat in einer schwierigen Lage. . . . daß es für den Holocaust keine Sprache gibt und keine Sprache geben kann. Der euro-päische Überlebende kann seine Leidensgeschichte nur in irgendeiner europäi-schen Sprache erzählen, doch diese Sprache ist nicht seine Sprache und auch nicht die der Nation, von der er sich die Sprache für seine Erzählung ausgeliehen hat") (Kertész, "Ich bin der Spuk" 46).

A particularly sophisticated description of Kertész and the Nobel Prize is the article by Thomas Steinfeld in the *Süddeutsche Zeitung*, "Bescherung. Imre Kertész in Stockholm: Eine Selbstauskunft und keine." In the piece, Steinfeld analyzes Kertész's acceptance speech and presents his opinion about both the writer as a person and his texts. Interesting is that Steinfeld accords Kertész an amicable personality that is tied to an intellectual sophistication worthy of the Nobel Prize. Steinfeld also proposes that the Swedish Academy and the audience at the acceptance speech did not, really, understand Kertész or his work. Steinfeld suggests that Kertész as an individual is deeply philosophical (in the context of understanding; on this, see Friedland) about the Holocaust and his own relationship with it, while at the same time in his work he comes to provoke an opposition—his and in general—to the postmodern notion that there is an author no more. Kertész argues, instead, for knowledge understood in the experience of the Holocaust. In Steinfeld's essay, the implicit and explicit criticism of the Swedish Academy and its not-fully understanding of the significance of Kertész's oeuvre is an exception in the otherwise positive accounts of Kertész's Nobel Prize in the German-language media.

A curious situation has occurred in the German media in relation to Kertész, after and since the 2003 war in Iraq, one that demonstrates ideological fault lines within German-language media. As Kertész states in an interview in the magazine *Newsweek*, "We need to define a European identity that loves America, because Europe stands in America's debt" (Kertész qtd. in Thiel 96). Consequently, Kertész is critical of the German and French stand on the war in Iraq. For obvious reasons, namely because Germany's objection to the U.S. war on Iraq, the German media does not report explicitly Kertész's statements about his opposition to the German and French negation of U.S. policies and actions. However, his criticism did become a media issue: At a high-profile conference, *Day of German Unity: German Anti-Americanism and Eastern European Pro-Americanism*, the official federal government celebration for the "Day of German Unity" on 3 October 2003 in Magdeburg, Kertész was one of the keynote speakers, where he objected to and criticized the German stand strenuously. In the *Frankfurter Allgemeine Zeitung* Kertész's views were described as follows: "Kertész complained about Europe's division over the Iraq War. It presumably reverted 'back to its old structures.' Suddenly the Iraqi dictator was able to let us forget who was a friend and who was an enemy. It came to 'ridiculous verbal battles' between supporters and opponents of the war. Kertész referred in this context to the fact that the Eastern European countries stood on the side of the United States and Great Britain. Poles and the Czechs were better able to remember Munich (1938) than most Western Europeans. Kertész also said that the fight against terrorism was a fight between good and evil, one that is just as important for Europe as it is for America, with, in his view, pacifism. Pacifism no answer to the challenge of terrorism, either" ("Tag der deutschen Einheit" 3). David Kaspar analyzes the response to Kertész in the German media thus: "Imre Kertész's criticism of Germany's Iraq policy is quoted by the German media, but not emphasized, and instead hidden in the texts of longer descriptions of the event. It is interesting to note that not a German publication, but the Swiss *Neue Zürcher Zeitung* printed the full speech of Imre Kertész. In contrast, U.S.-American critics of President George W. Bush such as Michael Moore or Susan Sontag can usually easily publish in German newspapers and magazines" (Kaspar <http://medienkritik. typepad.com/blog/netzeitung/>). I should like to note here that while the tone and amount of U.S.-American critical discussions of U.S. government decisions in U.S.-American media right after 9/11 and right after the 2003 invasion of Iraq suggest self-censorship of the U.S.-American media, in both instances this self-censorship has given way to the appearance of a large number of pro- and con-views, which can be seen, for example, in any issue of any day of the *New York Times* or the *Washington Post*. In contrast, in Germany, where Kertész's views have been always given ample latitude and exposure in the media, his view with regard to the 2003 Iraq war was given no attention beyond a few lines in the *Frankfurter Allgemeine Zeitung*. What this suggests is that in Germany, while cultural, historical, sociological, etc., as well as public discourse about and on the Holocaust are a given, this standard is not allowed to extend to a matter concerning current public opinion, such as the 2003 Iraq war. In other words, while there are instances of self-censorship in current U.S.-American media, the same can be observed in German media. Obviously, these occurrences of limitations, while they do not pose a threat to free speech, do pose serious questions about the power of media when it selects and self-censors matters not deemed appropriate in a climate of divided public opinion.

Overall, my reading of the media response to Kertész's Nobel Prize in German-language print media is that his texts and the Nobel Prize are described with sophistication and more than the usual knowledge about Central Europe and Hungary. As a result, the media response to Kertész's Nobel Prize represents critics' and the public's continued interest in the author's work and underlines the importance of his work in the contexts of literature, ideology and history. While this importance is understandably in the context of Germany's attention to matters relating to the Holocaust, tangential attention in the media, such as with regard to the eastward expansion of the European Union, the question of committed literature versus literature for the sake of literature, or the question of in-between-ness as a postmodern condition suggest a social and political impact of Kertész and the Nobel Prize that is duly registered in German media discourse. As to the problematic of my interpretation with regard to the media reception of the Nobel Prize in Hungary, the German media appears to be unawares of the blatant anti-Semitic discourse in Hungary. To my knowledge, the first item about this appeared in the weekly *Die Zeit* in its 3 June 2004 issue, with an article entitled "Die versteckten Juden," with the explanatory paragraph below the title of the article: "Hungary is home of the fourth largest community of Jews in Europe. With the freedom came a newly acquired self assurance in the younger generation. Yet, if someone confesses to his/her Jewish faith, risks still today being vilified" ("Ungarn ist die Heimat der viertgrößten jüdischen Gemeide in Europa. Mit der Freiheit ist ein neues Selbstbewusstsein in der jungen Generation erwacht. Doch wer sich zu seinem Glauben bekannt, riskiert auch heute noch, angepöbelt zu werden") (Schneider 15). While the attention to the situation of Hungarian Jews in *Die Zeit* is clearly an important step for the recognition of the matter in Hungary, in my opinion the article itself is of a very tentative and accommodating tone. That is, the author of the article, Richard Chaim Schneider, while exploring some of the issues, does not appear to be aware of the seriousness of anti-Semitism and its discourse in the country. And, overall, the same can be stated about the U.S.-American and Canadian media and their lack of attention to the situation in Hungary.

U.S.-American media reacted to the Nobel Prize in Literature awarded to Kertész similarly to the situation when Polish poet Wislawa Szymborska received the 1996 Nobel in Literature, with a resolute "Who?" The title of Stephen Kinzer's review, "America Yawns at Foreign Fiction" in the *New York Times*, says it all. Kinzer's review of the situation of foreign authors, gauged on the echo of Kertész's Nobel, is interesting also from a statistical point of view. Kinzer writes that "Readers in other developed countries still have appetites for translated literature. German publishers, for example, bought translation rights to 3,782 American books in 2002, while American publishers bought rights for only 150 books" (A1). And the media response was no different in Canada. In addition to the marked non-interest of the general public in foreign literature, critics whose interests would perhaps include the promotion of translated works are few. The reviews of Kertész after he received the Nobel show this clearly: Of the few reviews published in the U.S.-American and Canadian media, most were by critics of Hungarian descent, such as the Columbia professor emeritus István Deák, who published an extended review of Kertész and his work in the *New York Review of Book*, or George Szirtes, who published the review "Nobel Laureate Who?" in the journal *Maisonneuve: Eclectic Curiosity*. While Kertész was an unknown writer even among scholars of literature, let alone to the general public in Canada and in the U.S. before and when he received the Nobel, since then the moderate interest generated by the Nobel Prize has ebbed to a barely noticeable trickle and remains perhaps only among scholars interested in Holocaust literature (and where this interest includes Hungarian-language primary texts; the call for papers for the present volume on Kertész's work in the *PMLA: Publications of the Modern Language Association of America* and on several listserves resulted in moderate interest on the English-language landscape of scholarship: it would be unthinkable, in another case, to receive in total twenty-one papers for a volume on a Nobel Prize winner).

In my opinion, among the very few items in U.S.-American print media on Kertész's Nobel, it is Stefan Thiel's one-page interview with Kertész, "A Voice of Conscience" in *Newsweek* that is the most comprehensive. Of particular interest to me is Thiel's question to Kertész about the currency of terrorism and the divergence of Europe and the U.S. As introduced above, Kertész's response is one of mitigation between the two opposing positions—and the Thiel interview took place before the invasion of Iraq—where Kertész says: "We need to define a European identity that loves America, because Europe stands in America's debt" and continues with a clear and forceful warning that "We [Europeans] might be growing back together economically, but there are a lot of psychological traumas we haven't dealt with. The old nationalisms that exploded in the Balkan wars are a example of that. And Eastern Europe doesn't trust the EU, which waited much too long after 1989 to reach out. Back then we were all enthusiastic about a reunited Europe, and what happened? Instead we all watched powerlessly as Europe let genocide happen once again" (Kertész qtd. in Thiel 96). I read Kertész in in Thiel's interview as Kertész's indictment of Europe, based on his epistemological, psychological, and historical understanding of western modernity as an era of totalitarian horrors and on his understanding and verdict about the response to these horrors by the United States. Together with his view that "let's not forget that America is built upon the most beautiful of Europe's ideals," Kertész as a writer and here as a public intellectual expressing hi views in the press comes through with a powerful message both Europe and the U.S.—policy makers as well as the public—could or ought to appropriate. Here, the medium is not only the message but the message is content without the medium. . . .

In my selection of items from the Hungarian press I focus on pro-Kertész items because of the context and contexts the award in which his work is discussed and because anti-Kertész items are of lesser interest, owing to their undifferentiated and blatantly anti-Semitic and/or conservative nationalist ideologies (although, at the same time, these items are of course most important because of their existence per se; on the aspects of the conservative-nationalist and anti-Semitic reception of Kertész's Nobel, see Marsovszky; Young). As I suggested previously, although publications—either in content or with regard to their numbers—of anti-Kertész items in Hungary did not reach and did not gather interest in German- or English-language media, what these items suggest is that anti-Semitism in Hungary exists to an unacceptable level today (see Marsovszky; Young). In the context of Hungary's joining the European Union in 2004, the level of anti-Semitism that in public discourse in the media in Hungary ought receive due attention as an ominous situation that is unacceptable: In my view, the reception of the Kertész's Nobel Prize in the Hungarian media—pro and con—becomes a matter of importance for the European Union, de facto (and perhaps even de jure). Overall, the reception of the award in the Hungarian press is complicated to gauge because of the social and intellectual self-divide, increasingly so in the last several years, of the country into pro- and anti-Semitism that is played out in full force in the media (for a positive item in the Hungarian media, see also Bőhm, Vári, Koltai, and Várnai; with regard to the situation of populist right-wing matters in Central and Eastern Europe, see Chiantera-Stutte and Pető; in Hungary see Marsovszky; Young).

In Hungarian media, Gáspár Miklós Tamás's article "Kertész Imre magyar író Nobel-díjas. Zsidó" ("Hungarian Writer Imre Kertész, Jew, Receives the Nobel Prize") published in the daily *Magyar Hírlap* on 11 October 2002—one day after the announcement of the prize by the Swedish Academy—was the first article in the war of words and ideologies. Tamás (a well-known liberal philosopher and, since 2004, a representative of Hungary in the European Parliament) predicted in his article the coming onslaught of a national debate, which has played out and is still playing out two years after the award in Hungarian media. In newspapers and magazines with right-of-center or outright right-wing ideologies the award received brief but scathing criticism, as George Szirtes states laconically, "The political resonance of Kertész's prize is shown by the way parts of the Hungarian press have treated it. Although the distinction of the Nobel Prize had long been sought and might have been wildly welcomed as an overdue recognition of Hungarian writing, the main nationalistic right-wing paper reduced the news to a paragraph" (Szirtes <http://www.maisonneuve.org/print_article.php?article_id=88>). Indeed, media resonance in Hungary to Kertész's Nobel has been controversial and divided along ideological lines (for discussions on the current situation of nationalism and anti-Semitism in Hungary, see, e.g., Gerő, Varga, and Vince; Ozsváth; Suleiman; Tötösy de Zepetnek "And the 2002"; and the already referred to studies by Marsovszky; Young). The dividing lines are of course not simple but multi-level and multi-voiced, although I propose that in the anti-Kertész camp there are two—at times overlapping and coinciding, at times not—ideologies: one that is anti-Semitic of the first order and the other that is nationalistic in the best tradition of Hungarian self-referentiality, where the concept of and adherence to nation is understood as a co-referent of language, including literature. Here is one example: "*Fatelessness* is the work of a genius. Only, it is not Hungarian. Which is a problem, because Nobel Prize recipient Imre Kertész receives the Prize. In turn, for the literary canon this means that now he is the greatest Hungarian writer. He, who does not consider himself Hungarian" ("A *Sorstalanság* zseniális alkotás. Csak nem magyar. Ami azért baj, mert Kertész Imre nobeldíjas kap díjat. És ez a kánon szempontjából aztat jelenti, hogy mostantól Ő a legnagyobb magyar iró. Ő, aki nem tartja magát magyarnak") (Waltraute qtd. in Székely 7). The essentialist equation nation = culture, and, in the case of Hungary, nation = language & literature (this goes back to one of the greatest figures of Hungarian history, the nineteenth-century aristocrat István Széchenyi, who coined "it is in its language where the nation exists" ["nyelvében él a nemzet"], a credo of Hungarian nationalism ever since) has proponents also among pro-Kertész critics (see, e.g., Pallagi), although there are others who consider the award to be that of/for Kertész in the first instance and to be that of/for literature in the second, and then with the addition of "Hungarian" only as a last and accidental instance (see Bánó). Of course, the problem and unsavory in the opinion by the e-mail correspondent "Waltraute" is the blanket assumption that Kertész himself would claim that he is not Hungarian and the correspondent's belief that a Hungarian can be of one type only. Unfortunately, this belief is shared by a substantial number of the population in today's Hungary.

In my opinion, an important item is the article "Az eredendő történelmi bün" ("The Original Sin of History") in the culture magazine *Kritika* by Ákos Szilágy, who reads Kertész not as a Holocaust author but as an author of a post-Holocaust world which, in turn, is impregnated by and is based on the Holocaust understood as the human condition of modernity (as does Kertész himself). Szilágyi reads Kertész's texts as an interpretation of this human condition, the "mythology of nothingness" ("a semmi mitosza") as represented by the Holocaust (Szilágyi 7). And the world can exist only as a livable world if we recognize the universality of the Holocaust. Whether this view and opinion is in contradiction to the in many quarters accepted opinion that the Holocaust is unique in the history of humanity remains an open question, and further analysis of the Nobel Laureate's work is needed to come to an understanding of this problematic. Nevertheless, Szilágyi's analysis of Kertész's texts underlines what I propose to be the importance of the media reception of Kertész's works and the Nobel Prize, namely that Kertész and his work are unique because, despite their author's insistence on non-engagement, his merit is, precisely, the results of public discourse in the media about the un-speakability of the Holocaust in an innovative and until now un-explored way. This is the case especially in comparison with the majority of authors who write in fiction, in documentary, in autobiography, or in fictional autobiography, or who write about the Holocaust in the second generation of Holocaust victims or survivors. A further consequence of this public discourse in the media is the importance of the process from author to public intellectual per se, thus demonstrating the "power" of the media. Despite itself, there is poetry after the Holocaust, and Kertész shows us how in a new and innovative ways. Kertész's work is thus significant and needed not only as a text of literary, cultural, and social relevance, in the study of literature and culture, in Holocaust studies, and in history: His work is an eternal mark in Western culture, along with Wiesel, Lévi, Borowski, Nyiszli, Ember, Frank, (the just discovered) Némirovsky, and so many others.

Works Cited

Adorján, Johanna, and Nils Minkmar. "Liebe ist das Wichtigste." *Frankfurter Allge-meine Sonntagszeitung* (13 Oktober 2002): 21.

Bánó, András. "Kié az elismerés?" *Blikk* (12 October 2002):

Bittner, Jochen. "Deutschland: Wo jeder sich vor jedem fürchtet." *Die Zeit* 46 (7 November 2002): 10–11.

Bőhm, Ágnes, György Vári, Nelli Koltai, and Pál Várnai. "Köszöntjük a Nobel-Díjas Kertész Imrét!" ("We Congratulate the Nobel Laureate Imre Kertész!"). *Szombat* 10 (2002): 5–17.

Chiantera-Stutte, Patricia, and Andrea Pető. "Cultures of Populism and the Political Right in Central Europe." *CLCWeb: Comparative Literature and Culture* 5.3 (2003): <http://clcwebjournal.lib.purdue.edu/chiantera&peto03.html>.

Deák, István. "Stranger in Hell." *New York Review of Books* (25 September 2003): 65–67.

Felman, Shoshana. "Camus' *The Plague*, or a Moment to Witnessing." *Testimony: Crises of Witnessing in Literature, Psychoanalysis, and History*. Ed. Shoshana Felman and Dori Laub. New York: Routledge, 1992. 93–119.

Friedland, Amos. "Imre Kertész, Hegel, and the Philosophy of Reconciliation." *Imre Kertész and Holocaust Literature*. Ed. Louise O. Vasvári and Steven Tötösy de Zepetnek. West Lafayette: Purdue UP, 2005. 51–64.

Gerő, András, László Varga, and Mátyás Vince. *Anti-Semitic Discourse in Hungary in 2000*. Budapest: B'nai B'rith, 2001.

Gerő, András, László Varga, and Mátyás Vince. *Anti-Semitic Discourse in Hungary in 2001*. Budapest: B'nai B'rith, 2002.

H., Gy.-T.K. "Kelendőek lettek a Kertész-könyvek" ("Kertész Books Have Become Sought After"). *Napi Gazdaság* (11 Oktober 2002).

Kaspar, David. "German Media Reject Charge of Anti-Americanism/ Deutsche Medien weisen Vorwurf des Anti-Amerikanismus zurück." *Davids Medienkritik* (2004): <http://medienkritik.typepad.com/blog/netzeitung/>.

Kertész, Imre. *Fatelessness*. Trans. Tim Wilkinson. New York: Vintage, 2004.

Kertész, Imre. "Ich bin der Spuk." Trans. Kristin Schwamm. *Frankfurter Allgemeine Zeitung* 62 (14 March 2002): 46.

Kinzer, Stephen. "America Yawns at Foreign Fiction." *The New York Times* (26 July 2003): A17–19.

Lee, Mabel. "Nobel in Literature 2000 Gao Xingjian's Aesthetics of Fleeing." *CLCWeb: Comparative Literature and Culture* 5.1 (2003): <http://clcwebjournal.lib.purdue.edu/clcweb03–1/lee03.html>.

Marsovszky, Magdalena. "Imre Kertész and Hungary Today." *Imre Kertész and Holocaust Literature*. Ed. Louise O. Vasvári and Steven Tötösy de Zepetnek. West Lafayette: Purdue UP, 2005. 148–61.

Marsovszky, Magdalena. "Imre Kertész—einer von uns! Oder doch nicht? Kulturkampf und Identität in Ungarn." *Europas Mitte, Mitteleuropa, europäische Identität? Geschichte, Literatur, Positionen*. Ed. Barbara Breisach and Dorothee Rabe. Berlin: Logos, 2003. 137–53.

Marsovszky, Magdalena. "Der Antisemitismus in Ungarn. Nur Polit-Folklore?" *ha-Galil.com: Culture & News from Central Europe* (2002): <http://antisemitismus.juden-in-europa.de/osteuropa/ungarn.htm>.

Müller, Lothar. "Eine Wiedervereinigung." *Süddeutsche Zeitung* (*Feuilleton*) (12–13 October 2002): 11.

Némirovsky, Irène. *Suite française*. Paris: Denoël, 2004.

Nobel Prize in Literature, The: Laureates (2002): <http://www.nobel.se/literature/laureates/index.html>.

Ozsváth , Zsuzsanna. "Radnóti, Celan, and the Aesthetic Shifts in Central European Holocaust Poetry." *Comparative Central European Culture.* Ed. Steven Tötösy de Zepetnek. West Lafayette: Purdue UP, 2002. 51–69.

Pallagi, Ferenc. "Tizezer perc" ("Ten Thousand Minutes"). *Tallózó* (17 October 2002): 2726.

Radisch, Iris. "Die Glückskatastrophe. ZEIT-Gespräch mit dem Nobelpresisträger Imre Kertész über Berlin, den Antisemitismus, das Geld und die Erlösung." *Die Zeit* 43 (17 Oktober 2002): 45–46.

Schmidt, Uwe. "Poeta laureatus." *Thalia LiteraTouren Thalia Bücher* (2002): n.p.

Schneider, Richard Chaim. "Die versteckten Juden." *Die Zeit* (3 June 2004): 15–18.

Steinfeld, Thomas. "Ein Steinchen für Sisyphos." *Süddeutsche Zeitung (Feuilleton)* (11 October 2002).

Steinfeld, Thomas. "Bescherung." *Süddeutsche Zeitung (Feuilleton)* (9 Oktober 2002): 18.

Suleiman, Susan Rubin. "Central Europe, Jewish Family History, and *Sunshine.*" *Comparative Central European Culture.* Ed. Steven Tötösy de Zepetnek. West Lafayette: Purdue UP, 2002. 169–88.

Szilágyi, Ákos. "Az eredendő történelmi bün" ("The Original Sin of History"). *Kritika* (February 2003): 4–8.

Székely, R. Julianna. "A *Sorstalanság.* . . . Így írunk mi. (Idézetek az internetről)" ("*Fateless.* . . . And Thus We Write. [Quotations from the Internet]"). *Vasárnapi Hírek* (13 October 2002): 7.

Szirtes, George. "Nobel Laureate Who?" *Maisonneuve: Eclectic Curiosity* 3 (2003): <http://www.maisonneuve.org/print_article.php?article_id=88>).

"Tag der deutschen Einheit." *Frankfurter Allgemeine Zeitung* (4 October 2003): 3.

Tamás, Gáspár Miklós. "Kertész Imre magyar író Nobel-díjas. Zsidó" ("Hungarian Writer Imre Kertész, Jew, Receives the Nobel Prize"). *Magyar Hírlap* (11 October 2002): <http://www.magyarhirlap.hu/Archivum_cikk.php?cikk=57200&archiv=1&next=60>.

Taterka, Thomas. *Dante Deutsch. Studien zur Lagerliteratur.* Berlin: Erich Schmidt, 1999.

Thiel, Stefan. "A Voice of Conscience." *Newsweek* (6 January 2003): 96.

Tötösy de Zepetnek, Steven. *Comparative Literature: Theory, Method, Application.* Amsterdam: Rodopi, 1998.

Tötösy de Zepetnek, Steven. "Comparative Cultural Studies and the Study of Central European Culture." *Comparative Central European Culture.* Ed. Steven Tötösy de Zepetnek. West Lafayette: Purdue UP, 2002. 1–32.

Tötösy de Zepetnek, Steven. "And the 2002 Nobel Prize for Literature Goes to Imre Kertész, Jew and Hungarian." *CLCWeb: Comparative Literature and Culture* 5.1 (2003): <http://clcwebjournal.lib.purdue.edu/clcweb03–1/totosy03.html>.

Young, Judy. "The Media and Imre Kertész's Nobel Prize in Literature." *Imre Kertész and Holocaust Literature*. Ed. Louise O. Vasvári and Steven Tötösy de Zepetnek. West Lafayette: Purdue UP, 2005. 271–85.

Holocaust Literature and Imre Kertész

Paul Várnai

In order to place Imre Kertész's novel *Sorstalanság* (*Fatelessness*) in a comparative cultural context, I discuss briefly representative Hungarian and foreign works dealing with the Holocaust. Anna Frank's diary entry for Friday, 31 March 1944, reads: "Hungary is occupied by German troops. There are still a million Jews there. So they, too, will have had it" ("A német csapatok megszállták Magyarországot. Ott még egymillió zsidó él. Most aztán ők is sorra kerülnek") (187; I am quoting in all cases from the Hungarian; all subsequent translations from the Hungarian are mine, unless noted otherwise). Primo Lévi notes in his book *Survival in Auschwitz:* "Throughout the Spring convoys arrived from Hungary. One prisoner in two was Hungarian and Hungarian had become the second language in the camp after Yiddish" (l06). In his introduction to Tadeusz Borowski's *This Way to the Gas, Ladies and Gentlemen*, Jan Kott, the noted author of *Shakespeare: Our Contemporary*, comments: "At Auschwitz this was the most dreadful time. In May and June of 1944 more than four hundred thousand Jews from Hungary were gassed and burned" (Borowski 16). These are but a few examples of foreign works recording the predicament of Hungarian Jews (on Jewish-Hungarian history and on the history of the Hungarian Holocaust, see, e.g., Braham; Gerő; Kovács; Ozsváth; Suleiman). And Hungarian author György Moldova writes: "I didn't expect Horthy to put on the yellow star as did the king of Denmark, nor an expression of solidarity on the part of the government and the clergy as in Bulgaria. Yet, the way Hungarians deported 400,000 Jews from the countryside within a few weeks is certainly a world record" ("Nem vártam, hogy Horthy feltegye a sárga csillagot, mint ahogy feltette a dán király, vagy a főpapság és a kormány álljon ki értünk, mint Bulgáriaban, de ahogy a magyarok négyszázezer vidéki zsidót néhány hét alatt deportáltak, az mindenesetre világrekord") (65).

The destruction of much of Hungarian Jewry was particularly tragic as it took place in the last stages of war, when, with their limited resources, the Germans, more determined to complete the final solution than to win the war, would not have been able to carry out their mission without the help of the more than willing Hungarian authorities. This was the time when the Allies, in their concentration to achieve speedy victory, made little effort either to bomb the camps or slow down the advance of cattle cars, which, Béla Zsolt, author of *Kilenc koffer* (Nine

Suitcases) described as "The means of transportation tailored to my generation" ("A generációm testére szabott közlekedési eszköz") (60). In his article "A magyar holokauszt" ("The Hungarian Holocaust"), historian György Ránki singles out "sorstalanság" ("fatelessness") as Hungarian Jewry's particular tragedy. While "in Western Europe Jews have been able to share the fate of their nations, and those of Eastern Europe have interpreted their persecution as a fulfilment of some sort of a Jewish fate" ("A nyugat-európai izraeliták nemzetük sorsában osztoztak, a kelet-európaiak pedig úgy vélhették, üldöztetésükben valamiféle örök zsidó sors teljesedett be") (7), Hungarian Jews found themselves in the middle. Having shared Hungarian destiny consciously, they have only been deprived of it, concludes Ránki, by "the brutality of the Hungarian authorities and gendarmery" ("a magyar hatóságok, csendőrök brutalitása") (7). In more fortunate lands, Ránki argues further, the safeguarding of the country's independence coincided with democracy and the protection of human rights (on Ránki and the debate about the Hungarian Holocaust, see Kovács).

Among the works published shortly after the war on the subject of Auschwitz, at least two received international recognition. In his book *The Informed Heart*, Bruno Bettelheim makes reference to Olga Lengyel's *Five Chimneys*, and Miklós Nyiszli's *Auschwitz: A Doctor's Eyewitness Account* is a unique document written by Mengele's "assistant" about medical experiments performed on children. A recent U.S.-American film adaptation of Nyiszli's book bears the title *The Grey Zone*. In his 1991 public lecture "Hosszú sötét árnyék" ("Long Dark Shadow"), Kertész speculates on why Communist dictatorships played down the importance of the Holocaust. In fact, he says, it was only in those years he fully understood Auschwitz, for totalitarian regimes operate by the same mechanisms. And in a recent interview Kertész states that he wrote his novel *Fatelessness* about the Kádár regime, the more moderate Communist period between 1956–1988 (see Rádai). *A kudarc* (The Failure), another novel he wrote, is doubtlessly about the Kádár regime, but *Fatelessness?* Repressive as it was, "the best barrack in Eastern Europe" is not Auschwitz, and Kertész, as he repeatedly stated, wrote about a fifteen-year-old boy in the concentration camp. Following three decades of silence, Hungarian works of fiction staged a significant comeback in the 1970s. By then the children of yesterday had come of age. The works are often autobiographical, narrated from the fresh perspective of a child, combined with the more analytical viewpoint of the adult author. *Első évtized* (First Decade) by Pál Bárdos and *Hajtű-kanyar* (Hairpin Bend) by Mária Ember relate the deportation of some 22,000 Jews to Austria—the lucky exception to Auschwitz. Ember's much quoted motto: "The subject of this book is not Jewish destiny. What this book tells about is Hungarian history" ("Ennek a könyvnek a tárgya nem a zsidó sors. Amit ez a könyv elbeszél, az magyar történelem") (5) suggests, among other things, that the author intends to address the broader questions of the place of Jews in Hungary's past and present. Furthermore, what happened to Hungarian Jews in 1944 is not solely a Jewish issue. Alas, it still is, to a large extent: Gracia Kerényi (eminent mythologist Karl Kerényi's daughter, writer and translator of Polish), herself a survivor, told me once: "To Poles, Auschwitz is a Polish problem, to Hungarians, it is a Jewish problem." These and some other works of the period raise many relevant questions belonging more to history, sociology, and politics than to literature.

In *Terelőút* (Detour) by György Gera, the narrator returns to the Austrian village where he was once interned, decades later, and the indifference and hostility of the locals exasperates the returnee. (There is a similar theme in Kertész's short novel *Nyomkereső* [The Pathfinder], whose narrator vainly seeks a mass grave to find the body of his father, massacred in the area by the Nazis. He also deals with this episode in his book *Valaki más* [Someone Else].) *Elysium* by Imre Keszi is a moving novel about a ten-year-old boy in Auschwitz, modeled allegedly on the son of the eminent musicologist Bence Szabolcsi. Owing to his gymnastic skills and dexterity, Gyuri is selected for experiments. The camp, a world of make-believe, is organized rationally: good behavior is rewarded while disobedience is punished; only the existence of the camp is irrational.

While the relatively liberal climate of the 1970s produced little that was truly outstanding on the subject, the above works nonetheless kept the memory of the Holocaust alive. They were essentially anti-fascist, sentimental works, ending with liberation, conforming to the norms of the regime, and hence, they enjoyed certain popularity, while Kertész's novel, published in the same period, received little attention. The subject proved inexhaustible. In recent years, György Konrád, Mária Ember, László Márton, and Teréz Mózes, to mention but a few, produced more works about Jewish childhood and adult experience in 1944. I wish to single out *Elindulás és hazatérés* (Departure and Return) by György Konrád, where the author revisits his birthplace and recalls his miraculous survival at age eleven, as well as the novel *2000-ben fogunk-e még élni?* (Will We Be Still Alive in the Year 2000?) by Maria Ember, in which she remembers her childhood in the Hungarian provinces and relates the story of her deportation in 1944. Although I do not discuss poetry here, I should like to mention that the poetry of Ágnes Gergely, Magda Székely, and András Mezei on the subject is truly outstanding.

Among the vast number of prominent works written on the Holocaust outside of Hungary I would mention the unique diary of Etty Hillesum in Holland, *Interrupted Life,* and *Le Grand voyage* by Jorge Semprún in France, the prose of Ladislav Fuks and Arnost Lustig in Czechoslovakia, *Painted Bird* by the Polish-American Jerzy Kosinski, *Badenheim 39* by the Czernovitz-born Israeli Aharon Appelfeld, the poetry of Paul Celan (also from Czernovitz), Elie Wiesel's *Night*, and *Last of the Just* by André Schwarzbart in France. Kertész himself holds that only a handful writers were able to create lasting works about the Holocaust, and for him these include Paul Celan, Primo Lévi, Tadeusz Borowski, and the philosopher Jean Améry. They succeeded, he claims, because they found a new, valid, post-Auschwitz language (*A száműzött nyelv* 280–81). Borowski's *This Way to the*

Gas is likely the most compelling book of all. The author calls his work "a voyage to the limit of a particular experience" (25). In Borowski's Auschwitz stories, the difference between executioner and victim is reduced to a second bowl of soup, an extra blanket" (23). The unquestionable classic of Holocaust literature, Primo Lévi, wrote his text with great simplicity and objectivity. His insight into the psychology of human behavior is considerable. Himself a scientist, Lévi views the camp as a "pre-eminently gigantic biological and social experiment" where inmates are divided into the opposing groups of the saved and the drowned (79); and "Nowhere is man as polarized as in the camp," where "everyone is desperately and ferociously alone" (80) This desperate aloneness, especially of the intellectual, is among the subjects treated by Améry. His views—he is both a political and a Jewish survivor—are among the most tragic and bitter among the survivors. He fears that time will reject, discard the survivor's experience; it is he who will be a nuisance to the indifferent world, as Kertész puts it, "the unpacifyable and incorrigible reactionary" ("az igazi javíthatatlanok és megbékélhetetlenek") (*A száműzött nyelv* 78).

Kertész worked on *Sorstalanság* for thirteen years. Delayed by five years owing to its rejection, the novel was published finally in a censored form in 1975. Critical and public reception was modest until the writer György Spiró wrote an article in the journal *Élet és Irodalom* in 1983, creating some interest in intellectual circles. It is the kind of book, argued Spiró, which, "at first, goes unnoticed, yet, its value will increase in time. It offers something else that the reader is unused to, something essential, existential, hitherto nonexistent philosophical views" ("mű, amelyik nem kelt visszhangot ám értéke egyre nő, valami mást kapunk, többet mint szokványos regénytől, valami lényegit, egzisztenciálisat, még nem volt lét-filozófiát") (5). Nearly three decades later, the philosopher Ágnes Heller could justly call the novel "the only perfectly authentic, genuine Holocaust novel" ("ez az egyetlen tökéletesen autentikus holocaustregény") (6).

In his novels and essays Kertész uses repeatedly the notion of "idegenség" ("otherness"), a feeling of being an outsider, an exile. It is not surprising that affinities with Camus's *L'Étranger* or Franz Kafka have been noted (see, e.g., Koltai; Vasvári). This "életidegenség" (an otherness also in the context of alienation of life), did not originate with the concentration camp. In *A száműzött nyelv*, Kertész writes that in his childhood "my feeling was that I . . . was participant in a general, big lie, but that this lie is the truth and it is only my fault that I perceive it to be a lie" ("Az volt az érzésem, hogy valamilyen általános, nagy hazugság része vagyok, de hogy ez a hazugság az igazság, s csak az én bűnöm, hogy hazugságnak érzem") (278). This experience, as he realized later, was a protest against the semi-fascistic climate of the 1930s, which expected him to accept this personal menace as a normal fate. His whole education, the system of values he was brought up on, encouraged self-denial and obedience, slowly preparing him for extinction. In *Gályanapló* (Galley Boat-Log) he admits: "I hated my childhood, experienced my youth

(Nietzsche) as an 'illness'" ("Gyűlöltem gyermekkoromat, az ifjúságot (Nietzsche) 'betegségként' éltem át") (140). His family circumstances were equally unfavorable: he had an authoritarian and demanding father (here parallel can be found with Kafka's *Letter to His Father* and the son-father relationship in Károly Pap's *Azarel*, presently receiving world-wide recognition), and the time spent at a boarding school only furthered and confirmed his alienation.

Sorstalanság is a *Bildungsroman*, about growing up, of coming to awareness, and, in a way, an existential novel. The first sentence says it all: "Today I didn't go to school" ("Ma nem mentem iskolába") (7). His father is called up for forced labor and Uncle Lajos, a somewhat pretentious relative, assumes the dubious role of enlightening the youth: "The carefree, happy years of childhood are over" ("A gondtalan, boldog gyermekéveknek vége") (20), Gyuri (George) is told. Now he will be the head of the family and, most importantly, he will be part of the "common Jewish fate" ("a közös, zsidó sors részese") (20), a fate that "Jews must accept with submission and patience" ("zsidóknak belenyugvással és türelemmel kell fogadniok") (20), for it comes from God for their sins. While Gyuri is doing his best to digest all of this, it nonetheless goes a bit over his head. He cannot understand, for instance, what sins the uncle is talking about. In another conversation with a young girl acquaintance, Gyuri argues that Jews do not have any specific quality that sets them apart from Gentiles. What makes them different is that now they have to wear a yellow star. Short of that, their whole suffering lacks meaning. When the time comes to say goodbye to his father, the boy, as is common at his age, is ill at ease in expressing his feelings. He feels strange, alienated in his own family, trying, but does not know how to meet the expectations of adults around him, all of whom are treated with irony. Gyuri retains his distance and objectivity even when he himself is arrested, relating his experiences matter-of-factly and, at the same time, naively: "Next day a strange thing happened to me" ("Másnap egy kissé furcsa esetem volt") (35), one understatement of the many in this novel. On his way to work he is taken off the bus, along with other Jewish boys, by a policeman. When he joins the others, they all seem cheerful. From this point on, until much later, the protagonist accepts these unusual occurrences as normal, without the slightest surprise, indignation, or protest. In the world of the absurd, everything is normal, natural. His terse remarks, objectivity, adaptability, and cheerful disposition only stress the incongruity between reality and appearances. Captivity is accepted as merely "unusual." They are taken to a custom's house, then to a brick factory: "The policeman was content" ("A rendőr elégedettnek látszott"), and Gyuri could see immediately that "he had nothing against us" ("nincs ellenünk kifogása") (36), things appeared "acceptable." Presenting the story from the viewpoint of a perfectly naive and unassuming adolescent, without a definite set of values, makes events seem even worse: reality appears in a distorted mirror. When the gendarmerie takes over, at their rougher treatment Gyuri "felt like laughing . . . also with the passing thought that flew through my imagination, and this was the face of my stepmother when she realizes that tonight I would not show up for sup-per" ("nevethetnékem volt kissé . . . egy futó gondolattól is, ami éppen hogy átsu-hant a képzeletemen: s ez mostohaanyám arca volt, amikor ráeszmel majd, hogy ma este már bizony hiába számit rám a vacsorával") (49–50). When offered the op-tion of signing up for work, Gyuri is enthusiastic: he expects a life of order, activ-ity, new impressions, even fun, a way of life to his liking, an opportunity to see the world, all of which sounds like going on a picnic.When one of the boys steals away, Gyuri is surprised: "I saw no reason to escape" ("okot nem láttam rá, hogy elinaljak") (48), he comments. Besides, his "honesty" would not let him. Here we see an example of how concepts of the normal world are applied to the abnormal, making it ironic and grotesque. A rabbi, also deported, turns up among them, an-other authority figure, advocating again resignation, and reiterating the belief in the "Jewish fate," the issue Gyuri is contending with throughout the novel.

Being accustomed to descriptions of cruelty, moralizing, and sentimentality, the reader is struck by the low-key, uninvolved recounting of experiences. The cat-tle car is hugely overcrowded, but the boy is content that they are well-settled. In-human conditions are accepted as "normal" and "natural," key words in this book. Lack of water is, of course, a problem, and when an old woman dies of thirst Gyuri is quick to explain: "it is understandable, after all, she was old and sick" ("beteg meg öreg is volt, magam is érthetőnek találtam") (63). His earnestness leans to-wards the grotesque: the uncertainty of how long the train ride will take worries him: "They did not let us know at the brick factory" ("a téglagyárban nem tudat-ták") (50), he states matter-of-factly. When the station with the sign "Auschwitz-Birkenau" shows up, Gyuri notes dryly that he never studied about the place in geog-raphy. Once off the train, his first impressions are those of a Gulliver in Auschwitz. He mistakes the striped-outfitted Jews (Häftling-s) for common criminals. The manner in which he describes their lamentable appearance is reminiscent of Nazi cartoons. Here is the underdog's well-known identification with the oppressor: see-ing himself through their eyes, stereotyped: "they seemed Jewish in every way" ("csakugyan, zsidóknak látszottak, minden tekintetben") (66), concludes Gyuri, and, given his Hungarian middle-class prejudices, he probably means it. Their look inspires little confidence. He is almost reassured when, in contrast, he catches sight of the neat, well-kept Germans, radiating calm, corresponding to their previous im-age of being honest, orderly, punctual, and hard-working. He is surprised, how-ever, to notice sticks hanging at their sides that, at a closer look, turn out to be whips. His logic helps again: "after all, there are many convicts among us" ("meg aztán elvégre sok a fegyenc is körülöttünk, beláttam") (71). The infamous doctor Mengele is seen as appealing, with a good appearance, kind eyes and a soft, clear, cultivated voice, inspiring immediate confidence in the boy. Through their eyes the Jews, indeed, must have made a pitiful impression. Of course, there was a contrast not only between Germans and Jews but between German appearance and their true character. Consistent with his distorted logic, it is the Jews Gyuri finds fault with: they "embarrass" him, ask too many questions, do not seem to understand what is expected of them, are undisciplined, a "nuisance" in every way. On the whole, they are "sort of foreign" ("idegenszerűek") (66). His hero (or rather anti-hero) only gradually loses his fate. At this point he is still grateful for small mercies: the sight of a soccer field fills him with enthusiasm, and he expresses joy even seeing a tap with a sign "no drinking water" ("Kein Trinkwasser") (75).

At this early stage of initiation the adolescent feels like a guest: his reactions are those of a perceptive observer, a good pupil, trying to adjust to the unadjustable. His wish is to become a good slave. The narrator is painstakingly precise, specifying what he personally experiences, sees, notices, what he just heard by hearsay, what he was told. His generous use of verbs lends credibility to the story: "noticed," "heard," "deserved," "surprised me," "discovered," "informed us," "remembered," "I could barely distinguish," "realized," "I didn't find," "experienced," etc. The frequent use of "I could see" or "I could understand" ("beláttam"), is especially apparent: it shows how far one can go in self-deceit in reality and ironically. At first, a good sense of humor—black humor, that is—still helps. When the atrocious slop of dry vegetables (86) is served, the boys burst out laughing: "for the Hungarian stomach . . . it is of course strange" ("magyar gyomornak . . . persze szokatlan") (87), someone remarks, but then the Germans are masters of drying vegetables, and besides, it has a lot of calories and vitamins in it. But the timing of meals is strange. Gratitude is shown not so much for the soup but for the "gondoskodás" ("gesture of care") (85). In another understatement Gyuri mentions that clothing and shoes were "impractical;" they did not live up to expectation, an in-depth irony brought about by the contrast between the description and the shoes' actual condition. One of his concerns that he was unprepared for before Auschwitz is whether he did indeed accept his fate: "non scolae sed vitae discimus" (93). But if this is so, why did he not he learn about Auschwitz? he asks. "Well, it is not part of general culture, I had to admit" ("No meg nem is tartozik hozzá a műveltséghez, beláttam") (93). Realizing the existence of gas chambers sets him to thinking. To be sure, "all that is no joking matter" ("mindez mégse egészen tréfa") (91). Contemplating the deception, the ingeniousness of the whole procedure, fills him with respect, yet he detects some kind of a joke in it, a kind of "student prank" ("diákcsíny") (91).

After three days Gyuri is transferred to Buchenwald, than to Zeitz. The railway station at Buchenwald is "provincial and friendly" ("vidékies, barátságos") (99). His factual description of the place might have been taken from a guide book; it sounds most attractive, no wonder the boy "soon became fond of it" ("én is hamar megszerettem") (105)—although "there are strange places in Buchenwald" ("vannak furcsa helyek Buchenwaldban") (161)—while "Zeitz seemed a very tolerable place" ("Zeitz igen tűrhető helynek mutatkozott") (118). To me, one of the chief merits of this novel is its inexhaustible subtle irony, unique in Holocaust literature—with perhaps one exception, Lina Wertmuller's film *The Seven Beauties*. The irony and distance are most apparent in recounting his transfer to Zeitz: "I can say that there was nothing more troublesome, more exhausting than those tedious rituals we had to pass through, it seemed, every time we arrived at a new concentration camp" ("Mondhatom, hogy nincs vesződségesebb, nincs kimerítőbb dolog azoknál a nyűgös fáradalmaknál, melyeken mindannyiszor keresztül kell, úgy látszik, esnünk, valahányszor csak egy új koncentrációs táborba megérkezünk") (105). He calls Zeitz a "kinda' tiny, poor, remote, one could say country-side concentration camp" ("afféle kicsiny, szegényes, félreeső, amolyan, mondhatni, vidéki koncentrációs tábor") (105). All the same, he later recalls the time spent in there as "golden days" ("arany napok voltak") (121).

As the time passes, the ironical tone becomes gradually subdued, yielding to lyrical and philosophical reflections. While the rough words of command earlier sounded "pleasant" to his ears, now beating angers him, and when he feels a soldier's boots trampling on his body, he notes: "something broke in me irreversibly" ("valami megjavíthatatlanul tönkrement bennem") (138). The boy's attitudes change unnoticeably: first he advances from being a guest to a good slave, then hunger, exhaustion, physical pain, gradually overpower him, and he becomes irritable. It was impossible not to notice that people around him deteriorated, aged quickly, so much so that, in comparison, the civil population looked positively handsome. Gyuri is learning slowly the necessity of defying the system, as much as possible. What is also new here in Holocaust literature is that Kertész does not dwell on suffering; he avoids scenes of cruelty. He suggests, in fact, that those who could write about the Holocaust are no longer there and those who are there cannot write about it. Auschwitz, says the novel's protagonist, is characterized not so much by the word "terrible" but by the length of days, boredom, idle waiting, disgust. Hence the recurring reference to time: "On the whole, the day went by" ("Egészében, elmondhatom, a nap eltelt") (46), "Even in the train time had to be spent somehow" ("A vonatban is az időt kellett valahogyan eltöltenünk") (61), and again with irony and black humor, "in time one gets used even to slavery, the trouble is that they don't give us enough time" ("idővel a rabélethez is hozzászokhat az ember, az a baj, hogy nem adnak hozzá elég időt") (126). That is the essence of life in the concentration camp: the way time is spent, the endless, uneventful gray days, the boredom of it all. It may shock the uninitiated reader that, just as imagination, reminiscing, and dreaming can help in alleviating suffering, occasional moments of happiness can exist there.

Gyuri's perception and experience of life in the concentration camp remain those of an outsider, perhaps here, too, meant ironically and not only in a context of the horrors of the experience. This I understand in the context of Gyuri's alienation in his own family and community: he was reminded now and again that suffering was part of the "common Jewish fate," and throughout his time in the concentration camp is ambivalent toward his Jewishness. Yiddish-speaking Jews ostracize him in the camp because he does not understand their language; they call him a *segec*, a *gój*. Here, again, he experiences the pain of not belonging. He discovers being a Jew just when he is excluded for not being one. Later, when campmates are hanged for attempting to escape, these very Jews mumble the Kaddish, the prayer for the dead, and Gyuri, for the first time, regrets not to be able to pray in that language. When he is back in civilization, the situation is no different. To Gyuri, fatelessness is not about the Holocaust. Rather, it has wider implications: it is about the human condition. That is why the novel has been called an existential or a surrealist novel (see Heller 8).

However ironical, the concentration camp has conditioned Gyuri into a sense of feeling home there. Now that he is released, he recognizes the falseness of the world outside, of the world that learned nothing. While in the camp old words and concepts acquired new meaning, people outside cling to their old language. Gyuri disappoints people in refusing to talk about the horror and hell he experienced, refusing to short-change his experiences for political purposes. When his old family friends insist that he should forget about the past and start a new life, Gyuri objects vehemently. He had a life and he lived it; although it was forced upon him he has been honest in his given fate. Being deprived of it would mean losing the sense of it all. Yet he refuses to accept what he lived through as part of Jewish fate, for that would justify what was done to him. In the camp a fellow inmate suggested that the sign "U" on his chest meant *unschuldig* (innocent), rather than *Ungarn* (Hungary). Gyuri disputes the argument. Just as Borowski in his *This Way to the Gas*, Kertész also challenges the division into persecutors and victims. No one is innocent, including the survivor. According to Kertész, dictatorship deprives a person of his fate and responsibility, even his name: it infantilizes him. He shocks people when he tells them about their own share of responsibility.

Works Cited

Bárdos, Pál. *Első évtized* (First Decade). Budapest: Szépirodalmi, 1975.

Bettelheim, Bruno. *The Informed Heart*. New York: Avon, 1971.

Borowski, Tadeusz. *This Way to the Gas, Ladies and Gentlemen*. Trans. Barbara Vedder. New York: Penguin, 1976.

Braham, Randolph L. *The Politics of Genocide: The Holocaust in Hungary*. New York: Columbia UP, 1981. 2 vols.

Ember, Mária. *Hajtű-kanyar* (Hairpin Bend). Budapest: Szépirodalmi, 1974.

Ember, Mária. *2000-ben fogunk-e még élni?* (Will We Be Still Alive in 2000?). Budapest: Múlt és Jövő, 2001.

Frank, Anna. *Frank Anna naplója*. Trans. Trans. Erzsébet Solti. Bukarest: Kriterion, 1987.

Gera, György. *Terelőút* (Detour). Budapest: Magvető, 1972.

Gergely, Ágnes. *A tolmács* (The Interpreter). Budapest: Szépirodalmi, 1973.

Gerő, András. "Identities of the Jew and the Hungarian." *Imre Kertész and Holocaust Literature*. Ed. Louise O. Vasvári and Steven Tötösy de Zepetnek. West Lafayette: Purdue UP, 2005. 138–47.

The Grey Zone. Dir. Tim Blake Nelson. Toronto: Lions Gate Films, 2001.

Heller, Ágnes. "A *Sorstalanság* húsz év múlva" ("*Fatelessness* Twenty Years After"). *Múlt és Jövő* 4 (2002): 4–13.

Kertész, Imre. *Fatelessness*. Trans. Tim Wilkinson. New York: Vintage, 2004.

Kertész, Imre. *Gályanapló* (Galley Boat-Log). Budapest: Holnap, 1992.

Kertész, Imre. *Kaddis a meg nem született gyermekért* (*Kaddish for an Unborn Child*). Budapest: Magvető, 1990.

Kertész, Imre. "Long Dark Shadow." Trans. Imre Goldstein. *Contemporary Jewish Writing in Hungary: An Anthology*. Ed. Susan Rubin Suleiman and Éva Forgács. Lincoln: U of Nebraska P, 2003. 171–77.

Kertész, Imre. *Nyomkereső* (The Pathfinder). Budapest: Szépirodalmi, 1977.

Kertész, Imre. *Sorstalanság*. Budapest: Századvég, 1993.

Kertész, Imre. *A száműzött nyelv* (The Language of Exile). Budapest: Magvető, 2001.

Kertész, Imre. *Valaki más. A változás krónikája* (Someone Else: A Chronicle of the Change in Régime). Budapest: Magvető, 1997.

Keszi, Imre. *Elysium*. Budapest: Szépirodalmi, 1958.

Koltai, Kornélia. "Imre Kertész's *Fatelessness* and the Myth about Auschwitz in Hungary." Trans. Katalin Erdődi. *Imre Kertész and Holocaust Literature*. Ed. Louise O. Vasvári and Steven Tötösy de Zepetnek. West Lafayette: Purdue UP, 2005. 125–37.

Konrád, György. *Elindulás és hazatérés* (Departure and Arrival). Budapest: Noran, 2001.

Kovács, András. "The Historians' Debate about the Holocaust in Hungary." *Imre Kertész and Holocaust Literature*. Ed. Louise O. Vasvári and Steven Tötösy de Zepetnek. West Lafayette: Purdue UP, 2005. 138–47.

Lengyel, Olga. *Five Chimneys: The Story of Auschwitz*. 1946. Trans. Clifford Coch and Paul P. Weiss. Chicago: Ziff-Davis, 1947.

Lévi, Primo. *Survival in Auschwitz*. Trans. Stuart Woolf. New York: Collier Books, 1961.

Mezei, András. *A csodatevő és más történetek* (The Miracle Maker and Other Stories). Budapest: Szépirodalmi, 1984.

Moldova, György. *Szent Imre induló* (Saint Emery's March). Budapest: Magvető, 1981.

Nyiszli, Miklós. *Auschwitz: A Doctor's Eyewitness Account*. 1946. Trans. Tibère Kremer and Richard Seaver. New York: Fell, 1960.

Ozsváth, Zsuzsanna. "Radnóti, Celan, and the Aesthetic Shifts in Central European Holocaust Poetry." *Comparative Central European Culture*. Ed. Steven Tötösy de Zepetnek. West Lafayette: Purdue UP, 2002. 51–69.

Radnóti, Miklós. *Subway Stops*. Trans. Emery George. Ann Arbor: Ardis, 1977.

Rádai, Eszter. "A *Sorstalanság*ot a Kádár-rendszerről írtam" ("I Wrote *Fatelessness* about the Kádár Regime"). *Élet és Irodalom* 47.22 (2003): 8–10.

Ránki, György. "Magyar Holocaust" ("Hungarian Holocaust"). *Élet és Irodalom* 6 (1982): 7–8.

Spiró, György. "Non habent sua fata." *Élet és Irodalom* 7 (1983): 5.

Suleiman, Susan Rubin. "Central Europe, Jewish Family History, and *Sunshine.*" *Comparative Central European Culture.* Ed. Steven Tötösy de Zepetnek. West Lafayette: Purdue UP, 2002. 169–88.

Vasvári, Louise O. "The Novelness of Imre Kertész's *Sorstalanság (Fatelessness).*" *Imre Kertész and Holocaust Literature.* Ed. Louise O. Vasvári and Steven Tötösy de Zepetnek. West Lafayette: Purdue UP, 2005. 258–70.

Zsolt, Béla. *Kilenc koffer* (Nine Suitcases). Budapest: Magvető, 1980.

The Novelness of Imre Kertész's
Sorstalanság (Fatelessness)

Louise O. Vasvári

Imre Kertész said that living in the West in a free society, he probably would have not been able to write *Sorstalanság* (*Fatelessness*) but would have tried to produce a "showier fiction," by breaking up time and narrating only powerful scenes (see "Heureka!"; in this paper, while I quote from the Wilson and Wilson translation of *Sorstalanság*, *Fateless*, I am otherwise using the title of the correct translation by Tim Wilkinson, *Fatelessness*, a new translation that appeared after the writing of the present paper). Instead, he made his protagonist, György Köves (George Koves), who, like the author himself, returned to Budapest after the concentration camp to languish in the "dreadful trap of linearity," and instead of spectacular series of great and tragic moments, he made him live through everything that is oppressive and offers little variety, like life itself. Arguably the most shocking scene in the book is the description of the efficiently orchestrated selection process in Auschwitz, which took some twenty minutes. Kertész says that no matter how many survivors' accounts he read, they all agreed that everything proceeded all too quickly, but he remembered them differently, and augmented his own memory with Tadeusz Borowski's stark narrative, *This Way to the Gas, Ladies and Gentlemen* (see "Heureka!"). The example of the selection process illustrates how Kertész, by deliberately perverting the "serious" values of Holocaust literary culture, has produced a work that is unreadable within its aesthetic conventions. Kertész is, rather, a social realist who has nevertheless produced experimental fiction, the understanding of whose novelness must be sought in its primary debt to existentialism and to the postmodern novel.

In relation to Kertész's debt to existentialism, György Spiró noted most cogently that Kertész presents a "philosophy of existence which almost explodes the boundaries" (*Magániktató* 381; all subsequent translations are mine unless noted otherwise). Kertész has commented himself that in the camps he realized he could be killed at any moment and that it was this existential moment that became crucial to him as a writer (qtd. in Szántó, "Editorial Comment" 5). Kertész's fourteen-and-a-half-year-old protagonist and alter-ego, György Köves (or Gyuri, his name's diminutive), is the embodiment of this existential attitude; when imprisoned in a concentration camp and attempting to become a model prisoner he comes somehow to feel that his imagination could remain free. This attitude is further exemplified in the last part of the book, when on returning to Budapest after liberation, Köves is even angered by the attitude of self-victimization of two old acquaintances who survived there, Steiner and Fleischmann. Kertész's thematic debt to philosophical existentialism in *Fatelessness* can be expressed in the Heideggerian terminology *zum Tode sein* (to be destined for/delivered to death; see Wahl 45), but of more specific interest to me is his direct indebtedness to Albert Camus's existentialism of psychological isolation and anguish, as exemplified in *L'Étranger* (1944). As Kertész was starting to work on *Fatelessness*, *L'Étranger* was not yet available in communist countries due to Camus's anti-communism, but he apparently came upon a copy by chance in a Budapest second-hand shop and he has admitted it to have been one of the major influences on his own work (see Kertész, "A *Sorstalanság*ot" 8). In the following, I discuss the similarity of *Fatelessness* and *L'Étranger* as philosophical tracts masquerading as fiction as well as their startling degree of textual similarity, particularly at the very beginning and the very end of *Fatelessness*. In both novels everything is filtered exclusively through the consciousness of the first-person narrator. In my reading of *Fatelessness*, Köves is merely a younger model of Meursault, "the indifferent man," who does not have the ability to experience communion with the world, who shows an utter lack of emotion at his mother's death, and who accepts everything that happens to him with indifference (on this, see Daniel; Daruwalla 61).

Features of the postmodern novel evident in *Fatelessness* include intertextuality, subversion, and the mixing of genres, as well as of notions of stable identity, truthful introspection, unified selfhood, authentic memory, and the translatability of experience into language, and, most importantly, the questioning of grand narratives. While today postmodernity may not be news in relation to the novel in general, the overturning of every clichéd convention of Holocaust literature is still a very touchy issue, in particular among Jewish readers. It is precisely this "defamiliarization" of the Holocaust narrative and turning it into what Albena Lutzkanova-Vassileva refers to as "almost clinical discourse" (see at <http://clcwebjournal.lib. purdue.edu/clcweb01–1/lutzkanova-vassileva01.html>) and that makes Kertész's text difficult for a general readership, including in its translated versions. By some accounts when *Sorstalanság* was first published in Hungary in 1975 it met "a wall of silence," perhaps because of the subject matter (see Szántó, "Editorial Comment" 5–6). The literary and culture establishment took no notice of Kertész and his name was not listed in the 1983 *A History of Hungarian Literature* by Tibor Klaniczay, he was mentioned only in passing in the 1984 *Oxford History of Hungarian Literature* by Lóránt Czigány, and in the most recent history of Hungarian literature, Ernő Kulcsár Szabó's 1993 *History of Hungarian Literature between 1945–1991*, Kertész is still not mentioned. In sum, it was in the years after the 1989 demise of the Soviet and Communist empire in Central and Eastern Europe that he started to gain fame, his texts were translated into (mainly) German and other languages, and that his work was discussed in the context of postmodern literature in Hungary (see Balogh, <http://www.irodalmiakademia.hu/dia/diat/bio/kertesz_imre. html>).

As Gábor Szántó has explicated, for Kertész the individual in a state of fatelessness is one who has become totally beholden to the state (see "A katarzis reményében"). As his protagonist Köves, having been deprived of all possibility of personal choice, he is in the ultimate instance reduced to a less than human state and becomes part of the masses, which can be manipulated at will by totalitarian regimes, depriving him of sovereign identity, freedom, and human dignity, but also, at the same time, dangerously, seemingly freeing him of all personal responsibility. In this sense, Kertész, who is a survivor of both Nazism and Communism, has said that experiencing under Communism some of the same terrors he had had under Nazism had helped him understand, synthesize, and turn into literary form his earlier experiences, and helped him realize that all totalitarianisms are alike. In fact, more recently he has gone so far as to declare that he "actually" wrote *Sorstalanság* about the Kádár regime (see Kertész, "A *Sorstalanság*ot"), a seemingly outrageous claim and that one must take into account in the context that, along with a number of other Central and Eastern European writers under Communism, Kertész disguised his work about totalitarianism as an examination of Nazism. He said in another context that socialism for him was like Prousts's "petite madeleine," and, more specifically, that living as an adult under the logic of one kind of totalitarianism he depicted an adolescent in another totalitarian system and that "this turned the language of my novel into a highly allusive medium" ("Heureka!" 606, 608). In sum, the main problematic of *Fatelessness* and of Kertész's whole oeuvre is the question of what freedom humans have in totalitarian regimes.

As I mentioned previously, at first reading, *Fatelessness* plays a trick on readers by its deceptively similar structure to standard Holocaust narratives, whether categorized as fiction or nonfiction. In its overall tripartite division the first three chapters (74 pages) start off with the fourteen-and-a-half-year-old György Köves's seemingly familiar story of home life "before" deportation, the description of the *razzia* in which he is rounded up with other adolescent boys, and the oft-represented scene of Jewish internment in a Budapest brick factory before deportation. The bulk of the book (four chapters consisting of a total of 225 pages) is dedicated to the deportation experience, beginning with the inevitable scenes of the train trip to Auschwitz, the selection process, and, in the protagonist's case, further transfer to Buchenwald, Zeitz, and, ultimately, back to Buchenwald, where he is liberated. The brief final section, consisting of only one chapter of 31 pages, describing Köves's return to Budapest almost exactly one year later, is nevertheless the philosophical core of the work, where a now matured protagonist begins to have some interior life and to meditate on the concept of fatelessness and individual responsibility and to begin to come to terms with what it means to be a Jew. It is only this third part of *Fatelessness* that finally gives an explanation of the resigned and indifferent tone of the novel and of Köves's understanding of the main problematic of his existence, the freedom of man under totalitarianism of any sort. The book ends with Köves, once again feeling utterly bereft because no one who was not in the camps can understand him. "A sharp painful futile despair grasped [his] heart: 'homesickness' and he said to himself: 'Even back there, in the shadow of the chimneys, in the break between pain, there was something resembling happiness.' Everybody will ask me about the deprivation, the 'terrors of the camps,' but for me, the happiness, there will always be the most memorable experience. Perhaps, yes, that's what I'll tell them next time they ask me: about the happiness in those camps. If they ever do ask. And if I don't forget" (*Fateless* 190–91). This shocking ending, lamenting the lost "happiness" of the camps, has been explained by one critic as part of the instinct for self-preservation (see Basa). Perhaps, however, one needs to examine these lines from an existential perspective and relate it to the direct literary influence of Camus's *L'Étranger*. In the last pages Mersault, condemned to death by hanging for a senseless crime he committed and daily awaiting his execution, muses that his mother—about whom he otherwise expressed no feeling—used to say that one is never totally unhappy. He found that it was enough to cause him happiness every dawn not to hear approaching footsteps of the executioners. He concludes that, after all, since everyone has to die, eventually it matters little if one dies at thirty or at seventy, because it is always you who dies while others will live. So, ultimately, for Mersault, life, or death, and the belief in god, are equally unimportant, everything is unimportant. Mersault's last words are similar to Köves's memories of the camp: "J'ai senti que j'avais été hereux, et je l'étais encore" (178).

If, as the above factors with regard to the structure and plot of the text show, they are relatively conventional, in what, then, does the radical novelness of *Fatelessness* consist? To start with, let us consider the deliberate confusion of author/narrator/protagonist. The fate of the first-person narrator/protagonist and of the author—who conveniently share the first initial K. of their last name (along with Kafka, who, alongside Camus, is one of Kertész's major influences)—is in every major biographical detail indistinguishable (on this, see Basa, who nevertheless considers it a gross simplification to equate the two). One of the techniques Kertész uses to minimize the biographical identity between author and narrator is for the latter to downplay details that he would be expected to recall, such as exact dates or names of streets. So, for example, while Kertész was rounded up on 30 June 1944, his hero reports on that day only that "summer is now here," and rather than naming a certain street he says "near the square, where there is the tram stop" (*Fateless* 179; see also Karolle). Further, an extreme example of the biographical identity of Kertész and of his protagonist is the description in the novel of the hallucinatory near-death experience of Köves in Buchenwald, which forms the single longest and most narratively fragmented section of the work. The grotesque nature of the overlap between fact and fiction is underlined by Kertész's real-life experience when the director of the Buchenwald Memorial Center presented him with a copy of the daily report of the camp's prisoners for the day in which one Imre Kertész, Prisoner #64,921 is reported among the dead (see "Heureka!"). While—as Dorrit Cohn (4) suggests—in any first-person novel the degree of fact versus fiction separating the life of the real versus the implied author and the necessarily unreliable narrator is inevitably not a fixed quantity but variable and subject to a given reader's judgment, in *Fatelessness* Kertész may be imposing on readers a level of readerly responsibility that not all can tolerate. The degree of identity between author, narrator, and protagonist, and fact and fiction, in *Fatelessness*, then, presents the reader with the dilemma of ascertaining within what conventions to read this work (see Basa as to how not only average readers but some noted Hungarian critics have reacted with discomfort to the novel's generic liminality and the narrator's single voice).

In *A kudarc* (The Failure), Kertész provides in perfect postmodern novelistic fashion his own ironic commentary of the potential unreadability of *Sorstalanság* for many readers, reinforcing the novel's self-reflexivity by inventing an embedded reader and critic whose comments echo the judgments of Kertész's critics. In one scene the novel submitted by an aging author about his Holocaust experience is rejected by a "professional humanist" reader in a publishing house. The reader objects that some readers would find the work unreadable because it is too depressing, and that it is also unbelievable that a youth could remain so naïve for so long and, particularly, that he could remain so unmoved when he finally realizes the function of the crematoria (*A kudarc* 41–42). Kertész has also addressed the issue of the readability of his work in an interview with the satirical magazine *Magyar Narancs*, when he said that it was his aim to traumatize the reader into being forced to fill the interpretative gap lacking in the narrator (see Kertész, Interview <http://www.mancs.hu/index.php?gc.Page=public/hir.phg&id=757>).

In the oeuvre of a writer such as Philip Roth, which also centers on the question of Jewishness and the dichotomy of fact versus fictionality, from the beginning some critics and some members of the Jewish community have complained bitterly about how Roth portrays Jews. Roth's penchant for including a great deal of his public self and autobiography in his novels blurs the distinction between fiction and reality further. Although such literary paradoxes have become more acceptable today, even in Roth's case, when he published his *Portnoy's Complaint* in 1969—whose protagonist's year and place of birth and biographical details were virtually identical with that of the author's—it was much maligned, in particular by Jewish critics, as an unflattering caricature of American lower-middle-class Jewish life. Roth himself poked fun at his intentional diminishing of the barrier between fiction and reality in his l985 *Zuckerman Unbound*, where his alter-ego Nathan Zuckerman is accosted by strangers who cannot believe that the sex scenes in his *Carnovsky*, the alter-novel to *Portnoy's Complaint* in *Zuckerman Unbound*, were fantasy. Without a final source of truth or ultimate moral authority, fiction and reality for Zuckerman become interchangeable; as he says, "my life was coming to resemble one of those texts upon which certain literary critics . . . used to enjoy venting their ingenuity" (72). In *Zuckerman Unbound*, Roth writes that "they had mistaken impersonation for confession and were calling out to a character who lived in a book" (123). Thus, it is precisely the line between confession and impersonation that Roth exploits: The effect of postmodern and post-structuralist conceptions of textuality and the self is to subvert the distinction between autobiography and fiction. Roth, in the purportedly directly autobiographical *The Facts* and *Deception*, presents provocations to the reader to rethink the complicated relations between kinds of texts and between fact and fiction and their implications for the conception of the self (on this, see Goodheart).

Let us consider the opposite case, of fiction masquerading as fact, with regard to the widely acclaimed 1995 publication by the reputable German publisher Suhrkamp of a supposedly Holocaust memoir, *Bruchstücke*, which appeared in English by Random House as *Fragments: Memories of a Wartime Childhood*, by the Swiss Binjamin Wilkomirski. The work was translated into twelve languages and garnered numerous literary awards, among them the 1996 National Jewish Book Award for Autobiography and Memoir. Narrated primarily in the present tense in disjointed flashbacks, the author claimed to recount his fragmented memories from the perspective of a three-to-five-year-old child in the ghetto in Riga and camps in Poland. When, three years later, the work was discovered to be fiction by an author who was not even Jewish, Wilkomirski was vilified and declared a hoax, with the case unleashing an enormous amount of commentary (see, e.g., Bernard-Donalis; Mächler, who discusses memory and testimony; Eskin, who places the affair in a socio-historical context; Weinberg, who compares Wilkomirski with five other cases he considers fraudulent Holocaust testimonies, including that of Jerzy Kosinski). Essentially, Wilkomirski was pilloried for having broken the "autobiographical pact" (see Lejeune; Reiter), even as the much praised literary quality of his work remained, presumably, intact. Another question that has been raised in this context is whether false testimony could be an effective instrument. Interestingly, even among survivors there was at least one defender who claims that although the author may not have experienced the events, he compelled readers to "see" them (Lappin 61). The whole affair underlines the "exceptionally vexed" relationship between history, memory, and testimony, where victims of trauma never could during the events be fully aware of what was happening, so that their testimony becomes an oblique recounting (see Caruth 187; LaCapra 20–21).

Wilkomirski's novel, masquerading as memoir, and Kertész's "autobiographical" novel *Fatelessness*, then, represent opposing borderline cases of fictional versus historical life narratives. The genre has been variously called autofiction (Lecarme) or pseudo-autobiographical novel, a term used by Philippe Lejeune to emphasize the distinction between related kinds of autobiographical writing, including memoir, autobiographical poem, and diary, from autobiography proper. Lejeune defines the autobiographical novel as a fictional text in which the reader has reason to suspect, from the resemblances that he thinks he sees, that there is identity of author and protagonist, whereas the author has chosen to deny this identity. This definition fits well Kertész's own denial of autobiographical intent. In spite of the biographical identity between his own life and that of his protagonist, he has claimed in interviews that it is not an autobiographical book and that he never wanted to write about his own life (qtd. in Szántó, "Editorial Comment" 5). Andrew Baruch Wachtel defines pseudo-autobiography as a "first-person retrospective narrative based on autobiographical material, in which the author and the protagonist are not the same person" (3). Wachtel traces the form to Tolstoy's trilogy *Childhood* (1852), *Boyhood* (1854), and *Youth* (1857), where much of the fictional life of the narrator, Nikolai Irten'ev, was drawn from Tolstoy's own experience. In these novels the protagonist at the same time ends up being his own double because throughout the older Irten'ev comments on his past actions.

While Lejeune's and Wachtel's definitions of pseudo-autobiography give a useful generic starting point, Kertész's use of the form is far more complicated, because, unlike Tolstoy but similar to Wilkomirski, he thematizes the use of the French *passé composé,* or present perfect tense in startling ways, so as to give his fiction the additional immediacy of a diary. For example, the first line of the novel reads as if it had just happened: "Today I skipped school. That is, I went, but only to ask my teacher to excuse me from class. I gave him my father's letter asking if I could be excused for 'personal reasons.' My teacher wanted to know the reasons. I told him my father was being conscripted into the labor service" (*Fateless* 1). There follows a chapter describing the preparations for the father's departure and the description of the family farewells. The second chapter begins again in the present tense, with "It has been two months now since we said good-bye to my father. Summer is now here, but at school we were given vacations long ago, in the springtime. . . . For two weeks now I have been working" (21). The third chapter, although it narrates what occurs *the next day,* when Köves is rounded up and taken to the brick factory, switches to narration in the past tense (31), with the protagonist even mentioning that "his memory of later events is all hazy" (35). That is, here, as in Tolstoy, the narrator becomes his own double, narrating his own past. The rest of the book follows suit, with the last chapter beginning with "I came home at around the same time of the year as I had left" (173). Since it is only here that the now more mature survivor philosophizes about his camp experience, we again have a retrospective narrative of the older protagonist looking back on his younger self. Through its temporal play, then, the novel begins in a kind of diary form and continues as a retrospective pseudo-autobiography, where the distance between the narrating and past self gradually builds up, or what Spiró called the strange and unique amalgam of viewpoints ("In Art Only the Radical Exists" 34).

Presumably, Kertész himself might deny literary intention to the complex temporal disjunctures of *Fatelessness*, as he has claimed that writing about Auschwitz has, in a certain sense, suspended literature, and that in his writing the Holocaust could therefore never be presented in the past tense (see "Heureka!"). Literary intention, however, becomes inescapable when it becomes evident that the play with temporal perspective is a direct calque of the very first line "Aujourd'hui maman est morte" of *L'Étranger* (I thank Judit Zerkowitz for reminding me of this first line). Nor does the resemblance in the opening pages of both texts stop here, because as György Köves must ask permission to be absent from school from his teacher for "family" reasons, so Merseult upon receiving a telegram about his mother's death says, all in the future tense, that he will take the two-o'clock bus and will arrive in the afternoon, adding that he has just asked for two days' leave from his boss, who could not possibly refuse such a legitimate request. From the following page, however, the rest of the novel is narrated in the *passé composé*. Camus broke new ground in French narrative with this use of the *passé composé* rather than the *passé simple* because this tense can apply to very recent occurrence as a kind of dramatic present and colloquially can also replace the remote past (see Fletcher 211).

A second major problematic, related to that of the confusion of authorial and narrative voice, is that readers who are pulled into the game of fact versus fiction of the pseudo-autobiography are likely to be even far more disturbed by the voice of the protagonist, whom István Deák dubs "an optimistic boy, a modern Candide, who faces his hellish world with confidence and a sense of humor" (65). As Kertész predicted in *A kudarc* (The Failure), most readers will, instead, find at times absolutely irritating his childlike slowness to catch on to adult references around him. For example, he is mystified by the term *selyemfiú* (gigolo, literally "silk boy"), the nickname given to one of the boys rounded up with him, thinking the nickname appropriate because of the boy's slicked-back hair (*Fateless* 54). In another scene, when his friend Bandi Citrom refers to a gypsy guard as *homokos* ("faggot," i.e., homosexual), Köves says he does not understand the term, and when it is clarified for him by another derogatory synonym, *buzi*, he muses, "well, now I was somewhat more clear with the concept, approximately, I think" (96). However serious Köves's cluelessness about sexual matters, readers are likely to find far more annoying the boy's natural cowing to authority and his characterizations of the most reprehensible acts of authority figures with adjectives such as "understandable," "natural," and a series of similar terms, often tacked on to the end of a sentence (on this, see also Várnai). As in *A kudarc*, the reader's potential irritation is also thematized in the last section of *Fatelessness*, when Köves, on returning to Budapest from Buchenwald, meets a reporter on the trolley who wants to write his story. However, the poor man is soon frustrated by the boy's laconic answers, asking in frustration: "Why do you keep saying 'naturally,' son, he exclaimed, seeming to lose his temper, 'when you are referring to things that are not natural at all?' 'In a concentration camp,' I said, 'they are very natural.' 'yes, yes,' he gasped, 'it's true there, but . . . well . . . but the concentration camp itself is not natural'" (180). In fact, the word *természetesen* ("naturally" and its various synonymous expressions), probably the single most common word used by Köves, is used inevitably—not only in the camps but also before—in the most inappropriate contexts.

In his use and abuse of "naturally" and its synonyms Köves is again a direct heir of Meurseult in *L'Étranger*, who constantly uses terms such as "[tout] naturellement," "bien entendu," "sans doute," or "je ne pouvais pas m'empêcher de reconnaître" in contexts such as, for example, how he "naturally" had to understand that his boss was upset that by giving him two days' leave for his mother's funeral he was actually getting four days because she died on a Thursday, or that it was "natural" that his pimp neighbor would resort to punishing his girlfriend by beating her and that Mersault would later agree to provide false testimony on his behalf. Köves's existential stance towards life, or what Katherine M. Wilson (the translator, with Christopher C. Wilson, of *Fateless*) called "the voice of a witness" (11) is not one, as the interchange with the reporter might imply, that he developed through his bitter camp experiences, but rather the indifference and the emotional incapacity to connect, which he already demonstrates from the very beginning, where, for example, he finds it understandable that the local baker would have no choice but to dislike Jews, since in this way he would not have to feel guilty about cheating them. While in canonical Holocaust narratives the "before" chapter presents inevitably a kind of nostalgia for a lost Eden, all the better to contrast the horrors that are to follow, the explanation for Köves's indifferent reaction to his camp experiences is to be found in the total lack of emotional involvement and his psychological isolation from his family, which he demonstrates the last day before his father is sent to labor camp. Throughout the day, he can only pretend to show some involvement and is finally very relieved when, at the end of the evening, "perhaps from sheer exhaustion," he finds that his tears began to flow: "Whatever the reason, it happened the way it should have. My father also, I sensed, was pleased that it had happened" (20). This sentence illustrates that the minimal level of interaction that Köves is able to muster with his environment is not to feel, actually, but only to observe with satisfaction the effect that his mimicking of socially appropriate actions *seems* to elicit. Here, again, Köves's favorite reaction on such occasions, "I sensed he was pleased," is a calque of his predecessor Merseult's "il a eu l'air [mé]content" (64, 69).

The first chapter, characterized by Köves's detached and brutally clinical observation of his relatives, is, in its essence, no different from, for example, how he will judge his fellow prisoners in the Auschwitz line-up, some, like him, saved for the moment by the doctor making the selection, whom he "immediately trusted because he was very presentable and had an appealing, longish, clean-shaven face with rather narrow lips, and blue or gray but in any case light and benevolent-looking eyes" (63). While he judges the doctor in such favorable terms, contrast his view of one of the child victims: "And then my attention was caught by the terrible screams of a messy, curly-haired little boy dressed like a show-window mannequin as he tried to free himself from the arms of a blond woman, obviously his mother, with strange pulls, twitches, and convulsions. 'I want to go with Daddy' he screamed, shouted, and yelled, stamping his white-shoed feet with ridiculous impatience on the white gravel and the white dust" (60). Some eight hours after the *trillage* Köves begins to comprehend that those chimneys billowing smoke belong not to a factory but a crematorium that has already suffocated those new fellow arrivals who ended up in the other line. He thinks about several people he had noticed among them, including that child: "This was the end, doubtless of . . . the little boy with the white shoes and his blond mother" (82). But there was no time for sentimentality, "there was more talk of our future prospects, possibilities, and hopes than of the chimneys. At those times it was as if they weren't there. We paid no attention to them" (84). Kertész, with his deliberate and total elimination of multiple perspectives, has allowed the laconic voice of his immature teenage narrator to control the narrative, as well as to ventriloquize with irony the voice of all other characters we are allowed to hear. Since Köves accepts even the smoking chimneys—"it all depended on the way the wind blew, we admitted" (84)—without ever showing incredulity or grief, he is shocking his readers deliberately and forcing *them* to fill the narrative void of moral indignation. Kertész himself suggest in his "A holokauszt mint kultúra" and in his Nobel lecture that such an activity may have a cathartic function for his readers: "If the Holocaust has by now created a culture, as it undeniably has, its aim must be [to] give rise by way of the spirit of restoration, a catharsis. This desire has inspired me in all my creative endeavors" ("Heureka!").

Kertész also states in his Nobel lecture that "what happened to language in the twentieth century . . . has become unsuitable to convey concepts and processes that had once been unambiguous and real. Think of Kafka, think of Orwell, in whose hands the old language simply disintegrated" ("Heureka!" 612). Through Köves's last shocking words, Kertész attempts to illustrate the impossibility of conveying through ordinary language the experience of the camps to those who did not witness it. Thus, appropriating and experimenting with techniques of representation by writers such as Camus, Kafka, and Joyce, Kertész has created deliberately a new "traumatic" style with which to shock his readers into reacting. Through this deliberately confrontational style and fundamentally generically ambivalent work, whatever truth that is attained may be best expressed as a fiction of the truth. However, despite its self-reflexivity, Kertész's fiction contains a far wider concern than is associated customarily with Western postmodern literature; his range includes socio-political commentary and life outside the text. While the conventional Holocaust novel continues to flourish with second- and third-generation writers, Kertész has—as Philip Roth has done with the moribund ethnic novel—re-contextualized the conventions of the Holocaust novel of adolescence (a subgenre of *Bildungsroman*), thus giving rebirth to Holocaust narrative. Kertész's daringly innovative text functions as the ultimate Holocaust novel, which subverting the rhetorical and narrative myths of its predecessors through defamiliarization, irony, humor, and elements of self-parody.

Works Cited

Balogh, Endre. "Kertész Imre életrajza" ("Curriculum Vitae of Imre Kertész"). *Digitális Irodalmi Akadémia* (2004): <http://www.irodalmiakademia.hu/dia/diat/bio/kertesz_imre.html>.

Basa, Enikő Molnár. "Imre Kertész and Hungarian Literature." *Imre Kertész and Holocaust Literature*. Ed. Louise O. Vasvári and Steven Tötösy de Zepetnek. West Lafayette: Purdue UP, 2005. 11–23.

Bernard-Donalis, Michael. "Beyond the Question of Authenticity: Witness and Testimony in the *Fragments* Controversy." *PMLA: Publications of the Modern Language Association of America* 116.5 (2001): 1302–15.

Camus, Albert. *L'Étranger*. Paris: Gallimard, 1942.

Caruth, Cathy. "Unclaimed Experience: Trauma and the Possibility of History." *Yale French Studies* 79 (1991): 181–92.

Cohn, Dorrit. "Fictional *versus* Historical Lives: Borderlines and Borderline Cases." *Journal of Narrative Technique* 19 (1989): 3–23.

Czigány, Lóránt. *The Oxford History of Hungarian Literature*. Oxford: Oxford UP, 1984.

Daniel, Jean. "Innocence in Camus and Dostoevsky." *Camus's* L'Étranger *Fifty Years On*. Ed. Adele King. New York: St. Martin's, 1992. 36–46.

Deák, István. "A Stranger in Hell." *New York Review of Books* (25 September 2003): 65–68.

Daruwalla, K. N. "The Impact of *L'Étranger*: Oblique Reflections on an Oblique Novel." *Camus's* L'Étranger *Fifty Years On*. Ed. Adele King. New York: St. Martin's, 1992. 59–64.

Eskin, Blake. *A Life in Pieces: The Making and Unmaking of Binjamin Wilkomirski*. New York: Norton, 2000.

Fletcher, John. "*L'Étranger* and the New Novel." *Camus's* L'Étranger *Fifty Years On*. Ed. Adele King. New York: St. Martin's, 1992. 209–20.

Goodheart, Eugene. "Counterlives: Philip Roth in Autobiography and Fiction." *Novel Practices: Classic Modern Fiction*. By Eugene Goodheart. New Brunswick: Transaction Publishers, 2004. 161–74.

Karolle, Julia. "Imre Kertész's *Fatelesnesss* as Historical Fiction." *Imre Kertész and Holocaust Literature*. Ed. Louise O. Vasvári and Steven Tötösy de Zepetnek. West Lafayette: Purdue UP, 2005. 89–96.

Kertész, Imre. *Sorstalanság* (*Fatelessness*). Budapest: Magvető, 1975.

Kertész, Imre. *A kudarc* (The Failure). Budapest: Szépirodalmi, 1988.

Kertész, Imre. *Fateless.* Trans. Christopher C. Wilson and Katherine M. Wilson. Evanston: Northwestern UP, 1992.

Kertész, Imre. *A holokauszt mint kultúra. Három előadás* (The Holocaust as Culture: Three Lectures). Budapest: Századvég, 1993.

Kertész, Imre. Interview by Tamás Szőnyei. "Nem érzem magam téves helyen, amikor Németországban olvasok fel (Kertész Imre író)" ("I Do Not Feel Out of Place When I Read My Work in Germany [Imre Kertész, Writer]"). *Magyar Narancs* (*Archive*) (12 December 1996): <http://www.mancs.hu/index.php?gc.Page=public/hir.phg&id=757>.

Kertész, Imre. "Heureka!" Trans. Ivan Sanders. *PMLA: Publications of the Modern Language Association of America* 118.3 (2003): 604–14.

Kertész, Imre. "A *Sorstalanság*ot a Kádár-rendszerről írtam" ("I wrote *Fatelessness* about the Kádár Regime"). Interview with Eszter Rádai. *Élet és Irodalom* (30 May 2003): 3, 8.

Kertész, Imre. *Fatelessness.* Trans. Tim Wilkinson. New York, Vintage, 2004.

Klaniczay, Tibor. *A History of Hungarian Literature.* Budapest: Corvina, 1983.

Kulcsár Szabó, Ernő. *A magyar irodalom története 1945–1991 között* (History of Hungarian literature between 1945–1991). Budapest: Argumentum, 1993.

LaCapra, Dominick. *History and Memory after Auschwitz.* Ithaca: Cornell UP, 1998.

Lappin, Elena. "The Man with Two Heads." *Granta* 66 (1999): 7–65.

Lecarme, Jacques. "L'Autofiction. Un mauvais genre?" *Autofiction et Cie.* Ed. Serge Doubrovsky, Jacques Lecarme, and Philippe Lejeune. Nanterre: U Paris X-Nanterre, 1993. 231–42.

Lejeune, Philippe. *Le Pacte autobiographique.* Paris: Seuil, 1975.

Lutzkanova-Vassileva, Albena. "Testimonial Poetry in East European Post-Totalitarian Literature." *CLCWeb: Comparative Literature and Culture* 3.1 (2001): <http://clcwebjournal.lib.purdue.edu/clcweb01–1/lutzkanova-vassileva01.html>.

Mächler, Stefan. *Der Fall Wilkomirski über die Wahrheit einer Biographie.* Zürich: Pendo, 2000.

Reiter, Andrea. *Narrating the Holocaust.* Trans. Patrick Camiller. New York: Continuum, 2000.

Roth, Philip. *Portnoy's Complaint.* New York: Random House, 1969.

Roth, Philip. *Zuckerman Unbound.* New York: Farrar, Strauss & Giroux, 1981.

Roth, Philip. *The Facts: A Novelist's Autobiography.* New York: Farrar, Strauss & Giroux, 1988.

Roth, Philip. *Deception.* New York: Vintage, 1997.

Rüsen, Jörn. "Holocaust-Memory and Identity-Building: Metahistorical Considerations on the Case of (West-)Germany." *Disturbing Remains: Memory, History, and Crisis in the Twentieth Century.* Ed. Michael S. Roth and Charles S. Salas. Los Angeles: The Getty Research Institute, 2001. 252–70.

Spiró, György. *Magániktató* (Self-Recorder). Budapest: Szépirodalmi, 1985.

Spiró, György. "In Art Only the Radical Exists: Imre Kertész." *The New Hungarian Quarterly* 43 (2002): 29–37.

Szántó, Gábor. "A katarzis reményében. Kertész Imre kapta az irodalmi Nobel díjat" ("In the Hope of Catharsis: Imre Kertész Received the Nobel Prize"). *Szombat* 14.9 (2002): 3.

Szántó, Gábor. "Editorial Comment to Imre Kertész's 'Heureka!'" *Szombat* 16.8 (2004): 5–6.

Várnai, Paul. "Holocaust Literature and Imre Kertész." *Imre Kertész and Holocaust Literature*. Ed. Louise O. Vasvári and Steven Tötösy de Zepetnek. West Lafayette: Purdue UP, 2005. 247–57.

Wachtel, Andrew Baruch. *The Battle for Childhood: Creation of a Russian Myth*. Stanford: Stanford UP, 1990.

Wahl, Jean. *A Short History of Existentialism*. New York: The Philosophical Library, 1949.

Weinberg, Avraham. *Wilkomirski & Co. Im Land der Täter, im Namen des Volkes. Eine Dokumentation*. Berlin: Kronen, 2003.

Wilkomirski, Binjamin. *Fragments: Memories of a Wartime Childhood*. Trans. Carol Brown Janeway. New York: Random House, 1996.

Wilson, Katharine M. "Finding the Voice: Translating Imre Kertész." *American Translators' Association Source* 38 (2003): 1, 11.

The Media and Imre Kertész's Nobel Prize in Literature

Judy Young

The Nobel Prize—the crowning achievement of a literary career—is an opportunity for the overall assessment or reassessment of a writer's work and to situate him/her in a national or international literary and cultural context. Indeed, in the case of Imre Kertész, most international responses attempted to do exactly that. On 10 October 2002, when the prize was announced, the very first German article sets the tone: "The novel *Fatelessness* by the Hungarian writer Imre Kertész belongs to the most important works of European literature in this century" ("*Der Roman eines Schicksallosen* des ungarischen Schriftstellers Imre Kertész gehört zu den wichtigsten Werken der europäischen Literatur dieses Jahrhunderts") (Rathgeb). George Szirtes, writing in *The Times Literary Supplement*, characterizes the work as "an enormous effort to understand and find a language for what the Holocaust says about the human condition. For Kertész it is less a question of what happened, at one particular historical instant to the Jews as such; but what the phenomenon says about Europe in particular and humanity in general" (17). The specifically (Central) European nature of Kertész's work is noted by a number of scholars (see, e.g., Deák; Tötösy de Zepetnek, "And the 2002 Nobel Prize" <http://clcwebjournal.lib.purdue. edu/clcweb03–1/totosy03.html>). However, in Hungary reactions to the award lay bare a range of social, cultural, and political/ideological considerations. A review of the media responses in Hungary does not so much enlighten us about the writer or his place in Hungarian or European literature; rather, it tells us much about the political and ideological battles being fought in the country (on this, see also Marsovszky; Tötösy de Zepetnek, "Imre Kertész's Nobel Prize").

The analysis in this paper is based on the review of a cross section of print and electronic media between 10 October 2002 and the end of January 2003, with selected items after that date if they contribute to the particular point being made. I seek answers to two questions about Kertész's Nobel Prize: 1) What were the main media responses to the prize in Hungary? and 2) What was the effect of this prize on Kertész's work, his life, and on Hungarian literature and literary culture? This last question includes Kertész's own reaction to the prize and its meaning for him. The primary focus of this survey is the Hungarian press; this is partly because I am

271

making available material that is more often than not inaccessible due to the language, and also because I hope to make a contribution to an understanding of the current cultural-political climate in Hungary.

Although it is at times argued to the contrary, Kertész was well-known to the literary and literate public in Hungary (see, e.g., Marsovszky, "Imre Kertész and Hungary Today"). Since at least the 1990s, he was regularly named among the best writers in Hungary and although there was not much response to *Sorstalanság* (*Fateless* 1992; *Fatelessness* 2004) when it was first published in 1975, in later years there were many critical essays and reviews about him by a number of important literary and public figures, such as Péter Esterházy, François Fejtö, Ágnes Heller, György Konrád, Tamás Molnár Gábor, György Spiró, George Szirtes, and others. In addition, Kertész has won a number of major literary prizes in Hungary: Milan Füst 1983, Forintos 1986, Artisjus 1988, József Attila 1889, Tibor Déry 1989, Örley 1990, Soros 1992 and 1995, Sándor Márai 1996 and finally, in 1997, the Kossuth Prize, the major prize for contribution to the arts and sciences in Hungary. Since the Nobel Prize he has also been awarded the great cross of the Order of the Hungarian Republic. As is well known, since 1990 his work has received particularly positive notice in Germany, where all his works have appeared in translation, and where he has received a number of literary awards (most recently the Goethe medal), as well as special invitations to the Frankfurt, Leipzig, and Weimar book fairs. In the afterword to a well-timed book of essays about Kertész's work, which was prepared before but published just after the Nobel Prize in the fall of 2002, Sándor Radnóti explains that it was not the prize which focused the attention of the younger generation of scholars and critics; these scholars have been studying Kertész and his work all along for years (213).

In Hungary there was a veritable outpouring of press reactions immediately after the announcement on 10 October 2002, and news items and articles appeared in the major dailies, literary weeklies, and cultural and arts journals. Not only was the literary establishment mobilized, but journalists of all stripes, political writers of all persuasions, philosophers, historians, and even economists contributed to the barrage of coverage. Of the daily newspapers, *Népszabadság* (People's Freedom, the daily with the largest circulation and left of centre), *Magyar Hírlap* (Hungarian News), *Napi Gazdaság* (Daily Economy), and *Népszava* (People's Word) all had several items in the first week after the announcement of the Nobel. *Népszabadság* and *Magyar Hírlap* had the greatest number of articles in October and continuing into December. The latter published some sixty articles between 10 October and 27 December and maintained a dossier of these on its website as of March 2004 ("Kertész Imre Nobel-díjas író" ["Imre Kertész, Nobel Laureate"] <http://www. magyarhirlap.hu/cikk.php?cikk=57583>). *Magyar Nemzet* (Hungarian Nation), the conservative daily, was much more restrained. Its contributions concentrated generally on the negative, downplaying Kertész's worth as a writer or questioning his views on Hungary and Hungarian history. Of the weeklies, *Budapest Business, 168*

Óra (168 Hours), and *Világgazdaság* (World Economy) all covered the news. *Magyar Fórum* (Hungarian Forum), the weekly of the far right party MIEP: Magyar Igazság és Élet (Hungarian Life and Justice) published by writer-turned-politician and ideologue István Csurka, had only one article on the prize, and not much attention was paid to it in *Heti Válasz* (Weekly Response), the weekly associated most closely with the conservative party FIDESZ: Fiatal Demokraták Szövetsége (Federation of Young Democrats). The major liberal literary and political weekly, *Élet és Irodalom* (Life and Literature), had a large number of articles in each of the issues following the announcement. Other literary journals, such as *The New Hungarian Quarterly* and *Beszélő* (Speaker), devoted special sections to the award. The Jewish literary and cultural press carried several articles too, especially *Szombat* (Saturday [Shabbat]) and *Múlt és Jövő* (Past and Future).

Articles and news items which appeared right after the announcement of the prize in October in the two dailies *Népszabadság* and *Magyar Hírlap*, as well as in the weeklies *168 Óra* and *Élet és Irodalom* were congratulatory in tone and positive in content, and in an interview Péter Esterházy—one of Hungary's best-known authors—told of the spontaneous standing ovation with which the news of the award was received by the public at a literary event in the city of Pécs (Esterházy, "Kertész életműve" 2784). Elsewhere, Esterházy likened the prize to a miracle in a fairy tale ("Az örömről" 3). However, in response to a number of public pronouncements by Csurka and other ideologues of the right, many articles started defending Kertész as they responded to questions about who is a "true" and "authentic" Hungarian and who should really have been awarded the prize; about the lack of acknowledgment of the Holocaust in Hungary; about issues of national identity and the interpretation of Hungarian history; about Kertész's anti-Hungarian views; and even about Hungary's international political standing on the threshold of membership in the European Union. Within a week of the announcement, the Hungarian print media was awash in a strongly politicized discussion about the Nobel Prize, thus reproducing the same polarization vis-à-vis the award that characterizes everyday political life in Hungary. After the first week, most articles in the press were drawn into a heated debate and took sides pro or contra on the basis of their writers' ideological stance rather than on an assessment or appreciation of Kertész's oeuvre. It appears that the debate around the Nobel Prize was expropriated by the right, leaving those who were genuinely pleased at this honor or value the author's work in the position of having to react to real and perceived attacks on Kertész. Thus, what might otherwise have been an occasion for a celebration became another vehicle to inflame the ongoing national debate over unresolved issues.

The first defensive voices surfaced already on 13 October in *Vasárnapi Blikk* (Sunday View), where readers were reminded that if Csurka had had a say in it, Kertész's name would have been excluded from the list of those considered worthy of the prize. The writer of the article recounted how, at the time of the 2000 Frankfurt Book Fair, Csurka had declared that Kertész was not sufficiently Hungarian to represent Hungarian literature at the fair. Now, however, everyone was proud of him, and many recognized that the tragedy of the Holocaust touches all Hungarians (Pallagi 2726). The response came in Csurka's weekly, *Magyar Fórum*, in an article on 17 October by Zoltán Szőcs: "Auschwitz Received the Nobel Prize" ("Auschwitz Nobel-díjat kapott"), which was crudely political, aggressive, and full of anti-Semitic innuendo. Szőcs admonished the Hungarian news media for its "insane" and "sensational enthusiasm" towards Kertész and concluded: "I too congratulate Imre Kertész for this great international recognition but have to admit . . . I am really curious as to who will be the first Hungarian writer to receive the Nobel Prize and when" ("Magam részéről szintén gratulálok Kertész Imrének a magas nemzetközi elismeréshez, de be kell vallanom, egyre jobban furdalja az oldalamat a kiváncsiság: vajon mikor és ki lesz az első Magyar Nobel-díjas iró?") (2784). So, hardly a week after the announcement of the prize, the media entered the fertile territory of nationalist ideology. On 24 October in an article in *Népszabadság*, "Imre Kertész and the Right Wing" ("Kertész Imre és a jobboldal"), Péter Kóczián commented on the politicization of culture in Hungary and the instrumentalization in this process of a great literary figure. After noting that neither the two right-wing parties nor the right-leaning intelligentsia participated in the celebrations surrounding Kertész's Nobel Prize, Kóczián went on to say: "the prize is a momentous event, an exceptional moment in Hungarian culture . . . with its cold-shouldering, the right wing has turned the prize into yet another instrument in the struggle between the two camps. The politicians on the right continue to maintain the complete politicization of Hungarian culture" ("Kertész díja világraszóló esemény, a magyar kultúra kivételes pillanata. . . . Kertész hideg üdvözlésével a jobboldal a Nobel díjat is a táborok közötti küzdelem eszközévé alakította. A jobboldali politikusok a maguk részéről továbbra is fenntartják a kultúra teljes átpolitizáltságát") (2829). Typically for *Magyar Nemzet*, a sarcastic little piece appeared on 24 October—"The City Is in Pain" ("Fáj a város")—in which Kertész was attacked for saying that Budapest no longer provided him with the same existential support it had done in the past: "so then good-by and let's meet in Vladivostock if we have to" ("akkor viszontlátásra, találkozzunk Vladivosztokban, ha muszáj") (Pilhál 2830). There was an interview in the 24 October issue of *168 Óra* with Horace Engdahl, permanent secretary of the Swedish Academy. Engdahl noted that the academy was surprised to receive several emails a day from Hungary expressing displeasure at the award and alleging that the academy "had become the victim of an international conspiracy aimed at destroying Hungarian culture" ("a magyar kultúra megsemmisitésére törekvő nemzetközi konspiráció áldozatául esett") (qtd. in Dragos 2831).

The largest number of articles on and analyses of the prize were published in *Népszabadság* and in *Élet és Irodalom*, with the political relevance of the award having been quickly seized upon in these papers, too. For instance, Eszter Babarczy wrote that "Imre Kertész's Nobel Prize gave the Hungarian public and Kertész himself something to think about. The Nobel Committee could not have chosen a Hungarian writer who would have stirred up more anxiety and aggressiveness in us about who is 'us' and what this honor means. . . . Our pleasure was mixed . . . the press mirrored the dilemma which we face because we have not dealt with the tension between 'us' and 'them.' Hungarian anti-Semites went instantly into internet chat rooms debating the writer's 'Hungarianness,' using the cliché of a Jewish conspiracy, asking what is it that they need to confront. . . . Many people even asked to what degree the Nobel Prize of a writer is ours if he has a bad opinion about Hungarians and does not consider Hungary his home" ("Kertész Imre Nobel-díja feladta a leckét a magyar nyilvánosságnak s neki magának is. A Nobel-bizottság aligha választhatott volna magyar írót, aki jobban felkavarja ezt a szorongást és agresszívitást bennünk a 'mi' körvonalait és a dicsőség mibenlétét illetően . . . az örömbe üröm vegyült . . . a sajtóban már tükröződött az a dilemma, amelyet a 'mi' és a 'nem mi' közti feldolgozatlan feszültség állít elénk. A magyar antiszemiták rögvest ugrottak az internetes fórumokon, részint az író 'magyar' voltát vitatva, részint a zsidó összeesküvés szokott közhelyét hangoztatva, részint felháborodva azon, hogy ugyan mivel is kéne nekik szembenézniük. . . . Többen egyenesen azt kérdezték, vajon mennyire miénk egy olyan író Nobel-díja, aki rossz véleménnyel van a magyarokról, és nem tekinti hazájának Magyarországot") (19).

An article by Iván Bächer in the 26 October 2002 issue of *Népszabadság* summarized the divergent reactions to the prize in Hungary. Entitled "Kertészmagyarország" ("The Hungary of Kertész"), the article demonstrated the wide divide in national responses: On the one hand, the prize is "hymnic high praise" ("himnikus fölmagasztalás") while on the other "a well-placed kick in the butt" ("pontosan odatett hátsón rúgás") (36) and Bächer suggested that "This Nobel Prize has become the litmus test of the nation. It is true, there are two Hungarys. One is the Hungary of Imre Kertész. The other is the Hungary which eliminated him, his family, and those who shared his fate—or fatelessness—from the legal framework of the Hungarian state" ("Ez a Nobel díj a nemzet lakmuszpapirja lett. Mert igenis: két Magyarország van. Az egyik Kertész Imre Magyarországa. A másik az a Magyarország, amely Kertész Imrét, családját és sorstársait—vagy sorstalanságtársait—kiiktatta a Magyar államiság kereteiből") (36). In a very concise article ("Fate") ("Sors"), László Seres summarized many of the issues raised in the Hungarian press in the two months following the Nobel announcement, showing the vicissitudes of this Nobel Prize. He closed his analysis by suggesting that those who were bothered by the fact that a Jewish-Hungarian writer received the Nobel Prize should re-evaluate their sense of national identity so that Kertész could fit into it, too (Seres 3).

Among the numerous articles in *Élet és Irodalom* two are worthy of particular note. The first is an abbreviated version of the one-hour television program *Záróra* (Closing Hour) shown on Magyar TV II on 11 October 2002. Three well-known literary critics, Péter Balassa, Sándor Radnóti, and Ákos Szilágyi engaged in a wide-ranging discussion about the Kertész oeuvre. They noted that *Sorstalanság* was first accepted for publication as an "anti-fascist" narrative, thus placing it into the very ideological frame of reference that it attempted to break out of. The work has remained difficult for Hungarians to digest, perhaps because Hungary has not done the requisite "grieving work" ("gyászmunka") since Auschwitz, because Hungarian cultural memory does not include Auschwitz as a Hungarian catastrophe, and because no Hungarian writer other than János Pilinszky has made this integral to his work. One of the discussants suggested that Kertész's work was now helping to accomplish this *Vergangenheitsbewältigung* and that Kertész had translated the tragedy of Auschwitz into an aesthetic form describing the unspeakable in a "masterpiece" (qtd. in Mészáros 8). In the discussants' opinion, there were few Holocaust writers who could be compared with Kertész—Borowski, Celan, Lévi, and Wiesel were mentioned—since most other survivors wrote about their experiences as "witness" testimonies or as philosophical commentaries. Balassa argued that the Nobel Prize had a wise humanistic message too: Central and Eastern Europe should use this as an opportunity to learn to debate the past—as happened in Germany—so a renewal may occur (qtd. in Mészáros 8–9).

The second article, "Magyar lobogók" ("Hungarian Flags"), is a satire on another television program, *Éjjeli menedék* (Night Refuge), shown on 22 November 2002 on Magyar TV II (see Győri). In the article, the moderator, Gábor Matúz, spoke about Kertész and the Nobel Prize with writer Péter Szentmihályi Szabó and poet Kornél Döbrentei in the House of Hungarians in front of an invited audience of about one hundred. The two guests declared proudly to applause from the audience that they had not read anything by Kertész. The only one who admitted to having read him was the moderator. After explanations as to why Kertész should not have received the Nobel Prize, Döbrentei weighed in with a lengthy monologue that was so garbled that it hardly made any sense. It consisted of a list of grievances about Hungary's lost wars, lost territories, the Communist dictatorship, the 1956 uprising, the new government's financial plans, collective guilt, the Beneš decree, the many Hungarian dead on the Soviet front during the Second World War, and so on. The resentment and the injured tone were evident in a five-minute-long stream of consciousness that began with the injustice of the Treaty of Trianon and ended with "we have our own dead. And what is terrible is that someone achieves one of the world's greatest Nobel prizes [*sic*], the greatest and finest literary prize, through suggesting but not actually mentioning the collective guilt of a nation, that is why it hurts" ("Megvannak a magunk halottai. És borzasztó az, hogy ha valaki a világ egyik legnagyobb Nobel-díját [*sic*], a legnagyobb, előkelő irodalmi díját egy nép kollektiv bünösségének a ki nem mondott sugallásával éri el, ezért fáj") (qtd. in Győri 8). At this point the speaker's words were swallowed up in the audience's applause. In order to make their views a little clearer, Szentiványi mentioned current attempts to make Holocaust denial illegal and suggested that if that happened, "it will probably become illegal to deny Kertész's literary merit" ("akkor nyilván büntethetővé válik, hogy valaki Kertész Imre irodalmi érdemeit tagadja") (8). To this Döbrentei added: "everyone knows that we are terrorized by the taste of a minority, to which the said gentleman belongs . . . if we look at the list of Nobel Prize winners, [we see] that there is political compensation going on. This prize is awarded to those political directions and peoples which have been of service to this cosmopolitan community" ("azt mindenki tudja, hogy egy kissebbségi ízlésterror van, amelynek része az illető úr. [látnivaló] . . . ha végigtekintünk a Nobel-díjasok listáján, hogy politikai kompenzáció folyik. Olyan politikai irányzatok és népek kapják ezt a díjat, amelyek szolgálatot tettek ennek a kozmopolita közösségnek") (8).

Éjjeli Menedék was criticized in the press, and more than sixty intellectuals protested in writing (see "Tiltakozás" ["Protest"] <http://www.magyarhirlap.hu/cikk.php?cikk=60248>). According to *Magyar Hírlap* of 9 December 2002, the program made the news in other countries, too, for giving voice to anti-Semitic, racist, and far-right views. It was taken off the air after giving a platform in October 2003 to Holocaust denier David Irving, who was in Budapest, together with Jean-Marie Le Pen, at the invitation of István Csurka. The right reacted to this closure with accusations of lack of freedom of the press, and members of the far-right MIEP, with some of former prime minister Viktor Orbán's "civic" groups, demonstrated against the unfairness of this decision. Döbrentei used subsequently (not for the first time) one of these demonstrations to make an overtly anti-Semitic speech, as a result of which more than one hundred and sixty members of the Hungarian Writers' Union resigned in the spring of 2004 when the Union was unwilling to censure Döbrentei. As a postscript to this affair, Kertész wrote an extensive analysis of the Writers' Union debacle (see Kertész, "Jelentés").

An overview of the Hungarian media response to Kertész's Nobel Prize would not be complete without the Jewish-Hungarian cultural and literary press. I include here three significant contributions: The monthly *Szombat* and the quarterly *Múlt és Jövő* devoted special sections in two issues each to the news and to interpretations of the Laureate's work, while the quarterly journal *Remény* (Hope) contained a section on Kertész's work in its Winter 2002 issue. The November 2002 issue of *Szombat* has a picture of Kertész on its cover with the caption "Imre Kertész Has the Nobel Prize!" ("Kertész Imre Nobel-díjas!"), and the issue contains an editorial by the writer Gábor Szántó, who expressed the hope that the prize will lead to a "catharsis" of understanding and appropriate reception for the work in Hungary and in the world. Further, he stated, the prize should help "form historical understanding in Hungary" ("a magyar történelmi tudat formálásához") (3). The December issue of *Szombat* contains a whole section devoted to the analysis of Kertész's work. *Múlt és Jövő* published a rich collection of articles on the prize by some of Hungary's best-known intellectuals, including the philosopher Ágnes Heller, critics Mihály Vajda and Zsuzsa Selyem, and writers János Kőbányai and

György Dalos (see Kőbányai). In addition, Israeli writer Aharon Appelfeld contributed an analysis of Kertész's work interspersed with personal recollections (Appelfeld 33–38). The journal's editor, János Kőbányai, noted the importance of this event on the back cover in English: "Most of our current issue is dedicated to the Nobel Prize of Imre Kertész . . . the greatest recognition ever of Hungarian literary achievement. This achievement is about the memory of Auschwitz with which, like the tattooed numbers, Kertész's work has burnt the experience of Auschwitz into the memory of European culture. The prize clearly shows that Europe has understood and is willing to deal with the culmination of its modern history." The first issue of the same journal in 2003 continued to comment on the prize with several more articles, including one by Hungarian-born French thinker François Fejtö. There was a review of media responses to the Nobel in the German-language press by György Fehéri, who commented on the very positive reception there and the fact that Kertész was seen as a friendly, happy person. Fehéri noted that "it is grotesque but one has to say the Germans are lucky that they have an Imre Kertész" ("Groteszk kimondani, de szerencsések a németek, hogy van egy Kertész Imréjük") (71). One of the more unusual items in this issue reported about plans to publish *Sorstalanság* in Esperanto (in 8,000 copies) and in Lovari, one of the Roma languages spoken in Hungary (in 3,000 copies; the publisher is a Chinese immigrant to Hungary). The 2002 winter issue of *Remény* carried a photograph of Kertész on the cover and printed the congratulatory speech of the executive director of the Federation of Hungarian Jewish Communities, given at a large public event held by the Federation in Kertész's honor on 19 October 2002 (Zoltai 3–4). One might sum up these reactions by noting that the "Jewish" response is less overtly political in tone than the mainstream press.

Kertész was in Berlin when the prize was announced and thus he gave many interviews to the German-language media. There was strong reaction in Hungary, especially on the political right, to some of the statements he made to German or Swiss journalists. In the German-language media, virtually all reports were extraordinarily positive and did not shy away from dealing with tough questions (see, for instance Andreas Oplatka's piece in the *Neue Zürcher Zeitung* about the main theme of the Kertész oeuvre, the Holocaust, as taboo under Communism and as instrumentalized negatively in current political discourse in Hungary). Not only the major dailies but many local papers in the German-language press contained articles and commentary on the prize. In the period October–December 2002 there were almost as many articles in the *Frankfurter Allgemeine Zeitung* and the *Neue Zürcher Zeitung* as in the two main Hungarian dailies, and overall, the German press continued its preoccupation with Kertész's work much longer than the Hungarian press.

Much negative reaction in Hungary was occasioned by an interview published in the German weekly *Die Zeit* on 14 October. With reference to Martin Walser's most recent (and controversial) novel, Kertész said that he had seldom come across anyone in Germany who denied what was happening there in 1944. He attributed this to the confrontation with the past that had taken place in Germany. According to him, in Hungary this confrontation had not taken place and there was, instead, a conspiracy of silence: "You cannot imagine the conditions there. There is overt anti-Semitism. Self-professed Nazis, aggressive nationalists appear in the media and they are not as sophisticated as Herr Walser. It is almost as disgusting as in the late 1930s" ("Sie können die Zustände dort nicht vorstellen. Es herrscht offener Antisemitismus. Erklärte Nazis, aggressive Nationalisten treten in den Medien auf, die sind nicht so fein wie Herr Walser. Es ist beinahe so ekelhaft wie in den späten dreissiger Jahren") (qtd. in Radisch 45). In Hungary this statement played into the hands of conservative nationalists and those on the extreme right, who used the statement in the public media (e.g., in *Éjjeli Menedék;* see above), not only against Kertész, but more broadly to score points in their ongoing ideological struggle to regain some of what they perceived as moral support during the years of the conservative Orbán government (which lost the 2002 election). In fact, Kertész seems to have been both accurate and prescient, as in the meantime anti-Semitic statements and incidents have increased both in Hungary and elsewhere in Europe. In Hungary it is not unusual to find openly anti-Semitic articles in the far-right press, such as *Magyar Fórum* or *Magyar Demokrata,* and more coded ones in the mainstream *Magyar Nemzet.* Public radio and television have also carried exclusionary and at times hardly coded anti-Semitic messages. Noteworthy among recent cases of "hate-speech" is that of Lóránt Hegedüs, a Reform Church minister whose conviction for "inciting hatred against a community" (he called for the elimination of "Galician hordes" in an article) was overturned by an appeals court to a chorus of praise in *Magyar Fórum, Magyar Demokrata,* and other right-wing publications. On the other hand, eighty-four leading Hungarian intellectuals signed a public statement expressing their disappointment in the court's decision because its message to the world is that "in Hungary discrimination, racism and anti-Semitism are normal parts of public life" (Molnár <http://tinyurl.com/2hewg>).

To provide some answers to my second question—What was the effect of this prize on Kertész's work, his life, and on Hungarian literature and literary culture?—one cannot leave unexamined the Internet, an unending source of information about Kertész and his Nobel Prize. Here are a few summary comments from the vast available material. On <www.google.ca> in the spring of 2003 there were at least 58,000 references to Kertész, mostly in connection with the Nobel Prize, in a large number of languages ranging from the more common European ones to Chinese, Hindi, Korean, Turkish, and Vietnamese. In February 2004 there were still 60,000 or more references. Doing a Google search in early 2004 using Hungarian, there were 38,000 references citing articles, news items, and discussions, from newspapers, magazines, booksellers, press agencies, publishers from around the world, literary, cultural, and political journals, academic websites, the Nobel site and its links, international electronic media, Hungarian embassy websites abroad, the Frankfurt and Leipzig Book Fairs, academic conferences, and Jewish literary and other sites such as *centropa.org* and *Virtual Jerusalem*. Even tourism sites carried information about the award, as, for instance, *Budpocketguide.com,* which lists Kertész with such famous Hungarians as Otto von Habsburg, Kossuth, Puskás, Lehár, Bartók, and Pulitzer.

The Hungarian search engine <http://vizsla.origo.hu/> had over 45,000 references to Kertész in March 2004. As a result of the prize, the Digitális Irodalmi Akadémia (Digital Academy of Literature) decided to place all of Kertész's works on their public access website at <http://www.irodalmiakademia.hu/>. Another website for literature, the Kortárs Irodalmi Adattár (Database of Contemporary Authors), added much biographical and bibliographic information about Kertész after the Nobel Prize (see <http://www.kontextus.hu/kia/kia.php>). Kertész's Hungarian publisher Magvető created a Kertész website soon after the award at <http://kertesz.uw.hu> with a selection of quotes from a variety of papers from around the world and links to other sites. The Fokusz Online Internet bookstore achieved a record number of hits (400,000 during October 2002), as well as sales of Kertész's works after the Nobel announcement. Their Internet book sales in general were boosted by 20 percent (see Sebők <http://www.she.hu/main.php?form=cikk&id=2974>).

As a result of the general media attention in Hungary, the publisher Magvető immediately produced a new and complete edition of Kertész's work, including the Stockholm lecture. In the first few weeks after the announcement 70,000 copies of *Sorstalanság* were sold and 50,000 more printed for Christmas. The Hungarian best-seller list for the year 2002 contained six of Kertész's works among the top twenty, with *Sorstalanság* at the top of the list. Altogether 210,000 copies of the novel were sold between 10 October and the end of December, more than any other book in living memory (see V.L.M., <http://lists.topica.com/lists/netszemle/read/message.html?mid=805358572>). The novel *Sorstalanság* (and Kertész generally) was recommended for use in teaching in Hungarian high schools and certainly at the university level. The Ministry of Culture provided a copy for each of 3,800 public libraries; they also sent the complete works to seventeen Hungarian cultural centers abroad. The Ministry of Education sent the book to 4,492 state elementary and high schools. At the same time the mayor of Budapest sent each high school in the city a copy (these items were reported in *Népszabadság* [11 December 2002]: 11). Legislation was passed quickly to change existing tax laws so the writer would not have to pay tax on the roughly $1 million prize. The film of *Sorstalanság*, which had already been planned before the prize, obtained significant funding (920 million forints) from the Hungarian government and is being worked on as an international co-production (on this, see Portuges). Rights to the film script have been bought by China, France, Spain, and the U.S. Foreign-language rights to the new novel *Felszámolás* (*Liquidation)* were sold by the German publisher upon news of the Nobel Prize to Brazil, France, Greece, Holland, Italy, Poland, Portugal, Spain, and the U.S., and to more countries since then. Kertész was made an honorary citizen of Budapest, and *Magyar Hírlap* declared him "Man of the Year" for 2002.

So what is the meaning of this Nobel Prize for Kertész himself and for Hungarian literature and cultural life? On the purely factual, materialistic side, we have seen that the writer and his work have been catapulted onto the world stage. Recognition, financial security, and a measure of happiness have come his way, although with characteristic irony it is a "catastrophe of happiness" that has been showered on him; out of sheer goodness people have placed little rocks of Sisyphus in his path. He wants above all to continue writing and hopes the prize will give him the freedom to do so: "[the prize] has not changed my life—in essence—I don't want it to change" ("az én életemen ez—ami a lényeget illeti—tulajdonképpen nem változtat, nem akarom, hogy változtasson" ("A *Sorstalanság*ot a Kádár-rendszerről írtam" 3). Inevitably, the prize makes him review the meaning of his work; much of his Nobel lecture deals with how he came to be a writer, his loneliness, and the difficulty of creating art using the subject matter that has most occupied him. He accepts that he is a "Holocaust writer" on condition that the Holocaust is recognized as a metaphor for the human condition in general and the collapse of European civilization in particular (see Kertész, "Eureka!").

As for Hungarian literature and Hungarian society in general, some claim that "gradually the reception of Imre Kertész's Nobel Prize will have its own literature at home; this is really a debate about how Hungarians—readers and non-readers—received the news of Kertész's Nobel Prize, and how his work was viewed before and after, and, of course, inevitably: whether Kertész likes Hungarians. And if he does not, is it his prerogative not to?" ("Lassan külön irodalma lesz Kertész Imre Nobel-díja hazai recepciójának, a vitának, amely egyebek között arról szól, hogy miként fogadták a magyarok—olvasók és nem olvasók—Kertész Nobel-díjának hírét, s miként viszonyult a kritika az életműhöz annak előtte és annak utána, na és ahogy mondani szokás: arról is, hogy szereti-e Kertész a magyarokat. És ha nem, jogában áll-e nem szeretni?" (Szigethy <http://lists.topica.com/lists/netszemle/read/message.html?mid=805392697>). Although this question did indeed occupy many in Hungary, especially those—such as Döbrentei—who carry within them a sense of grievance and resentment, the Nobel Prize was, nevertheless, the biggest event of the season according to an opinion survey carried out by the Median survey research company. The survey found that 90 percent of those asked had heard of the prize, 43 percent considered it one of the five most important events to touch the lives of Hungarians. The only Hungarian event that was more "newsworthy" at the time was a record high lottery prize (see Szigethy <http://lists.topica.com/lists/netszemle/read/message.html?mid=805392697>). Kertész himself understands that his Nobel Prize is also a sign of distinction for Hungarian literature and, in turn, an opportunity to review the European and Hungarian past (Kertész, "Endlich Sicherheit" <http://tinyurl.com/3bgzh>). He ac-

knowledges this "educational" aspect of his work and in his interview with Eszter
Rádai, comments on the general acceptance of *Sorstalanság* as a Holocaust novel
that is supposed to help Hungarian society confront its past. The Hungarian media
understood this lesson also: "Consciously or unconsciously, the writer's thoughts
must circle around the political-moral divisiveness which characterizes Hungary's
attitude to its own historical past on the national question. This debate in Hungary
was precipitated not least by the Kertész Nobel Prize which, on the one hand, divides
society, but on the other, encourages and strengthens those forces which—together
with Kertész—have pledged themselves to truth on the path to (Western) Europe"
("A Nobel-díjas író gondolatai tudatosan-öntudatlanul a körül a politikai-morális me-
gosztottság körül forognak, amely a mai Magyarországot a nemzeti kérdésben a saját
történelmi multhoz való viszonyulásában jellemzi. Magyarországon ezt a vitát nem
utolsósorban Kertész Nobel díja robbantotta ki, amely egyrészt megosztja a társa-
dalmat, másrészt bátorítja, gyarapítja azokat az erõket, amelyek—Kertésszel együtt
—elkötelezettek az igazság, a (Nyugat)-Európa irányába való nyitas iránt") (Dunai
11).

The Nobel Prize has put Hungary on the world map, at least briefly, and
Hungarian culture has benefited by having Kertész's works translated and published around the world. More importantly perhaps, the admiration for or antagonism to the prize have become part of a public discussion, at times bitter and un-
civilized, which might be considered the first steps in a process of *Vergangenheitsbewältigung*. Efforts are underway in Hungary to memorialize the Holocaust in
appropriate ways, to teach about it in schools and slowly perhaps to confront the
past. A recent survey carried out by polling agency Szonda Ipsos on Holocaust
awareness in Hungary found that only 2 percent of the adult population is well informed about the Holocaust and 16 percent is totally uninformed. The most serious
fact uncovered was that among the least informed were young people between the
ages of 18 and 25 (see Cs. K., <http://www.nol.hu/cikk/145535/>). So there is a
long way to go. But the confrontation with Kertész's work and the meaning of the
Nobel Prize may, indeed, be beneficial in this process. By the spring of 2003 the
media debates about the prize had died down in Hungary and Kertész is no longer
"on the agenda." While he remains highly valued as a writer, the media has
dropped him in favor of other, more exciting matters of the moment. The right-
wing and nationalist groupings have found other issues with which to pursue their
essentialist and exclusionary discourse. Kertész, too, will presumably continue, despite his Nobel Prize, to chisel away at his rock of Sisyphus.

Works Cited

Appelfeld, Aharon. "Kain és Ábel narratívája. Kertész Imre Nobel-díjáról" ("The Nar-
    rative of Cain and Abel: About Imre Kertész's Nobel Prize"). Trans. János
    Kőbányai. *Múlt és Jövő* 4 (2002): 33–38.

Babarczy, Eszter. "Nobel-dilemma—itt az alkalom" ("The Dilemma of the Nobel: An Opportunity"). *Népszabadság* (19 October 2002): 19.

Bächer, Iván. "Kertészmagyarország" ("The Hungary of Kertész"). *Népszabadság* (26 October 2002): 36.

Cs.K. "A többség nem hallott Dachauról" ("The Majority Has not Heard of Dachau"). *Népszabadság* (6 February 2004): <http://www.nol.hu/cikk/145535/>.

Deák, István. "Stranger in Hell." *New York Review of Books* (25 September 2003): 65–67.

Digitális Irodalmi Akadémia (Digital Academy of Literature): <http://www. irodalmiakademia.hu/>).

Dragos, Erzsébet. "A 17-es székben" ("In Chair Number 17"). *Tallózó* 14 (31 October 2002): 2830–31.

Dunai, Péter. "Üzenet a magyaroknak Stockholmból" ("Message to the Hungarians from Stockholm"). *Népszabadság* (11 December 2002): 11.

Esterházy, Péter. "Kertész életműve a 20. század egyik legmagasabb pontja" ("Kertész's Oeuvre Is One of the High Points of the Twentieth Century"). *Tallózó* (24 October 2002): 2784.

Esterházy, Péter. "Az örömről" ("About Happiness"). *Élet és Irodalom* 46 (25 October 2002): 3.

Fehéri, György. "Miért szeretik Kertész Imrét Németországban?" ("Why Do They Like Imre Kertész in Germany?"). *Múlt és Jövő* 1 (2003): 70–75.

Fejtö, François. "Kicsoda Kertész Imre?" ("Who Is Imre Kertész?") *Múlt és Jövő* 1 (2003): 67–68.

Győri, J. László. "Magyar lobogók" ("Hungarian Flags"). *Élet és Irodalom* 46 (29 November 2002): 8.

K.Cs. "A többség nem hallott Dachauról" ("The Majority Has Not Heard of Dachau"). *Népszabadság* (6 February 2004): <http://www.nol.hu/cikk/145535/>.

Kertész, Imre. "Endlich Sicherheit." faz.net (10 October 2002): <http://tinyurl.com/ 3bgzh>.

Kertész, Imre. "Eureka! The 2002 Nobel Lecture." Trans. Ivan Sanders. *World Literature Today* 77.1 (2003): 4–8.

Kertész, Imre. *Fatelessness*. Trans. Tim Wilkinson. New York: Vintage, 2004.

Kertész, Imre. "Jelentés a költészet birodalmából. Egy mítosz vége" ("Report from the Empire of Poetry: End of a Myth"). *Élet és Irodalom* 48 (2 April 2004): 3.

Kertész, Imre. *Sorstalanság* (*Fatelessness*). Budapest: Szépirodalmi, 1975.

Kertész, Imre. "A *Sorstalanságot* a Kádár-rendszerről írtam" ("I Wrote *Fatelessness* about the Kádár Régime"). Interview with Eszter Rádai. *Élet és Irodalom* (30 May 2003): 3, 8.

"Kertész Imre Nobel-díjas író" ("Imre Kertész, Nobel Laureate"). *Magyar Hírlap* <http://www.magyarhirlap.hu/cikk.php?cikk=57583>.

Kóczián, Péter. "Kertész Imre és a jobboldal" ("Imre Kertész and the Right Wing"). *Tallózó* 14 (31 October 2002): 2829.

Kortárs Irodalmi Adattár (Database of Contemporary Authors): <http://www.kontextus. hu/kia/kia.php>.

Kőbányai, János, ed. *Múlt és Jövő* 4 (2002): 4–56.

Marsovszky, Magdalena. "Imre Kertész—einer von uns! Oder doch nicht? Kulturkampf und Identität in Ungarn." *Europas Mitte, Mitteleuropa, europäische Identität? Geschichte, Literatur, Positionen.* Ed. Barbara Breisach and Dorothee Rabe. Berlin: Logos, 2003. 137–53.

Marsovszky, Magdalena. "Imre Kertész and Hungary Today." Trans. Eszter Pásztor. *Imre Kertész and Holocaust Literature.* Ed. Louise O. Vasvári and Steven Tötösy de Zepetnek. West Lafayette: Purdue UP, 2005. 148–61.

Mészáros, Sándor, ed. "Hírérték és kulturális emlékezet" ("News Value and Cultural Memory"). *Élet és Irodalom* (25 October 2002): 8–9.

Molnár, Bálint. "Drawing Red Lines" *Transitions OnLine: Central Europe Review* (9 January 2004): <http://tinyurl.com/2hewg>.

Oplatka, Andreas. "Das lange Warten in Ungarn" ("The Long Wait in Hungary"). *Neue Zürcher Zeitung* (11 October 2002): Feuilleton.

Pallagi, Ferenc. "Tízezer perc" ("Ten Thousand Minutes"). *Tallózó* 14 (17 October 2002): 2726.

Pilhál, György. "Fáj a város" ("The City Is in Pain"). *Tallózó* 14 (31 October 2002): 2830.

Portuges, Catherine. "Imre Kertész and the Filming of *Sorstalanság* (*Fatelessness*)." *Imre Kertész and Holocaust Literature.* Ed. Louise O. Vasvári and Steven Tötösy de Zepetnek. West Lafayette: Purdue UP, 2005. 182–94.

Radisch, Iris. "Die Glückskatastrophe. ZEIT-Gespräch mit dem Nobelpreisträger Imre Kertész über Berlin, den Antisemitismus, das Geld und die Erlösung." *Die Zeit* (17 Oktober 2002): 45–46.

Radnóti, Sándor. "Utószó—a Nobel-díj után" ("Epilogue: After the Nobel Prize"). *Az értelmezés szükségessége. Tanulmányok Kertész Imréről* (The Necessity of Interpretation: Studies on Imre Kertész). Ed. Tamás Scheibner and Zoltán Gábor Szűcs. Budapest: L'Harmattan, 2002. 211–17.

Rathgeb, Eberhard. "Porträt. Imre Kertész, ungarischer Schriftsteller." *Frankfurter Allgemeine Zeitung* (10 October 2002): Feuilleton.

Sebők, János. "Kertész Imre az Interneten is 'arat'" ("Imre Kertész is 'Reaping Success' on the Internet, Too"). *She.hu* (22 November 2002): <http://www.she.hu/ main.php?form=cikk&id=2974>.

Seres, László. "Sors" ("Fate"). *Népszabadság* (10 December 2002): 3.

Szántó, Gábor T. "A katarzis reményében" ("Hoping for Catharsis"). *Szombat* 14.9 (November 2002): 3.

Szigethy, András. "Szereti-e Kertész a magyarokat?" ("Does Kertész Like Hungarians?") *Népszabadság*, (30 January 2003): <http://lists.topica.com/lists/netszemle/ read/message.html?mid=805392697>

Szirtes, George. "Who Is Imre Kertész?" *Times Literary Supplement* (18 October 2002): 18.

Szőcs, Zoltán. "Auschwitz Nobel-díjat kapott" ("Auschwitz Received the Nobel Prize"). *Tallózó* 14.43 (24 October 2002): 2784.

"Tiltakozás az *Éjjeli Menedék* Kertész-műsora ellen" ("Protest Against the Kertész Program on *Éjjeli Menedék*"). *Magyar Hírlap* (16 December 2002): <http://www. magyarhirlap.hu/cikk.php?cikk=60248>.

Tötösy de Zepetnek, Steven. "And the 2002 Nobel Prize for Literature Goes to Imre Kertész, Jew and Hungarian." *CLCWeb: Comparative Literature and Culture* 5.1 (2003): <http://clcwebjournal.lib.purdue.edu/clcweb03–1/totosy03.html>.

Tötösy de Zepetnek, Steven. "Imre Kertész's Nobel Prize in Literature and the Print Media." *Imre Kertész and Holocaust Literature*. Ed. Louise O. Vasvári and Steven Tötösy de Zepetnek. West Lafayette: Purdue UP, 2005. 232–46.

V.L.M. "Kertész Imre hat könyve a sikerlistán" ("Six Books by Imre Kertész on the Bestseller List"). *Népszabadság* (27 January 2003): <http://lists.topica.com/lists/ netszemle/read/message.html?mid=805358572>.

Zoltai, Gusztáv. "Kertész Imre." *Remény* (Hope) 5.4 (2002): 3–4.

Book Review Article: Jewish Identity and Anti-Semitism in Central European Culture

(Books by Lamping, Gilman and Steinecke, Goltschnigg and Steinecke, Suleiman and Forgács, and Wallas)

Barbara Breysach

As we know, Jewish thought and cultural production played over the centuries a significant role particularly in Central and Eastern European culture, and the Jews, a poly-lingual and culturally productive minority, often played the role of mediators. In the last few years a good amount of scholarship has been published about Jewish literature in the various languages of the region. German-language Jewry is the starting point for an exploration of this geo-cultural space. In this review article, I present a number of volumes published more recently of both primary texts and criticism: Dieter Lamping, ed., *Identität und Gedächtnis in der jüdischen Literatur nach 1945* (Berlin: Erich Schmidt, 2003), Sander L. Gilman and Hartmut Steinecke, eds., *Deutsch-jüdische Literatur der neunziger Jahre: Die Generation nach der Shoah* (Berlin: Erich Schmidt, 2002), Dietmar Goltschnigg and Hartmut Steinecke, eds., *Essays über österreichische, deutsche und jüdische Literatur* (Berlin: Erich Schmidt, 2000), Susan Rubin Suleiman and Éva Forgács, eds. *Contemporary Jewish Writing in Hungary: An Anthology* (Lincoln: U of Nebraska P, 2003), and Armin A. Wallas, ed. *Jüdische Identitäten in Mitteleuropa. Literarische Modelle der Identitätskonstruktion* (Tübingen: Niemeyer, 2002).

    Contemporary Jewish Writing in Hungary: An Anthology, edited by Susan Rubin Suleiman and Éva Forgács within the series Jewish Writing in the Contemporary World (series editor is Sander L. Gilman), suggests a productive and lively Jewish-Hungarian literary scene but where the shadows of annihilation and the concentration camp experience are very much present. In the Second World War and in particular with the German occupation of Hungary in 1944, the Hungarian authorities cooperated with the national socialist regime and, as a consequence, two-thirds of the Jewish-Hungarian population were murdered. Today, about 100,000 Jews live in Hungary (more than that if we count the secularized and assimilated Jewry) and form one of the largest Jewish communities in Central and Eastern Europe. The Jewish-Hungarian literature of today goes back to the period of Jewish-Hungarian assimilation between 1867 and 1914, followed by the period between the two world wars when legalized anti-Semitism took hold in Hungary. For example, it is during the latter period when the brilliant texts of prose author Károly Pap were published, a text of whom is included in the volume (Pap perished in the concentration camp at Bergen-Belsen). In addition to some well-known names, such as Imre Kertész, György Konrád, and Péter Nádas, the volume by Suleiman and Forgács includes a number of authors little or not at all published and consequently unknown in the English-speaking world.

In the volume, Örkény's *Minute Stories* reflects the trauma of the Holocaust and the ideological, social, and moral abyss of post-Second World War Hungary. For example, Örkény's *One-Minute Biography* presents an unfinished and disabled ego, one that could never realize its potentials given by birth. One can read this text as an expression of Jewish-Hungarian *post-histoire:* The destructive ways of history are illustrated by the autobiographical "I," where the author is condemned to lead a secondary and secret existence, disabled and at the same time superimposed on the "primary" existence. Örkény's text makes me think of the Polish writer Hanna Krall, whose work is centered around the problem of memory. Péter Nádas and Imre Kertész stress that Jewish-Hungarian literature in its entirety should not be considered a "minor literature" (that is, in the context of Deleuze and Guattari) but instead as world literature, thematically and formally. Suleiman and Forgács selected an excerpt from Kertész's *Sorstalanság* (the selection occurred before Kertész received the Nobel Prize); and from Nádas, who had spent many years in Berlin and had found there early recognition that was instrumental for his artistic development, they selected the short story "The Lamb," in my opinion a narrative masterpiece, written in the 1960s. This short story—translated into English here for the first time—anticipates the breakup of the (autobiographical) narrative perspective, which led Nádas later in his novel *The Book of Memories* (trans. Ivan Sanders) to achieve his distinctive narrative style. Mr. Roth, a Jew and bizarre outsider in a housing project area, especially in the view of children, steps out of his hidden and stigmatized existence only through his sudden—possibly suicidal—death. In the story children and teenagers act as catalysts of the inner social dynamics of the society described. Already the word "Jew" indicates ambiguity, insecurity, or defense, and becomes a non-word, which then indicates a taboo. Thus, Nádas's short story expresses the double negation of Jewish existence in post-Second World War Communist Hungary. To me, the text remains until today a text full of disturbing double meanings. Dramaturgically, it is centered around everyday life, but in a deeper sense it describes the cultural silence about Jewish identity. With the exception of Mária Ember the Jewish-Hungarian authors represented in the anthology are predominantly writers of fiction. Ember wrote the first memoir of a Holocaust survivor published in Communist Hungary, although the memoir was presented in a fictional form. In the new edition of 1994, Ember then interprets her Holocaust text as a contribution to "Hungarian history," apparently to avoid the danger of a Jewish-Hungarian niche literature and thus exclusion by the virulent anti-Semitic sections in Hungary active today.

The texts in the volume by Suleiman and Forgács suggest to me that, similar to the situation in Poland (see Antony Polonsky and Monika Adamczyk-Grabowska, eds., *Contemporary Jewish Writing in Poland*), Jewish-Hungarian literature appears to have emerged from the status quo of taboo with regard to Jewish identity and that this slow emergence occurred with the last years of Communist rule. At the same time, tragically, the end of Communist rule in 1989 brought not only liberation from Soviet colonial rule in Hungary and in the other countries of the region but also a culture clash where latent anti-Semitism gained much support. The background of this acute development is explained briefly by Suleiman and Forgács in their introduction to the volume. And I should like to add that after the Nobel Prize of Imre Kertész in 2002, this culture clash became evident in the nationalist and right-wing media active today in Hungary (see, e.g., in the present volume by Marsovszky; Tötösy de Zepetnek; Young). In my opinion, the volume is a significant contribution to the landscape of English translations from an otherwise neglected part of the world. In the selection of texts, the editors' concentration on authors who remained in Hungary and are alive today (or died only recently) is important because their texts reflect clearly the post-1989 situation of culture in the country. One question remains for me, however, and this is whether the texts in the collection should be inscribed exclusively as Jewish-Hungarian literature or whether they would be best located in a conceptualization of a variety of Hungarian literatures, together with Sándor Márai, Antal Szerb, or Dezsö Kosztolányi and others, all important representatives of Hungarian literature on the German book market. Of course, this is a question touching on the larger theme of the national versus the pluri-cultural understanding of culture and literature.

The collection *Jüdische Identitäten in Mitteleuropa* was published in the Niemeyer series *conditio judaica*, edited by Armin A. Wallas following a symposium held at the University of Klagenfurt (at the University of Klagenfurt, Armin A. Wallas was a prolific scholar of Central and Eastern European culture with focus on matters Jewish, who died tragically in 2002). The volume's theme is the plurality/variety of Jewish cultures in Central Europe. In his introduction, Wallas differentiates between the Jewish cultures of Central and Eastern Europe and argues that Jewish people's culture as a formative current would have developed only in Eastern Europe. Material of the volume is wide-ranging and features multicultural Trieste, Croatia, Serbia, German-language Galician, Czech, Moravian, Hungarian, and Austrian authors. An eye catcher is the special importance accorded to the avant-garde and modernity as an artistic alternative between the options of the full assimilation of Jews or cultural or political Zionism. Modernity in artistic production opened a space to Jewish authors where they were able to draft the self/own as an Other. This way they could avoid artistically the compulsion to decide for themselves for one or another form of Jewish existence. In other words, Jewish self-consciousness develops itself frequently in the darkness of individual conscience, beyond the possibility of definition, as Michael A. Meyer, following Freud, points out.

Of special interest for an understanding of Central European Jewish culture are the intra-Jewish debates treated in the contributions of the Wallas's "Kulturzionismus, Expressionismus und jüdische Identität. Die Zeitschriften *Jerubaal* und *Esra* als Sprachrohr und Diskussionsforum der zionistischen Jugendbewegung in Österreich" (61–100) and Andreas Herzog's "Ludwig Strauß und Ernst Sommer als Vertreter der jüdischen Renaissance. Ein Beitrag zur Buber-Rezeption" (47–60). Herzog regards Ludwig Strauß and Ernst Sommer as representatives of a Jewish Renaissance. In Strauß, Herzog sees correctly the search for original Jewish creativity and the detachment "von der geistigen Knechtschaft des Deutschtums" ("from the intellectual serfdom of Germandom" (53). However, in my opinion this characterization leaves the Hölderlin scholar Strauß out and reduces him to his "Jewish intellectuality." Strauß's German-Jewish bi-culturality is certainly one of the most original positions within cultural Zionism. Wallas discusses in his paper, "Kulturzionismus, Expressionismus und jüdische Identität," the connection between Jewish renaissance and expressionist awakening. This is underlined not only by the remarkable number of Jewish expressionists, such as Else Lasker-Schüler, Albert Ehrenstein, Alfred Wolfenstein, Kurt Hiller, Max Brod, and Franz Werfel, but also the existence of such journals as *Jerubaal* and *Esra* testifies to the connection between Jewish messianism interpreted as the modern and expressionist bathos of change.

I was intrigued in the volume in particular by the discussion about Trieste Jewry. The collection succeeds here not only in presenting scholarship about a cultural sphere in the south of Habsburg Central Europe, but also in presenting a variety of methodologies, including the analysis of bourgeois family history as well as theories of writing and feminist. This includes also papers in the field of the history of ideas, such as about the melancholic and skeptic humanism of Guido Voghera and his son Giorgio. Renate Lunzer's essay, "Hungerküstler gegen Menschenfresser. Zur Theorie der ethischen Antiselektion bei Guido und Giorgio Voghera" (301–10) analyzes this, pointing in equal measure to Schopenhauer, a specific Habsburg cultural mentality, and the Jewish experience. Like his father before him, Giorgio Voghera emigrated to Palestine at the end of the 1930s and left in 1948 before the state of Israel was founded. To him, anti-Semitism appeared to be a standard of society, present not in economic or social conflicts or in intolerance towards religion. Rather, anti-Semites are human beings who aim permanently at conquest, aggression, violence, and struggle, and are unable to value the Jewish mentality towards life, a mentality that has sometimes been defined as Christian. The contributions by Anna Millo (on the Vivante family), by Christian Benussi (on female Jewish writers in the twentieth century), by Edgar Sallager (on Italo Svevo), and by Renate Lunzer—the latter two being also translators of Italo Svevo and Giorgio Voghera into German—illuminate the literature of Trieste Jewry in their papers written in Italian and thus a specific variety of literature in Habsburg Central Europe.

Psychoanalysis is employed in this volume in Edgar Sallager's contribution, "Implizites Judentum und Psychoanalyse bei Italo Svevo" (283–300). However, as psychoanalysis was introduced in the preface as an interpretative model of Jewish identity in Central Europe, I was expecting more in-depth discussion on the topic. Claudio Magris and Angelo Ara postulate in their cultural history of Trieste— *Triest: Eine literarische Hauptstadt in Mitteleuropa*, trans. Maria Gschwend Ragni —that psychoanalysis would be "Trieste's grand contribution to Italian culture" and mention both Vogheras in this context. Sallagher's study now puts Svevo's "implizites Judentum" (implicit Jewry) and the importance of psychoanalysis for his work into a basic connection, especially for the interpretation of his late novel *La Conscienza dei Zeno* (1923). All of Svevo's novels have protagonists who appear to be weak in action and will, skeptical, and without drive. Sallagher interprets this as the "Jewish essence" of Svevo's texts, as a reflection of the nonsense of Jewish endeavors towards assimilation and integration. His interpretation of Svevo thus upgrades the role of the Jewish experience in his work and defines this as a tendency towards self-control, as the ability for self-recognition and self-irony, but also as a tendency to masochism and the conviction of the relativity of human cultural achievements. This is plausible insofar as Sallagher understands the status and locus of Jews as being in-between cultures. Svevo therefore wrote to live and experience while he situated psychoanalysis as therapy with words. Svevo was a master of raising the autobiographical in this manner to art, so that it was included and at the same time hidden and estranged. Trieste played a hidden role in the writing of a famous elective Trieste citizen, James Joyce, in his novel *Ulysses* and its the image of the city; in Voghera's and Svevo's prose Trieste becomes the capital of a tired Europe. And Tamás Lichtman, in his paper, "Jüdische Identitätsfragen und -konflikte in der ungarischen Literatur am Beispiel von Károly Pap" (127–42), argues that there is no "Jewish" literature in Hungarian as a specific body of text. Instead, there is Jewish literature in Hungary, which consists of works written in Hebrew and Jiddish. With this opinion Lichtman contradicts the approach of Suleiman and Forgács in the anthology I introduced above. In my view, Lichtman's attempt to be more precise is only partially helpful, because the perspective of Jewish-Hungarian literature does not exclude in any way the proposition that Pap belongs to Hungarian literature at the same time. Unfortunately, the volume contains no contributions on Jewish literature in Poland, a literature that experienced an upswing comparable to the developments in Hungary from the end of the nineteenth century to the first third of the twentieth century.

The conceptual confusion about the loci and definition of Jewish literature appears to be fully accomplished in the title of a collection on Egon Schwarz's essays, put together by Dietmar Goltschnigg and Hartmut Steinecke, eds., *Essays über österreichische, deutsche und jüdische Literatur*. And the confusion increases when Arthur Schnitzler and Heinrich Heine are designated as "Jewish literary men" (although they are regarded, respectively, in general, as Austrian-Jewish and German-Jewish writers). But this was probably only a lapsus within the title, as Schwarz himself clarifies in his essay "Der 'Beitrag' der Juden zur deutschen Literatur" (55–73): primarily, the possibility of choice between Germanness and Jewishness has led to the productivity of German-Jewish literature. This would include different affinities being side by side respectively, a double nationality: "As the 'hyphenated American' undoubtedly exists, so were our writers both in their conscience both German and Jewish, and there was a need for cataclysmic developments to separate this unity" (59; all subsequent translations from the German are mine). Schwarz is aware of the problem that subordinations become questionable if there are no more "religious and linguistic barriers" (57). A few pages later Schwarz discusses the tradition of anti-Semitic literary history and quotes Adolf Bartels's thesis that "the Jews wanted to replace the real German culture by a German-Jewish fictitious culture. . . . The Jews imagine that they administer the intellectual property of the German people, although they just change it and destroy it thereby" (70). The position of Schwarz rises to the challenges of German-Jewish literary and intellectual history only conditionally in the face of the fact that Bartels's anti-Semitism anticipated the cultural policy of the National Socialist regime and also in the face of contemporary anti-Semitism. Perhaps Schwarz bases his thoughts on his own apparently positive experience of exile in the U.S. and his being a mediator between the two continents, resulting in his postulate about the acceptance of Jews as "wanderers" between worlds of nations. While I do not doubt that the overcoming of national thinking would be the basis necessary for both modernity and postmodernity, at the same time transnationality ought not to be linked unreflected and exclusively to Jewish existence. In this context, Schwarz argues convincingly that anti-Jewish thought in the 1920s was mostly anti-modern as well. This is proven paradigmatically by Bartels's invectives against the S. Fischer publishing house, for example. In his essay "Paradigmen eines grenzenlosen Antisemitismus" (74–91), Schwarz devotes himself to two "classics" of racial anti-Semitism, by Eugen Dühring and Edouard Drumont. The Frenchman Drumont—emulating his countryman de Gobineau—argues in his book *La France juive* (1886) that Jews are different and alien to the French, that they lack artistic and intellectual originality. Drumont denies that Jewish writers and artists could have freedom, beauty, and moral greatness. He spreads also the stereotype used later again and again, namely that the sharp, but intellectually and artistically nonproductive "Jewish intelligence" is in fact limited. The case of Dühring and his book *Die Judenfrage als Rassen-, Sitten- und Kulturfrage mit einer weltgeschichtlichen Antwort* (1881) is an interesting source for research on anti-Semitism, because the atheist Dühring planned to found an anti-Jewish-Christian substitute for religion by the creation of a "German church." Dühring negated not only the German Jewry and Jewry as such, but also the Christianity of his time. He understands religion as "a sum of people's fantasies, which embody the desires and main concerns of the respective people" (85). Dühring's thesis of the supremacy of national identity against higher religious ethics anticipates National Socialist ideology and the disastrous merger of a state-friendly part of the Protestant church with the national socialist regime. Schwarz's reading of both anti-Semitic standard works is stimulating and close to the text—and the only essay in the volume not published previously.

Schwarz is an expert of Austrian-Jewish literature and he demonstrated this with his incisive papers on Werfel, Schnitzler, and Hofmannsthal. Schwarz negates the anti-Semitic cultural theory of Drumont as seen in his paper "Artur Schnitzler und das Judentum" (133–51), where he postulates that Schnitzler had become a model case of successful assimilation because of his Jewish-Hungarian origin, followed by his predominance in German-speaking Vienna's literary scene and theater life, because of the high esteem of his work by Freud, and because of his independence from the psychoanalytical approach. Schwarz describes Austrian anti-Semitism, which was widespread among both the bourgeoisie and the aristocracy and argues that Schnitzler is no representative of the so-called self-hating Jew. Schwarz uses the example, for instance, of the scenic sequence in Schnitzler's play *Reigen* where he discusses both anti-Semites and Jews. The scandal around his play made Schnitzler sensitive for his fate as an Austrian Jew. Schwarz shows that Schnitzler was not only denied musical competence, but there was also the opinion in Vienna's literati circles that a Jew would not be capable of portraying an Austrian lieutenant as in his short story "Leutnant Gustl." The novel *Der Weg ins Freie* and the play *Professor Bernhardi* emerged during the first decade of the twentieth century as incisive texts and Schwarz locates these correctly in the context of Schnitzler's dealing with anti-Semitism in Viennese society at the time. In the novel, Schnitzler created in the playwright Bermann an alter ego and he lets him discuss with a Zionist the fate of the many immigrant Eastern European Jews, whose problems were much more drastic than those of the bourgeois Jews. Even successful and socially respected Jews became uncertain existentially or were threatened by latent and manifest mechanisms of exclusion. Schwarz summarizes his view of Schnitzler thus: "He [Schnitzler] was saved from the worst. He died in time. Only a few years later he would have been driven without consideration of age or the right to have a home into exile or into the gas chamber by those whom he had portrayed recognizably" ("Das Ärgste blieb ihm [Schnitzler] erspart. Er starb rechtzeitig. Nur wenige Jahre später wäre er ohne Rücksicht auf Alter und Heimatrecht von denen, die er erkannt hatte, ins Exil oder in die Gaskammer getrieben worden") (51). The portrait of Schnitzler is one of the most sensitive and knowledgeable texts in this volume: One does not have to interpret Schnitzler exclusively in regard to his Jewishness, but it is valid for him, too, that "all [were]

Jewish in one respect: we moved in Jewish circles, our friends, our physician, our lawyer were Jews" (150). Freud's son Martin wrote about the assimilated Viennese Jewry that if one defines the cultural assimilation of the Jewish intelligentsia as a way of translating oneself into another world, then the more narrowly defined social environment was an exception, resulting in repercussions on the literature of the Austrian Jews. This way the argumentation justifies the notion of an Austrian-Jewish literature.

Franz Werfel, as Schwarz shows in his essay "'Ich war also Jude! Ich war ein Anderer!' Franz Werfels Darstellungen der sozio-psychologischen Judenproblematik" (152–62) was attracted by Catholicism and was famous, predominantly, as a poet. He was, according to a horrifying statement in a letter by Rainer Maria Rilke, a representative of the "hypocrisy of Jewish intelligence, which is detached everything that binds us together, but is nevertheless capable of talking about it" ("Verlogenheit der jüdischen Mentalität, die von allem losgelöst ist, was uns bindet, und die es dennoch fertigbringt, davon zu reden"). Rilke had high esteem for Werfel's work, but he rejected him personally as a representative of Jewish. And Werfel's immediate social experience was also affected by the exclusion of the Jewry. This left traces in his work, as Schwarz points out, especially in the short story "Pogrom" (1926). While the comedy *Jakobowsky und der Oberst,* dealing with Jewish topics as well, became a worldwide success, the much more pessimistic "Pogrom" remained unknown, although it is in many ways a continuation of Werfel's successful novel *Die vierzig Tage des Musa Dagh*—insofar as a protagonist alienated from his cultural origins reflects critically on his assimilation. Schwarz impresses in his essays not as a theorist, but as an analyst of potential cultural conflicts and as a subtle expert of German- and Austrian-Jewish literary history.

Dieter Lamping is the editor of the volume *Identität und Gedächtnis in der jüdischen Literatur nach 1945*, a collection of papers from a conference held at the University of Mainz in 2000. The starting point of the essays are texts predominantly in German, although other topics are Jewish-American (Philip Roth, Cynthia Ozick, Paul Auster, Erica Jong) and Jewish-British literature (Harold Pinter). "Holocaust literature is predominantly, but not exclusively Jewish literature" (9) writes Lamping in his introduction. He continues to state that the Holocaust would as well be an occasion "to pose the question for Jewish identity anew" (11). Lamping refers to Michael A. Meyer, who writes about Enlightenment, anti-Semitism, and Zionism as the power field that constituted Jewish identity. Undoubtedly, one has to add the experience of annihilation as a fourth factor, and this is the point of reference for the essays of this volume. Alvin H. Rosenfeld questions in "The Jewish Writer at the End of Time" (17–28) literature on the Shoah as end-of-time literature and texts and summarizes using the example of the epic *Dos lid funm oysgemergelten yidishn folk* by Icchak Kacenelson: "The song the Holocaust poet will sing . . . is a halting and almost broken one, the song of a people doing its best to keep from passing out of history, unremembered and un-mourned" (qtd. in Lamping 27). Elrud Ibsch in her contribution, "Der Holocaust im literarischen Experiment" (29–45) goes back to historians' debates, such as the debate between Hayden White and Carlo Ginsburg and to Saul Friedländer's warning of the relativization of the factual by concentration on the linguistic expression: "It appears . . . that literary works which use allegoric elements to present the Shoah have to keep enough direct references to the 'real' events to avoid the possibility of total disjunction, of too much allegoric distance" (qtd. in Lamping 31). Ibsch argues against this, saying that the narrative prose of the Holocaust would often build on postmodern, anachronistical, and provocative positions with a large resonance. This can be confronted with Rosenfeld's primacy of authentical testimony. In regard to Imre Kertész, she stresses the epistemological experiment, in regard to Edgar Hilsenrath the Jewish identity as object of the experiment; in Romain Gary's novel, *La Danse de Gengis Cohn*, she sees a cynical rewriting of history, and in David Grossman's novel *Stichwort: Liebe*, Ibsch discovers the search for a language which comes to terms with the disturbed communication between the generations.

Andreas Solbach shows in his brilliant study on Jean Améry, "Über Zwang und Unmöglichkeit, Jude zu sein: Jean Amérys Testimonium" (62–89), how the author deals narratively with his experience of torture. Solbach interprets Améry's descriptions of the experience of torture as a form of representation of suffering that is not pure *narratio* any more, but *argumentatio* in the context of classical rhetoric. Améry thus became not only the narrator of the Holocaust but also a post-Holocaust thinker. The influence of existentialism on Améry is apparent, but it is even more interesting to understand how torture—or aging as well—is interpreted as a form of being-in-the-world in Améry's writing: "According to this the ego is always there where the world ends; whoever fights in the world, becomes an ego by this: There where the essence is, there is no world, but time; there where world is, there is no essence" ("Demnach ist das Ich immer erst dort, wo die Welt aufhört; wer in der Welt kämpft, wird dadurch erst zum Ich: Dort, wo das Wesen ist, ist keine Welt, sondern Zeit, dort, wo Welt ist, kein Wesen") (76). Solbach interprets Améry's reflections on torture also in the context of Christian topoi: "The situation of the tortured is the situation of the crucified, who is crucified as a Jew and expelled as a Jew from the community by the Pharisees. . . . The central precondition for the forgiving of sins, is according to a Christian understanding, the sincere conscience of sin. . . . Améry demands nothing else from the German people as condition for understanding" ("Die Situation des Gefolterten ist die Situation des Gekreuzigten, der als Jude gekreuzigt und als Jude von den Pharisäern aus der Gemeinschaft verstoßen wird. . . . Die zentrale Voraussetzung der Möglichkeit der Vergebung der Sünden ist nach christlichem Verständnis das aufrichtige Sündenbewußtsein. . . . Nichts anderes verlangt auch Améry vom deutschen Volk als Bedingung der Verständigung") (73). Solbach's interpretation is supreme to the struggle between the postmodern understanding of literature and those who evaluate authentic testimony as the intrinsic Holocaust text. On the one hand, he upgrades the hidden non-realist, non-narrative element in Améry's texts and, on the other hand, he admits models of interpretation that are older than these debates.

If it is true that the memory of a historical trauma includes talking about previous catastrophes, and if these assumptions are always referring to the European-Jewish history of catastrophes, then there is a double reason to ask how American literature participates in the Jewish search for identity after 1945. This is the focus of Alfred Hornung's paper, "*Hungerkünstler* und die jüdisch-amerikanische Literatur: Kafka, Roth, Auzick, Auster" (116–26), where his starting point is the influence of Franz Kafka on postwar American literature. From 1971 to 1976 Philip Roth had visited Prague until the Czechoslovak authorities refused entry to him. Roth regards Kafka in his essay "I Always Wanted You to Admire My Fasting, or, Looking at Kafka" in the context of annihilation, as one of the potential victims, which include Kafka's sisters: "Skulls chiseled like this one were shelved by the thousands from the ovens; had he lived, his would have been among them, along with the skulls of his three younger sisters" (Roth 224). Roth assigns himself herewith to the generation of survivors. Nevertheless, to him Kafka is primarily a Jewish world author from Prague and secondarily a representative of Jewish Central Europe. Hornung interprets Roth's story "The Breast" (1973) as exceeding Kafka by the word becoming flesh, but according to Hornung Roth could also be read in a postmodern understanding as an ironic repetition of Kafka. Roth's transformed person says about himself that "Beyond sublimation. I made the word flesh. I have out-Kafkaed Kafka. He could only imagine a man turning into a cockroach. But look what I have done" (72–73). However, already Kafka's narrator stressed that the metamorphosis was no dream, whereas his protagonist, who changed into a beetle, had no voice himself. This is different from Roth's version. To Roth himself there is no substantial meaning of the difference between modernity and postmodernity, as he clarified in an interview at the end of the 1980s: "There is nothing 'modernist,' 'postmodernist' or the least bit avant-garde about the technique. We are all writing fictitious versions of our lives all the time, that however subtly or grossly falsified, constitute our hold on reality and are the closest thing we have to the truth" (qtd. in Lamping 121) and this could be understood in a postmodern context.

Andreas Wittbrod devotes himself in his study to the German-French author Georges-Arthur Goldschmidt, who grew up and lived in Hamburg until the Nazi takeover. As a boy, his parents sent him to a boarding school in France, and he survived there, whereas both parents perished in the Holocaust. Goldschmidt's rescue had a bitter taste, not only because of the murder of his parents, but also because he became a victim of frequent and arbitrary physical punishment in school. "Meine Identität," Goldschmidt said in an interview with the German author Hans-Ulrich Treichel, "ist die Freiheit" ("My identity is freedom") (qtd. in Lamping 200). But this does not imply, as Wittbrod suggests, that this principle explains the sophisticated writing of Goldschmidt, which estranges the concreteness of the real world by a morbid and weird color. For me, the "freedom" Goldschmidt is talking about seems to be new and perhaps hitherto unknown, as the terrifying being-in-the-world, which revealed itself to Améry under torture. The volume is perhaps best summarized as stating that Jewish writing is about a collective rejection of a Jewish postmodernity by insisting on writing about values and reality.

Sander L. Gilman and Hartmut Steinecke are the editors of the volume *Deutsch-jüdische Literatur der neunziger Jahre: Die Generation nach der Shoah*, also based on a conference in 2000. The material in the volume features both younger and older Jewish authors from the three German-speaking countries, e.g., Esther Dischereit, Barbara Honigmann, Daniel Ganzfried, and Henryk M. Broder, while others are objects of literary analysis in the papers, including Robert Schindel, Maxim Biller, Chaim Noll, and Doron Rabinovici. Central Europe as a point of reference of the writing of these authors appears to be less obvious in the papers of this volume. In German cultural memory conflicts are coined strongly by the polarity of the German-Jewish perpetrator and victim, so that Central Europe as a common cultural space has lost its weight. The Jews who had emigrated to Germany up to the first third of the twentieth century and had assimilated there came from Central and Eastern Europe and their cultural memory was closely linked to this Europe. The history of cultural Zionism shows that German Jews such as Alfred Döblin were searching for their roots when traveling to the Jewry of the furthest reaches of Eastern Europe. Gilman and Steinecke's volume, however, starts on a level prior to the importance of the Jewry in Central and Eastern European culture. According to Steinecke, Gershom Scholem had already doubted this importance for the time before 1933, when he questioned the myth of German-Jewish symbiosis: "Long into the 1980s the avoidance of these adjectives [German-Jewish] dominated, in order to avoid the suspicion that one was—even subconsciously—propagate National Socialist labels" ("Bis weit in die achtziger Jahre herrschte die Vermeidung dieser Adjektive [deutsch-jüdisch] vor, um nicht in den Verdacht zu geraten, man führe, und sei es unbewusst, nationalsozialistische Etikettierungen fort") (11). His conclusion is correct, but the reason for it in my opinion is only partially so, because, according to National Socialist ideology and its construction of antagonisms, "German-Jewish" culture did not exist at all. Rather, one should talk about the impossibility of Jewish existence in Germany after 1945, as Esther Dischereit has put it elsewhere. In 1992, Sander L. Gilman was one of the first to raise the question as to why the "category of the 'Jewish writer' in the postwar discussion" in Germany has been avoided conspicuously and consistently: "Who killed the remaining Jews in current German culture and why?" ("Wer brachte die restlichen Juden in der heutigen deutschen Kultur um und warum?") (qtd. in Gilman and Steinecke 12). Gilman concludes that the avoidance of the designation led to an avoidance of German-Jewish identity. This phase was followed by the conscious positioning of the second and third generation of Jews in Germany.

The place of this literature by Jews is questioned again by Jews with regard to German, by the authors themselves as well as by such people as the Germanist Andreas Kilcher, who characterizes the position of Maxim Biller in his paper this way: "Der deutsch-jüdischen Literatur als Residuum des Goethe- und Kleist-Deutschland hält er eine dezidiert jüdische Literatur in deutscher Sprache entgegen, eine Literatur, die sich kulturell scharf von der deutschen abgrenzt" ("He confronts the German-Jewish literature of Goethe's and Kleist's Germany with a definite Jewish literature in German language, which demarcates itself from German literature" (146). Kilcher stresses the difference from Jewish writers in exile, and Biller would insist on a "marginality" on the scene, whereas Rabinovici would want to find a "Jewish" storytelling. In reality, Rabinovici talks of a "demarcation line" that separates some of the Jewish-German writers from Austrians and Germans (144). Biller claims for himself hatred with a therapeutical effect. He writes in an article for the *Süddeutsche Zeitung* in 1995 that "German literature will never again be synonymous with Jewish literature. . . . We live with them, we work with them, we laugh with them—but we will be divorced people forever" ("die deutsche Literatur [wird] nie mehr zum Synonym für jüdische Literatur werden. . . . Wir leben mit ihnen, wir arbeiten mit ihnen, wir lachen mit ihnen—aber wir werden auf immer geschiedene Leute sein") (qtd. in Gilman and Steinecke 144).

It may be a matter of opinion whether the above formulates a state of being or a position of "dissimilation," relevant for cultural theory, as Kilcher thinks. One could also conclude: This is differentiated because of the difference. Difference becomes the lead notion of cultural memory and produces an enormous mirroring of both sides at the same time. The possibility of new stereotypes is reflected sovereign and ironically most clearly in Esther Dischereit and is thus overcome. If she writes, for instance, about a conversation with a young Turkish woman and the latter's anger about the cliché of Turkish women wearing headscarves, "We smile like two people whose secret is known by no one else. Probably there is no purpose in publishing secrets" ("Wir lächeln wie zwei, von deren Geheimnis sonst keiner weiß. Wahrscheinlich ist es zwecklos, Geheimnisse zu veröffentlichen") (221). Consequently, there are differences beyond manifestations of identity, even if they are of that kind, that being Jewish might decrease during breakfast, as Dischereit says to a school class. This way, European thinking gets a space within Dischereit's German-Jewish reflection of herself. We should let the individual decide whether this is more or less Central European. In my opinion, the papers in Gilman and Steinecke's volume do not succeed in summarizing literary and scholarly positions on the topic of German-Jewish identities, but at the same time they point to a fruitful discussion with all its preliminaries and detours.

Essential for all five volumes seems to be that they point to significant challenges for Jewish identity and Jewish literature in Central Europe. They may of course also be regarded as an example of the problems of other ethnic and cultural minorities in Europe. But still the discussion of Jewish exile and European-Jewish identity after the Shoah is a field comprised of many and various concepts of identity and how they are represented in literature. It is simply not possible to set up a list of categories which would allow us positively to call a literary text or a cultural event "Jewish" or Jewish German." Jewish-European literatures, then, are situated within an ongoing debate. Unfortunately, also the opposite strategy seems to be less than optimal, namely the silence on Jewish existence that characterized most European cultures. If we look at German scholars such as Lamping, Steinecke, Wallas, or Gilman—who, as a U.S.-American scholar, is very much present in the debates of the German-speaking scholarship—we see an astonishing competency in describing a contradictory situation, one that does not fail to produce also ironic aspects. Recently, during a conference on Jewish-German Studies at the Potsdam Moses Mendelssohn Centre in October 2004, Gilman proposed considering the Jewish diaspora and its cultural parameters also as a potential case study for the Islamic diaspora, a proposal certain to invite further discussion and debates.

Works Cited

Deleuze, Gilles, and Félix Guattari. *Kafka. Für eine kleine Literatur.* Trans. Burkhart Kroeber. Frankfurt: Suhrkamp, 2002.

Dischereit, Esther. "Gespräch mit Wolfgang Benz." *Übungen jüdisch zu sein. Aufsätze.* By Esther Dischereit. Frankfurt: Suhrkamp, 1998. 199–214.

Dühring, Eugen Carl. *Die Judenfrage als Rassen-, Sitten- und Kulturfrage mit einer weltgeschichtlichen Antwort.* Karlsruhe: H. Reuter, 1881. 2nd.ed.

Freud, Martin. "Who Was Freud?" *The Jews of Austria. Essays on Their Life, History and Destruction.* Ed. Josef Fraenkel. London: Vallentine-Mitchell, 1967. 197–211.

Gilman, Sander L. *Jüdischer Selbsthaß. Antisemitismus und die verborgene Sprache der Juden.* Trans. Isabella König. Frankfurt: Jüdischer Verlag, 1993.

Gilman, Sander L., and Hartmut Steinecke, eds. *Deutsch-jüdische Literatur der neunziger Jahre. Die Generation nach der Shoah.* Berlin: Erich Schmidt, 2002.

Goltschnigg, Dietmar, and Hartmut Steinecke, eds. *Essays über österreichische, deutsche und jüdische Literatur.* Berlin: Erich Schmidt, 2000.

Krall, Hanna. "Briefly Now." *Contemporary Jewish Writing in Poland.* Ed. Antony Polonsky and Monika Adamczyk-Grabowska. Lincoln: U of Nebraska P, 2001. 303–11.

Lamping, Dieter, ed. *Identität und Gedächtnis in der jüdischen Literatur nach 1945.* Berlin: Erich Schmidt, 2003.

Magris, Claudio, and Angelo Ara. *Triest. Eine literarische Hauptstadt in Mitteleuropa.* Trans. Maria Gschwend Ragni. München: Carl Hanser, 1987.

Marsovszky, Magdalena. "Imre Kertész and Hungary Today." *Imre Kertész and Holocaust Literature.* Ed. Louise O. Vasvári and Steven Tötösy de Zepetnek. West Lafayette: Purdue UP, 2005. 148–61.

Marsovszky, Magdalena. "Imre Kertész. Einer von uns—oder doch nicht? Kulturkampf und Identität in Ungarn." *Mitteleuropa, Europas Mitte, Europäische Identität, Literatur—Geschichte—Positionen.* Ed. Barbara Breysach. Berlin: Logos, 2003. 137–53.

Meyer, Michael A. *Jüdische Identität in der Moderne.* Frankfurt: Jüdischer Verlag, 1992.

Milbauer, Asher Z., and David Watson. "An Interview with Philip Roth." *Reading Philip Roth.* Ed. Asher Z. Milbauer and David Watson. London: Palgrave Macmillan, 1988. 1–12.

Polonsky, Antony, and Monika Adamczyk-Grabowska, eds. *Contemporary Jewish Writing in Poland: An Anthology.* Lincoln: U of Nebraska P, 2001.

Rilke, Rainer Maria. "Brief an Marie von Thurn und Taxis (21.10.1913)." *Rainer Maria Rilke und Marie von Thurn und Taxis. Briefwechsel.* Trans. Egon Schwarz. Zürich: Niehaus, 1951. Vol. 1, 45–46.

Roth, Philip. "I always Wanted You to Admire My Fasting, or, Looking at Kafka." *Reading Myself and Others.* By Philip Roth. New York: Farrar, Straus and Giroux, 1975. 247–70.

Suleiman, Susan Rubin, and Éva Forgács, eds. *Contemporary Jewish Writing in Hungary: An Anthology.* Lincoln: The U of Nebraska P, 2003.

Tötösy de Zepetnek, Steven. "Imre Kertész's Nobel Prize in Literature and the Print Media." *Imre Kertész and Holocaust Literature.* Ed. Louise O. Vasvári and Steven Tötösy de Zepetnek. West Lafayette: Purdue UP, 2005. 232–46.

Wallas, Armin A., ed. *Jüdische Identitäten in Mitteleuropa. Literarische Modelle der Identitätskonstruktion.* Tübingen: Niemeyer, 2002.

Young, Judy. "The Media and Imre Kertész's Nobel Prize in Literature." *Imre Kertész and Holocaust Literature.* Ed. Louise O. Vasvári and Steven Tötösy de Zepetnek. West Lafayette: Purdue UP, 2005. 271–85.

A Bibliography of Imre Kertész's Oeuvre and Publications about His Work

Steven Tötösy de Zepetnek

1. Imre Kertész's Oeuvre (in Hungarian and in Translation)

Kertész Texts Online: *Digitális Irodalmi Akadémia* <http://www.irodalmiakademia.hu>.

Kertész, Imre. "À qui appartient Auschwitz?" *Nouvelle Revue Française* 551 (September 1999): 223–30.

Kertész, Imre. *Az angol lobogó* (The English Flag). Budapest: Holnap, 1991.

Kertész, Imre. *Un Autre. Chronique d'une métamorphose*. Trans. Natalia Zaremba and Charles Zaremba. Arles: Actes Sud, 1999.

Kertész, Imre. *Bezosudovos* (*Fatelessness*). Trans. Eva Kroupová. Bratislava: Slovart, 2000.

Kertész, Imre. "A boldogtalan huszadik század" ("The Unhappy Twentieth Century"). *A száműzött nyelv* (The Exiled Language). By Imre Kertész. Budapest: Magvető, 2001. 11–44.

Kertész, Imre. "El coraje de la razón Giorgio Pressburger." Trans. Hugo Beccacece. *Suplemento Cultura La Nación* (7 September 2003): 1, 3.

Kertész, Imre. *Dank des Preisträgers. Leipziger Buchpreis zur Europäischen Verständigung 1997*. Frankfurt: Suhrkamp, 1997.

Kertész, Imre. *Die englische Flagge. Erzählungen*. Trans. György Buda and Kristin Schwamm. Reinbek bei Hamburg: Rowohlt, 1999.

Kertész, Imre. "Entrevistas en dos tiempos: El sobreviviente Javier Rodríguez Marcos." Trans. Hugo Beccacece. *Suplemento Cultura La Nación* (13 October 2002): 2.

Kertész, Imre. "Entrevistas en dos tiempos: El vencedor Dario Fertilio." Trans. Hugo Beccacece. *Suplemento Cultura La Nación* (13 October 2002):1–2.

Kertész, Imre. *Essere senza destino*. Trans. Barbara Griffini. Milano: Feltrinelli, 1999.

Kertész, Imre. *Être sans destin*. Trans. Natalia Zaremba and Charles Zaremba. Arles: Actes Sud, 1996.

Kertész, Imre. "Eureka! The 2002 Nobel Lecture." Trans. Ivan Sanders. *World Literature Today* 77.1 (2003): 4–8.

Kertész, Imre. "Failure." *The New Hungarian Quarterly* 30 (1989): 59–73.

Kertész, Imre. *Fateless*. Trans. Christopher C. Wilson and Katharina M. Wilson. Evanston: Northwestern UP, 1992.

Kertész, Imre. *Fatelessness*. Trans. Tim Wilkinson. New York: Vintage, 2004.

Kertész, Imre. *Felszámolás* (*Liquidation*). Budapest: Magvető, 2003.

Kertész, Imre. *Het fiasco*. Trans. Henry Kammer. Amsterdam: Van Gennep, 1999.

Kertész, Imre. *Fiasko*. Trans György Buda and Agnes Relle. Reinbek bei Hamburg: Rowohlt, 1999.

Kertész, Imre. *Fiasko*. Trans. Ervin Rosenberg. Stockholm: Norstedt, 2000.

Kertész, Imre. "The Freedom of Self-Definition." Trans. Ivan Sanders. *Witness Literature: Proceedings of the Nobel Centennial Symposium*. Ed. Horace Engdahl. New Jersey: World Scientific, 2002. 33–43.

Kertész, Imre. *Galärdagbok* (Galley Boat-Log). Trans. Ervin Rosenberg. Stockholm: Norstedt, 2002.

Kertész, Imre. *Galeerentagebuch*. Trans. Kristin Schwamm. Reinbek bei Hamburg: Rowohlt, 1993.

Kertész, Imre. "*Galley Boat-Log* (*Gályanapló*): Excerpts." Trans. Tim Wilkinson. *Imre Kertész and Holocaust Literature*. Ed. Louise O. Vasvári and Steven Tötösy de Zepetnek. West Lafayette: Purdue UP, 2005. 97–110.

Kertész, Imre. *Gályanapló* (Galley Boat-Log). Budapest: Holnap, 1992.

Kertész, Imre. *Eine gedankenlänge Stille, während das Erschiessungskommando neu lädt*. Trans. György Buda. Reinbek bei Hamburg: Rohwolt, 1999.

Kertész, Imre. "Das Geheimnis der Diktatur." Interview with Stefan Speicher. *Berliner Zeitung* (6 November 2004): Magazin.

Kertész, Imre. *Eine Geschichte. Zwei Geschichten. Imre Kertész mit Péter Esterházy*. Trans. Kristin Schwamm and Hans Skirecki. Salzburg: Residenz, 1994.

Kertész, Imre. *A gondolatnyi csend, amíg a kivégzőosztag ujratölt* (The Moment of Silence while the Execution Squad Reloads). Budapest: Magvető, 1998.

Kertész, Imre. "Heureka!" Trans. Ivan Sanders. *PMLA: Publications of the Modern Language Association of America* 118.3 (2003): 604–14.

Kertész, Imre. "Der Holocaust als Kultur." *Eine Gedankenlänge Stille, während das Erschießungskommando neu lädt*. Trans. György Buda. By Imre Kertész. Reinbek bei Hamburg: Rowohlt, 1999. 54–69.

Kertész, Imre. *A holokauszt mint kultúra. Három előadás* (The Holocaust as Culture: Three Lectures). Budapest: Századvég, 1993.

Kertész, Imre. "Hommage à Fejtö." Trans. Irene Rübberdt. *Sinn und Form: Beiträge zur Literatur* 53.1 (2001): 41–47.

Kertész, Imre. "Ich bin der Spuk." Trans. Kristin Schwamm. *Frankfurter Allgemeine Zeitung* 62 (14 March 2002): 46.

Kertész, Imre. *Ich ein anderer*. Trans. Ilma Rakusa. Berlin: Rowohlt, 1998.

Kertész, Imre. *Un instante di silencio en el peredón. El Holocausto como cultura*. Trans. Adam Kovacsics. Barcelona: Herder, 1999.

Kertész, Imre. *Jegyzőkönyv. Kertész Imre Esterházy Péterrel* (Sworn Statement: Imre Kertész with Péter Esterházy). Budapest: Magvető, 1993.

Kertész, Imre. "Jelentés a költészet birodalmából. Egy mítosz vége" ("Report from the Realm of Poetry: The End of a Myth"). *Élet és Irodalom* (2 April 2004): 3.

Kertész, Imre. "Jerusalem, Jerusalem: Reflections Sparked by the Sight of a War-torn City." *Logos* (2003): <http://www.logosjournal.com/kertesz.htm>.

Kertész, Imre. *Lelo goral* (*Fatelessness*). Trans. Miriam Alcazi. Tel Aviv: Am Oved, 1994.

Kertész, Imre. *Kaddijs for et ikke fodt barn.* Trans. Ove Lund. Oslo: Pax, 2000.

Kertész, Imre. *Kaddijs voor een niet geboren kind.* Trans. Henry Kammer. Amsterdam: Van Gennep, 1994.

Kertész, Imre. *Kaddis a meg nem született gyermekért* (*Kaddish for an Unborn Child*). Budapest: Magvető, 1990.

Kertész, Imre. *Kaddiš za nenarozené dítě* (*Kaddish for an Unborn Child*). Trans. Dana Gálová. Praha: Hynek, 1998.

Kertész, Imre. *Kaddisch für ein nicht geborenes Kind.* Trans. György Buda and Kristin Schwamm. Berlin: Rowohlt, 1992.

Kertész, Imre. "Kaddish a meg nem született gyermekért" ("Kaddish for an Unborn Child"). *The New Hungarian Quarterly* 32 (1991): 42–55.

Kertész, Imre. *Kaddish for a Child Not Born.* Trans. Christopher C. Wilson and Katharina M. Wilson. Evanston: Hydra Books, 1997.

Kertész, Imre. *Kaddish for an Unborn Child.* Trans. Tim Wilkinson. New York: Vintage, 2004.

Kertész, Imre. *Kaddish för ett ofött barn.* Trans. Ervin Rosenberg. Stockholm: Norstedt, 1996.

Kertész, Imre. *Kaddish for et ufødt barn.* Trans. Péter Eszterhás. Roskilde: Batzer & Co., 2002.

Kertész, Imre. *Kaddish por uma criança não nascida.* Trans. Raquel Abi-Sâmara. Rio de Janeiro: Imago, 1995.

Kertész, Imre. *Kaddish pour l'enfant qui ne naîtra pas.* Trans. Natalia Zaremba-Huzsvai and Charles Zaremba. Arles: Actes Sud, 1995.

Kertész, Imre. *A kudarc* (The Failure). Budapest: Szépirodalmi, 1988.

Kertész, Imre. "The Language of Exile." Trans. Ivan Sanders. *The Guardian* (19 October 2002): <http://books.guardian.co.uk/review/story/0,12084,814056,00.html>.

Kertész, Imre. *Liquidation.* Trans. László Kornitzer und Ingrid Krüger. Frankfurt: Suhrkamp, 2003.

Kertész, Imre. *Liquidation.* Trans. Tim Wilkinson. New York: Knopf, 2004.

Kertész, Imre. "Long Dark Shadow." Trans. Imre Goldstein. *Contemporary Jewish Writing in Hungary: An Anthology.* Ed. Susan Rubin Suleiman and Éva Forgács. Lincoln: U of Nebraska P, 2003. 171–77.

Kertész, Imre. *Mannen utan öde* (*Fatelessness*). Trans. Maria Ortman. Stockholm: Norstedt, 1998.

Kertész, Imre. "Megdöbbenés, csupa megdöbbenés . . ." ("Astonishment, Nothing But Astonishment . . ."). *Élet és Irodalom* (8 October 1999): 8.

Kertész, Imre. *Meine Rede über das Jahrhundert* (My Speech about the Century). Hamburg: Hamburger Ed., 1995.

Kertész, Imre. *Mensch ohne Schicksal*. Trans. Jörg Buschmann. Berlin: Rütten & Loening, 1990.

Kertész, Imre. "Mon oeuvre *Être sans destin* est une métaphore du régime de Kádár." Interview by Eszter Rádai. Trans. J. Fühling. *Bulletin Trimestriel de la Fondation Auschwitz* 80–81 (2003): 209–19.

Kertész, Imre. Interview by Tamás Szőnyei. "Nem érzem magam téves helyen, amikor Németországban olvasok fel (Kertész Imre író)" ("I Do Not Feel Out of Place When I Read My Work in Germany [Imre Kertész, Writer]"). *Magyar Narancs* (*Archive*) (12 December 1996): <http://www.mancs.hu/index.php?gc.Page=public/hir.phg&id=757>.

Kertész, Imre. "A Nobel-díjat zavaró repülésnek éreztem" ("I Felt the Nobel Prize a Distracting Flight"). *Heti Világ* (6 September 2003): 47–48.

Kertész, Imre. *A nyomkereső. Két regény* (The Pathfinder: Two Novels). Budapest: Szépirodalmi, 1977.

Kertész, Imre. *Onbepaald door het lot* (*Fatelessness*). Trans. Henry Kammer. Amsterdam: Van Gennep, 1994.

Kertész, Imre. "Proces-verbal." *Europe-Revue Littéraire Mensuelle* 79 (2001): 152–68.

Kertész, Imre. "Rakusa I. 'Meine Einzige Identität'." *Sinn und Form: Beiträge zur Literatur* 50.2 (1998): 165–77.

Kertész, Imre. *Le Refus*. Trans. Natalia Zaremba-Huzsvai and Charles Zaremba. Arles: Actes Sud, 2001.

Kertész, Imre. "La Restitution des documents carbonisés par un traitement de calcination (thermique)." *Avant-texte, texte, après-texte*. Ed. Louis Hay and Péter Nagy. Budapest: Akadémiai, 1982. 65–67.

Kertész, Imre. *Roman eines Schicksallosen*. Trans. Christina Viragh. Berlin: Rowohlt, 1996.

Kertész, Imre. *Schritt für Schritt. Drehbuch zum Roman eines Schicksallosen*. Trans. Erich Berger. Frankfurt: Suhrkamp, 2002.

Kertész, Imre. *Sin destino*. Trad. Trans. Judith Xantus Szarvas. Barcelona: Plaza y Janés, 1996.

Kertész, Imre. *De skæbnelose* (*Fatelessness*). Trans. Péter Eszterhás. Kobenhavn: Forum, 1996.

Kertész, Imre. "Someone Else: A Chronicle of the Change in Régime." Trans. Tim Wilkinson. *Common Knowledge* 10.2 (2004): 314–46.

Kertész, Imre. *Sorstalanság* (*Fatelessness*). Budapest: Szépirodalmi, 1975.

Kertész, Imre. *Sorstalanság. Filmforgatókönyv* (*Fatelessness*: Film Script). Budapest: Magvető, 2001.

Kertész, Imre. "A *Sorstalanság*ot a Kádár-rendszerről írtam" ("I Wrote *Fatelessness* about the Kádár Régime"). Interview with Eszter Rádai. *Élet és Irodalom* (30 May 2003): 3, 8.

Kertész, Imre. *Steg för steg*. Trans. Maria Ortman. Bromma: Fripress, 1985.

Kertész, Imre. "Sworn Statement: A True Story." *The New Hungarian Quarterly* 42 (2001): 45–58.

Kertész, Imre. *A száműzött nyelv* (The Exiled Language). Budapest: Magvető, 2001.

Kertész, Imre. "A száműzött nyelv" ("The Exiled Language"). *A száműzött nyelv* (The Exiled Language). By Imre Kertész. Budapest: Magvető, 2001. 274–97.

Kertész, Imre. "The Union Jack." Trans. Tim Wilkinson. *The Hungarian Quarterly* 48 (2002): 3–28.

Kertész, Imre. "The Union Jack." Trans. Tim Wilkinson. *Leopard V. An Island of Sound: Hungarian Poetry and Fiction before and beyond the Iron Curtain*. Ed. George Szirtes and Miklós Vajda. London: Harvill, 2004. 86–116.

Kertész, Imre. *Los utracony* (*Fatelessness*). Trans. Krystyna Pisarska. Warsawa: W.A.B., 2002.

Kertész, Imre. *Valaki más. A változás krónikája* (Someone Else: A Chronicle of the Change in Régime). Budapest: Magvető, 1997.

Kertész, Imre. "A végső kocsma. Feljegyzések" (The Ultimate Pub: Notes.). *Élet és Irodalom* (21 December 2001): 3–4.

Kertész, Imre. "Wem gehört Auschwitz?" *Die Zeit* (19 November 1998): 55.

Kertész, Imre. "Wem gehört Auschwitz?" *Eine Gedankenlänge Stille, während das Erschießungskommando neu lädt*. Trans. György Buda. By Imre Kertész. Trans György Buda. Reinbek bei Hamburg: Rowohlt, 1999. 145–54.

Kertész, Imre. "Wenn die Freudenfeuer verglimmen. Europa in der Generalprobe: Rede zur Feier der deutschen Wiedervereinigung." Trans. Kristin Schwamm. *Neue Zürcher Zeitung* (4 October 2003): Feuilleton.

Kertész, Imre. "Who Owns Auschwitz?" Trans. John MacKay. *Yale Journal of Criticism: Interpretation in the Humanities* 14.1 (2001): 267–72.

Kertész, Imre. *Eine Zurückweisung*. Potsdam: Vacat, 1995.

2. Publications about Imre Kertész's Work

Anonymous. "*Fatelessness* by Imre Kertész." *complete review: a literary saloon and site of review* (2004): < http://www.complete-review.com/reviews/magyar/kertesz5.htm>.

Anonymous. "Hungary's Kertesz Writes about Survival under Communism." *EUbusiness.com* (20 April 2004): <http://www.eubusiness.com/afp/040420021357.cv0awuut>.

Anonymous. "Imre Kertész." *Time* (21 October 2002): 90.

Anonymous. "Imre Kertesz at the *complete review*." *complete review: a literary saloon and site of review* (2004): <http://www.complete-review.com/authors/kertesz.htm#biblio>.

Anonymous. "Kertesz Turns 75." *complete review: a literary saloon and site of review* (9 November 2004): < http://www.complete-review.com/saloon/archive/200411a. htm#jl3>.

Anonymous. "A magyar irodalom ünnepe" ("Celebration of Hungarian Literature). *Magyar Hírlap* (11 October 2002): 5.

Anonymous. "Sampling Imre Kertész." *New York Times* (11 October 2002): A8.

Anonymous. "Tag der deutschen Einheit." *Frankfurter Allgemeine Zeitung* (4 October 2003): 3.

Anonymous. "Translators to Discuss Prize Winner." *Edmonton Journal* (9 December 2002): C7.

Aczél, Tamás. "Letter from Budapest." *World & I* 6.3 (1991): 430–37.

Adelman, Gary. "Getting Started with Imre Kertész." *New England Review* 25.1–2 (2004): <http://cat.middlebury.edu/~nereview/Adelman.html>.

Adorján, Johanna, and Nils Minkmar. "Liebe ist das Wichtigste. Der Literatur-Nobelpreisträger Imre Kertész übers Schreiben, die Diktatur, Martin Walser und das Glück, nirgends dazuzugehören." *Frankfurter Allgemeine Sonntagszeitung* (13 October 2002): 21.

Appelfeld, Aharon. "Die Erzählung von Kain und Abel." *Sinn und Form: Beiträge zur Literatur* 55.2 (2003): 201–11.

Babarczy, Eszter. "Nobel-dilemma—itt az alkalom" ("The Dilemma of the Nobel: An Opportunity"). *Népszabadság* (19 October 2002): 19.

Babarczy, Eszter. "The Nobel Dilemma—Now Is the Time to Speak!" Trans. János Széky. *transcript: European internet review of books and writing* (2002): <http://www.transcript-review.org/sub.cfm?lan=en&id=107>.

Bächer, Iván. "Kertészmagyarország" ("The Hungary of Kertész"). *Népszabadság* (26 October 2002): 36.

Balassa, Péter. "A hang és a látvány. Miért olvassák a németek a magyarokat?" ("Voice and Mirage: Why are Germans Reading Hungarians?"). *Jelenkor: Irodalmi és művészeti folyóirat* 7–8 (1995): 664–68.

Balla, Zsófia. "Ajándék. Kertész Imre Nobel-díjas" ("A Gift: Imre Kertész, Nobel Laureate"). *Élet és Irodalom* (25 October 2002): 3.

Bán, András Zoltán. "A Trilogy of Fatelessness." *The New Hungarian Quarterly* 32.124 (1991): 36–41.

Bánó, András Zoltán. "Kié az elismerés?" *Blikk* (12 October 2002): 13.

Basa, Enikő Molnár. "Imre Kertész and Hungarian Literature." *Imre Kertész and Holocaust Literature*. Ed. Louise O. Vasvári and Steven Tötösy de Zepetnek. West Lafayette: Purdue UP, 2005. 11–23.

Basse, Michael. "Auschwitz als Welterfahrung. Der ungarische Schriftsteller Imre Kertész." *Merkur: Deutsche Zeitschrift für Europäisches Denken* 53.6 (1999): 559–64.

Bazsányi, Sándor. "A boldogtalanság retorikája" ("The Rhetoric of Unhappiness"). *Holmi* 12 (1998): 1744–47.

Bazsányi, Sándor. "Rosszízü mondatok" ("Sentences with a Bad Taste in the Mouth"). *Beszélő* (November 2002): 18–19.

Berkes, Erzsébet. "Az ésszerű lét nyomorúsága" ("The Misery of Meaningful Life"). *Mozgó Világ* 11 (1990): 118–21.

Bikácsy, Gergely. "Öntagadás mint műalkotás. Kertész Imre, avagy a nevetés kegyelme" (Self-denial as Aesthetics: Imre Kertész, or, the Mercy of Laughter"). *Orpheus* (1993): 162–69.

Björksten, Christel. "Kertész dubbla verklighet." *Horisont* 50.3 (2003): 47–49.

Bőhm, Ágnes, György Vári, Nelli Koltai, and Pál Várnai. "Köszöntjük a Nobel-Díjas Kertész Imrét!" ("We Congratulate the Nobel Laureate Imre Kertész!"). *Szombat* 10 (2002): 5–17.

Bojtár, Endre. "Die Winterreise des Sisyphos." Trans. Éva Zádor. *Der lange, dunkle Schatten. Studien zum Werk von Imre Kertész.* Ed. Mihály Szegedy-Maszák and Tamás Scheibner. Wien: Passagen, 2004. 327–41.

Books and Writers: Imre Kertész (1929-) (2002): <http://www.kirjasto.sci.fi/kerte.htm>.

Borcza, Ágnes Z. "Egy Nóbel-díj margójára" ("On the Margins of a Nobel Prize"). *Magyar Nemzet* (5 November 2002): 6.

Breitenstein, Andreas. "Schöne Tage in Buchenwald: Imre Kertész' *Roman eines Schicksallosen.*" *Neue Zürcher Zeitung* (27 April 1996): 67.

Clamens, G. "Nobel Prize winner Imre Kertész and the Auschwitz Experience: A Reading of His Works." *Temps Modernes* 58 (2003): 300–06.

Clavel, André. "Le Primo Lévi magyar." *L'Express* (21 November 2002): Livres.

Cohen, George. Review of Imre Kertész's *Kaddish for a Child Not Born. Booklist* 93.21 (1997): 1797.

Cohen, Sara D. "Jewishness in Hungary, Imre Kertész, and the Choice of an Identity." *Imre Kertész and Holocaust Literature.* Ed. Louise O. Vasvári and Steven Tötösy de Zepetnek. West Lafayette: Purdue UP, 2005. 24–37.

Csáki, Judit. "Auschwitz by the Minute: Reflections on the Anti-Semitic Discourse Surrounding Nobel Prizewinner Imre Kertész's Reception in Hungary." Trans. Andrea Megyes. *Anti-Semitic Discourse in Hungary in 2002–2003.* B'nai B'rith Budapest, 2004: 189–209.

Csáki, Judit. "Sors és sorstalanság. Beszélgetés Kertész Imrével" ("Fate and Fatelessness: A Conversation with Imre Kertész"). *Kritika* 3 (1992): 24–26.

Czarny, N. "*Être sans destin.* Kertész, I. Zaremba, C., et Zaremba, N." *Quinzane Littéraire* (16 April 1998): 10–11.

Dalos, György. "Felszámolás" ("Liquidation"). *168 Óra* (11 September 2003): 31.

Dalos, György. "Parallel Lives: Günther Grass and Imre Kertész in Conversation with György Dalos." *The New Hungarian Quarterly* 45 (2004): 34–47.

Dávidházi, Péter. *Az értelem szükségszerűsége. Tanulmányok Kertész Imréről* (The Necessity of Meaning: Studies on Imre Kertész). Budapest: L'Harmattan, 2002.

Dávidházi, Péter. "Bedrängnisvolle Vergangenheit im Hafen der nachträglichen Redaktion. Schicksalsdeutung im *Galeerentagebuch* von Imre Kertész." Trans.

Éva Zádor. *Der lange, dunkle Schatten. Studien zum Werk von Imre Kertész.* Ed. Mihály Szegedy-Maszák and Tamás Scheibner. Wien: Passagen, 2004. 237–46.

Davis, Robert Murray. Review of Imre Kertész's *Kaddish for a Child Not Born. World Literature Today* 74.1 (2000): 205.

Deák, István. "Stranger in Hell." *New York Review of Books* (25 September 2003): 65–67.

Dérczy, Péter. "A történetnek nincs vége" ("The Story Has Not Yet Ended"). *Élet és Irodalom* (19 September 2003): 25.

Dés, Mihály. "Celebración universal del fracaso." *Letras Libres* 4.49 (2003): 52–54.

dpa. "Lex Kertész." *Frankfurter Allgemeine Zeitung* (7 November 2002): Feuilleton.

Eaglestone, Robert. "The Aporia of Imre Kertész." *Imre Kertész and Holocaust Literature.* Ed. Louise O. Vasvári and Steven Tötösy de Zepetnek. West Lafayette: Purdue UP, 2005. 38–50.

Eder, Richard. "Piercing the Veil Surrounding a Captive Writer." *The New York Times* (18 August 2003): B6.

Eigner, Gerd-Peter. "'Ein kleines Drama des Beleidigtseins': Kertész und wir." *Horen: Zeitschrift für Literatur, Kunst und Kritik* 42.2 (186) (1997): 81–85.

Emmerich, Wolfgang. "Keine 'sinngebung des Sinnlosen': Kertész lesen." *Horen: Zeitschrift für Literatur, Kunst und Kritik* 42.2 (186) (1997): 78–80.

Esterházy, Péter. "Kertész életműve a 20. század egyik legmagasabb pontja" ("Kertész's Oeuvre is One of the High Points of the Twentieth Century"). *Tallózó* (24 October 2002): 2784.

Esterházy, Péter. "Az örömről. Documentation. Kertész Imre Nobel-díjas" ("About Joy: Documentation about Nobel Laureate Imre Kertész"). *Élet és Irodalom* (25 October 2002): 3.

Falbo, M. Anna. Review of Imre Kertész's *Kaddish for a Child Not Born. Library Journal* 122.10 (1997): 149.

Fehéri, György. "Miért szeretik Kertész Imrét Németországban?" ("Why Do They Like Imre Kertész in Germany?"). *Múlt és Jövő* 1 (2003): 70–75.

Fejtö, François. "Kicsoda Kertész Imre?" ("Who is Imre Kertész?"). *Múlt és Jövő* 1 (2003): 67–68.

Fenyves, Miklós. "Holocaust als Kultur—ein Traum der Wendezeit? Über Imre Kertész." *Engagierte Literatur in Wendezeiten.* Ed. Willi Huntemann, Malgorzata Klentak-Zablocka, Fabian Lampart, and Thomas Schmidt. Würzburg: Königshausen & Neumann, 2003. 269–80.

Fenyvesi, Charles. "Living the Unlivable." *U.S. News & World Report* (21 October 2002): 59.

Flower, Dean. Review of Imre Kertész's *Fateless.* *Hudson Review* 46.2 (1993): 397–98.

Földényi, F. László. "'Große Wahrhaftigkeit.' *Roman eines Schicksallosen* von Imre Kertész." Trans. Hans Skirecki. *Der lange, dunkle Schatten. Studien zum Werk von*

Imre Kertész. Ed. Mihály Szegedy-Maszák and Tamás Scheibner. Wien: Passagen, 2004. 103–15.

Földényi, F. László. "A Large Truth." *Common Knowledge.* 7.1 (1998): 7–14.

Földes, Anna. "Nem csak Kertészről van szó." *Élet és Irodalom* (31 January 2003): 12–13.

Fried, Ilona. "Sors nélküli lét. Kertész Imre regénye Olaszországban" ("Existence without Fate: Kertész's Novel in Italy"). *Élet és Irodalom* (18 July 2001): 12.

Fried, István. "A naplóíró Kertész Imre. Vázlat a *Gályanapló*ról" ("The Diarist Imre Kertész: A Scetch on the Galley Boat-Log"). *Irodalomtörténet* 84.3 (2003): 337–47.

Fried, István. "Der Tagebuchautor Imre Kertész. Skizze zum *Galeerentagebuch.*" Trans. Éva Zádor. *Der lange, dunkle Schatten. Studien zum Werk von Imre Kertész.* Ed. Mihály Szegedy-Maszák and Tamás Scheibner. Wien: Passagen, 2004. 247–62.

Friedland, Amos. "Imre Kertész, Hegel, and the Philosophy of Reconciliation." *Imre Kertész and Holocaust Literature.* Ed. Louise O. Vasvári and Steven Tötösy de Zepetnek. West Lafayette: Purdue UP, 2005. 51–64.

Friedland, Amos. Review of Imre Kertész's *Liquidation,* trans. Tim Wilkinson. *Globe and Mail* (27 November 2004): D43.

Gács, Anna. "Egy különös regény. Kertész Imre: *Gályanapló*" ("A Peculiar Novel: Imre Kertész's Galley Boat-Log"). *Jelenkor: Irodalmi és művészeti folyóirat* 35.10 (1992): 857–60.

Gács, Anna "Mit számít ki motyog? A szituáció és autorizáció kérdései Kertész Imre prózájában" ("What Does It Matter Who is Muttering? Questions about Situation and Authorization in the Prose of Imre Kertész"). *Jelenkor: Irodalmi és művészeti folyóirat* 45.12 (2002): 1280–95.

Gács, Anna. "Was zählt's wer vor sich hin murmelt? Fragen über die Situation und Autorisation in der Prosa von Imre Kertész." Trans. Christine Rácz. *Der lange, dunkle Schatten. Studien zum Werk von Imre Kertész.* Ed. Mihály Szegedy-Maszák and Tamás Scheibner. Wien: Passagen, 2004. 263–92.

Gahse, Zsuzsanna. "Das Unerwartete und Imre Kertész. Eine Laudatio." *Die Horen: Zeitschrift für Literatur, Kunst und Kritik* 42.2 (1997): 67–73.

Gamel, Kim. "Auschwitz Survivor Awarded Nobel Prize for Literature: Swedish Academy Singles out Imre Kertesz's 1975 Debut Novel *Fateless.*" *The Vancouver Sun* (11 October 2002): A11.

Garam, Katalin, and János Járai. "Sors és szabadság. Stockholmi tudósítás az irodalmi Nobel-díj átadásáról" ("Fate and Freedom: Report on the Nobel Prize Award in Stockholm"). *168 óra* (19 December 2002): kultúra.

Garam, Katalin, and János Járai. "Kertész Magda a férjéről és a Nobel-díjról" (Magda Kertész about Her Husband and the Nobel Prize"). *168 óra* (19 Decem-ber 2002): kultúra.

Gömöri, George. Review of Imre Kertész's *Gályanapló. World Literature Today* 67.2 (1993): 412.

Graf, Hansjörg. "'Ein durchaus erträglicher Ort': Imre Kertész's *Roman eines Schicksallosen*." *Süddeutsche Zeitung* (6 April 1996): 27.

Gusev, Iu. "Znak osventsima: O tvorchestve Imre Kertesza, laureata Nobelevskoi premii po literature." *Voprosy Literatury* 3 (2003): 124–51.

Gustafsson, Madeleine. "Imre Kertész: A Medium for the Spirit of Auschwitz." Trans. Victor Kayfetz. *Nobel e-Museum* (2003): <http://www.nobel.se/literature/articles/gustafsson/index.html>.

György, Péter. "A *Sorstalanság* egy mondatának értelmezéséhez" ("On the Analysis of a Sentence in *Fatelessness*"). *Orpheus* 4 (1991): 39–49.

György, Péter. "A holokauszt közös emlékezet" ("The Holocaust Is Collective Memory"). *Beszélő* (November 2002): 15–17.

György, Péter. "A hajléktalan" ("The Homeless"). *Élet és Irodalom* (12 September 2003): 3–4.

Győrffy, Miklós. "An Age of Unborn Children." Review of Imre Kertész's *Felszámolás* (Liquidation) and Endre Kukorelly's *TündérVölgy avagy Az emberi szív rejtelmeiről* (Fairy Valley, or, On the Mysteries of the Human Heart). *The New Hungarian Quarterly* 43.172 (2003): 134–36.

Győrfy, Miklós. "A kő és a hegy. Kertész Imre: *A kudarc*" ("The Rock and the Mountain: Imre Kertész's *The Failure*"). *Jelenkor: Irodalmi és művészeti folyóirat* 10 (1989): 985–87.

Győrffy, Miklós. Review of Imre Kertész's *A kudarc*. *The New Hungarian Quarterly* 30.114 (1989): 182–187.

Győrffy, Miklós. Review of Imre Kertész's *Az angol lobogó*. *The New Hungarian Quarterly* 33.125 (1992): 124–128.

Hage, Volker. "Vom Glück in der Hölle." *Der Spiegel* 42 (2002): 48.

Halkó, Gabriella. "Nem próféta a saját hazájában" ("No Prophet in His Own Country"). *Színes Mai Lap* (11 Oktober 2002):

Häupl-Seitz, Helga, and Helmut Schneider. "Gespräch mit Imre Kertész. In der Erinnerung . . ." *Wien Live: Das Kulturmagazin für Wien* (4 November 2003): 12–15.

Heller, Ágnes. "*A holokauszt mint kultúra*. Kertész Imre könyvéről" ("The Holocaust as Culture. About the Book by Imre Kertész") *Az idegen* (The Foreigner). By Ágnes Heller. Budapest: Múlt és Jövő, 1997. 92–101.

Hernádi, Miklós. "Kertész Imréhez, meggyőződésből" ("To Imre Kertész, with Conviction"). *Élet és Irodalom* (11 January 2002): 18–20.

Hima, Gabriella. "Kertész Imre: *A kudarc*." *Alföld: Irodalmi, művészeti és kritikai folyóirat* 6 (1989): 86–88.

Jagow, Bettina von. "Mythische Denkmuster in der Nachzeit der Shoah. Erinnerung zwischen Fiktion und Wahrheit in Imre Kertész' *Roman eines Schicksallosen* und Roberto Benignis Film *La vita è bella*." *Topographie der Erinnerung. Mythos im strukturellen Wandel*. Ed. Bettina von Jagow. Würzburg: Königshausen & Neumann, 2000. 237–60.

Jagow, Bettina von. "Representing the Holocaust, Kertész's *Fatelessness*, and Benigni's *La vita è bella*." Trans. Sabine Prechter. *Imre Kertész and Holocaust Literature*. Ed. Louise O. Vasvári and Steven Tötösy de Zepetnek. West Lafayette: Purdue UP, 2005. 76–88.

Kállai, István. "Apám, amit írtál, zseniális" ("Buddy, What you Wrote Is Genial"). *Kritika* (December 2002): 26–27.

Kálmán, C. György. "Kertész közöttünk. Az ÉS könyve decemberben" ("Kertész among Us: The Book by *ÉS* [*Élet és Irodalom*] in December"). *Élet és Irodalom* (13 December 2002): 29.

Kalocsai, Katalin. "Még létre sem jött, mikor már elveszett. Az identitás építésének nehézségeiről egy szélsőségesen fenyegetett helyzetben" ("It Did not Yet Materialize When It Was Already Lost: About The Construction of an Identity in Highly Endangered Situation"). *Az értelmezés szükségessége. Tanulmányok Kertész Imréről* (The Necessity of Interpretation: Studies on Imre Kertész). Ed. Tamás Scheibner and Zoltán Gábor Szűcs. Budapest: L'Harmattan, 2002. 53–66.

Kaposi, Dávid. "Egy diákcsíny margójára. Kertész Imre: *Sorstalanság*" ("On the Margins of a Student's Practical Joke: Imre Kertész's *Fatelessness*"). *Irodalomtörténet* 84.3 (2003): 348–66.

Kaposi, Dávid. "Kertész kontra Kertész." *Thalassa: Pszichoanalízis – társadalom – kultúra* 14.1 (2003): 3–24.

Kaposi, Dávid. "Narratívátlanság. Kulturális sémák és a *Sorstalanság*" ("Narrativelessness: Cultural Schematas and *Fatelessness*"). *Az értelmezés szükségessége. Tanulmányok Kertész Imréről* (The Necessity of Interpretation. Studies on Imre Kertész). Ed. Tamás Scheibner and Zoltán Gábor Szücs. Budapest: L'Harmattan, 2002. 15–51.

Kaposi, Dávid. "'Narrativeless': Cultural Concepts and the [sic] *Fateless*." *SPIEL: Siegener Periodicum zur Internationalen Empirischen Literaturwissenschaft* 21.1 (2002): 89–105.

Kaposi, Dávid. "Narrativlosigkeit. Kulturelle Schemata und der *Roman eines Schicksallosen*." Trans. Éva Zádor. *Der lange, dunkle Schatten. Studien zum Werk von Imre Kertész*. Ed. Mihály Szegedy-Maszák and Tamás Scheibner. Wien: Passagen, 2004. 67–102.

Kappanyos, András. "Was übersetzbar ist und was nicht." Trans. Christine Rácz. *Der lange, dunkle Schatten. Studien zum Werk von Imre Kertész*. Ed. Mihály Szegedy-Maszák and Tamás Scheibner. Wien: Passagen, 2004. 117–25.

Karasek, Manuel, and Ulrich Gutmair. "Die Harmlosigkeit des Grauens." *Voice of Germany: netzeitung.de* (10 October 2002): <http://www.netzeitung.de/voice ofgermany/210622.html>.

Karolle, Julia. "Imre Kertész's *Fatelesnesss* as Historical Fiction." *Imre Kertész and Holocaust Literature*. Ed. Louise O. Vasvári and Steven Tötösy de Zepetnek. West Lafayette: Purdue UP, 2005. 89–96.

Kaspar, David. "German Media Reject Charge of Anti-Americanism / Deutsche Medien weisen Vorwurf des Anti-Amerikanismus zurück." *Davids Medienkritik* (2004): <http://medienkritik.typepad.com/blog/netzeitung/>.

Kelemen, Pál. "Fremderfahrung und Gedächtnis bei Imre Kertész." *Der lange, dunkle Schatten. Studien zum Werk von Imre Kertész.* Ed. Mihály Szegedy-Maszák and Tamás Scheibner. Wien: Passagen, 2004. 211–35.

Kertzer, Adrienne. "Reading Imre Kertész in English." *Imre Kertész and Holocaust Literature.* Ed. Louise O. Vasvári and Steven Tötösy de Zepetnek. West Lafayette: Purdue UP, 2005. 111–24.

Kinzer, Stephen. "America Yawns at Foreign Fiction." *The New York Times* (26 July 2003): A17–19.

Kirk, Karl Peter. "Hungary's Nobel Prize Winner Remains Critical Towards Homeland." *ABC News.com* (18 October 2002): <http://core.ujcfedweb.org/content_display.html?ArticleID=62804>.

Klein, Judith. "'. . . als wäre ich selbst der Dichter': Übersetzen als Thema und Metapher literarischer Texte (an Beispielen von Isaak Babel, Aharon Megged und Imre Kertész)." *LiLi: Zeitschrift für Literaturwissenschaft und Linguistik* 25.99 (1995): 155–60.

Kóczián, Péter, and Erzsébet Dragos. "Kertész Imre és a jobboldal" ("Imre Kertész and the Right-Wing"). *Tallózó* (24 October 2002): 2829–31.

Kőbányai, János. *Az ember mélye. Írások Kertész Imréről a Múlt és Jövőben* (The Depths of Man: Writings on Imre Kertész in *Múlt és Jövő*). Budapest: Múlt és Jövő, 2003.

Koltai, Kornélia. "Imre Kertész's *Fatelessness* and the Myth about Auschwitz in Hungary." Trans. Katalin Erdődi. *Imre Kertész and Holocaust Literature.* Ed. Louise O. Vasvári and Steven Tötösy de Zepetnek. West Lafayette: Purdue UP, 2005. 125–37.

Kornis. Mihály. "Sors" ("Fate"). *Élet és Irodalom* (18 October 2002): 4.

Kovács, Lóránt Béla. "Az időbeliség tapasztalatának módosulásai Kertész Imre *Sorstalanság* című regényében" (Modifications of the Experience of Time in Imre Kertész's Novel *Fatelessness*). *Az értelmezés szükségessége. Tanulmányok Kertész Imréről* (The Necessity of Interpretation: Studies on Imre Kertész). Ed. Tamás Scheibner and Zoltán Gábor Szűcs. Budapest: L'Harmattan, 2002. 67–75.

Lányi, Dániel. "A *Sorstalanság* kisérletete" ("The Attempt of *Fatelessness*"). *Holmi* 7.5 (May 1995): 665–74.

Lassen, Morten. "At grave sig en grav i skyerne: Skæbne og identitet i Imre Kertész' forfatterskab." *Kritik* 160 (2002): 50–57.

Leaf, Jonathan. "Another Nobel Winner You've Never Heard of." *Weekly Standard* (28 October 2002): 37–38.

Lurincz, Iva. "An Ordinary Day at Auschwitz." *Sydney Morning Herald* (23 November 2002): 1–2.

Mahlmann-Bauer, Barbara. "Von weltliterarischem Rang. Das Oeuvre des diesjährigen Literaturnobelpreisträgers Imre Kertész." *Literaturkritik* 12 (2002): 9–38.

Mahlmann-Bauer, Barbara. "Imre Kertész' Gottesbild in seinen Tagebuchauf-
zeichnungen *Galeerentagebuch* und *Ich—ein anderer*." *Colloquium Helveticum*
34 (2003): 267–301.

Margócsy, István. "... valami más ... Kertész Imre: *Valaki más*" (... Something Else
... Imre Kertész's *Someone Else*." *Élet és Irodalom* (6 June 1997): 17.

Margócsy, István. "'Minden nincs meg.' A megfogalmazás kalandja" ("'Nothing Is
Done': The Adventure of Composition"). *Az értelmezés szükségessége. Tanulmányok Kertész Imréről* (The Necessity of Interpretation: Studies on Imre
Kertész). Ed. Tamás Scheibner and Zoltán Gábor Szűcs. Budapest: L'Harmattan,
2002. 199–210.

Margócsy, István. "'Es ist nicht alles da.' Das Abenteuer des Erzählens." Trans. Éva
Zádor. *Der lange, dunkle Schatten. Studien zum Werk von Imre Kertész*. Ed.
Mihály Szegedy-Maszák and Tamás Scheibner. Wien: Passagen, 2004. 313–25.

Marsovszky, Magdalena. "Aus der Rezeption des Nobelpreises für Imre Kertész in
Ungarn. 'Geschmacksterror einer Minderheit'." *haGalil Online* (6 December
2002): <http://www.klick-nach-rechts.de/gegen-rechts/2002/12/kertesz.htm>.

Marsovszky, Magdalena. "Imre Kertész and Hungary Today." Trans. Eszter Pásztor.
Imre Kertész and Holocaust Literature. Ed. Louise O. Vasvári and Steven Tötösy
de Zepetnek. West Lafayette: Purdue UP, 2005. 148–61.

Marsovszky, Magdalena. "Imre Kertész—einer von uns! Oder doch nicht? Kulturkampf und Identität in Ungarn." *Europas Mitte, Mitteleuropa, europäische Identität? Geschichte, Literatur, Positionen*. Ed. Barbara Breisach and Dorothee Rabe.
Berlin: Logos, 2003. 137–53.

Márton, Gábor. "A *Sorstalanság* folyamatossága" ("The Continuity of *Fatelessness*").
Népszabadság (21 October 1985): 7.

Megyesi, Gusztáv. "Szép, kicsi ország" ("Beautiful, Small Country"). *Élet és Irodalom*
(18 October 2002): 1.

Mészáros, Sándor. "Hírérték és kulturális emlékezet" ("News Value and Cultural
Memory"). *Élet és Irodalom* (25 October 2002): 8–9.

Molnár, Gábor Tamás. "Fikcióalkotás és történelemszemlélet; Kertész Imre: *Sorstalanság*" ("The Creation of Fiction and the Perspective of History: Imre Kertész's *Fatelessness*"). *Alföld: Irodalmi, művészeti és kritikai folyóirat* 47.8 (1996): 57–71.

Molnár, Sára. "A fogolylét poétikája. Kertész Imre: *Jegyzőkönyv*" ("Poetics of the Prisoner's Existence: Imre Kertész's *Sworn Statement*"). *Az értelmezés szükségessége.
Tanulmányok Kertész Imréről* (The Necessity of Interpretation: Studies on Imre
Kertész). Ed. Tamás Scheibner and Zoltán Gábor Szűcs. Budapest: L'Harmattan,
2002. 167–98.

Molnár, Sára. "Imre Kertész's Aesthetics of the Holocaust." *Imre Kertész and Holocaust Literature*. Ed. Louise O. Vasvári and Steven Tötösy de Zepetnek. West Lafayette: Purdue UP, 2005. 162–70.

Murányi, Gábor. "'A Nobel-díjat zavaró repülésnek éreztem.' Interview with Imre
Kertész" ("'I Felt the Nobel Prize a Distracting Flight': Interview with Imre
Kertész"). *Heti Világgazdaság* (6 September 2003): 47–48.

Murányi, Gábor. "Egyenlőre még tanulóvezető vagyok. 1994-es beszélgetés Kertész Imrével" ("For Now I am Only Learning to Drive: Conversation in 1994 with Imre Kertész"). *Kritika* (April 2003): 14–16.

Müller, Lothar. "Eine Wiedervereinigung." *Süddeutsche Zeitung (Feuilleton)* (12–13 October 2002): 11.

Nad', Ishtvan. "Ot vynuzhdennoi uchasti-k vyboru sud'by. O tvorchestve Imre Kertesza." Trans. Sergeii Vol'skii. *Zvezda* 7 (2003): 188–202.

Nádas, Péter. "Kertész munkája és a témája" ("Kertész's Work and Thematics"). *Élet és Irodalom* (18 October 2002): 3.

Nádas, Péter. "Imre Kertész's Work and His Subject." *The New Hungarian Quarterly* 43.168 (2002): 38–40.

Nagy, Ferenc. "The First Hungarian Nobel Laureate of the 21st Century." *The Hungarian Observer* Special Issue (2002): 22–23.

Nagy, Péter Sz. "Holokauszt vagy soa? Két monográfia Kertész Imréről" (Holocaust or Shoah? Two Monographs about Imre Kertész"). *Kritika* (November 2003): 9–11.

Nirenstein, Susanna. "Aki megmenekült Auschwitz poklából" ("One Who Escaped the Hell of Auschwitz"). Trans. György Petöcz. *Élet és Irodalom* 46.42 (18 October 2002): 4.

Oplatka, Andreas. "Festtag in Ungarn. Reaktionen auf Imre Kertész' Nobelpreis." *Neue Zürcher Zeitung* (12 October 2002): 3.

Orecklin, Michele. "A Nobel Effort." *Time Europe* (21 October 2002): 76.

Ököli, Tünde. "Literary Portrait of a Laureate." *Africa News Service* (16 October 2002): 20.

Orlando, Mejía Rivera. "Imre Kertész y el territorio mítico de Auschwitz." *Revista Universidad de Antioquia* 271 (2003): 66–71.

Pályi, András. "Derült égből Nobel-díj" ("Nobel Prize Out of the Clear Sky"). *Élet és Irodalom* (18 october 2002): 7.

Pályi, András. "Mindenki zsidó. Kertész Imre: *Felszámolás*" (Everyone is Jewish: Imre Kertész's *Liquidation*). *Kritika* (November 2003): 7–9.

Peguy, Marie. "The Dichotomy of Perspectives in the Work of Imre Kertész and Jorge Semprún." *Imre Kertész and Holocaust Literature*. Ed. Louise O. Vasvári and Steven Tötösy de Zepetnek. West Lafayette: Purdue UP, 2005. 171–81.

Pelle, János. "A *Sorstalanság* új élete" ("The New Life of *Fatelessness*"). *Heti Válasz* (11 October 2002): 8.

Portuges, Catherine. "Imre Kertész and the Filming of *Fatelessness*." *Imre Kertész and Holocaust Literature*. Ed. Louise O. Vasvári and Steven Tötösy de Zepetnek. West Lafayette: Purdue UP, 2005. 182–94.

Pór, Péter. "Ein jüdischer *Candide* im Reich des Bösen. Gedanken zur Lektüre von Imre Kertész' *Roman eines Schicksallosen*." *Schweizer Monatshefte* 84 (2004): 40–44.

Pór, Péter. "Köves Gyuri utazása a Rossz birodalmában. Megjegyzések Kertész Imre *Sorstalanság* című regényének értelmezéséhez" ("The Travels of George Köves in the Empire of the Evil: Comments on Imre Kertész's *Fatelessness*"). Trans. József Bende. *Vigília* 69 (2004): 840–49.

Pór, Péter. "Un ingénu dans le domaine du Mal. Pour lire les *Êtres sans destin* d'Imre Kertész." *Esprit* 310 (2004): 84–93.

Pór, Péter. "Ein jüdischer 'Candide' im Reich des Bösen." *Schweizer Monatshefte* 84.5–6 (2004): 40–45.

Proksza, Ágnes. "Döntés és ítélet. Kertész Imre: *Sorstalanság*" ("Decision and Judgment: Imre Kertész's *Fatelessness*). *Az értelmezés szükségessége* (The Necessity of Interpretation). Ed. Tamás Scheibner and Zoltán Gábor Szűcs. Budapest: L'Harmattan, 2002. 77–102.

Proksza, Ágnes. "Entscheidung und Urteil. Imre Kertész: *Roman eines Schicksallosen*." Trans. Karl Vajda. *Der lange, dunkle Schatten. Studien zum Werk von Imre Kertész*. Ed. Mihály Szegedy-Maszák and Tamás Scheibner. Wien: Passagen, 2004. 139–66.

Radics, Viktória. "Az ember mélye. Kertész Imre: *Sorstalanság*" ("The Depth of Man: Imre Kertész's *Fatelessness*"). *Életünk* 1 (1988): 80–85.

Radisch, Iris. "Die Glückskatastrophe. ZEIT-Gespräch mit dem Nobelpresisträger Imre Kertész über Berlin, den Antisemitismus, das Geld und die Erlösung." *Die Zeit* 43 (17 Oktober 2002): 45–46.

Radisch, Iris. "Luck and Catastrophe." *World Press Review* (January 2003): 32.

Radnóti, Sándor. "Auschwitz mint szellemi életforma" ("Auschwitz as a Mental Form of Life"). *Holmi* 3 (1991): 370–78.

Radnóti, Sándor. "Utószó—a Nobel-díj után" ("Epilogue: After the Nobel Prize"). *Az értelmezés szükségessége. Tanulmányok Kertész Imréről* (The Necessity of Interpretation: Studies on Imre Kertész). Ed. Tamás Scheibner and Zoltán Gábor Szűcs. Budapest: L'Harmattan, 2002. 211–17.

Radnóti, Sándor, and László Szörényi László. Interview. "Áldjuk a Jóistent, hogy nekünk adott tanút" ("Bless the Good Lord for Having Given Us a Witness). *Beszélő* (January-February 2003): 30–36.

Radnóti, Sándor. "Auschwitz als geistige Lebensform. Imre Kertész: *Kaddisch für ein nicht geborenes Kind*." Trans. Éva Zádor. *Der lange, dunkle Schatten. Studien zum Werk von Imre Kertész*. Ed. Mihály Szegedy-Maszák and Tamás Scheibner. Wien: Passagen, 2004. 181–94.

Rathgeb, Eberhard. "Porträt. Imre Kertész, ungarischer Schriftsteller." *Frankfurter Allgemeine* Zeitung (10 October 2002): Feuilleton.

Ratkovčić, Rosana. "Danilo Kiš, Imre Kertész, and the Myth of the Holocaust." Trans. Irina Krlić. *Imre Kertész and Holocaust Literature*. Ed. Louise O. Vasvári and Steven Tötösy de Zepetnek. West Lafayette: Purdue UP, 2005. 195–204.

Reid, Calvin. "Kertész Awarded Literature Prize." *Publishers Weekly* (14 October 2002): 19.

Riding, Alan. "A Holocaust Survivor at Home in Berlin: Nobel Hero Insists Hungary Face Its Past." *New York Times* (4 December 2002): E1, E5.

Riding, Alan. "Nobel for Hungarian Writer Who Survived Death Camps." *New York Times* (11 October 2002): A1, A8.

Rosenbaum, Thane. "The Survivor Who Survived." *New York Times* (12 October 2002): A21.

Rosenberg, Ervin. "Világkisebbségi helyzet" ("Global Minority"). Interview with Eszter Rádai. *Élet és Irodalom* (18 October 2002): 5.

Rudtke, Tanja. "'Eine kuriose Geschichte.' Die Pikaro-Perspektive im Holocaustroman am Beispiel von Imre Kertész' *Roman eines Schicksallosen*." *Arcadia: Zeitschrift für Vergleichende Literaturwissenschaft* 18 (1983): 43–57.

Sanders, Iván. "Kemény dió" ("Hard Nut"). *Élet és Irodalom* (4 January 2002): 15–17.

Sándor, Iván. "Szemben Wittgenstein mesterrel" ("Face-to-Face with Master Wittgenstein"). *Élet és Irodalom* (18 October 2002): 3.

Sándor, Iván. "Mi a magyar (író) most? A Nobel-díj-szindróma" ("What Does it Mean to Be a Hungarian [Writer] Now? The Nobel Prize Syndrome"). *Élet és Irodalom* (21 February 2003): 5.

Sándor, Zsuzsanna, György Spiró, Katalin Garam, György Dalos, Péter Léner, and Ákos Szilágyi. "Címlap. Nobel-díjas magyar" ("Title Page: Hungarian with Nobel Prize"). *168 óra* (17 October 2002): 24–33.

Sárközi, Bence. "A díjra érdemes ember" ("A Man Worthy of the Prize"). *Remény* 5.4 (2002): 5–10.

Scheibner, Tamás. "Az önmagától megfosztott én. Kertész Imre: *Jegyzőkönyv*" ("The Self-Deprived Self: Imre Kertész's *Sworn Statement*." *Irodalomtörténet* 84.3 (2003): 367–79.

Scheibner, Tamás. "Das um sich selbst gebrachte Ich. Imre Kertész: *Protokoll*." Trans. Andrea Egyed. *Der lange, dunkle Schatten. Studien zum Werk von Imre Kertész.* Ed. Mihály Szegedy-Maszák and Tamás Scheibner. Wien: Passagen, 2004. 293–311.

Scheibner, Tamás. "Mítosz és ideológia. Paradoxitás Kertész Imre esszéiben" ("Myth and Ideology: Paradoxes in the Essays of Imre Kertész"). *Jelenkor* 46.5 (2004): 555–62.

Scheibner, Tamás. "Imre Kertész's *Jegyzőkönyv* (*Sworn Statement*) and the Self Deprived of Itself." Trans. Sean Lambert. *Imre Kertész and Holocaust Literature.* Ed. Louise O. Vasvári and Steven Tötösy de Zepetnek. West Lafayette: Purdue UP, 2005. 205–19.

Scheibner, Tamás, and Zoltán Gábor Szűcs, eds. *Az értelmezés szükségessége. Tanulmányok Kertész Imréről* (The Necessity of Interpretation: Studies on Imre Kertész). Budapest: L'Harmattan, 2002.

Schein, Gábor: "Összekötni az összeköthetetlent" ("Connecting the Inconnectible"). *Az értelmezés szükségessége. Tanulmányok Kertész Imréről* (The Necessity of Interpretation: Studies on Imre Kertész). Ed. Tamás Scheibner and Zoltán Gábor Szűcs. Budapest: L'Harmattan, 2002. 103–18.

Schein, Gábor. "Das Unverbindbare verbinden. Anmerkungen zu Prosa von Imre Kertész." Trans. Karl Vajda. *Der lange, dunkle Schatten. Studien zum Werk von*

Imre Kertész. Ed. Mihály Szegedy-Maszák and Tamás Scheibner. Wien: Passagen, 2004. 165–80.

Schlink, Bernhard. "Anfang der Kritik. Eine Laudatio auf den Schriftsteller Imre Kertész." *Kultur* (10 November 2002): Literatur.

Schmal, Dániel. "Kiket legjobb lett volna sohse látnotok" ("Those Whom It Would Have Been Better Not to See"). *Pannonhalmi Szemle* 3 (1994): 100-07.

Schmidt, Uwe. "Poeta laureatus. Der Literaturpreisträger 2002." *Thalia LiteraTouren* (2002): n.p.

Schmidt-Dengler, Wendelin. "Schritt für Schritt." *Wien Live: Das Kulturmagazin für Wien* (4 November 2003): 16–17.

Selyem, Zsuzsa. "Irodalom és irodalom—a mellérendelés etikája" ("Literature and Literature: The Ethics of Coordination"). *Pannonhalmi Szemle* 9.3 (2001): 75–97.

Shrivastava, Anjana. "Imre Kertész und das Glück." *Voice of Germany: netzeitung.de* (10 December 2002): <http://www.netzeitung.de/voiceofgermany/218623.html>.

Spiró, György. "Non habent sua fata. A *Sorstalanság*—ujraolvasva" ("Non habent sua fata: *Fatelessness*—Reread"). *Élet és Irodalom* 30 (1983): 5.

Spiró, György. "In Art Only the Radical Exists: Imre Kertész." *The New Hungarian Quarterly* 43 (2002): 29–37.

Spiró, György. "Örüljünk!" ("Let Us Rejoice!"). *168 óra* (17 October 2002): 26–27.

Steinfeld, Thomas. "Bescherung." *Süddeutsche Zeitung (Feuilleton)* (9 Oktober 2002): 18.

Steinfeld, Thomas. "Ein Steinchen für Sisyphos." *Süddeutsche Zeitung (Feuilleton)* (11 October 2002): 19.

Summers-Bremner, Eluned. "Imre Kertész's *Kaddish for a Child Not Born*." *Imre Kertész and Holocaust Literature*. Ed. Louise O. Vasvári and Steven Tötösy de Zepetnek. West Lafayette: Purdue UP, 2005. 220–31.

Szántó, Gábor T. "Interjú Kertész Imrével" ("Interview with Imre Kertész"). *Szombat* 4 (1994): 35.

Szegedy-Maszák, Mihály. "Der Außenstehende und der Betroffene: Die Ironie des Verstehens." Trans. Karl Vajda. *Der lange, dunkle Schatten. Studien zum Werk von Imre Kertész*. Ed. Mihály Szegedy-Maszák and Tamás Scheibner. Wien: Passagen, 2004. 127–38.

Szegedy-Maszák, Mihály, and Tamás Scheibner, eds. *Der lange, dunkle Schatten. Studien zum Werk von Imre Kertész*. Wien: Passagen, 2004.

Szilágyi, Ákos. "2000-beszélgetés Kertész Imrével (1995)" ("2000-Conversation with Imre Kertész [1995]"). *2000* 11 (2002): 5–11.

Szilágyi, Ákos. "Az eredendő történelmi bűn" ("The Original Sin of History"). *Kritika* (February 2003): 4–8.

Szilágyi, Ákos. "Die historische Erbsünde. Auschwitz als 'idealer Ausgangspunkt' in den Romanen von Imre Kertész." Trans. Christine Rácz. *Der lange, dunkle Schatten. Studien zum Werk von Imre Kertész*. Ed. Mihály Szegedy-Maszák and Tamás Scheibner. Wien: Passagen, 2004. 343–64.

Szilágyi, Márton. Review of Kertész Imre: *Kaddish a meg nem született gyermekért*. *Alföld: Irodalmi, művészeti és kritikai folyóirat* 41.12 (December 1990): 72–73.

Szirák, Péter. "A szük az most tágasabb" ("The Narrow is Wider Now"). *Kortárs* 11 (1992): 96–100.

Szirák, Péter. "Emlékezés és példázat Lengyel Péter, Kertész Imre és Szilágyi István elbeszélő prózájában" ("Memory and Exemplification in the Prose of Péter Lengyel, Imre Kertész, and István Szilágyi"). *A népiségtől a posztmodernig. Tanulmányok korunk irodalmáról* (From the *népiség* to the Postmodern: Studies on Contemporary Literature). Ed. I. Bitskey. Debrecen: Kossuth, 1997. 71–93.

Szirák, Péter. "Emlékezés és példázat. A létezés negatív aspektusa (A Kertész-olvasás)" ("Memory and Exemplification: The Aspect of Negative Existence [The Reading of Kertész]"). *Folytonosság és változás* (Continuity and Change). By Péter Szirák. Debrecen: Csokonai, 1998. 82–88.

Szirák, Péter. "A megérthetetlen megőrzése. Kertész Imre *Sorstalanság*áról" ("Preservation of the Incomprehensible: About Imre Kertész's *Fatelessness*"). *Magyar Lettre* (Winter 2002–2003): 1–2.

Szirák, Péter. *Kertész Imre. A pesszimizmus: bátorság* (Imre Kertész. Pessimism is Courage). Bratislava: Kalligram, 2003.

Szirák, Péter. "Die Bewahrung des Unverständlichen. Imre Kertész: *Roman eines Schicksallosen*." Trans. Karl Vajda. *Der lange, dunkle Schatten. Studien zum Werk von Imre Kertész*. Ed. Mihály Szegedy-Maszák and Tamás Scheibner. Wien: Passagen, 2004. 17–66.

Szirtes, George. "Who is Imre Kertész?" *Times Literary Supplement* (18 October 2002): 17–18.

Szirtes, George. "Nobel Laureate Who?" *Maisonneuve: Eclectic Curiosity* 3 (2003): <http://www.maisonneuve.org/print_article.php?article_id=88>).

Takács, Ferenc. "Erdő, halál, írtás" ("Forest, Death, Destruction"). *Kortárs* 6 (1990): 153–55.

Takács, Géza. "Olvasónaplók a *Sorstalanság*ról" ("Diaries about *Fatelessness*"). *Beszélő* (November 2002): 20–34.

Takáts, József: "Citrom Bandi védelmében. Vári György *Sorstalanság*-értelmezéséről" ("In the Defense of Bandi Citrom: On György Vári's Interpretation of *Fatelessness*"). *Jelenkor* 46.5 (2004): 548–54.

Tamás, Gáspár Miklós. "Kertész Imre magyar író Nobel-díjas. Zsidó" ("Hungarian Writer Imre Kertész, Jew, Receives the Nobel Prize." *Magyar Hírlap* (11 October 2002): 5.

Teslár, Ákos. "Élni és (újra)írni. Morál és poétika *A kudarc*ban" ("Live and [Re]Write: Morals and Poetics in The Failure"). *Az értelmezés szükségessége. Tanulmányok Kertész Imréről* (The Necessity of Interpretation: Studies on Imre Kertész). Ed. Tamás Scheibner and Zoltán Gábor Szűcs. Budapest: L'Harmattan, 2002. 151–66.

Thiel, Stefan. "A Voice of Conscience." *Newsweek* (6 January 2003): 96.

Thomka, Beáta. "Narrative Identität im *Roman eines Schicksallosen*. Das Werk des Imre Kertész und sein Kontext in der zeitgenössischen ungarischen Prosa." *Neohelicon: Acta Comparationis Litterarum Universarum* 30.2 (2003): 105–17.

Tötösy de Zepetnek, Steven. "And the 2002 Nobel Prize for Literature Goes to Imre Kertész, Jew and Hungarian." *CLCWeb: Comparative Literature and Culture* 5.1 (2003): <http://clcwebjournal.lib.purdue.edu/clcweb03–1/totosy03.hml>.

Tötösy de Zepetnek, Steven. "Imre Kertész's Nobel Prize in Literature and the Print Media." *Imre Kertész and Holocaust Literature*. Ed. Louise O. Vasvári and Steven Tötösy de Zepetnek. West Lafayette: Purdue UP, 2005. 232–46.

Turai, Tamás. "A hiten túl, a pusztulás előtt" ("Beyond Faith, Before Destruction"). *Jelenkor: Irodalmi és művészeti folyóirat* 34.4 (1992): 310–16.

Vaderna, Gábor. "A lehetséges egyetlen regény. Kertész Imre: *A kudarc*" ("The Only Possible and Only Novel: Imre Kertész's The Failure"). *Az értelmezés szükségessége. Tanulmányok Kertész Imréről* (The Necessity of Interpretation: Studies on Imre Kertész). Ed. Tamás Scheibner and Zoltán Gábor Szűcs. Budapest: L'Harmattan, 2002. 137–49.

Vaderna, Gábor. "Der einzig mögliche Roman. Imre Kertész: *Fiasko*." Trans. Christine Rácz. *Der lange, dunkle Schatten. Studien zum Werk von Imre Kertész*. Ed. Mihály Szegedy-Maszák and Tamás Scheibner. Wien: Passagen, 2004. 195–209.

Varga, László. "Barcelona—s közben egy magyar Nobel-díj" ("Barcelona and in the Meantime a Hungarian Nobel Prize"). *Élet és Irodalom* (25 October 2002): 10.

Vári, György. "A *Sorstalanság* történelemszemléletéről" ("About the Historical Perspective of *Fatelessness*"). *Élet és Irodalom* (18 October 2002): 7.

Vári, György. "Cselekményesítés, történelmi tapasztalat és a fenséges művészete" ("The Art of Plot, Historical Experience, and the Sublime"). *Az értelmezés szükségessége. Tanulmányok Kertész Imréről* (The Necessity of Interpretation: Studies on Imre Kertész). Ed. Tamás Scheibner and Zoltán Gábor Szűcs. Budapest: L'Harmattan, 2002. 119–36.

Vári, György. *Kertész Imre. Buchenwald fölött az ég* (Imre Kertész: The Sky above Buchenwald). Budapest: Kijárat, 2003.

Várnai, Pál. "A száműzött nyelve. Olvasónapló Kertész naplóiról és esszéiről" ("The Language of the Exile: About Kertész's Diaries and Essays"). *Szombat* (October 2002): 15–17.

Várnai, Paul. "Holocaust Literature and Imre Kertész." *Imre Kertész and Holocaust Literature*. Ed. Louise O. Vasvári and Steven Tötösy de Zepetnek. West Lafayette: Purdue UP, 2005. 247–57.

Vásárhelyi, Mária. "Nobel-díj—történeti keretben" ("The Nobel-Prize in a Historical Setting"). *Élet és Irodalom* (18 October 2002): 6.

Vasvári, Louise O. "The Novelness of Imre Kertész's *Fatelessness*." *Imre Kertész and Holocaust Literature*. Ed. Louise O. Vasvári and Steven Tötösy de Zepetnek. West Lafayette: Purdue UP, 2005. 258–70.

Weinzierl, Ulrich. "Verstörendes Glück. Imre Kertész in der Schule des Grauens." *Frankfurter Allgemeine Zeitung* (30 March 1996): B5.

Wilkinson, Timothy. "Kaddish for a Stillborn Child? Translating Imre Kertész." *The New Hungarian Quarterly* 43 (2002): 41–43.

Wilson, Katharine M. "Finding the Voice: Translating Imre Kertész." *American Translators' Association Source* 38 (2003): 1, 11.

Wilson, K.M., and R.M. Davis. Review of Imre Kertész's *Kaddish for a Child Not Born. World Literature Today* 74.1 (2000): 205.

Wirth, Imre. Review of Imre Kertész's *Kaddis a meg nem született gyermekért." Vigília* 11 (1990): 876–77.

Wirth, Imre. *Sorstalanság = 7 x 7 híres mai magyar regény (Fatelessness = 7 x 7 Famous Hungarian Novel Today).* Budapest: Móra, 1997.

Young, Judy. "The Media and Imre Kertész's Nobel Prize in Literature." *Imre Kertész and Holocaust Literature.* Ed. Louise O. Vasvári and Steven Tötösy de Zepetnek. West Lafayette: Purdue UP, 2005. 271–85.

Note: I thank Clare Callaghan, Magdalena Marsovszky, Tamás Scheibner, Louise O. Vasvári, and Tim Wilkinson for their assistance with the above bibliography.

Index

Bioprofiles of Contributors

Tonin Baltus is a retired secondary school teacher who taught English at high schools in Ales (Gard), Figeac (Lot), and Lodève (Herault) in France. Baltus is the translator of Marie Peguy's "The Dichotomy of Perspectives in the Work of Imre Kertész and Jorge Semprún" in the collected volume *Imre Kertész and Holocaust Literature*. Ed. Louise O. Vasvári and Steven Tötösy de Zepetnek. West Lafayette: Purdue UP, 2005. He lives in Lodève.

Enikő Molnár Basa received her Ph.D. in comparative literature from the University of North Carolina Chapel Hill and worked until her retirement as a senior cataloger in the Serial Records Division of the Library of Congress. In scholarship, Basa has published numerous articles in learned journals, newspapers, and magazines as well as volumes in the Twayne series on Sándor Petőfi, Mihály Csokonai Vitéz, Imre Madách, Kálmán Mikszáth, and Ferenc Molnár, and in the series of the Finnisch-Ugrisches Seminar at the University of München on Dezső Kosztolányi and Miklós Radnóti. Basa is now working on a book examining Hungarian literature in the context of political and social commitment.

Barbara Breysach teaches German and comparative literature at Viadrina University where she also serves as coordinator of the European Fellows Program at the Collegium Polonicum. Her interests in research include German and German-Jewish literature and culture from 1800 to the present, Polish and Polish-Jewish literature in the twentieth century, and comparative studies of Central European literatures and she has published widely in these areas of scholarship. Currently, she is investigating the context of literary language and violence in the works of Herta Müller and Marguerite Duras.

Sara D. Cohen received her M.A. in Central and South-East European Studies from the School of Slavonic and East European Studies at University College London in 2003. While at SSEES, she served as editor of the journal *Slovo*. In 2003 Cohen co-organized the SSEES conference *Four Empires and an Enlargement: Transfiguring Perspectives and Images of Central and Eastern Europe* and she is one of the editors of a collected volume with the papers of the conference. Since 2004 Cohen is a Foreign Service Officer with Foreign Affairs Canada.

Robert Eaglestone teaches literature at Royal Holloway, University of London. His interests in scholarship include Holocaust literature and testimony, ethics, historiography, Carter, Beckett, Derrida, Agamben, Levinas, archaeology, postmodern-ism and science. His numerous publications in these fields include *The Holocaust and the Postmodern* (2004), *Postmodernism and Holocaust Denial* (2001), *Doing English* (1999, 2nd ed. 2002), *Ethical Criticism: Reading after Levinas* (1997). Eaglestone is series editor of *Routledge Critical Thinkers* and a literary advisor to the British Council. In his current research, Eaglestone is project leader of a British Academy funded project, *Literary Encounters between the United Kingdom and Hungary: Contrasting Memories, Cultural Dialogues.*

Katalin Erdődi translates from Hungarian into English texts in the humanities, pub-lic administration, and public relations. She has received her diploma in public ad-ministration and international relations from the University of Economic Sciences and Public Administration, Budapest, in 2004. In 2001–02 Erdődi studied on a fel-lowship at the University of Santiago de Compostela. Currently, she is working at the Trafó House of Contemporary Arts, Budapest. Erdődi is the translator of Kornélia Koltai's "Imre Kertész's *Fatelessness* and the Myth about Auschwitz in Hungary" in the collected volume *Imre Kertész and Holocaust Literature.* Ed. Louise O. Vasvári and Steven Tötösy de Zepetnek. West Lafayette: Purdue UP, 2005.

Amos Friedland completed his Ph.D. in philosophy with a dissertation entitled *Forgiveness, Reconciliation, and the Remains of Resentment* at New School Uni-versity in 2002. The dissertation is on forgiveness and resentment in Hegel and in post-Holocaust thought and literature, with focus on Imre Kertész's work. Cur-rently, Friedland holds a Social Sciences and Humanities Research Council of Canada fellowship at McGill University, where he is at work on a book on for-giveness and geopolitics in the twentieth century, a book on Emil Fackenheim and the imperatives of post-Holocaust thought, and a book investigating the legal his-tory underlying the Palestinian-Israeli conflict. He has also published a number of philosophical and political articles on these same themes.

András Gerő teaches history at Eötvös Loránd University where he also serves as director of the Institute of Habsburg History. He also teaches at Central European University and has been invited visiting professor at the University of Pennsylvania and at Amsterdam, Columbia, and Utrecht universities. Gerő has published widely articles and books in Hungarian, German, and English, and he is editor of the *Bu-dapest Quarterly.* His most recent publications include *Unfinished Socialism* (1999), *Emperor Francis Joseph, King of Hungarians* (2001), and *Imagined His-tory* (2005).

Bettina von Jagow holds a doctorate in modern German literature from the Univer-sity of München and a Lic.Phil. in theater studies from the Université de la Sor-bonne Nouvelle. Currently, she is DAAD (German Academic Exchange) Fellow at the Institute for Jewish Studies, University of Basel. Her recent publications include *Poetische Skizzen einer Ästhetik des Mythischen. Poetologien des Erinnerns im Werk von Ingeborg Bachmann* (2003) and she is co-editor, with Florian Steger, of *Differenzerfahrung und Selbst. Bewußtsein und Wahrnehmung in Literatur und Geschichte des 20. Jahrhunderts* (2003), *Repräsentationen. Medizin und Ethik in Literatur und Kunst der Moderne* (2004), and *Literatur und Medizin im europäischen Kontext. Ein Lexikon* (2005).

Julia Karolle received her Ph.D. in German from the University of Wisconsin-Madison in 2001. Following a visiting appointment at Purdue University, since 2002 she teaches German literature at John Carroll University. Her interests and publications include linguistic issues in dialect in standard-language literature and German literature by non-native authors, turn-of-the-century newspapers, Karl May, detective novels, and novels on the 1989 German *Wende*. Karolle serves on the Modern Language Association Division on Linguistic Approaches to Literature 2004–08.

Adrienne Kertzer teaches English literature at the University of Calgary. Winner of the F.E.L. Priestley Prize for "Fugitive Pieces: Listening as a Holocaust Survivor's Child," Kertzer is author of numerous papers on children's literature and Holocaust representation. Her book, *My Mother's Voice: Children, Literature, and the Holocaust* (2002), won the Canadian Jewish Book Award for Scholarship on a Jewish Subject and the Children's Literature Association Honor Book Award for Literary Criticism in Children's Literature. Her recent publications include the introduction to Playwrights Canada's two-volume collection of Holocaust plays, *A Terrible Truth: Anthology of Holocaust Drama* (2004), a paper, "The Problem of Childhood, Children's Literature, and Holocaust Representation," in the volume *Teaching the Representation of the Holocaust* (2004), and the entry "Holocaust Literature for Children" in the *Oxford Encyclopedia of Children's Literature* (forthcoming).

Kornélia Koltai teaches ancient Hebrew at Eötvös Loránd University. Her translations from the Hebrew into Hungarian include *Atyák mondásai—Pirqé ávot*, a collection of previously unpublished rabbinical writings in the early seventeenth century by Simon Péchi and she has published articles on the works of Imre Kertész and György Konrád in various journals. Koltai has studied on a fellowship at the Hebrew University of Jerusalem and she is now working on her doctoral dissertation on Simon Péchi.

András Kovács teaches sociology at Central European University in the Nationalism Studies Program and the Jewish Studies Program. His interests in scholarship include the study of Jewish identity and anti-Semitism in post-war Hungary, memory and identity, and socio-economic attitudes and politics. Kovács's more recent publications include "Changes in Jewish Identity in Modern Hungary" in *Jewish Identities in the New Europe* (1994) "Anti-Semitism and Jewish Identity in Post-Communist Hungary" in *Anti-Semitism and the Treatment of the Holocaust in Postcomunist Eastern Europe* (1994), and "Jewish Groups and Identity Strategies in Post-Communist Hungary" in *New Jewish Identities* (2003).

Irina Krlić works as a free-lance interpreter and translator for The International Criminal Tribunal in The Hague, The World Council of Churches, World Learning Inc., the Jasenovac Memorial, NONA Women's Multimedia Centre, etc., and teaches English as a foreign language in Zagreb, where she resides. Krlić is the translator of Rosana Ratkovčić's "Danilo Kiš, Imre Kertész, and the Myth of the Holocaust" in the collected volume *Imre Kertész and Holocaust Literature*. Ed. Louise O. Vasvári and Steven Tötösy de Zepetnek. West Lafayette: Purdue UP, 2005.

Sean Lambert resides in Budapest and River Falls, Wisconsin. Lambert has translated numerous articles and books from Hungarian to English, most recently Szabolcs Szita's *A zsidó mentőbizottság és az SS embervásár* as *The Jewish Rescue Committee and the SS Human Trade* (2005) and Tamás Scheibner's "Imre Kertész's *Jegyzőkönyv* (*Sworn Statement*) and the Self Deprived of Itself" in the collected volume *Imre Kertész and Holocaust Literature*. Ed. Louise O. Vasvári and Steven Tötösy de Zepetnek. West Lafayette: Purdue UP, 2005.

Magdalena Marsovszky is working towards her doctorate in media and politics at Viadrina University. At the same time, she works in culture management and as a freelance journalist in München. Her publications are in the fields of socio-political criticism of Hungarian culture, culture and media policy, anti-Semitism, and the country's integration in the European Union. In 1999 Marsovszky received an award from the Hungarian Academy of Sciences for her *Währungsunion gleich Kulturunion*, a study about Hungary's culture policies in the context of the country's integration in the European Union. Marsovszky is active in various cultural and political associations, for example, she is advisory board member of the Bavarian branch of the Kulturpolitische Gesellschaft (Society for Culture Policy).

Sara Molnár received her doctorate with a dissertation on Imre Kertész from Lajos Kossuth University in 2002. Her areas of interest and publications include Central European literature and culture, contemporary literary theory, and history of literature and she has published papers in these fields in Hungarian, German, and English. Currently, she works as a free-lance translator, editor, and critic in Budapest and Vienna.

Eszter Pásztor is a translator and managing director at Németh & Pásztor International Communication Consulting in Budapest. She translates English to Hungarian and Hungarian to English in a number of fields including the banking industry, legal and constitutional matters, tax and insurance laws, accounting, and the pharmaceutical industry. Pásztor is the translator of Magdalena Marsovszky's "Imre Kertész and Hungary Today" in the collected volume *Imre Kertész and Holocaust Literature*. Ed. Louise O. Vasvári and Steven Tötösy de Zepetnek. West Lafayette: Purdue UP, 2005.

Marie Peguy teaches secondary school in Clermont l'Herault and is also appointed to teach at the Institut Universitaire de Formation des Maîtres in Nîmes. She is working towards her doctorate in comparative literature with a dissertation about Kertész, Semprún, and Applefeld at the University of Montpellier under the supervision of Jeanne-Marie Clerc. Her interests and publications include medieval literature, especially the troubadour lyrics, and her book, *Lo ferm Voler, Essai sur la lyrique des troubadours* was published in 1991. Peguy is also active in promoting writing and arts in secondary schools and cultural associations.

Catherine Portuges teaches film studies and comparative literature at the University of Massachusetts Amherst where she also serves as director of the film program. Her more recent publications include *Screen Memories: The Hungarian Cinema of Márta Mészáros* (1993) and papers in the collected volumes *Writing New Identities: Gender, Nation & Immigration* (1996), *Cinema, Colonialism, Postcolonialism* (1996), *Borders, Exiles, and Diasporas* (1998), *Comparative Central European Culture* (2001), *Minarik, Sonnenschein és a többiek. Zsidó sorsok magyar filmen* (2001), and *24 Frames: Central Europe* (2005).

Sabine Prechter holds a doctorate in English linguistics and she has taught linguistics, intercultural communication, German, and publishing at various universities in Germany the United Kingdom. Her latest publications include the Spanish version of the presentation of the Documentation Center of the Nürnberg Party Rally Grounds and a paper "Discourse Markers in School Discourse" in the volume *Festschrift for David Heath* (2004). In her current research, Prechter focuses on aspects of alternative motivation and evaluation strategies in foreign language teaching. Prechter is the translator of Bettina von Jagow's "Representing the Holocaust, Kertész's *Fatelessness*, and Benigni's *La vita è bella*" in the collected volume *Imre Kertész and Holocaust Literature*. Ed. Louise O. Vasvári and Steven Tötösy de Zepetnek. West Lafayette: Purdue UP, 2005.

Rosana Ratkovčić, an art critic and theorist, works as museum curator in Zagreb. Her interests in scholarship include Feminist Studies and Medieval Studies. Ratkovčić is member of the Centre for Women's Studies in Zagreb and serves on the editorial board of *Treća* (The Third), a journal of the Center. Her recent publications include "Novi stalni postav Memorijalnog muzeja Spomen područja Jasenovac" ("The New Permanent Exhibition in the Jasenovac Memorial Museum") in *Povijest u nastavi* (2004), "Gender Transgression of Space and Time" in

Patterns of Visibility, a catalogue of the Croatian exhibition at the 50th Venice Bi-
ennale, (Ed. Leonida Kovač) (2003), and "Through the Visible and the Invisible"
in *Orshi Drozdik / Passion after Appropriation* (Ed. Leonida Kovač) (2003).

Tamás Scheibner is working towards his doctorate in comparative literature at Eötvös Loránd University. His interests in scholarship include twentieth-century Hungarian literature, literary theory, and the work of Jorge Luis Borges. He is the editor
of the series Dayka Books on the history of Hungarian literature with L'Harmattan.
Scheibner's recent publications include the edited volumes *Az értelmezés szükségessége* (The Necessity of Interpretation) with Z.G. Szűcs (2002) and, with with
Mihály Szegedy-Maszák, *Der lange, dunkle Schatten. Studien zum Werk von Imre
Kertész* (2004).

Eluned Summers-Bremner teaches literature and women's studies at the University
of Auckland. Her numerous publications are on literary and psychoanalytic topics
including recent papers in the journals *New Formations* (2001), *Dalhousie Review*
(2004), *The Journal of Narrative Theory* (2005) and in the collected volume *Comparative Cultural Studies and Michael Ondaatje's Writing* (2005). Currently, she is
writing a cultural history of insomnia and is at work on two other book-length projects, on the role of memory in the imagination of human and exile and on the contemporary function of the fantasy of childhood.

Steven Tötösy de Zepetnek <http://clcwebjournal.lib.purdue.ed/totosycv.html>
taught comparative literature at the University of Alberta 1984–2000 and after
moving to the U.S. in 2000, he teaches, concurrently, at the University of Halle-
Wittenberg comparative culture and media studies. Author of numerous papers and
books published on both sides of the Atlantic and in Asia, Tötösy's next book is
Comparative Cultural Studies (2005). Tötösy is editor (founding) of the journal
CLCWeb: Comparative Literature and Culture <http://clcwebjournal.lib.purdue.
edu> and series editor of Books in Comparative Cultural Studies, both published
by Purdue University Press.

Paul Várnai has taught for some thirty years Russian and East European literatures
at Carleton University. His interests in scholarship range from Canadian literature
and culture to Russian, Hungarian, and Jewish-Hungarian literature and he has
published widely in these fields. His more recent papers include "Sohasem
járhatunk jól" ("We Can Never Have It All") in *Szombat* (2003) and "Remélem,
odaát nagyon erős a szeretet" ("I Hope Love is Very Strong in the Next World")
also in the journal *Szombat* (2003). Since his retirement, Várnai focuses on Jewish-
Hungarian literature and his own autobiography. He lives in Ottawa and Budapest.

Louise O. Vasvári taught 1973–2002 Hispanic literatures and comparative literature at the State University of New York, Stony Brook. Her interests include folk-

lore, medieval literature, translation theory, and sociolinguistics (all informed by gender theory) and she has published widely in these areas. Her most recent book is *The Heterotextual Body of the "Mora Morilla"* (1999) and she has published, with Louise Haywood, a companion to the *libro de buen amor* (2004). Vasvári has taught also at the University of California, Berkeley, at the Central European University, and currently teaches at New York University. She lives in New York and Budapest.

Tim Wilkinson was born and educated in the U.K. and in the 1970s has lived and worked in Hungary for several years. He has translated a range of works on Hungarian history and culture, including Éva Balázs's *Hungary and the Habsburgs 1765–1800* (1997) and Domokos Kosáry's *Hungary and International Politics in 1848–1849* (2003). In recent years Wilkinson has been involved with contemporary Hungarian literature and has published translations of three novels by Imre Kertész, *Fatelessness*, *Kaddish for an Unborn Child*, and *Liquidation* (all 2004) as well as shorter texts by Péter Esterházy, Endre Kukorelly, Zsolt Láng, Lajos Parti Nagy, and Péter Nádas. He lives in London.

Judy Young has taught German language and literature and has worked for over twenty-five years in the Canadian Government's multiculturalism programs, most recently as Special Advisor on Multiculturalism in the Department of Canadian Heritage. During the last ten years she has undertaken joint projects in Central and East Europe in the management of cultural diversity, with respect to the elimination of discrimination and the participation of minorities in the social, political, and cultural life of the society in which they live. She has presented papers and published in these fields, for example "No Longer 'Apart'? Multiculturalism Policy and Canadian Literature" in *Canadian Ethnic Studies / Études ethniques au Canada* (2001). She lives in Ottawa.